IRELAND and S
1600–185

IRELAND
and
SCOTLAND
1600–1850

Parallels and Contrasts
in Economic
and Social Development

Edited by
T. M. DEVINE
and
DAVID DICKSON

JOHN DONALD PUBLISHERS LTD
EDINBURGH

ISBN 0 85976 089 8

Exclusive distribution in the United States of
America and Canada by Humanities Press Inc.,
Atlantic Highlands, NJ 07716, USA.

Phototypeset by H.M. Repros, Glasgow.
Printed in Great Britain by Bell & Bain Ltd., Glasgow.

Preface

IN 1976 an exploratory seminar on comparative aspects of Irish and Scottish economic and social development was held in Trinity College, Dublin. The success of this venture and the publication of the proceedings, *Comparative Aspects of Irish and Scottish Economic and Social History* (Edinburgh, 1977), edited by L. M. Cullen and T. C. Smout, encouraged historians on both sides of the Irish Sea to acknowledge the value of the comparative approach in contributing to a fuller understanding of the evolution of the two societies.

As a result, a second seminar, supported like the first by the Social Science Research Council, took place in Strathclyde University from 16–18 September, 1981. The organisers of this meeting sought not only to maintain the contacts earlier achieved but to broaden and deepen the issues under discussion. The second seminar placed even greater emphasis on the central question of the divergence of the two societies after c.1780, during which time Scotland moved successfully towards industrialisation while Ireland experienced the horror of the Great Famine and mass emigration. The factors which shaped this contrasting development, after an earlier phase of similar types of expansion in Scotland and Ireland, are examined in several of the papers that follow.

Moreover, the Strathclyde seminar intended to focus on themes which had been neglected at the Dublin meeting (such as relations with England, urban comparisons, religion and migration) and to highlight issues, such as rural social and economic change, which the first conference indicated might be of special importance. The virtual absence of papers on foreign trade and industrial change from the seminar proceedings simply reflects the fact that these subject areas were given extensive coverage in 1977. All the papers presented at the Strathclyde seminar are printed in this volume. The final chapter represents our joint reflections on both the papers and the discussions which took place at the seminar itself.

We are happy to record our thanks for the generous financial assistance provided by the Social Science Research Council, without which the conference could not have taken place. Three graduate students at Strathclyde University, Allan Gunning, Mary McHugh and William Sloan, gave valuable help in the duplication of papers and the general organisation of the proceedings. John Tuckwell of John

Donald Ltd. guided two somewhat wayward editors with his customary patience and professional skill. Our final and main debt is to Louis Cullen and Christopher Smout who first saw the value in comparing Irish and Scottish development and encouraged us to proceed further with the study they had pioneered.

T. M. Devine, Glasgow.
David Dickson, Dublin.

Contents

S.S.R.C. Conference on Irish and Scottish Economic and Social Development, 1600–1850

Strathclyde University
16–18 September, 1981

PARTICIPANTS

Professor Michael Anderson, Professor of Economic History, University of Edinburgh

Professor John Butt, Professor of Economic History, University of Strathclyde

Professor R. H. Campbell, Professor Emeritus of Economic History, University of Stirling

Professor Aidan Clarke, Associate Professor of History, Trinity College, Dublin

Dr. Leslie Clarkson, Reader in Economic and Social History, the Queen's University of Belfast

Dr. Laura E. Cochran, Formerly Columba Research Fellow, St. Edmund's House, University of Cambridge

Professor D. C. Coleman, Formerly Professor of Economic History, University of Cambridge and Fellow of Pembroke College

Brenda Collins, Junior Research Fellow, Institute of Irish Studies, the Queen's University of Belfast

Dr. Sean Connolly, Lecturer in History, New University of Ulster, Coleraine

W. H. Crawford, Keeper of Material Culture, Ulster Folk and Transport Museum

Professor L. M. Cullen, Professor of Modern Irish History, Trinity College, Dublin

Dr. A. J. G. Cummings, Lecturer in History, University of Strathclyde

Dr. T. M. Devine, Senior Lecturer in History, University of Strathclyde

Dr. David Dickson, Lecturer in Modern History, Trinity College, Dublin

Dr. R. A. Dodgshon, Lecturer in Geography, University College of Wales, Aberystwyth

Raymond Gillespie, Research student, Trinity College, Dublin

Malcolm Gray, Formerly Reader in Economic History, University of Aberdeen

Allan Gunning, Research student, University of Strathclyde

J. R. Hume, Lecturer in History, University of Strathclyde

Dr. Gordon Jackson, Reader in Economic History, University of Strathclyde

Graeme Kirkham, Research student, Trinity College, Dublin

Professor Joseph Lee, Professor of Modern History, University College, Cork

Bruce P. Lenman, Senior Lecturer in Modern History, University of St. Andrews

Dr. D. G. Lockhart, Lecturer in Geography, University of Keele

Professor Rosalind Mitchison, Professor of Social History, University of Edinburgh

Professor Joel Mokyr, Associate Professor of Economics, Northwestern University, USA

Dr. C. W. Munn, Lecturer in Economic History, University of Glasgow

Dr. Patrick O'Flanagan, Lecturer in Geography, University College, Cork

Dr. Cormac Ó Gráda, College Lecturer in Economics, University College, Dublin

Professor Eric Richards, Professor of History, Flinders University, Australia

Dr. Peter Roebuck, Senior Lecturer in History, New University of Ulster, Coleraine

William Sloan, Research student, University of Strathclyde

Peter Solar, Lecturer in Economic History, University of York

Professor T. C. Smout, Professor of Scottish History, University of St. Andrews

Dr. David Stevenson, Senior Lecturer in History, University of Aberdeen

Dr. J. H. Treble, Senior Lecturer in History, University of Strathclyde

Dr. R. Weir, Lecturer in Economic History, University of York

Dr. I. D. Whyte, Lecturer in Geography, University of Lancaster

D. M. Woodward, Senior Lecturer in Economic History, University of Hull

Part I

Ireland and Scotland, 1600–1800

1

Ireland and Scotland: The Seventeenth-Century Legacies Compared

Rosalind Mitchison

NEITHER Scotland nor Ireland can be studied for the seventeenth century without attention to their relationships to England and to the effects on both countries of decisions made in England. By contrast with England their economies were undeveloped. The three countries did not naturally complement each other in products: their crops were much the same, and stock similar, though there were notable differences in the availability of minerals. Such complementary features as existed came from the effects of English specialisation and English wealth. Scotland and Ireland sought in England a wide variety of metal goods, industrial necessities, household comforts and some expensive luxuries. English appetites wanted more meat than could advantageously be produced on English soil, English overseas activities came to be sustained by salt beef, and the sophistication of English transport on imported tallow and leather. English concentration on the manufacture of woollens left a market for linen. Yet at the same time these imported goods could also be produced in England, and interest groups of English producers might gain the ear of Parliament. Even if the identification by such groups of a threat to their interests might be mistaken, the response to their demands could lead to the sudden restriction of the market. Examples of such events are the imposition of duties on Scottish cattle, linen, salt and skins, and the bans on Irish cattle in the 1660s. Woodward has given us a glimpse of the estimates made in England of the scale of the Scottish cattle trade which may have inspired restrictive legislation — estimates which, whether right or wrong about the balance of trade between the two countries, show the Scottish cattle exports at a level near to the Irish.[1] It is worth remembering that there was no natural community of interest between Ireland and Scotland, and that the Scots followed the lead of the English in banning Irish cattle in 1667, adding salt beef and grain to the prohibition in 1672.[2]

In the modern world countries with big, protectionist neighbours can expand their trade by specialisation, and can encourage, by protection, import substitution. But both courses are difficult when the customs staff is scanty and corrupt and the industrial base weak. There is also the policy of expanding the economy by increasing internal traffic. Again complementarity is important. In Ireland, though there are gradients in rainfall, temperature and soil conditions, they are not such as to make for marked differences in the capacity to grow crops. In Scotland such differences did exist, between the various valleys and plains and the upland areas of Highlands and Borders. But until well on in the eighteenth century the Highland area sent out very little to the rest of the country except manpower.

We need, for real understanding of the seventeenth century, a few more reliable figures. One area of controversy, with remarkably wide alternative estimates, is Irish population. For Scotland the picture of population change in the seventeenth century is obscure, but the signs suggest much less than in Ireland. We have some information on grain prices, but not good series of cattle prices for either country or for their English markets, a serious gap not only because of the agricultural implications but also because cattle products were important elements in industry and transport.[3] There is difference of opinion on the relative scales of town life. It has been asserted that in the first half of the century towns in Scotland were bigger than those in Ireland. Dublin did not then compare with Edinburgh, though it was to do so later. A trio of Irish secondary towns, Cork, Limerick and Waterford, may have ranked near to those of Scotland: Dundee, Aberdeen and Glasgow. (The relationship of the share of customs and excise borne by the Irish three in 1664 to Dublin's is the same as that of the Scottish three to Edinburgh's in 1649).[4] The label of a town in both countries still included many which could be covered by the disparaging remark that Thomas Tucker made about some Scottish burghs as deserving 'no other appellation than village'.[5] Estimates of Dublin at the end of the century give it a population of between fifty and sixty thousand, but there is some doubt about these, since a household size of six is implied, which is larger than that assigned by Gregory King to London.[6] By then Edinburgh and her satellite Leith had over 17,000 hearths, and may have approached 50,000 people. The expansion of burgess entry in Edinburgh after 1660 suggests that the Scottish capital had recovered from the loss of the royal court.[7] Both capitals were by then large enough to have a beneficial effect on the surrounding rural area.

But the relative size of the urban sector, even allowing for the fact that much time of townsmen was spent in agriculture, is not a helpful measure of the state of the economy. What we need is some measure of the market economy, and there seems no doubt that this was bigger in Ireland than in Scotland. A sign of the lack of market orientation in Scotland is the large role of payment in kind. Rentals from this period showing a mixture of money rents, grain rents and services, often include arrangements for the conversion of grain into money, but the tendency for these to be 'at the highest fiar' suggests a preference on the part of the landowner for grain. In practice even the ostensible money rent might be paid in cattle. The system of restriction of burghs and markets, which did not weaken until the 1670s, also implies a narrow market sector. So does the difficulty which the country found in maintaining enough exports to pay for her vital imports. By contrast Ireland had a much bigger and more adjustable range of major exports, and showed the capacity to develop alternatives to fill at least a large part of the gap when a commodity was blocked. Her sales to the continent and the English colonies also show a more flexible approach than the Scottish, and so does her move to linen for the English market later. The failure of the Scots to expand cattle exports to England enough to fill up the place of Ireland after 1667 is significant. Every indicator supports the statement of Cullen that the Scottish economy was the more primitive of the two.[8] Also, where similar commodities were offered for exchange by both countries, the Scottish product was inferior: an example is the English official customs valuation of Irish cattle at 40% above Scottish. Scotland offered good quality material for sale only when, as in the case of coal, basic geological processes had done the work.

Both countries experienced a drastic social change in the seventeenth century. The old society of Ireland, which has been described by Hayes-McCoy, is remarkably similar in its values and priorities to that shown in Scotland by Wormald.[9] The standard aristocratic aim in both countries was the building up of lordship by various kinds of tie, and the adherents of a lord might be kinsmen, clients or mere neighbours. In Ireland this system was impinged upon in the Elizabethan land settlement, when lands had to be surrendered to the Crown, to be regranted on new tenure. The great Cromwellian land grab of the 1650s took this much further, and destroyed traditional landownership, and with it lordship. The amount of land held by intruders in plantations was nearly doubled, changing from 41% of the total in 1641 to 78% in 1688.[10] Many of the new settlers did not stay, but their mobility merely encouraged the process by which land became a commodity to be bought and sold, and used in a purely commercial spirit. Ireland thus passed suddenly and traumatically from a society where land was the basis of social relationships and of the life-style of a community to one where it was a commercial asset available for sale or exploitation. Profit had become more important than prestige and power. The change in Scotland was less sudden or total. It resulted from the revolutionary mid-century. The aristocracy, which had made the revolution of 1638–41 in alliance with the clergy, because it had lost confidence in the willingness of the Crown to respect its rights in land and influence, learned the hard way, by exclusion from office, financial loss, clerical intransigence, the rising independence of lairds and, finally, foreign domination, that it was advisable, for the future, to co-operate with the central government. Though the behaviour of Scottish noblemen as late as the reign of William III made it almost impossible to maintain a stable political system,[11] they had ceased to make bands and to claim the right to call upon their supporters to 'ride and gang' with them when they made a display of strength. But in abandoning the priorities of old-fashioned lordship, they did not immediately transfer their full attention to profit.

There is need for further study of the attitudes and decisions of landowners in Scotland in the restoration period, to see how far this change had gone. One aspect of change was the blurring of distinctions of tenure. Before the Great Rebellion the class of lairds was split between 'barons', that is tenants in chief, and lairds who 'held of a subject superior'. In the restoration period both become 'heritors', that is landowners with parochial responsibilities, a definition which took its importance from the legislation of 1633 defining the payment of stipends. It also gained from the new office of Commissioner of Supply, open to owners of fairly small estates, irrespective of feudal status. In the eighteenth century the courts were to push this change of emphasis further by stressing the rights of property over those of superiority.[12] A recent doctoral thesis on landowners in Forfarshire shows that the big estates were taking a slightly more professional approach to the career of factor, and in some cases raising rents. Factors were expected to produce accounts, even if belatedly, and were less likely than in the past to share the surname of the landowner. Even the relatively backward Airlie estate was using men not of 'the Name'; the progressive Panmure estate was pressing the tenants to expand grain production.[13]

There is a succession of probable stages by which landowners may perceive and act on a desire for greater wealth. They can attempt to raise the revenue of estates by cornering specific activities, notably sales of produce, they can squeeze up rents until the tenants refuse to pay or leave, and they can face the more difficult issue of how to increase total productivity, which usually means reorganisation. The cornering policy, carried out by many in the restoration period, led to the creation of new market centres and burghs, so that though the motive was often monopolistic, carried out on a wide scale it aided trade and may have caused expansion. In particular the Act of 1672, which allowed burghs outside the select group of royal burghs to engage in foreign trade, may have been generally beneficial. A document from the Atholl estate shows the monopolistic approach at a later date. It is a plan of 1708 for 'improving' the estates of the Duke of Atholl, not so much by change in methods of production but by compelling the tenantry to use only the Duke's market at Logierait, even for the smallest of purchases or sales. Though it also recommended technical improvements in the manufacture of linen, it did not consider the possibility of raising agricultural productivity.[14] But before the end of the seventeenth century there was some landowning concern for increased agricultural productivity — it is shown in the enabling legislation.

Whyte has pointed out that the agrarian legislation of this period, for instance that empowering owners to break up commonties, was all in the interests of the landowner class.[15] But reorganisation does not appear yet to have become a popular policy. Probably what was holding it back was the glut conditions which Smout and Fenton show to have existed at this time.[16] A system of rents in kind with prices low held the peasantry in a predetermined pattern of cropping and encouraged scourging, while it gave little incentive for reorganisation. In the Highlands evidence from selected estates shows little pressure to obtain a bigger return, though there was a new stress on the money component of the rent. For instance, the McLeod estates in Harris after 1680 saw a rise in this part of the rent, though there were still accepted returns of a traditional kind, such as the demand for as much victual, butter, cheese, wine, ale and acquavitae as a gentleman might require for one night's stay 'albeit he were 600 men in companie'.[17]

Scotland also experienced 'modernisation' in government. The experience of the revolutionary wars had led to the creation of a more adequate system of taxation. A single one of the covenanting government's devices for raising money had brought in more than twice the traditional royal revenue.[18] Of long-term significance was the creation of the Commissioners of Supply as an element in county government independent of magnate power and with their remit based on taxation. There was also an attempt, admittedly only partially successful, in the 1690s to make the poor law work.[19] At both central and local levels a more effective if limited system of government was being built up, and local control by the gentry on the English model but with enhanced power to the landowner was to be the eighteenth-century system. Such economic developments as happened in the first forty years of the eighteenth century in Scotland were in the realm of economic infrastructure, particularly in communications and banking, so the improvement in administration, the more effective raising of supply and the acceptance of higher standards of law and order must all be seen as contributing to these changes and so to economic growth. It was in the 1650s that a government in Scotland established its ability to control the Highlands when it so chose, though the later Stuarts and early Hanoverians did not choose to exercise this power.[20] There was some deliberate, if gradual, infusion of English ideas and systems, not always beneficial. For instance the legal rate of interest was lowered to conform with the English. Before 1641 the rate was 10% and frequently disregarded: by the end of the 1690s it stood at 5%, probably too low for the risks of enterprise in a backward economy. The reduction of the claims of lordship released small proprietors from the burden of riding attendance on great men, and gave them control of their own time, even while their continued demands for services denied such freedom to their tenantry. Intermarriage of the nobility with the English in the last quarter of the century may have increased the concern of many for higher money incomes. This is as yet an unexplored area, but one would expect the introduction of the pattern of relatively large dowries and settlements as used by the English, which could place heavy burdens on an estate overendowed with female dependents, to provoke a concern for higher income.

The social revolution seems to have been much more complete and rapid in Ireland, producing a landowning class with little in the way of personal links with the mass of the population in many areas, in fact often estranged from it by religious differences. Even if many of the original 'adventurers' sold their lands, about a third of the men of 1642 were still in possession in 1660, and some of these were true tycoons, men of commercial background and a purely commercial spirit.[21] The expansion of the cattle trade and trade in other cattle products, wool and grain, are all evidence of the response of landholders to economic opportunity. In the long run, however, this new type of landowner may have been less economically advantageous, by the alienation of those who actively worked the land. Agrarian reorganisation, when it came in Scotland, depended for success on the active participation of the peasantry and general acceptance of a change in status and work pattern, by which tenant farmers might become either agricultural labourers or an industrial work force. The rareness of protest or resistance to change in lowland Scotland is striking.[22] The Irish peasantry were less prepared than the Scottish to be deprived of a stake in the land. But in the later decades of the seventeenth century the intruded landowner class in Ireland seems to have been an important element, probably the most important element, in that country's economic adaptation and growth.

Even if still backward, the rural economy of Scotland was working better in 1690 than it had been in 1640. The step down in grain prices discernible in the runs of fiars prices was over 30% between the 1650s and the 1660s, and suggests improved relations between the supply of food and the people to consume it.[23] This could be the result of a fall in population rather than a rise in production, but only if the known reasons for population loss are assessed at improbably high levels. Scottish emigration to Ireland is now recognised as relatively small before the 1680s: Wentworth's figures, which ranged from 50,000 to 150,000 for the 1630s, and Petty's of 80,000 entering between 1650 and 1672, both seem impressionistic rather than quantitative. The plague in the 1640s was severe, but had little impact outside the towns and their immediate peripheries. There are statements of increased acreage of crops in the 1660s and evidence of more regular grain exports.[24] The fall in prices, while it discouraged reorganisation, at least made for less undernourishment. Appleby has argued for a shift in the terms of trade between pastoral and arable products in north-west England in the mid-seventeenth century, which improved conditions there.[25] We cannot say as yet whether cattle prices rose, but a fall in grain prices would mean that food could more easily be brought in to upland areas. The movement towards similarity in the movements of grain prices suggests easier purchase. Low prices for primary products meant that both the Irish and the Scottish economies had their exports mainly in the low price sector, but at least people could afford to eat.

At some point anyone trying to understand the Irish economy has to grapple with the problem of Irish population change. Ireland has not yet been a field for the use of the new demographic techniques developed by the French historians and taken further by the Cambridge group of demographers. Probably the source material is inadequate for such an approach. Little attention has been given to the period before 1740.[26] The main sources for the seventeenth century are colourful contemporary statements, the various calculations of William Petty and the hearth tax returns. Any set of figures implies extraordinary buoyancy, even when the old, catastrophic estimates of the impact of the Great Rebellion are discounted. Partly this is explained by the economy rather than by Irish fertility: English and Scots settled in Ireland whenever the price of land was low. Current estimates of the Scots settling in James VI's reign stand at 10,000, and by 1652 perhaps 20,000 altogether. Another four or five thousand a year may have been coming in for much of the 1690s.[27] Altogether this movement from Scotland may have done much to keep Scottish population from expansion in the seventeenth century. English population was similarly held down by supplying Ireland and the colonies.

The latest figures for Irish population, which of course include immigrants, are those of Cullen, derived partly from Connell:[28]

    1641 2.1 million
    1672 1.7 million
    1687 2.17 million
    1712 2.8 million

The 1712 figure is based on hearth tax records which show 349,849: the tax was not farmed out and so the house number may be accurate. The 1687 figure is adjusted from Petty's interpretation of tax material. Both assume a household size of over five. Cullen accepts Connell's 1712 figure as 'plausible', and notes that it gives a rate of seventeenth-century growth similar to that found elsewhere in Europe. This table implies an increase from 1687–1712 of approximately 1% a year. It is unlikely that an early modern population could achieve more than half this rate by natural increase, so these figures would imply a total immigrant cohort in this period of 300,000. If comparison with other countries is to be used as part of the approach to Irish population, we should consider an alternative comparison of household size. The 32 parish listings collected for England by Laslett for the period 1684–1705 average out (that is have a mean of means) at 4.79 people to a house. Early eighteenth-century Irish material, outwith Dublin, gives figures of between 4.3 and 5.[29] If Laslett's household size is applied to the 1712 hearth tax material, the total population suggested would be 1.676 million. This could be set against Petty's figure of 1.3 million for 1687, to give a slightly higher annual rate of increase than Connell's, but it would not require an immigrant cohort of over 200,000. These alternative figures are suggested with great hesitation. The important feature of any estimates for Irish population in this period is that they all show that both by procreation and by immigration people were giving a vote of confidence in the Irish economy which they were denying to the Scottish.

Were these estimates of the future wrong? The alternative figures, if accepted, suggest that Irish population went on growing rapidly at a time when the Scottish was increasing very slowly, until the Scottish population started to grow more rapidly about 1750. The Scottish economy had certainly ended the seventeenth century in difficulties, partly through an unusual and devastating period of bad weather, in longer terms by the closing of foreign markets. The policy attempted in 1681 of import substitution cannot be held to have succeeded.[30] But Scotland still had the opportunity to act in what she conceived to be her own interests. By 1700 the Scottish Privy Council had ceased to act independently of the English ministry,[31] but the Parliament, which had been gaining in independence since 1660, could still make trouble and force concessions from England.[32] Even if we accept the statement of Riley that the Wine Act of 1703 had no connection with anything but revenue gathering,[33] the subsequent renewal of wool exports to Europe and the Act anent Peace and War were clearly hostile to England. Though, even before the Union the Scots had managed to breach England's control of her colonial trade, the economic growth of Scotland in the eighteenth century must be largely attributed to the terms of the settlement of 1707 which she had been able to force from England.

Ireland obtained some specific concessions within the control system of the Navigation Acts, and it suited England to allow her colonies to receive Irish provisions. But Ireland had not only English protectionism, as had Scotland, to contend with. She had English intervention in her own internal and external affairs. The two conspicuous examples of this are the legislation following the end of war in 1691, the 'penal laws', and the Woollen Act of 1699. The penal laws came from an Irish protestant Parliament, but such a body existed only because English power installed it. The situation was a colonial one. It is difficult to assess the direct economic effects of these laws. The policy of destroying, or forcing down, the Catholic gentry, and the continuation of earlier land settlement policies affected land use only indirectly. The limitation of leases to Catholics of only 31 years duration has been considered discouraging to development, while it lasted.

Maureen Wall has said 'few Catholics would be encouraged to extend their businesses or to invest'.[34] But development was not capital-intensive at this time. It would be only the expensive manipulation of water power at the end of the eighteenth century, when the restriction no longer held, that would have found 31 years too short.

The Woollen Act was a more serious matter. Irish sheep produced good wool, and the cloth from it was capable of competing with English, particularly in the 1690s when Irish land values were low. Prohibition of this export prevented this. Cullen has pointed out that the Act was not 'the consequence of official English policy'.[35] But it was the sort of thing that the interest system of the English Parliament made possible. The Rent Restriction Acts of the British Parliament in this century were not intended to destroy the private building of houses for working-class tenancy, but that has been their effect. In the same way that the actions of the British Parliament constrained the American colonies in the eighteenth century, by banning industries once they had successfully surmounted initial difficulties, and so prevented industrial development, the Woollen Act made it clear to the Irish that they would not gain by developing industries which competed with the English. This tacit warning underlay the emphasis put by both Ireland and Scotland on the expansion of their linen industries. However much there might be joint English and Irish interests — and Irish prosperity was itself an indirect English interest — in a situation of conflict the direct English interests would prevail in the British Parliament. The English connection, which made for economic growth in the seventeenth century, would exact a price later.

So the seventeenth-century legacies of Ireland and Scotland can be contrasted. In one case there had been adaptation and economic expansion, but the long-term prospects were clouded by the political status imposed, and by the possible alienation of much of the population from the governing group. As a great Irishman was to say, 'Men may be injured in their prides as well as in their pockets.' In the other case economic growth had been slight, but institutional innovation and social adjustment had laid the foundation for later development.

REFERENCES

1. D. Woodward, 'Anglo-Scottish trade and English commercial policy during the 1660s', *Scottish Historical Review* LVI, 1977, pp. 153–174, and 'The Anglo-Irish livestock trade of the Seventeenth Century', *Irish Historical Studies* XVIII, 1972–73, pp. 489–523.

2. *Register of the Scottish Privy Council* 3rd series, II (Edinburgh 1909), p. 253; *Acts of the Parliaments of Scotland* VIII (Edinburgh 1820), p. 61.

3. M. W. Flinn, ed., *Scottish Population History from the Seventeenth Century to the 1930s* (Cambridge 1977) Appendix B gives a selection from the known runs of annual county fiars prices; Aidan Clarke, 'The Irish Economy 1600–60', in T. W. Moody, F. X. Martin and F. J. Byrne, eds., *A New History of Ireland* III, *Early Modern Ireland* (Oxford 1976) (hereafter *Early Modern Ireland*), pp. 168–186 brings out the importance of pastoral products for Ireland.

4. *Calendar of State Papers, Ireland, 1663–5* (London, 1907), pp. 460–1; T. C. Smout, *Scottish Trade on the Eve of Union* (Edinburgh, 1963), p. 282.

5. 'Report by Thomas Tucker upon the settlement of the revenues of excise and custom in Scotland AD MDCLVI', *Miscellany* (Scottish Burgh Record Society, Edinburgh 1881), p. 18.

6. D. V. Glass, 'Two Papers by Gregory King', in D. V. Glass and D. E. C. Eversley, eds., *Population in History* (London 1965), pp. 201-2; J. G. Sims, 'The restoration, 1660-85', p. 440 and L. M. Cullen, 'Economic trends 1660-91', p. 390, in *Early Modern Ireland*.

7. Flinn, *Scottish Population History*, p. 191. The burgess entry figures have been collected by Mrs Joyce McMillan as part of work for a doctoral thesis at Edinburgh University.

8. L. M. Cullen, *Anglo-Irish Trade* (London 1968), p. 39.

9. G. A. Hayes-McCoy, 'Gaelic Society in Ireland in the late sixteenth century', in G. A. Hayes-McCoy, ed., *Historical Studies* IV (London 1963), pp. 45-61; Jenny Wormald, *Court, Kirk and Community* (London 1981), ch. 2.

10. Karl S. Bottigheimer, *English Money and Irish Land* (Oxford 1971), p. 3.

11. P. W. J. Riley, *King William and the Scottish Politicians* (Edinburgh 1979), p. 3, describes the attitude of the greater nobles as 'purely selfish': this view ignores the obligations of an individual nobleman to his power base.

12. R. M. Mitchison, 'Patriotism and national identity in eighteenth century Scotland', in T. W. Moody, ed., *Historical Studies* XI, *Nationality and the Pursuit of National Independence* (Belfast 1978), ch. 4.

13. J. McFaulds, 'Lands and their Ownership in Forfarshire, 1660-88', (Unpublished Ph.D. thesis, University of Glasgow, 1980).

14. 'Proposals Presented to the Duke of Atholl 22 Jan. 1708', Edinburgh University Library MS, DC.1.37.1/3. This has been shown to me by Miss Leah Leneman.

15. Ian Whyte, *Agriculture and Society in Seventeenth Century Scotland* (Edinburgh 1979), ch. 4.

16. T. C. Smout and A. Fenton, 'Scottish Agriculture before the Improvers', *Agricultural History Review* XIII, 1965, pp. 73-93.

17. C. Horricks, 'Economic and Social Change in the Isle of Harris, 1680-1754', (Unpublished Ph.D. thesis, University of Edinburgh 1974), p. 190.

18. D. Stevenson, 'The Financing of the Cause of the Covenants, 1638-51', *Scottish Historical Review* LI, 1972, pp. 89-123.

19. R. M. Mitchison, 'The Making of the Old Scottish Poor Law', *Past and Present* 63 (1974), pp. 58-93.

20. F. D. Dow, *Cromwellian Scotland 1651-1660* (Edinburgh 1979), chs. 3, 6, 8.

21. P. J. Corish, 'The Cromwellian Régime 1650-60', *Early Modern Ireland*, p. 372; Bottigheimer, *English Money and Irish Land*, pp. 154-7.

22. T. C. Smout, *A History of the Scottish People* (1969), p. 360; T. M. Devine, 'Social Stability in the Eastern Lowlands of Scotland during the Agricultural Revolution', in T. M. Devine, ed., *Lairds and Improvement in the Scotland of the Enlightenment* (Glasgow 1979), pp. 59-60.

23. The average level of fiars for oatmeal in Perthshire and oats in East Lothian dropped respectively 31% and 34% between these two decades.

24. Smout and Fenton, 'Scottish Agriculture', pp. 81-2.

25. A. P. Appleby, *Famine in Tudor and Stuart England* (Liverpool 1978), pp. 161-2.

26. The exception is the important paper by L. M. Cullen, 'Population Trends in Seventeenth Century Ireland', *Economic and Social Review* 6, 2, 1974-5.

27. M. Perceval-Maxwell, *The Scottish Migration to Ulster in the Reign of James I* (London 1973), p. 207; L. M. Cullen, 'Population Trends', p. 153.

28. L. M. Cullen, 'Economic Trends 1660-91', *Early Modern Ireland*, p. 389; K. H. Connell, *The Population of Ireland 1750-1845* (Oxford 1950), p. 25.

29. P. J. Laslett, *Household and Family in Past Time* (Cambridge 1972), pp. 130-1; K. H. Connell, *Population of Ireland*, pp. 14, 20.

30. W. R. Scott, *The constitution and finance of English, Scottish and Irish joint-stock companies* (Cambridge 1912) III, pp. 138-62.

31. This is evident from the typescript of its *Acta* which I have been able to study by courtesy of the staff of the Scottish Record Office.

32. C. S. Terry, *The Scottish Parliament* (Glasgow 1905), pp. 145-9; W. Ferguson, *Scotland: 1689 to the Present* (Edinburgh 1968), pp. 8-9.

33. P. W. J. Riley, 'The Scottish Parliament of 1703', *Scottish Historical Review* XLVII (1968), p. 149.

34. Maureen Wall, 'Catholics in Economic Life', in L. M. Cullen, ed., *The Formation of the Irish Economy* (Cork 1968), p. 41.

35. L. M. Cullen, *An Economic History of Ireland since 1660* (London 1972), pp. 34-7.

2

The English Connection and Irish and Scottish Development in the Eighteenth Century

T. M. Devine

BOTH Scottish and Irish society were profoundly influenced by English political, economic and cultural connections in the eighteenth century. Indeed, Scottish historians have long argued that the relationship with England was the *sine qua non* ⟶ ✗ of Scottish commercial and industrial success in the decades following the achievement of the Parliamentary Union of 1707. The principal staples and supports of economic advance, the trade in cattle, transatlantic commerce and the linen manufacture, seemed to rest securely on the privileges of free trade and protection afforded in the Union. As one writer has put it, 'When after the 1780s the Scottish economy was resting on a basis laid by achievements apparently its own, it was in reality resting on a foundation established through Union with England'.[1] The thesis is persuasive and becomes doubly so when the more subtle relationships with England are considered. English technology was of crucial importance to the growth of the Scottish lead, coal and cotton industries while 'English methods' became very rapidly an integral part of the process of agrarian 'improvement' in rural Scotland.[2] The British empire provided a new range of career opportunities for ambitious Scots in military and administrative service, merchanting and medicine, and much of the resulting income percolated through the Scottish economy in consequence of the adventurers' habit of returning to their homeland with the profits of their varied enterprises.[3] Furthermore, the Scottish élite became increasingly open to English cultural influences through the immense popularity of eighteenth-century London periodicals and the stimulus of closer political connections.[4] This provided a new dynamic of competitive emulation which helped to release energies for social and economic improvement among the indigenous governing class. Indeed, without the advantages conferred by full union and the English connection, Scotland seemed likely in 1700 to face a bleak future sunk in the economic doldrums as the terms of trade in continental Europe began to move ruthlessly and decisively against her traditional activities.[5]

There seems little doubt of the central importance of the Anglo-Scottish Union in Scottish economic expansion before 1770, but it is more difficult to determine the exact relationship between the English connection and *structural change* in economic activity after c.1780. Historians traditionally assert that in the later period

✗: an Essential ingredient.

a mix of indigenous strengths and English economic pressures serves to explain the more fundamental and important transition from a society firmly rooted in a phase of proto-industrialisation to one in which the motors of growth were located in new manufacturing and urban development. Comparison with the Irish experience in this area of analysis is invaluable. Irish society was subject to a similar range of influences from England but, in the period after c.1780, and especially after 1815, reacted differently to them and, instead of structural change on the Scottish model, eventually endured the horror of widespread famine and the trauma of mass emigration. Comparison of the origins of this divergence helps to clarify the relative importance of indigenous and external factors in Scottish success. It is useful to begin with a discussion of the precise political relationship which each country had with England in the eighteenth century and to ask whether the particular form which this tie assumed in each case is perhaps itself sufficient to account for differentials in economic performance.

I

In essence the new English political connection with Scotland was forged in 1707 for strategic reasons in order to secure the northern flank against the feared threat of French and Jacobite attack.[6] Superficially at least, the end of the Scottish parliament in that year also implied the end of Scottish independence, since ultimate authority now derived from a London executive and Westminster legislature in which Scottish representation was numerically weak and politically subservient. Yet the reality of power relationships was somewhat different. Scottish 'independence' in the seventeenth century had been more apparent than real. Sir John Clerk, writing in 1730, may have put the point in extreme terms but his verdict contained a core of truth: 'As to our civil government [before 1707], it was an entire state of dependence on the councils of England. We had frequent sessions of Parliament, a constant Privy Council, a Treasury and Exchequer, but all these subservient to such administrators as the chief ministers in England thought fit to recommend to the Sovereign'.[7] Scotland had retained control over economic policy through Parliament and Privy Council in the era of the Union of the Crowns but none over foreign policy and precious little over the conduct of her commercial affairs abroad, as the notorious 'Darien Disaster' graphically illustrated. Moreover, after 1707, Scotland had free access to English domestic and colonial markets and at the same time enjoyed the protection of British tariffs which proved the keys to growth in her premier manufacture of linen. Yet this bonus was achieved with only marginal sacrifice in real political power. Essentially the Union was successful because it was incomplete and enhanced rather than eroded the traditional authority of the Scottish governing class. In no sense was Scotland merged with England. The great institutions of law, education and the Scottish Kirk, the primary sources of nationality rather than a Parliament which had only lost its ancient impotence two decades before Union, were preserved intact. The existing privileges of landowners and royal burgh merchants were maintained. The changes in the treason law and the Patronage Act, passed after Union, served only to buttress the existing influence of the landowning élite, while the ensuing 'semi-independence' allowed this class to promote Scottish interests through the formation of such bodies as the Board of Trustees for Manufactures and Fisheries, the Society of Improvers and the Committee for the Annexed Forfeited Estates.[8] Thus, as the political relationship between England and Scotland became clearer by the middle decades of the eighteenth century, it was apparent that Scotland had obtained vital commercial privileges while retaining an indigenous élite with an enhanced apparatus of power and also the survival of a series of institutions which both defined her nationality and provided the social base for modernisation. In no sense, therefore, could Scotland be described as an English colony, a characterisation often applied to eighteenth-century Ireland.

Ironically, Ireland did acquire the separate Parliament which Scotland lacked in the eighteenth century. As in the Scottish case, London was in theory the ultimate source of power, but specifically Irish interests were not neglected because London generally avoided direct legislative interference. Moreover, the increasing political initiative taken by the Anglo-Irish meant that the Dublin Parliament began to devote greater attention to economic matters. The Irish economy eventually enjoyed enthusiastic parliamentary support for transportation development, bounties on corn exports and significantly, in the later eighteenth century, protection for the infant indigenous cotton manufacture.[9] For unlike Scotland, Ireland in the eighteenth century possessed its own import and export duties and customs service and was able to provide a separate tariff system which was not completely synchronised with or subordinate to that of England. On the other hand, while Irish linen, provisions (after the 1750s) and shipping were given favoured treatment in the English market, Irish merchants were legally barred from importing certain 'enumerated' goods from the colonies before 1780, and unilateral advantages were often conceded in the Irish tariff system to English products especially in the early eighteenth century.

Indeed, the mere existence of a separate Irish Parliament could not conceal the fact that the relationship between England and Ireland was a profoundly colonial one. The native governing class had been destroyed in the troubles of the seventeenth century and the confiscation of their lands resulted in the emergence of deep social, religious and political divisions between the native population and the new dominant Anglo-Irish élite over vast tracts of the countryside. Ireland's colonial and dependent status was also exemplified by the settlement of immigrants from protestant England and Scotland, recently estimated at about 27 per cent of the total population in the early eighteenth century, and by the notorious 'Penal Laws', repealed only in 1778.[10] These sought to exclude the native catholic majority from landownership and the professions, and contributed to the development of social fissures in the community which had no parallel in Scotland. The colonial status of Ireland can also be discerned in the acquisition of lands by English and Scottish gentlemen, several of whom already owned property in Britain and as 'absentees' have been regarded until recently as a parasitical class diverting rental to external consumption rather than energetic investment in Ireland.[11] A case can be argued, then, that in the realm of political economy the English connection was more favourable to Scottish development than to Irish because the Scots obtained commercial privileges without southern interference. Can such a thesis be sustained and, in particular, can the precise form assumed by the English connection in each case help to account for the divergence in economic development between the two countries in the later eighteenth and early nineteenth centuries?

II

Both Scotland and Ireland gained successively through their commercial association with England in a number of similar ways of which the most striking example of a mutual bonus was in linen manufacturing. In 1693 and 1696 special English tariffs were imposed on French goods which were virtually prohibitive as far as manufactured goods were concerned and which remained in force until the Eden Treaty of 1786. Linen imports from both Ireland and Scotland developed to replace these and later Dutch and German substitutes. Irish linen expansion was aided by the removal of duties in 1696 and Scottish by the Union of 1707. Further measures, including the abolition of the Irish export duty on linens, creation of linen boards in both countries and the provision of export bounties, meant that by 1774 most of the linen used in England and her colonies came from within the British Isles.[12] By the 1760s an estimated 60 to 70 per cent of linen manufactured within Scotland for public sale was sold within the English domestic and colonial markets, while in 1758 linen cloth and yarn made up 80 per cent of total Irish exports to Great Britain.[13] In fact, Irish growth was even more spectacular than that experienced in Scotland. Here was a development which was entirely dependent on English commercial policy. There was no market for an export industry of such magnitude outside the protected walls of the British Empire and, as recent research on the Scottish manufacture has shown, expansion occurred primarily through favourable tariffs and bounties, not through productivity gains which reduced costs.[14]

Yet, at the same time, behind the apparent similarity of experience the historian immediately encounters a major difference in the eventual evolution of the two industries. In Ireland, linen can be interpreted as a major force perpetuating the era of proto-industrialisation and, partially at least, a regional factor in the fragmentation of land units which was a basic cause of the Irish disaster of the mid-nineteenth century.[15] But in Scotland the industry has enjoyed a dramatically different historiography, being regarded as the source of enterprise, capital and labour for cotton, the 'leading sector', which ushered in the age of industrialisation and future prosperity.[16] Plainly only indigenous elements can explain this contrasting development.

English markets for Scottish and Irish livestock and provisions were instrumental in the growth of rural income in the two societies. If anything, however, the English connection in this respect favoured Ireland rather than Scotland. In the eighteenth century the Scottish trade in food products to England and her colonies was essentially in live cattle, fish and only to a lesser extent in grain. The famous black cattle trade to the south was not, *pace* Adam Smith, the key to agrarian change in Scotland. Indeed, the expansion of the trade in the eighteenth century came about partly because it did not require fundamental improvements either in the productive process or in existing transportation systems. The business was based on cattle-rearing not fattening, and the cattle travelled to market on the hoof along the drove roads. It can be argued that the cattle trade merely perpetuated the archaic societies of the Highlands and Galloway whence most beasts originated and which maintained a stubborn resistance to fundamental improvement into the nineteenth century.

The indigenous multiplier effects of the provision and grain trades from Ireland to Great Britain and her colonies were probably more extensive, and in this sense the late seventeenth-century Cattle Acts, which prohibited the export of Irish live cattle to England, were a paradoxical bonus in the long term. The provision trade, centred on Cork and Waterford, nearly tripled in volume between 1700 and 1765 and had important backward linkages in the growth of barrelling and packaging facilities and in the intricate expansion of inter-regional trade within Ireland.[17] Again, there is no parallel in Scotland of the sustained penetration of Irish grain into England (and Scotland) in the later eighteenth century, especially after 1806 when the English market was thrown open to Irish corn.[18] Despite the greater stimulus to Irish rural products from market expansion in England and Irish supply responsiveness, no systematic reorganisation of agriculture along Scottish lines occurred. A massive swing to tillage did take place but no 'agricultural revolution' was achieved.[19] Once again, therefore, one is presented with differences in development which can only primarily be explained by indigenous factors within the two societies.

The Scots, unlike the Irish, enjoyed direct access to the English colonies and, in consequence, built up highly lucrative re-export trades in tobacco and sugar. Ireland, excluded for most of the eighteenth century from the privilege of direct colonial commerce, had no re-exports to compare with this Scottish bonus. Undoubtedly, the Scottish tobacco trade, accounting for 40 per cent of imports and 50 per cent of overseas exports in 1762, cannot be neglected in any analysis of eighteenth-century Scottish growth. It was a key element in Scotland's favourable balance of trade, widened the manufacturing base of west central Scotland, provided a stimulus to banking development and encouraged investment in agriculture through merchant purchases of land.[20] It is unlikely, however, to be a central factor in explaining why Scotland drew rapidly ahead of Ireland in the later eighteenth century. For one thing, Scottish success in the trade was not solely dependent on the Union, which merely provided an opportunity for a growth rate which rested ultimately on the efficiency of Scottish trading practices and hence on indigenous sources of enterprise. Secondly, the impact of industrial investment by tobacco merchants began to weaken in relative terms after c.1780, precisely at the time when the Scottish economy began to pull ahead.[21] Third, the Irish provision trade to the colonies had substantial and beneficial income and employment effects on both regional rural and urban economies which partly compensated for the lack of a trade in re-exports. Fourth, the Irish were granted direct access to the USA and the British plantations in the 1780s but continued to depend on Great Britain for most of their tobacco and sugar, a trend which can possibly be interpreted in terms of enterprise limitations in Ireland as well as conditions of comparative advantage within the two merchant communities.[22]

There is probably more merit in the view that the 'colonial' apparatus of 'Penal Laws', alien settlement and land confiscation handicapped the Irish economy. There is a consensus that in the short term the 'new' Irish landlord class in the seventeenth century, with no emotional or patriarchal ties with the indigenous peasantry, could promote efficient practice and more rational use of land resources.[23] In the longer term, however, the existence of social, racial and religious gulfs between many landlords and their dependent tenantry may have impeded the easy transmission of 'improving' ideas and provided more encouragement for resistance to change on the part of the peasantry in a way which was less likely to happen in the culturally homogeneous society of lowland Scotland. Certainly there was no Scottish parallel to the widespread incidence of Irish agrarian discontent in the later eighteenth century which, while primarily fuelled by land hunger, often had sectarian ramifications and overtones.[24] The mere existence of such fissures in society may have discouraged the thinning of the rural population — often an integral feature of improvement in Scotland — because of the effect on social stability which such policies might have produced.

There is now, however, less force in the old argument that absentee English landlords drained Ireland of her wealth. The material demands of the absentee in both Scotland and Ireland often produced a need to extend the revenue-producing capacity of the estate and in that sense were a positive force for change. Equally residence in itself did not always or necessarily guarantee action.[25] In fact absenteeism was a characteristic and inevitable feature of *British* landed society in the eighteenth century because primogeniture ensured that eldest sons inherited scattered estates.[26] However, absenteeism was a political issue in Ireland because the estates from which landlords absented themselves often came to them through confiscation. As we shall see in more detail later, there do appear to have been significant differences in the policies of Irish and Scottish landlords, but it is more difficult to assert that these were mainly due to the racial origin of landed families.

Finally, both Irish and Scottish producers relied heavily on English technical invention in both industry and agriculture, a reflection of England's more advanced economic condition, geographical proximity and particular commercial relationships with the two other societies. Belfast and Glasgow, for example, had historic connections with Yorkshire and Lancashire in the fine yarn trade and these undoubtedly helped the rapid diffusion of knowledge of the new cotton technology in the later eighteenth century in these two towns.[27] Furthermore, the Scots borrowed substantially from England in other fields, varying from iron-making and lead-smelting to coal-mining and agricultural technique. But English investment and innovation in Scotland, relevant in the early days of cotton-spinning and iron-making, were quickly superseded by vigorous native initiatives which often improved rapidly on southern models.[28] The best-known instances were in cotton;

Kelly of New Lanark was the first to apply power to Crompton's mule, and Snodgrass of Glasgow invented the scutching machine for cotton wool, both in the 1790s. Similar advances were made in steam-engine design, in steamship propulsion and in agricultural technology, where some of the most revolutionary designs, such as Small's plough and Meikle's threshing machine, were notable instances of Scottish ingenuity. There is no similar record of technical achievement in Ireland, and it is noteworthy how derivative was such innovation as there was there; interestingly too Scotland rather than England quickly became the source of techniques which were later adopted across the Irish Sea.[29] This is eloquent testimony either of the differing social values in the two countries or of the contrasting levels of economic development which in Scotland created a context where the need for labour-saving innovation became more pressing.

To sum up: it would seem apparent that the nature of the English connection with Scotland and Ireland is not in itself sufficient to explain the striking differences in economic performance between the two societies in the later eighteenth century and afterwards. While no precise measurement of the impact of English policy, market, technology and capital is possible a rough judgement suggests that the Scots did gain over the Irish because their social structure and cohesion was not disturbed by English conquest and confiscation. Against this, however, has to be set the fact that Irish producers of linen, beef and grain seem to have exploited English demand more successfully and consistently than their counterparts in Scotland. The key point, nonetheless, is the fact that the particular *response* to the English connection was critically dependent on indigenous social, geographical, economic and cultural traditions in each country. Put simply, Scottish society possessed more of the prerequisites for successful modernisation in the eighteenth century than Ireland.

III

In their provocative analysis of the comparative development of Scotland and Ireland, Cullen and Smout assert, principally on the basis of export figures, that, at the beginning of the eighteenth century, 'Ireland seemed to hold more promise of a bright economic future than Scotland'.[30] The sources on which their calculations depend are hazardous and incomplete and it is quite possible that the statement exaggerates the economic equality of the two societies before c.1750. A number of other indicators suggest that Scottish superiority was not suddenly established in the later eighteenth century but had been developing for some time before that. First, Irish peasant society presents an image of much greater levels of destitution than normally prevailed in lowland Scotland in the early eighteenth century. Holdings were abandoned in large numbers in years of crisis: Kerry and Sligo, two counties far apart and representative of poor, but by no means the poorest, areas in Ireland, show reductions in the hearth-money returns by as much as a third in the crisis of the 1740s.[31] This suggests a society which lacked sufficient surplus for savings and contrasts markedly with the resilience of rural society in Scotland where food shortage, not crisis, was experienced in 1756, 1776, 1782–3 and 1799 and where, in the lowlands at least, such habitual abandonment of buildings had long since disappeared.[32] For whatever reason the Scots seem already to have accumulated the reserves to maintain themselves in years of difficulty. Second, one gains the impression that town growth was more significant in Scotland by the later seventeenth century. As L. M. Cullen has recently suggested: 'there was a fundamental contrast between the largely unurbanised Irish society (of the later seventeenth century) and the small-scale but closely-knit urban life, the many 'royal boroughs yoken on end to end' of lowland Scotland . . . the poorness, smallness and isolation of Irish towns is eloquent testimony to the backwardness of Irish society'.[33] Third, and most importantly, the balance of population to resources probably favoured Scotland by the mid-eighteenth century. The precocious development of the linen manufacture and potato cultivation in Ireland can both be interpreted in these terms. Their pattern of expansion in Ireland resembles the proliferation of bi-employments in the north-west Scottish highlands rather than the superficially similar developments of the lowland zone. Linen production in Ireland, and especially in the poorer areas of that island, was primarily a means of increasing income in a society where population was already growing rapidly and standards falling. It thus tended to cause fragmentation of holdings in many parts as it became embedded within the farming structure.[34] In lowland Scotland, on the other hand, the richer areas such as the Lothians had hardly any textile tradition at all because a supplementary source of income of this type was less necessary. Where spinning and weaving elsewhere did become established they tended to concentrate in the cottages of farm servants or in villages, not in the homes of leaseholders.[35] In Scotland, therefore, linen production and farming income became insulated and there was little temptation for landlords to sub-divide units in the Irish fashion to maximise income from textile production.[36] Such a strategy was more typical of the Highland landed class who did encourage in that poorer society a smallholding system linked to kelping, fishing and illicit whisky-making. Significantly, too, the deprived north-west of Scotland was the Scottish home of the potato, not as an item in crop rotation but as a primary source of subsistence.[37]

If, on this evidence, Scotland was already a richer society by the mid-eighteenth century, developments thereafter merely increased her lead. Central to the process of differential advance post-1750 (and possibly before that date) was the contrasting rate of population growth. Over the period 1755 to 1821 Scottish population grew at a rate of 0.77 per cent per annum, while some recent calculations suggest an Irish rate of over 1.5 per cent per annum or more than twice as fast as that in Scotland.[38] Even this remarkable difference considerably underestimates the contrast in demographic pressure in the two societies because Scotland was also more successful in removing a proportion of its rural population from crop cultivation, where marginal productivity was close to zero, to industrial work in the towns and villages. The social consequences were plain: in Ireland population growth produced a pattern of farm fragmentation in densely settled areas and in more advanced farming districts an oversupply of labour and a decline in real wages.[39] In Scotland, the relatively slow rate of demographic expansion meant less pressure on land resources (except in the north-west highlands where population rose more rapidly and arable lands were scarcer) and rising real wages as farmers competed for labour with industrial producers.[40] In turn, with a buoyant home market, manufacturing growth was sustained in a fashion impossible in Ireland where rural incomes became depressed as the eighteenth century proceeded.[41]

It is easier to speculate on the effects than on the origins of this fundamentally important contrast in the demographic experience of the two societies. Sub-division of land was undoubtedly easier in Ireland than in lowland Scotland, and this may have contributed to earlier marriage through a greater facility in the setting up of separate holdings temporarily viable through potato cultivation and bi-employments.[42] Irish landlords have often been blamed through hindsight for allowing this potentially disastrous development. But landlords were less powerful than their critics allowed, and clandestine sub-division in defiance of estate authority was often practised. Partible inheritance apparently lay deep in the social institutions of the population, and its economic value exerted a powerful attraction for a population which was unlikely to find much in the way of long-term alternative employment off the land. In any case, Irish age at marriage seems to have been abnormally low by European standards, a pattern well established before the eighteenth century.[43]

Scottish social values and institutions were more conducive to economic growth in a wider sense. The apparent facility with which the economy recovered after 1770 from crises such as that of the American War of Independence and proceeded to exploit new avenues in West India trade, European commerce and East Indian connections reflected a society capable of rapid adjustment to new opportunities for profit and enterprise.[44] The Irish economy was encouraged by parliamentary assistance and landlord initiative but the population, even at élite levels, do not seem to have accepted growth as a social goal in the enthusiastic manner of the Scots. The great Scottish institutions of law, church and education partly inspired and at the same time reflected this approach. Legal thought evolved to accommodate the new demands of the emerging capitalist economy. Viscount Stair, in his *Institutions* of 1681, emphasised that man's obligations, not only to God but to the public interest, were 'anterior to and inductive' of property. By 1751, however, Lord Bankton was arguing, contrary to Stair, that property is anterior and that society really came into existence to protect property.[45] The same assumptions filtered through into the intellectual assumptions of the political economists who taught in the same universities and frequented the same clubs as the lawyers. The reader of the *Wealth of Nations* is left in no doubt that the main function of a country's legal system is to protect private property. At the more mundane level of burghal law and practice, equally important advances had occurred before the later eighteenth century. By the 1730s, the old legal constraints on entry to trade and apprenticeship seem to have been abandoned in practice in the larger towns, and competition rather than privilege became the governing influence on social status.[46]

In the age of the 'Moderates', the weight of the established church was thrown behind the cause of economic reform. The new rationalism of the Scottish Enlightenment quickly permeated some branches of the local parish ministry, not simply in the sense that Calvinism was able to accommodate the new realities of a commercial society but also, and more fundamentally, in the way in which many of the clergy enthusiastically commended material progress as a reflection of the will of God. In the *Old Statistical Account,* for instance, ministers were inclined to emphasise the contribution of religion, sobriety and industry to beneficent economic change. This was an important element in the legitimisation of growth. Of course, at a deeper level of analysis, no one can deny the relevance to Scottish economic success of the Calvinist inheritance and the social values it promoted. Historians dispute its precise influence, but there is a fair amount of agreement that it helped to strengthen the commercial virtues by encouraging social action and seriousness of purpose. As R. H. Campbell has argued: '. . . the social action was one in which the individual, as one of the elect, could find himself called to be a direct and active agent of God's Will. In that way the individual was a partner of the Almighty, a junior partner, but still a partner, and so was provided with a major incentive to the utter self-confidence and assurance in his actions which is necessary for a successful entrepreneur'.[47] There is less controversy over the importance of the elementary educational system, which was itself an integral feature of the Calvinist tradition. Schooling in the eighteenth century was not free nor was it compulsory, yet attendance in the lowlands was widespread. The system was one means by which the discipline of regular work was inculcated. The link achieved between parish and burghal schools and the universities was a route to social mobility for the *petite bourgeoisie* who made up the majority of students in higher education.[48] Trinity College, Dublin on the other hand had a mainly genteel intake and failed to develop vocational subjects when they were flourishing in the Scottish universities.

Little is known about the specific effect of basic educational skills upon growth, but it is likely that as a shift occurs to a more dynamic economic system, literacy acquires new value. The praise bestowed by contemporaries on Scottish farmers and labourers for their intelligent use of new methods and work patterns might suggest that literacy encourages processes of rationalism, raises expectations and stimulates the examination of alternatives. Comparison with Ireland reveals striking contrasts: in rural Ireland in 1841 only two-fifths of men over twenty-five years and less than a sixth of the women declared an ability to read and write.[49] Might this help to explain the technological conservatism and the aversion to risk of which Irish farmers were traditionally accused? Certainly current evidence suggests the survival of flail, spade and reaping hook in nineteenth-century Irish agriculture, but this might reflect the low labour cost structure of Irish farming (relative to Scottish) as much as anything else.[50]

Finally, some attention must be given to the three social groups, landlords, tenant farmers and merchant classes, in both Ireland and Scotland, who were primarily responsible for directing the course of economic change. The obvious contrast between an Irish Protestant landed class out of sympathy with a loyal Catholic peasantry and a Scottish landed élite with strong connections and much influence over its tenantry has already been mentioned. Equally significant were major differences in the composition of the landed classes. The large number of small estates in lowland Scotland permitted the relatively easy promotion of successful merchants, colonial adventurers, lawyers and military men to landed status. As non-landed fortunes rapidly accumulated in the period after 1750, so the speed and

extent of this penetration increased.[51] Two-thirds of Roxburghshire changed hands
and one-third of Renfrewshire between 1760 and 1815.[52] The widespread diffusion
of urban wealth in the lowlands ensured that the pattern was not simply limited to
the counties around Glasgow and Edinburgh though it was certainly more common
in the central zone.[53] Such a social change brought new ideas, fresh horizons and
more money to Scottish agriculture. No similar development occurred in Ireland.
Irish adventurers, especially successful Catholics, tended not to return home to a
landed estate in the Scottish fashion. Only in the Galway area and to some extent
around Cork and Belfast did similar relationships form to those which were
commonplace around every large Scottish town.[54] Connections were equally weak in
the opposite direction. The Anglo-Irish tended to identify closely with land and to
seek careers outside trade. Ironically, this helped to sustain business immigration
from Britain to the Irish towns, of which the influx of Scots into Irish wholesale
trade and manufacture was a particularly striking feature.[55] This partly reflected
contrasting attitudes to commerce among the Scottish landed classes. The
coincidence of small estates, traditions of primogeniture and the limited number of
more desirable professional posts in the law and the church ensured that the
younger sons of lairds saw trade as an entirely respectable and acceptable
occupation. In turn, this two-way contact between land and trade meant that a
deeply ingrained commercialism developed within the Scottish laird class.[56]

There were other differences. Scottish landlords were renowned for their
enormous traditional and legal powers. They had an accepted right to control the
organisation of the farm structure through the medium of the baron court, and
legislation of the Scottish Parliament in the later seventeenth century had both
strengthened these proprietorial privileges and given increased legal power to
enclose and consolidate. The delicate ties of hierarchy and dependence within the
social structure of their estates were maintained through their influence over
education, poor relief and church appointments as well as by hereditary privilege.
This helped to ensure the extraordinarily peaceful transition to capitalist agriculture
which was such a striking feature of the Scottish agricultural revolution.[57] Their
links with the world of the intellectuals through close association with the legal
classes, residence in Edinburgh for the season and attendance at university helped
to develop systematic ideas about the reorganisation of agriculture as both a morally
enlightened and materially beneficial course of action.[58] Eric Hobsbawm has
recently shown that the remarkable characteristic of the Scottish improvers and
agronomists was the intellectual lucidity with which they viewed the task of rural
transformation and their vehement but often uncritical condemnation of all
practices associated with what they perceived as the old feudal régime of reciprocity
and communalism.[59] The 5th Duke of Argyll spoke for his class when he asserted in
1800: '. . . farms should be divided so that every man may have his own separate
farm to manage and improve in his own way, and the skilful and industrious may
reap the benefit of their labours and knowledge and at the same time be examples to
others.'[60] Scottish landowners were committed to reorganisation of traditional
agriculture along the lines of consolidation into compact farms and utterly opposed
to sub-division as an unmitigated moral evil and enemy of agrarian efficiency.

Irish landowners cannot easily be classified because, like the Scots, there were significant local variations in estate practice and landlord personality but, as in Scotland, some common characteristics emerge.[61] Irish landlords were often confronted with a hostile tenantry whom they were perhaps unwilling to alienate further by attempting radical surgery on their estates. It is relevant to note that they sometimes had to take into account the sectarian mix of their estate populations when formulating improvements. Eviction was less common in Ireland before 1815, but there was more rural violence.[62] The division of labour and function between landlord and tenant in Scotland was notably different from that in Ireland. In Scotland the landlord assumed financial responsibility for the maintenance and extension of roads, farm buildings and outhouses, leaving the tenant to concentrate on labour management, crop rotations and animal husbandry. In Ireland, much more of the burden for 'fixed capital' improvement tended to fall on the shoulders of the tenant.[63] Landlord ability to influence the direction of change was further limited by the very long leases, often for three lives, which proliferated on Irish farms and by the 'middleman' system of tenure which, while important in the effective pursuit of agrarian operations, especially in pastoral regions, was conducive to the practice of uncontrolled sub-division in a social context of rising population.[64]

All this tended to create an effective barrier to even the most enthusiastic of Irish improvers. Recent work on Ulster has shown how committed reformers were ultimately overwhelmed by the appetite for land of a rapidly increasing peasant population, traditions of partible inheritance, the weakness of alternatives to landholding and the temptations of easy income before 1815 from a smallholding economy based on linen, cattle and grain sales.[65] Indeed, it would be difficult to argue that the striking differences between Irish and Scottish agricultural systems by 1800 were solely or even mainly due to contrasts in landlord performance.[66] Ultimately, what mattered was the response of the tenants because increasing yields depended on their adjustments to land use, crop selection and livestock preferences. In Scotland, highland and lowland landowners were equally committed to raising the revenue-producing capacity of their estates, but the greater success of the latter was due primarily to the existence on their properties of a much larger pool of tenant farmers capable of adjustment and vigorous response to new ideas. Here perhaps lay a crucial difference from the social structure of rural Ireland, at least outside favoured regions in the province of Munster and some other parts. The Scottish capitalist farmer did not emerge fully formed in the last quarter of the eighteenth century from the plans of often dilettante improving landlords who were occasionally more interested in elaboration than efficiency. Consolidation of farm units had been underway on a considerable scale since the seventeenth century and this, by c.1780, had produced in lowland Scotland groups of tenants well capable of responding to market trends and better methods after that date.[67] Indeed, the outlines of the conventional 'improved' farm were already present in several favoured areas — even outside the well-known example of East Lothian — by the middle decades of the eighteenth century. Interestingly, sub-tenancy on these farms, rapidly abandoned after 1780, was somewhat different from the smallholding structure in the central and western areas of Ireland. Often Scottish sub-tenants held the merest fragments of land and so had no option but to seek work on larger units for long periods in the year to gain a full subsistence. They had evolved to an intermediate rank which gave them a social position between that of peasant and agricultural labourer. Sub-division was thus partly prevented because sub-tenancies were effectively tied in with the specific labour needs of the larger farms and were altered when these changed after 1780.[68]

The Scottish tenant farming class were then provided with fresh incentives as the market for their products increased but it also did so for their Irish counterparts in the later eighteenth century. One key factor explaining different responses was that each group faced a quite different labour supply position. Labour was easy to come by in an Ireland experiencing high population growth and slow urban expansion. In lowland Scotland, however, population rose much more slowly while industrial and town growth proceeded apace. Irish farmers had less need to look for more productive methods as their labour costs fell in real terms; Scottish farmers on the other hand were confronted with sharp increases in wage levels as they competed with towns and industry. They reacted by organising labour more efficiently and produced by 1815 the classic Scottish structure of a small corps of dedicated, well-paid, full-time employees, the ploughmen, and a much larger number of poorly paid seasonal workers recruited mainly from Ireland, the Highlands and neighbouring towns and villages.[69] The contrast, therefore, which emerged between Ireland and the Scottish lowlands was reminiscent of that which developed between England north and south of the Trent line. In southern England, as in rural Ireland, there was a similar combination of rising population, decaying ancient manufacturing industry, slow migration and low labour efficiency, suggesting that it was the spatial concentration of new industry in Britain which was the decisive conditioning factor in agrarian development rather than the more dramatic and better documented intervention of landlord personalities.[70]

The roots of the Scottish achievement in urban and industrial growth, at least until the widespread use of steam-power after 1800, lay to a significant extent in the business resources and risk capital of the nation's commercial classes. It was not so much that Scotland had more investment capital than Ireland; rather it may be that there was more of it in the hands of the venturesome and the enterprising.[71] Again, the contrast between the two societies cannot be painted wholly in black and white terms. Irish merchants and producers, though constrained within the Navigation System to a greater extent than the Scots, were nevertheless able to take full advantage of national comparative advantage in provision supply and linen manufacture. However, the contrasts with the Scottish merchant community perhaps remain still more conspicuous than the parallels.[72] Irish traders tended mainly to do business on a commission basis, especially in English commerce, though less so in their European activities. The Scots normally traded on their own account but since the later seventeenth century had been effectively tapping London financial resources to help them do so. Mercantile activity in Ireland seemed more passive and dependent than in Scotland: the energetic fashion in which the Scots moved from emphasis on American trade before 1780 and then to

Caribbean, European and Asian connections is striking in this respect though, it might be added, the Scots trading community by then had the 'irresistible bundles of products of the Industrial Revolution'[73] to offer their customers. By contrast with the Scots, the capitals of Irish merchants were low, and while banking in Scotland, outside the chartered institutions, was dominated by the merchant class, the system in Ireland was more likely to be supported by landowners.[74] Recent work has drawn attention to the array of small capitalists in domestic industry and inland trade in lowland Scotland whose numbers rose rapidly in the later eighteenth century.[75] It was from this social group that the enterprise and finance for the textile revolution primarily derived.

IV

It is entirely accurate to assert that a central reason for the Scottish achievement of industrialisation was the country's favourable natural endowment of coal and raw materials in close proximity to navigable water. Yet proven advantages in such resources cannot in themselves adequately explain why Scotland drew so rapidly ahead of Ireland in the period before 1815 if only because, in the eighteenth and early nineteenth centuries, such factor endowments played a much less crucial part in Scottish industrial expansion than they were to do after 1830. The argument of this paper has been that the origins of the different rates of growth lie deeper and go much further back in time than some have suggested. Both societies from the mid-seventeenth century were faced with the challenge and stimulus of English competition, markets, cultural influences and technological ingenuity and reacted to them in dramatically contrasting ways. These responses were conditioned by the prevailing social structure, value systems, and business regimes of Ireland and Scotland and, perhaps most fundamentally of all, by the fact that by the early decades of the eighteenth century the two countries were already at somewhat different stages of development.

REFERENCES

1. R. H. Campbell, *Scotland since 1707* (Oxford, 1965), p. 42.

2. See, *inter alia*, B. F. Duckham, 'English influences on the Scottish Coal Industry, 1700–1815', in J. Butt and J. T. Ward, eds., *Scottish Themes* (Edinburgh, 1976), pp. 28–45; T. C. Smout, 'Lead-mining in Scotland, 1650–1859', in P. L. Payne, ed., *Studies in Scottish Business History* (London, 1967), pp. 103–35; J. E. Handley, *The Agricultural Revolution in Scotland* (Glasgow, 1963); H. Hamilton, *An Economic History of Scotland in the Eighteenth Century* (Oxford, 1963).

3. T. M. Devine, 'An Eighteenth Century Business Élite: Glasgow West India Merchants, 1750–1815', *Scott. Hist. Rev.*, LVII 1978, pp. 40–63; *idem*, 'The Scottish Merchant Community, 1680-1740', in R. H. Campbell and A. Skinner, eds., *The Origins of the Scottish Enlightenment* (Edinburgh, 1982); L. Timperley, 'The Pattern of landholding in Eighteenth Century Scotland', in M. L. Parry and T. R. Slater, eds., *The Making of the Scottish Countryside* (London, 1980), pp. 137–154.

4. John Clive, 'The Social Background to the Scottish Renaissance', in N. T. Phillipson and Rosalind Mitchison, eds., *Scotland in the Age of Improvement* (Edinburgh, 1970), pp. 225-244.

5. T. C. Smout, *Scottish Trade on the Eve of Union, 1660-1707* (Edinburgh, 1963).

6. P. W. J. Riley, *The Union of England and Scotland* (Manchester, 1980).

7. T. C. Smout, ed., 'Sir John Clerk's observations on the present circumstances of Scotland 1730', in *Miscellany of the Scottish History Society* X (Edinburgh, 1965), p. 184.

8. Alexander Murdoch, *The People Above: Politics and Administration in Mid-Eighteenth Century Scotland* (Edinburgh, 1980).

9. F. G. James, *Ireland in the Empire, 1688-1770* (Cambridge, Mass. 1973), pp. 190-127; L. M. Cullen, *Anglo-Irish Trade 1660-1800* (Manchester, 1968), pp. 1-28; E. M. Johnston, *Ireland in the Eighteenth Century* (Dublin, 1974), pp. 54-55.

10. L. M. Cullen, *The Emergence of Modern Ireland 1660-1900* (London, 1981), p. 87.

11. The basis of the revised view of the absentee landlords can be found in David Large, 'The Wealth of the Greater Irish Landowners, 1750-1815', *Irish Historical Studies*, XV (1966-7), pp. 22-41; A. P. W. Malcolmson, 'Absenteeism in Eighteenth Century Ireland,' *Irish Economic and Social History*, I (1974), pp. 15-30; W. A. Maguire, *The Downshire Estates in Ireland, 1801-1845* (Oxford, 1972).

12. R. Davis, 'English Foreign Trade 1700-1774', *Econ. Hist. Rev.* 2nd ser., XV (1963), pp. 286-7; N. B. Harte, 'Protection and the English Linen Trade', in N. B. Harte and K. Ponting, eds., *Textile History and Economic History* (Manchester, 1973), pp. 108-9.

13. A. J. Durie, 'The Markets for Scottish Linen, 1730-1775', *Scott. Hist. Rev.*, LII, (1973), pp. 30-49; Cullen, *Anglo-Irish Trade*, p. 51

14. A. J. Durie, *The Scottish Linen Industry in the Eighteenth Century* (Edinburgh, 1979), pp. 143-166.

15. W. H. Crawford, 'Landlord Tenant Relations in Ulster, 1609-1820', *Irish Economic and Social History* II (1975), pp. 12-16.

16. J. Butt, 'The Scottish Cotton Industry during the Industrial Revolution, 1780-1840' in L. M. Cullen and T. C. Smout, eds., *Comparative Aspects of Scottish and Irish Economic and Social History 1600-1900* (Edinburgh, 1977), pp. 116-128.

17. D. Dickson, 'Economic Development in Scotland and Ireland in the Eighteenth Century: Some thoughts on the Irish Case', Paper presented at the Economic History Society Conference, University College, Swansea, 1978; J. Mannion, 'The Waterford Merchants and the Irish-Newfoundland Provisions Trade, 1770-1820' in L. M. Cullen and P. Butel, eds., *Négoce et Industrie en France et en Irelande aux XVIIe et XIXe Siècles* (Bordeaux, 1980), pp. 27-43.

18. Raymond H. Crotty, *Irish Agricultural Production* (Cork, 1966), pp. 18-20; Laura E. Cochran, 'Scottish Trade with Ireland in the Eighteenth Century', Paper presented at the Economic History Society Conference, Loughborough University, 1981.

19. Sometimes reorganisation of farm structure on the Scottish pattern was attempted in areas of dense settlement but achieved little as population pressures increased. See D. McCourt, 'The Decline of Rundale, 1750-1850', in Peter Roebuck, ed., *Plantation to Partition* (Belfast, 1981), pp. 119-139.

20. The impact is discussed in detail in T. M. Devine, 'The Colonial Trades and Industrial Investment in Scotland 1700-1815', *Econ. Hist. Rev.*, 2nd ser. XXIX (1976), pp. 1-13, and idem, 'Colonial Commerce and the Scottish Economy 1730-1815', in Cullen and Smout, eds., *Comparative Aspects*, pp. 177-189.

21. *Ibid.*

22. Cullen, *Anglo-Irish Trade*, p. 19.

23. Donald Woodward, 'A comparative study of the Irish and Scottish livestock trades in the seventeenth century', in Cullen and Smout, eds., *Comparative Aspects*, p. 157.

24. T. Desmond Williams, ed., *Secret Societies in Ireland* (Dublin, 1973), pp. 13-25, 26-35; J. J. Lee, 'Patterns of Rural Unrest in Nineteenth Century Ireland', in L. M. Cullen and F. Furet, eds., *Ireland and France: 17th-20th Centuries* (Paris, 1981), pp. 223-237. For

the Scottish contrast, see T. M. Devine, 'Social Stability in the Eastern Lowlands of Scotland during the Agricultural Revolution, 1780-1840', in T. M. Devine, ed., *Lairds and Improvement in the Scotland of the Enlightenment* (Glasgow, 1979), pp. 59-70.

25. See references in note 11 and R. H. Campbell, 'The Scottish Improvers and the Course of Agrarian Change in the Eighteenth Century', in Cullen and Smout, eds., *Comparative Aspects*, pp. 204-215.

26. Peter Roebuck, 'Absentee Landownership', *Agricultural History Review* XXI (1973), pp. 11-14.

27. C. H. Lee, *A Cotton Enterprise 1795-1840: a History of McConnell and Kennedy* (Manchester, 1972), pp. 23-46; G. Kirkham, 'Economic Diversification in a Marginal Economy: a Case Study', in Roebuck, ed., *Plantation to Partition*, pp. 64-65.

28. T. C. Smout, 'Scotland and England: is Dependency a Symptom or a Cause of Underdevelopment?' *Review* III (1980), pp. 621-622.

29. J. S. Donnelly, *The Land and the People of Nineteenth Century Cork* (London, 1975), p. 11; E. R. R. Green, *The Lagan Valley 1800-50* (London, 1949), p. 98.

30. Cullen and Smout, eds., *Comparative Aspects*, p. 4.

31. Cullen, *Emergence of Modern Ireland*, pp. 30, 41-2, 90.

32. T. C. Smout, 'Famine and Famine-Relief in Scotland', in Cullen and Smout, eds., *Comparative Aspects*, pp. 21-30; I. D. Whyte, *Agriculture and Society in Seventeenth Century Scotland* (Edinburgh, 1979), pp. 7-28. Even in the north-western islands, the most primitive part of Scotland in the seventeenth century, little trace of this practice survives. See Frances J. Shaw, *The Northern and Western Islands of Scotland: their Economy and Society in the Seventeenth Century* (Edinburgh, 1980), *passim*.

33. Cullen, *Emergence of Modern Ireland*, p. 26.

34. Crawford, 'Landlord-Tenant Relations', p. 12; Eric L. Almquist, 'Mayo and Beyond: Land, Domestic Industry and Rural Transformation in the Irish West', *Irish Economic and Social History*, V (1978), p. 72.

35. Malcolm Gray, 'Scottish Emigration: the Social Impact of Agrarian Change in the Rural Lowlands, 1775-1875', *Perspectives in American History*, VII (1973), pp. 150-153.

36. T. C. Smout argues that it was the ease with which flax could be grown in Ireland which tied the proto-industrial family to the land, whereas in Scotland flax was largely imported from the Baltic, the weaver bought his raw material and became a specialist in the village. This might have been an additional influence contributing to the wider demographic pressures which are seen here as the central factors in the contrast between the two societies. See T. C. Smout, 'Centre and periphery in history — Scotland', *Journal of Common Market Studies*, XVIII (1980), p. 266.

37. James Hunter, *The Making of the Crofting Community* (Edinburgh, 1976); T. M. Devine, 'The Rise and Fall of Illicit Whisky-Making in Northern Scotland, 1780-1840', *Scott. Hist. Rev.*, LIV (1975), pp. 155-177.

38. S. Daultrey, D. Dickson and C. Ó'Gráda, 'Eighteenth Century Irish Population: New Perspectives from Old Sources', *Journal of Economic History*, XII, 3 (Sept. 1981).

39. For a discussion of a regional example of this process around the city of Cork, see D. Dickson, 'Property and Social Structure in eighteenth century South Munster', in Cullen and Furet, eds., *Ireland and France*, pp. 129-138.

40. For Scottish agrarian wages between 1740 and 1798, see Valerie Morgan, 'Agricultural Wage Rates in late Eighteenth Century Scotland', *Econ. Hist. Rev.*, 2nd ser., 24 (1971), pp. 181-201. For the period 1800 to 1840, see T. M. Devine, 'Social Stability and Agrarian Change in the Eastern Lowlands of Scotland, 1810-40', *Social History*, III (1978), pp. 331-346; *idem*, 'The Demand for Agricultural Labour in East Lothian after the Napoleonic Wars', *Trans. E. Lothian Antiquarian and Natural History Soc.*, Vol. 16, 1979, pp. 49-61; Ian Levitt and Christopher Smout, *The State of the Scottish Working Class in 1843* (Edinburgh, 1979), pp. 70-99.

41. Cullen, *Emergence of Modern Ireland*, p. 171.

42. There may well be contrasts in marriage ages. In Ireland they appear to have hovered around 22 years for males and 20 for females (Cullen, *Emergence of Modern Ireland,* p. 83). Material on the subject is fragmentary for eighteenth-century Scotland, but such data as do exist indicate substantially later ages at marriage: a mean 'rural' age for women in Central Ayrshire of 26; Laggan parish (Inverness) 29 to 32 for men and between 27 and 30 for women; Lochcrutton (Kirkcudbright) average age at marriage 33 for men and 24 for women. See Michael Flinn, ed., *Scottish Population History from the 17th century to the 1930s* (Cambridge, 1977), pp. 274–9.

43. L. M. Cullen, 'Population Trends in Seventeenth Century Ireland', *Economic and Social Review,* 61 (1974–5).

44. T. M. Devine, 'The American War of Independence and Scottish Economic History', in Owen Dudley Edwards and George Shepperson, eds., *Scotland, Europe and the American Revolution* (Edinburgh, 1976), pp. 61–65.

45. Peter Stein, 'The General Notions of Contract and Property in Eighteenth Century Scottish Thought', *Juridical Review* (1963), pp. 3–4, 11–12.

46. T. M. Devine, 'The Business Class of the Scottish Towns in the later Seventeenth and Early Eighteenth Centuries', in T. R. B. Dicks and G. Gordon, eds., *Studies in Scottish Urban History* (forthcoming).

47. R. H. Campbell, *The Rise and Fall of Scottish Industry, 1701–1939* (Edinburgh, 1980), p. 28. For other discussions of Calvinism and economic development, see Gordon Marshall, *Presbyteries and Profits* (Oxford, 1980); S. A. Burrell, 'Calvinism, Capitalism and the Middle Classes', *Journal of Modern History,* XXXII (1960); T. M. Devine and S. G. E. Lythe, 'The Economy of Scotland in the Reign of James VI: a Revision Article', *Scott. Hist. Rev.* 50 (1972), pp. 91–106.

48. W. H. Matthew, 'The Origins and Occupations of Glasgow Students', *Past and Present* 33 (1966).

49. C. Ó Gráda, 'On Some Aspects of Productivity Change in Irish Agriculture, 1845–1926'. Paper presented to the Seventh International Economic History Congress, Edinburgh University, 1978, p. 10.

50. *Ibid.*

51. Timperley, 'Pattern of Landholding', pp. 148–9.

52. Sir John Sinclair, *Analysis of the Statistical Account of Scotland* (1825), I, p. 175; Thomas Somerville, *My Own Life and Times 1741–1814,* (Edinburgh, 1861), pp. 359–60.

53. T. Donnelly, 'The Economic Activities of the Aberdeen Merchant Guild, 1750–1799', *Scottish Economic and Social History* I (1981), pp. 35–38; Timperley, 'Pattern of Landholding', pp. 148–9.

54. L. M. Cullen, 'Merchant Communities, the Navigation Acts and Irish and Scottish Responses', in Cullen and Smout, eds., *Comparative Aspects,* pp. 165–176.

55. Cullen, *Emergence of Modern Ireland,* pp. 16, 127–8, 189, 248.

56. Devine, 'Scottish Merchant Community'.

57. Devine, 'Social Stability during the Agricultural Revolution,' pp. 59–70.

58. N. T. Phillipson, 'The Social Structure of the Faculty of Advocates in Scotland, 1661–1840', in Alan Harding, ed., *Lawmaking and Lawmakers in British History* (London, 1980).

59. E. J. Hobsbawm, 'Capitalisme et Agriculture: Les Réformateurs Écossais au XVIIIe Siècle', *Annales* (1979), pp. 580–601.

60. The 5th Duke of Argyll's Instructions to Mr. Duncan Campbell as Chamberlain of Tiree (1800), in Eric R. Cregeen, ed., *Argyll Estate Instructions* (Edinburgh 1964), p. 51.

61. This is well brought out in Maguire, *The Downshire Estates, passim.*

62. Lee, 'Patterns of Rural Unrest', in Cullen and Furet, eds., *Ireland and France',* pp. 223–237; McCourt: 'Decline of Rundale', in Roebuck, ed., *Plantation to Partition,* p. 137.

63. Maguire, *Downshire Estates,* pp. 70–71 and sources mentioned therein.

64. D. Dickson, 'Middlemen', in T. Bartlett and D. W. Hayton, eds., *Penal Era and Golden Age* (Beifast 1979), pp. 162–185.

65. McCourt, 'Decline of Rundale', in Roebuck, ed., *Plantation to Partition*, pp. 119–139. Again the comparison with similar landlord disappointments in the Scottish highlands is a compelling one.

66. Irish landlords founded villages, sponsored rural industry and supported tenurial change but they had much less room for manoeuvre than their Scottish counterparts. See, for example, Ingeborg Leister's study of Tipperaray, *Das Werden Der Agrarlandschaft in der Grafschaft Tipperary, Irland* (Marburg, 1963). Racial and religious links between landlord and peasantry were not necessarily conducive to successful development. Connaught, where a Catholic landholding rump survived, was probably the most conservative part of Ireland in the eighteenth century. See J. G. Simms, 'Connaught in the Eighteenth Century', *Irish Hist. Studies*, XI (1958–9), pp. 119–124.

67. I. Whyte, 'The Emergence of the New Estate Structure', in Parry and Slater, eds., *The Making of the Scottish Countryside*, pp. 117–136; R. A. Dodgshon, 'The Removal of Runrig in Roxburgh and Berwickshire', *Scottish Studies*, 16 (1972), pp. 121–7; J. di Folco, 'The Hopes of Craighall and Land Investment in the Seventeenth Century', in Devine, ed., *Lairds and Improvement*, pp. 1–10.

68. Devine, 'Social Stability during the Scottish Agricultural Revolution', pp. 59–60.

69. T. M. Devine, 'Agrarian Change in Ireland and Scotland in the Eighteenth Century', Paper presented at the Economic History Society Conference, University College, Swansea, 1978, pp. 8–10. Production rose markedly in both societies but in Western and Northern Ireland such increments often derived from small-scale intensive farming related to potato cultivation. Yields tended therefore to be increased through the *intensification of labour* rather than (as in lowland Scotland) through the greater efficiency of a given unit of labour input. By the 1840s the contemporary agricultural statistician, William Burness, concluded that the ratio of arable acres to each labourer in Scotland was about 20 whereas in Ireland it was almost 3. See W. Burness, 'Our Agricultural Labourers: English, Irish and Scotch', *Journal of Agriculture*, new ser. 1849–51, p. 450 and the important French exercise in early productivity comparisons, Leonce de Lavergne, *Essai sur l'Economie Rurale de l'Angleterre, de l'Ecosse et de l'Irlande* (Paris, 1854).

70. Eric L. Jones, 'The Constraints on Economic Growth in Southern England, 1650–1850', in *Third International Conference of Economic History: Munich, 1965* (Paris, 1974), V, pp. 423–30.

71. One is struck, for example, by the more significant role played by landowners in banking and industrial development in Ireland compared to Scotland.

72. This paragraph is based mainly on Cullen, *Anglo-Irish Trade;* D. Dickson, 'The Cork Merchant Community in the Eighteenth Century: a Regional Perspective', in Cullen and Butel, eds., *Négoce et Industrie*, pp. 45–50; Devine, 'Scottish Merchant Community'; *idem, The Tobacco Lords* (Edinburgh, 1975), pp. 3–34.

73. Ralph Davis, 'English Foreign Trade, 1700–74', *Econ. Hist. Rev.*, 2nd ser. XV (1963), p. 298.

74. C. W. Munn, *The Scottish Provincial Banking Companies 1747–1864* (Edinburgh, 1981), pp. 152–163.

75. A. Dickson and W. Speirs, 'Changes in Class Structure in Paisley, 1750–1845', *Scott. Hist. Rev.* LIX (1980), pp. 54–72.

Part II

Rural Themes

3

Some Aspects of the Structure of Rural Society in Seventeenth-Century Lowland Scotland

I. D. Whyte and K. A. Whyte

A GOOD deal is known about the rural society which emerged in Scotland during the later eighteenth and nineteenth centuries, although even here there is still ample scope for debate on fundamental issues.[1] The variety and abundance of sources for the nineteenth century have allowed detailed studies to be made of the complex social hierarchies and interactions which existed even within single farmsteads.[2] But comparatively little is known about the structure of rural society in early-modern Scotland before the onset of more rapid social and economic changes in the later eighteenth century. Likewise it is not clear to what extent pre-Improvement Scottish rural society varied spatially due to influences such as landownership patterns, the nature of the agricultural economy, patterns of rural industry and proximity to urban markets, or whether cultural differences between the Highlands and the Lowlands also involved contrasts in rural social structure.

Past interpretations of pre-Improvement Scottish rural society have been based on two closely linked models of rural settlement and farm structure, the hamlet cluster and the ferm toun.[3] These have often been viewed as having been relatively uniform in character throughout the country. Recent research has, however, suggested that reality was more complex. Even at a local level settlements could differ considerably in size and function, while there are indications of regional contrasts in farm structure.[4] The nature and evolution of rural settlement in medieval and early-modern Scotland has yet to be explored in depth, but there are obvious implications for the study of rural society in the variations which have so far been identified.

In addition, the extent to which Scottish rural society corresponded with or differed from that in other parts of Britain at this period has not been considered in detail. Some obvious contrasts with England have been noted in passing, such as the dominance in Scotland of large estates and the comparative unimportance of small owner-occupiers.[5] Equally, comparisons have been drawn between rural settlement patterns in Scotland, particularly the West Highlands, and Ireland, suggesting that there might have been parallels between the social structure of these areas.[6] The tenant status of husbandmen under absentee landowners in many parts of Ireland at this time may echo conditions on some Scottish estates.[7]

Demographic crises caused by famines persisted into the late seventeenth century in Lowland Scotland and into the nineteenth century in the West Highlands, long after they had vanished from England.[8] The extent to which this produced contrasts in population characteristics with England and similarities with Ireland has not yet been fully explored. It is unclear whether or not there were differences in demographic measures such as age at marriage, family and household size and population mobility between early-modern Scotland and the more thoroughly researched conditions in England, though there are some indications of contrasts such as the suggestion that rural households were larger in Scotland than in England.[9]

The greatest proportion of husbandmen in early-modern Scotland were tenant farmers, yet we know little about them. Some old assumptions regarding tenancy, such as the supposed lack of written leases and the prevalence of tenancy at will during the seventeenth century, have been modified by recent research,[10] but this still leaves unanswered many questions regarding tenancy and tenant farming. To what extent was there continuity of tenure under the systems of short leases, whether written or verbal, which were common in the seventeenth century? How geographically and socially mobile were the tenantry? How frequently did holdings pass from father to son, and what became of tenants' sons who were unable to obtain a holding? Under what circumstances did tenants face eviction? To what extent were farmers able to accumulate capital reserves to tide them over bad years? The answers to such questions also have implications for other strata of rural society about which we know even less: the cottars, farm servants and labourers who were dependent upon the tenantry.

In the past it has been customary to dismiss as inadequate the source material available for the detailed study of the rural economy and society of early-modern Scotland. Certainly the documentary record is poorer than that of England in many respects: for example, few well-kept Scottish parish registers exist before the late seventeenth century. Nevertheless, Scottish archives have strengths as well as weaknesses. The dominance of large estates has resulted in the survival of many voluminous collections of estate papers. These are a major source of information on rural conditions, and though they have received increasing attention in recent years, their full potential has yet to be exploited.[11] In addition, other sources which are capable of shedding light on rural society, such as the Register of Sasines, the testaments and inventories lodged with Commissary Courts, and Kirk Session records, have still to be studied in detail.

The first part of this paper considers some general questions regarding the structure of rural society in seventeenth-century Scotland. The second part reports some preliminary findings of a research project which is investigating in detail the structure of a single rural community. An attempt is made to show the kind of information which can be obtained by using estate papers in conjunction with other sources, and some possible frameworks for further research on Scottish rural society at this period are suggested.

An obvious source of information on rural society in late seventeenth-century Scotland is the poll tax records of the 1690s. These have been frequently referred to in general terms,[12] but have not been analysed exhaustively from the standpoint of social structure. There are good reasons for this: apart from being fragmentary, the returns are not the mirror of rural society which they have sometimes been assumed to be. They have limitations which reduce their usefulness for studying social structure. First, people who were too poor to pay the poll — an unknown but possibly significant proportion of the population — were omitted. Second, children under the age of 16 were exempted and were only listed for the wealthiest families. Third, the recording of children over 16 who lived with their parents appears to be deficient.[13] Nevertheless, the returns have the advantages of a fairly standard format and reasonable spatial coverage while listing people, albeit sometimes ambiguously, at levels of society about which other sources say little. Interpreted with care, they provide a general indication of variations in the make-up of rural society between different areas and of contrasts within social groups.

However, another problem with the poll lists is that the designations which they use for different social groups vary from one district to another and do not necessarily match those of other sources. It is thus necessary to try and rationalise such designations before attempting further analysis. It must also be appreciated that the socio-economic classification used by the tax commissioners oversimplified a society whose gradations were complex and often overlapping. Table 1 tries to standardise the terms used in the poll lists and other sources such as the 1656 list of the Justices of the Peace for Midlothian.[14]

The socio-economic position of tenants is easiest to establish, as their poll was directly proportional to their rents. The poll lists show that in many lowland parishes tenants and their families formed a fairly small proportion of the recorded population. If only male heads of household and unmarried men (excluding children over 16 living at home) are considered, in lowland Aberdeenshire tenants formed only 20–25% of recorded adult males in many parishes.[15] The real figures are likely to have been lower, as any omissions would probably have been below the level of tenant. In some Berwickshire parishes the figure was as low as 15%, as was also the case in many West Lothian and Midlothian parishes.[16]

In remote parishes in upland Aberdeenshire the situation was different. In Glenbucket tenants made up 81% of recorded adult males and in Cabrach 48%. In the poor Cabrach especially the use of the term 'small tenant' for most people who rented land expresses fundamental differences in the make-up of the community from eastern lowland areas. It typifies a rural society which was probably widespread in the eastern Highlands where townships containing many small tenants holding direct from a proprietor or from intermediate tacksmen were normal.[17] Such small tenants were probably more comparable to substantial lowland cottars than to larger lowland tenants. The figures for Renfrewshire indicate a pattern intermediate between the eastern Highlands and Lowlands, with tenants making up 30–40% of the recorded active males in many parishes.[18] Smaller family holdings were more frequent here than in lowland Aberdeenshire or the Lothians.

The blurring of distinctions between different social groups was probably increased by lack of homogeneity within the tenantry. An examination of holding valuations from the poll tax returns illustrates the variations which occurred and the resulting differences in the tenantry. Most parishes contained a wide range of holding valuations but the balance varied. Renfrewshire was characterised by a predominance of smaller holdings with rents ranging from £20 to £40 Scots. In some parishes fragmentation had gone further and a significant proportion of tenants occupied holdings rented at £10 Scots or less, probably equivalent to many cottar holdings elsewhere. Renfrewshire, as in later times, had a greater proportion of small lairds and owner-occupiers than many parts of eastern Scotland.[19] The existence of such proprietors, who sometimes had additional occupations as tradesmen, must have further blurred social distinctions. In Lochwinnoch parish, for example, the mean rental value of lands held by small feuars was only £33 Scots against £26 Scots for tenant farmers.

In many Aberdeenshire parishes the majority of holdings were valued at between £50 and £75 Scots. Although full data are not available for the Lothians and Berwickshire, indications are that in many parishes both in the pastoral uplands and the arable lowlands average valuations were higher, some individual holdings being three times the highest valuation recorded in many Aberdeen and Renfrewshire parishes. The influence of landownership patterns and the policies of individual proprietors in shaping farm structure and hence rural social structure may be discerned, sharp variations in mean rents sometimes occurring between neighbouring estates. Broader regional variations may be related to various influences including land capability, population density and access to urban and overseas markets for agricultural produce.

Clearly a high proportion of the rural population over much of Lowland Scotland was below the tenant class. The terminology used for such people in the poll tax lists varies and it is difficult to decide to what extent this reflects real social differences or merely inconsistencies between different tax commissioners. For example, the Aberdeenshire lists record substantial numbers of 'cottars' and 'subtenants', differentiating them from farm servants who received wages. The latter group were almost never recorded as married, and it is reasonable to assume that they lived in the tenants' households while the cottars and subtenants did not. The Midlothian lists record cottars, ordinary farm servants and also married farm servants, sometimes referred to as hinds.[20] In the Renfrewshire lists relatively few cottars and subtenants appear. Instead, two categories of male farm servants occur, those who received annual wages and those who were only paid for work in harvest. It is difficult to judge whether people in the latter group lived in or not.

The records of the Justices of the Peace for Midlothian in 1656 contain a more complex hierarchy than the Midlothian poll tax lists (Table 1), showing that the latter simplify and perhaps distort social structure. In this list 'servants' include hinds, half hinds, herds, shepherds, taskers and domestic or in-servants. Men in all but the last group were normally married with their own house, kail yard and grazing rights. The hind and half hind, shepherd and herd also received some arable land. All these classes of servant were paid additional wages in kind or money. Clearly all of them, apart from domestic servants, were really cottars as they lived outside the tenants' households, subletting small portions of land in return for providing labour. It is uncertain what distinction the Midlothian poll tax lists made

TABLE 1. *Socio-economic designations used in the poll tax returns and other sources*

Designation	Definition	Variants
Landowner	Holding land by charter. May also lease land.	Owner Occupier: 'Bonnet Laird', Feuar, Portioner.
Customary tenant	Renting holding direct from proprietor but with prescriptive right to pass holding to heir.	Kindly Tenant, Rentaller.
Tenant	Renting holding direct from proprietor. Recorded in rentals.	General: Husbandman, Gudeman Small tenants: crofter, Pendicler Estate Officers: the barony officer sometimes had a specific croft. The baillie, chamberlain, factor were often tenant farmers as well. Gentlemen, 'Mr': some larger tenants styled themselves thus in the poll lists and paid a heavier poll. Millers: Mills and the lands attached to them were generally rented. Smiths: a rented smallholding often went with a smithy. Tradesmen: with smallholdings were sometimes listed primarily as tradesmen in the poll lists.
Cottar, subtenant	Living separately from tenants' households. Holding some land and/or grazings in return for labour. Sometimes receiving wages in addition.	Aberdeenshire poll tax, Cottar, Grassman, Grasswoman, subtenant Midlothian J.P.'s list 1656: Whole Hind, Half hind, tasker, herd, shepherd General: most tradesmen
Farm servant	Living in tenants' households. Landless. Paid in money, kind and board. Work primarily agricultural.	Midlothian J.P.'s list 1656: Domestic or in-servant. Renfrewshire poll tax lists: servant, harvest servant. General: hireman, hirewoman.

Domestic servant
  male or
  female
	Living in household of landed proprietor. Work not primarily agricultural.	

Specialist servant	Attached to household of landed proprietor but living separately.	E.g. Gardener

Tradesman	May be: 1. small tenant
	       2. cottar
	       3. landless
	       4. son living in household of above.	

Labourer	Living separately. May or may not have some land/grazing rights. Primarily dependent on wage labour but not sufficiently specialist or skilled to be classed as tradesman in poll lists.	Midlothian J.P.'s list 1656: Barrowman, Cowan, Mason, Slater, Common workman or labourer. Renfrewshire poll tax lists: Workman

between hinds and cottars but perhaps the latter, while subletting land, were less closely tied to a tenant in terms of the labour which they provided and did not receive additional wages. If so, such distinction was of degree rather than kind and should not be over-stressed.

It is not clear to what extent the Midlothian servant hierarchy applied elsewhere. Thus, although it may be tempting to equate Renfrewshire harvest servants with Midlothian taskers, the temptation should be resisted. The Renfrewshire male harvest servants are virtually never recorded as having been married. If such people had not been living-in servants, one would have expected a substantial proportion of them to have been married, and even if the poll tax lists had been severely deficient in their listing of the wives of such men, it is unlikely that they would have failed to register them so consistently. The fact that harvest servants were recorded under the names of particular tenants rather than separately, as were cottars, also supports the suggestion that they lived in. It is more likely that in Renfrewshire cottars and subtenants formed a smaller proportion of the rural population than in Midlothian or lowland Aberdeenshire due to the frequency of smaller holdings making entry into the lower ranks of the tenantry easier and the need for extra labour less acute.

The backbone of rural society in most areas, often forming between 40% and 60% of male heads of household and single men in the poll tax lists, were cottars and tradesmen. A high proportion of rural craftsmen were probably cottars. This is sometimes explicit in designations such as 'cottar and tradesman'. Some craftsmen were small tenants paying rents direct to a proprietor but they seem to have been comparatively few in number.

It is evident, though, that below the level of tenant social distinctions were blurred. Living-in servants should not necessarily be viewed as a separate group inferior in status to cottars and subtenants. Carter has stressed when considering farm servants in Aberdeenshire in later times that servants and crofters formed a cycle within the peasantry.[21] It is likely that at this period too living-in servants were generally young. This can often be demonstrated from the Aberdeenshire poll tax lists where many servants are referred to as boys or girls. A considerable proportion of these servants, once they were married, probably became cottars.

The element of the rural population which was landless is difficult to determine as landlessness was not necessarily an absolute concept. Some distinction may have existed between cottars who held some arable land and those who had only grazing rights and a kail yard, but it is not likely to have been a sharp one. At the bottom of the cottar class many of the Aberdeenshire grassmen and grasswomen may have been truly landless. While male living-in servants were also landless, this may often have been only a temporary state. Such men formed 15–20% of male heads of household and unmarried males in many lowland Aberdeenshire parishes, though the figures fell to 8 or 9% in upland parishes like Glenbucket and Cabrach. Most Renfrewshire parishes, with their many small family holdings, came in between. In parts of the Lothians and Berwickshire, where large holdings were frequent, unmarried living-in male servants, along with male domestic servants in the households of landed proprietors, formed up to 40% of heads of household and single adult males. Tenants of large farms like Bonitoun in Ratho parish, West

Lothian, extending to 14 oxgates, could employ six unmarried male servants in addition to married servants and cottars, though three or four was more common.[22] In such areas the transition from living-in servant to cottar may have been harder due to the smaller proportion of cottarages, and this may have further limited upward movement from the cottar to the tenant group, suggesting that social differentiation had proceeded further than in other parts of Scotland. The relationships between types of rural economy, landownership patterns, holding size and rural social structure were complex and are still far from clear, so conclusions such as these must be tentative.

A notable feature of the poll tax lists is the rarity with which people who could be termed landless labourers are mentioned. The 'workmen' of the Renfrewshire returns and some of the Aberdeenshire grassmen may fit into this category, but overall they formed a small proportion of the recorded population. Many unlisted poor people may have provided casual labour, but much skilled and semi-skilled work was probably done by people listed as cottars. The impression is that relatively few people supported themselves by piece work or day labour without the adjunct of at least a nominal foothold on the land. Some tradesmen, especially near large burghs, may have been full-time workers whose connection with the land was confined to helping with the harvest, but the frequent designation 'cottar and tradesman' in the poll tax lists suggests that industrial workers often had some land.

It is harder to establish the exact position of women in rural society from the poll tax lists and other sources, but it is clear that married women were often regarded as adjuncts to their husbands. Single women fall into two categories, domestic and farm servants who were probably mostly single and young, and female cottars and grasswomen, often widows, whose sources of livelihood are rarely indicated. Female tenants of smallholdings did occur, but it was uncommon to find women leasing a substantial farm. When this occurred, one suspects that the arrangement was merely temporary following the death of a husband and awaiting the transfer of the holding to another male tenant.

The poll tax returns are tantalisingly incomplete in coverage and variable in content. Nevertheless they provide a general perspective of Scottish rural society, prompting a number of questions and providing a starting point for more detailed investigations. They show a society with numerous gradations but where the distinctions between strata were not clear-cut. People in different groups most often have overlapped in terms of wealth, though how far status, occupation and wealth were linked is uncertain. Rural society appears to have been relatively undifferentiated compared with that of seventeenth-century England, though there are signs that polarisation was developing in some areas, notably the south-eastern lowlands. A high proportion of the rural population still had a foothold on the land. This must have provided a degree of cohesion, for example in subsistence crises like those which followed the harvest failures of the later 1690s, though inevitably perspectives must have varied depending on the position of individuals within the social hierarchy.

Spatial differences in social structure are, however, evident. In areas like Orkney, upland Aberdeenshire and, to a lesser extent, Renfrewshire, the peasantry appear to have been relatively homogeneous. In parts of the Lothians, Berwickshire and lowland Aberdeenshire, where commercial elements in agriculture were linked with cereal production for urban markets and for export, farm structures with fewer tenants and larger holdings were linked with a society in which social differentiation was more marked and in which the 'landless' element may have been larger. To some extent such contrasts may merely reflect different organisational responses to the economic potential of the land, but in another sense they can be viewed as a progression in an evolutionary sequence.

It is hard to decide how homogeneous this social structure was in practice. The statutes relating to the safeguarding of tenants, which attempted to set controls on the mobility of farm servants, suggest that there were clashes of interest between these groups.[23] Cottars appear to have been more dependent on the tenantry and may, of necessity, have identified more closely with their interests. While the social gulf between tenant and landowner was often wide, particularly where estates were large, there are indications that in some areas at least the upper ranks of the tenantry were identifying themselves more closely with the interests of the landowners than with the lower ranks of the peasantry by the end of the seventeenth century. This is suggested by the fact that some tenants styled themselves 'gentlemen' in the poll tax returns. While such elements were probably only weakly developed at this time, they were a foretaste of the re-orientation of rural society which was to occur during the later eighteenth and nineteenth centuries.

Nevertheless, the poll tax records present only a single cross-section in time. While they may indicate the existence of spatial patterns in the composition of rural society, they do not show what processes were active in producing such variations. A fuller understanding of the workings of Scottish rural society at this time can only be obtained by more detailed local studies using data which cover time as well as space.

No intensive studies of rural communities in early-modern Scotland have so far been undertaken, although in England such research has provided valuable insights into the nature of rural society in the sixteenth, seventeenth and eighteenth centuries.[24] This may be partly due to the belief that data are inadequate in coverage and quality to permit such research. Collections of estate papers, however, contain information on many aspects of the lives of tenant farmers, a group which, as has been shown, occupied an important position in rural society. Where particularly good sets of estate documents can be linked with other sources such as parish registers, wills and court records, light can be shed on many aspects of rural society which are not illuminated by general surveys like the one above. In order to develop further the theme of geographical and social mobility in Scottish rural society, some preliminary results will be presented of a project which focuses on an estate possessing an unusually complete run of accounts and rentals extending from the early seventeenth to the early eighteenth centuries.[25]

The major part of the estates of the Earls of Panmure, including the baronies of Ballumbie, Carmyllie, Downie, Innerpeffer, Kellie and Panmure, were located in Angus along the coastal plain between Dundee and Arbroath, extending inland on to the lower eastern slopes of the Sidlaw Hills. During the seventeenth century most tenants on the estate paid their principal rents in grain, and the estate exported considerable quantities of oats and bere with some wheat to Edinburgh and other east-coast burghs. Tenants in the higher-lying barony of Carmyllie paid rents in money and were probably more oriented towards pastoral farming.

The continuous series of rentals allows the length of tenancy for every husbandman on the estate to be calculated. Data have so far been extracted for the four contiguous baronies of Carmyllie, Downie, Innerpeffer and Panmure between 1650 and 1714. The mean length of tenancy in these baronies during this period was 9.3 years. This figure, though, conceals considerable variability: 11.8% of completed tenancies were for a single year and 33.4% were of two to five years' duration. On the other hand, 18.7% were of 11 to 20 years' duration and 11.8% of over 20 years. This suggests that elements of both stability and mobility existed within the tenantry, some farmers occupying the same holding for a substantial part of their working lives while others held land on the estate for only a brief period. The variation is not related to differences in holding size. If tenants in Downie, Innerpeffer and Panmure baronies are ranked according to how much grain they paid in their principal rents, then the tenants of smaller holdings paying under 10 bolls had a comparable distribution of length of tenancy with farmers on the largest holdings paying over 40 bolls.

What influences lay behind the high rate of turnover among this cross-section of the tenantry? Does it indicate a high level of mobility within rural society and, if so, to what extent were geographical and social mobility involved? One means of examining geographical mobility is to look at the origins of Panmure tenants recorded in surviving leases:[26] 65% of the seventeenth-century leases were renewals to sitting tenants; 18% recorded moves from other farms within the same barony and only 3.5% from other baronies; 13.5% of the tenants had come from outside the estate. The migration distances of this last group were short with a mean of 3.7 miles and a maximum of 8.5 miles. This suggests that geographical mobility operated over limited distances, and the rentals indicate that once a man had been entered as the tenant of a particular holding on the estate, he tended to remain there. Returning to the evidence of the rentals, only 14.7% of the tenants recorded between 1650 and 1714 moved to other farms within the four baronies. Some of the elements involved in the geographical mobility of tenant farmers are suggested in Fig. 1.

Socio-economic mobility among Panmure tenants coincided with geographical mobility when they moved from one holding to another on a different farm. Moves to larger holdings on other farms accounted for 21% of the total changes in holding sizes in the four baronies between 1650 and 1714 and moves to smaller holdings 21.5%. 57.5% of changes in holding size did not involve the re-location of the tenant. Of the available options the most popular was multiple leasing (36% of total changes). This involved a tenant who occupied one holding or farm leasing portions of an adjacent but separate farm. A counterpart of this within the same farm was engrossing, where a tenant originally occupying only a fraction of a farm enlarged his share or took over the entire unit. This accounted for 11.5% of total changes in

Some Elements in the Geographical Mobility of Tenants in Early-Modern Scotland

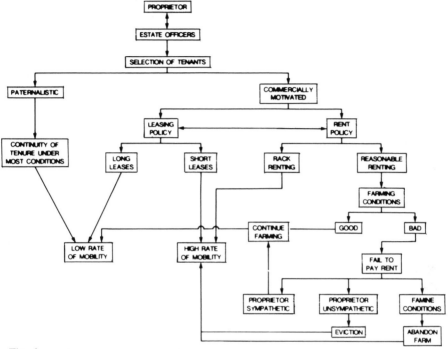

Fig. 1

holding size while the reverse process, whereby a tenant reduced his share of a farm, was equally common (10%).

The importance of changes in holding size without re-location of the farmer may indicate a desire to minimise the risks inherent in a tenant altering his enterprise. Multiple leasing and engrossing involved expanding from a base of land whose qualities were known, and working with familiar neighbours. Presumably this would have been the preferred option, all other things being equal. A move to another holding, even only a mile or two away, involved the greater risk of working land whose soils, drainage and exposure had not been assessed personally, and co-operating with different neighbours. This may have been a major influence behind the low rate of geographical mobility among farmers during their period as Panmure tenants, and may also help to account for the very short distances which were involved when re-location occurred. Tenants, because of their greater commitments to terms of rents and their greater capital inputs, had more to lose from an injudicious move than other social groups.

Elements of geographical mobility among the wider rural community can be demonstrated by marriage patterns. In Carmyllie parish, for example,[27] 43% of the marriages between 1684 and 1709 involved bridegrooms who were not resident within the parish. The marriage distances indicate, however, that 85% of the bridegrooms who were not residents within Carmyllie parish came from adjacent parishes. The remaining 15% all originated from within the Angus lowlands save for one man from Glenbervie 26 miles away in Kincardineshire. It is harder to isolate patterns of migration among specific groups below the tenant level. The movement of tenants from one farm to another must often have involved the re-location of cottars, as leases and details of evictions show that cottars frequently moved with their masters. Unmarried farm servants may have been even more mobile. Acts of Parliament which attempted to protect tenants from servants who left before the end of their agreed term suggest that farm servants were not tied as closely to their employers by personal and economic bonds and may have been more footloose. It is hoped that further work integrating data from estate papers, parish registers and other sources will provide more information about migration patterns for different groups within rural society.

A high turnover rate of tenants could be interpreted as indicating that many husbandmen, after a short stay on the Panmure estates, moved to holdings on neighbouring estates. This is impossible to check in the absence of information from the records of other landowners, but the low level of geographical mobility of tenants within the Panmure estates suggests that this was probably not a major factor. Another possible explanation is that many people entered tenancies at a relatively advanced period in their working lives, perhaps when their children were old enough to supply a good deal of labour. Ultimately it should be possible to test this hypothesis, using information drawn from parish registers. A third possibility is that there was a good deal of movement between the tenantry and the cottar class. This can be shown by examining leases in order to find instances where a person receiving a lease is stated to have been previously resident on a particular farm on the estate yet does not appear there in the rentals. Such people cannot have been tenants and their leases must record their entry into the tenantry. Out of 13 such instances, five of the people concerned were definitely or probably the sons of tenants. This is stated in two leases, and for the others a tenant with the same surname can be identified on the same farm in the years immediately preceding the granting of the lease. For the remaining eight there was no such record, and it is probable that some at least were cottars, though some may have come originally from tenant families.

While the rents of the holdings being taken by people in these two groups varied, the mean rent for sons of tenants was 48 bolls of victual and for the rest 23.5 bolls. Despite the small sample size, this suggests that there may have been a tendency for the sons of tenants entering farming directly to secure larger holdings than people moving up from cottarages. This may have been due to the influence of their fathers with the estate factor, but such newcomers may also have been more experienced in farm management and better capitalised than men who had previously been cottars. It is interesting to note that in the leases two of the sons of tenants were described as third sons, showing that it was possible for younger sons of tenants to acquire holdings. The evidence suggests that people who came into the tenant group from below may have found it harder to obtain a substantial holding. It can also be postulated that such people may not have risen as high and may have been more likely to have reverted to cottar status. The mean length of completed tenancy for the sons of tenants was 30 years against 14 for the other group, but again it must be emphasised that the sample is small and that further research is needed before these suggestions can be confirmed.

The barony of Panmure and Panbride parish were virtually co-extensive. Thus, if Panmure tenants can be identified in the Panbride parish register either before or after their period of tenancy, it is possible to pick out people who were moving into or out of the tenantry. Unfortunately the Panbride register[28] does not commence until 1690 and only records baptisms. The run of years before the series of estate records terminates in 1714 is short and only a proportion of people moving into and out of the tenantry are likely to have appeared in the register as fathers or witnesses. Nevertheless, 20 people can be identified as previous residents who acquired a tenancy during this period. Only six of these took over substantial holdings, the rest leasing pendicles and smallholdings. Ten people are recorded as still living in the parish after relinquishing a tenancy: again six had been pendiclers. To some extent this may mirror farm structures in Panmure barony which had more smallholdings than the other baronies on the estate, but it suggests that in this instance movement into and out of the tenant class was most active at lower levels. Given what has been written about variations in length of tenure in relation to holding size, other mechanisms must be proposed to account for situations where a previous resident of a parish suddenly became tenant of a large holding and worked it for only a limited number of years.

The overall picture presented of this particular rural community is one in which elements of geographical mobility existed at a local scale, varying in importance between different groups. Socio-economic mobility occurred within the tenantry and also between this group and others in rural society. The extent and importance of such movements is not yet clear and it is hoped that further research will provide more information on the processes which affected various forms of mobility such as the influence of family structure and the extent to which capital accumulation was possible at different levels of society. Some of the preliminary results suggest that there may have been more than one socio-economic cycle within rural society at this time (Fig. 2). As well as one where a farm servant became a cottar after marriage and his children in turn started off their working lives as farm servants, a more extended cycle may have existed in which a man started as a farm servant, became a cottar after marriage, and acquired a tenancy after his children were old enough to provide labour. If the children subsequently left home, a tenant could have maintained the labour supply with which to work his holding by employing farm servants or he could have moved to a smaller tenancy and perhaps in old age to a cottage as a 'grassman'. Such a cycle could have been short-circuited at various points: for example by a tenant's son succeeding to his father's holding. If such cycles existed they would have had the effect of binding rural society together more closely. This exploratory paper has, however, only outlined some of the problems and possible approaches to the study of early-modern Scottish rural society and its conclusions have been limited. Nevertheless, it is hoped that it has not only served to show some of the complexities which existed but that it has also indicated some potential directions for future research.

Some Elements of Social Mobility in Rural Society in Early Modern Scotland

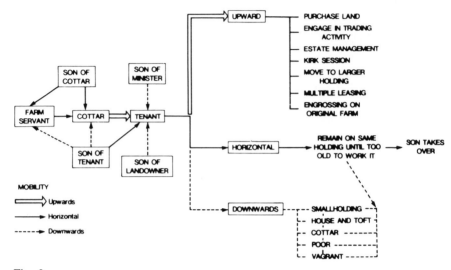

Fig. 2

REFERENCES

1. I. Carter, *Farm life in North East Scotland 1840–1914* (Edinburgh 1979).

2. *Ibid.*

3. E.g. G. Kay, 'The landscape of improvement', *Scot. Geogr. Mag.* 78 (1960), pp. 100–11; J. B. Caird, 'The making of the Scottish rural landscape', *Scot. Geogr. Mag.* 80 (1964), pp. 72–80.

4. I. D. Whyte, *Agriculture and society in seventeenth-century Scotland* (Edinburgh 1979), pp. 137–62; I. D. Whyte, 'The evolution of rural settlement in Lowland Scotland in medieval and early-modern times: an exploration', *Scot. Geogr. Mag.* 97 (1981).

5. T. C. Smout, *A history of the Scottish people 1560–1830* (London, 1972 edn.), p. 176.

6. J. H. Johnson, 'Crofting settlement types in North West Scotland', *Geogr. Rev.* 48 (1959), pp. 554–66; H. Uhlig, 'Old hamlets with infield-outfield systems in western and central Europe', *Geogr. Annual* 43 (1961), pp. 285–312.

7. T. W. Moody, F. X. Martin, F. J. Byrne, eds., *A new history of Ireland. III. Early-modern Ireland 1534–1691.* (Oxford 1976), pp. 154–5.

8. M. W. Flinn, ed., *Scottish population history* (Cambridge 1977).

9. *Ibid.*, p. 196.

10. I. D. Whyte, 'Written leases and their impact on Scottish agriculture in the seventeenth century', *Agric. Hist. Rev.* 27, (1979), pp. 1–9.

11. Whyte *Agriculture and society*, p. 5.

12. A. Geddes & T. Forbes, 'Rural communities of fermtoun and baile in the lowlands and Highlands of Aberdeenshire,' *Aberdeen University Review* 32 (1947), pp. 98–104; Smout, *Scottish People*, pp. 135–7; K. Walton, 'The distribution of population in Aberdeenshire in 1696', *Scot. Geogr. Mag.* 66 (1975), pp. 17–25.

13. Flinn, ed., *Scottish Population*, pp. 56–7.

14. C. H. Firth, ed., *Scotland and the Protectorate 1654–9* (Scot. Hist. Soc., Edinburgh 1899), pp. 405–8.

15. J. Stuart, ed., *List of pollable persons within the shire of Aberdeen 1696* (Spalding Club, Aberdeen 1844), 2 vols.

16. Scottish Record Office (S.R.O.), E.70 series.

17. Whyte, *Agriculture and society,* pp. 142–5.

18. D. Semple, ed., *Renfrewshire poll tax returns* (Glasgow 1864).

19. L. Timperley, in M. L. Parry & T. R. Slater, eds., *The making of the Scottish countryside* (London 1980), pp. 137–54.

20. S.R.O., E.70 series.

21. Carter, *Farm Life,* p. 109.

22. S.R.O., E.70/8/16.

23. *Acts of the Parliaments of Scotland* IV (1621), p. 623.

24. For example, D. G. Hey, *An English rural community: Myddle under the Tudors and Stuarts* (London 1974); M. Spufford, *Contrasting communities: English villagers in the sixteenth and seventeenth centuries* (Cambridge 1974); K. Wrightson and D. Levine, *Poverty and piety in an English village, Terling 1525-1700* (London 1979).

25. S.R.O. Dalhousie muniments, GD 45/18/1.

26. S.R.O. GD 45/18/148–415.

27. S.R.O. O.P.R. 276/1.

28. S.R.O. O.P.R. 316/1.

4

Agricultural Change and its Social Consequences in the Southern Uplands of Scotland, 1600–1780

Robert A. Dodgshon

UPLAND areas have the reputation of being sectors of economic retardation if not backwardness, stubborn refuges for old practices, institutions and values. General discussions of agricultural change rarely accord them more than a few lines, and then only to use their manifest conservatism to set off lowland advancement. Some writers seem imbued with the ideas of Sir Cyril Fox, whose *The Personality of Britain* typecast upland areas as a zone of cultural absorption and continuity whereas lowland areas formed a zone of successive change and replacement.[1] Upland areas having been cast almost conceptually in the role of laggard sector, pioneering change has not been looked for there nor is it expected. Change is conceded only as a nineteenth-century phenomenon, when their crises-ridden economies were swept aside by what one recent writer has called the 'backwash' effects of the industrial and agricultural revolutions of lowland Britain.[2] For some areas, this was undoubtedly the case. However, to extend such a conclusion over all upland areas serves more to confuse than to clarify the problem. We need to keep in mind J. Thirsk's argument concerning the experience of upland-pasture (and livestock-woodland) districts in England during the sixteenth and seventeenth centuries. Population growth, abundant waste and weak manorialism helped to foster important adjustments to their rural economy, with the widespread development of both commercial stock farming and domestic industry.[3] Such shifts were not necessarily born out of a spirit of improvement. Indeed, domestic industry seems to have flourished widely in an atmosphere of supply rather than demand economics, with survival being uppermost in the peasant mind rather than any eagerness to exploit the full opportunities of the marketplace. But whatever the verdict, it hardly lends support to those who see upland economies as lying relatively dormant prior to the nineteenth century.

These ideas have a bearing on what happened to the rural economy of the Southern Uplands from 1600 to 1800. Seen from the vantage point of a late eighteenth-century Improver's Movement, the Southern Uplands have the appearance of a laggard sector. Innovations which diffused through adjacent lowland areas like the Merse from the 1750s and '60s onwards — including enclosure, turnips, sown grasses, new breeds of livestock, improved ploughs, etc. — only began to penetrate upland areas during the 1790s and 1800s. Except for his contribution to the Improved Cheviot, the upland farmer seemed always one or two steps behind his lowland counterpart. Noted upland improvers, like Lord Napier, were generally active during the early nineteenth century, bettering the breed of their flocks, draining and re-seeding pasture, planting shelter belts, erecting sheep stalls and providing new steadings for their tenants and shepherds. Yet, in a sense, this sort of comparison with lowland areas creates a false perspective. It construes the problem solely in terms of the eighteenth-century Improver, with his search for a better, more productive husbandry, and ignores basic structural problems concerning the orientation of the farm economy. Put simply, the shift from medieval to modern patterns of farming in Scotland can be broken down into two broad categories of change. The first involved the commercialisation of the farm economy. This was essentially a structural adjustment involving a reduction in tenant numbers per farm (so as to create larger, more commercially viable units), a redirection of the farm economy away from subsistence towards a more active marketing strategy and the conversion of all rents in kind to cash. I regard this last point as a central issue. So long as tenants were committed to paying rents in kind, then they were for the most part insulated from the market and its spirit of mind. Such marketing as the peasant did engage in was a matter more of householding or rectifying imperfections in his farm economy, than of profiteering. Those landowners who collected vast quantities of rent in kind were obviously better placed to market produce. But with so much rent in kind forming bundles of produce that were fixed in both content and size by custom, even they found it difficult to be genuinely responsive to markets. The second broad category of change comprised those innovations which are conventionally linked with the Improvers: namely, new crops, breeds, systems of husbandry and enclosure.

I have made the distinction between these two categories of change because I feel it has a bearing on any comparison between the Southern Uplands and adjacent lowland areas. The point I particularly wish to make is that whereas lowland areas undoubtedly had the initiative with regard to the second type of change, the same is not true of the first type. There is a case to argue that by the middle decades of the eighteenth century — when the Improving Movement supposedly began — upland farms were more attuned to the market economy than lowland ones. The explanation for this state of affairs needs to be sought in the history of large-scale, commercial sheep farming. Three stages are proposed: the *first* concerns its pioneer inception as a farm enterprise in the Southern Uplands, the *second* concerns the conflict which arose between its continuing growth and the subsistence needs of the local community, and the *third*, the resolution of this conflict in favour of sheep farming and the social consequences which this had for the farming community.

The Establishment of Commercial Sheep Farming

The starting point for any history of Border sheep farming is with the abbeys. Following their foundation in the eleventh century, abbeys like Melrose, Jedburgh and Kelso soon acquired extensive holdings of upland pasture in the Cheviots, upper Teviotdale and Eskdale, on either side of Galawater and around the upper reaches of Yarrow and Ettrick Waters. Contemporary accounts give some sense of scale to their involvement, with an abbey like Melrose having as many as 12,000 sheep from which it reputedly harvested 50 sacks of wool per year.[4] But for all the documentation of monastic sheep farming, we still lack any kind of perspective on what happened when the abbeys drew back from the direct farming of their estates over the fourteenth and fifteenth centuries. Documentary light is only restored with the flurry of material that accompanied their dissolution.[5] Even at this point, though, the survival of large-scale sheep farming on their estates relies more on general comments about the region as a whole than on any freshly available manuscript sources. However, what is both clear and important is that a number of Border families gained from the windfalls of land that resulted from their dissolution. The not inconsiderable properties of Melrose and Kelso abbeys, for instance, passed largely into the hands of the Scotts and Kerrs respectively and contributed greatly to what later became the Buccleuch and Roxburgh ducal estates.

Other sheep or gerss farms boasted different roots. Many were established on disafforested land. A rental of 1376 for the Morton Lordship records large numbers of farms in upper Liddesdale and along Hermitage Water (i.e. Broadlie and Gorrenbury) that had previously been *Foresta*.[6] The most fully documented case of disafforestation is that of Ettrick. Established in the twelfth century, it embraced most of the old county of Selkirk. As with all royal forests, strict control was exercised via forest courts and a network of rangers and foresters. As late as the 1490s, it was still 'thochit expedient [at Ettrick] that thair be na telin, sawin, delfyne or ony maner of corne within the forsaid forest'.[7] Such restraint, though, did not automatically extend to livestock. Indeed, King James IV (1488–1513) reportedly had over 20,000 sheep in Ettrick at one point. During the opening years of the sixteenth century, Crown policy altered and the possessors of the various foresters' stedes were told 'to tak thair steidis and malingis in few-ferme . . . for it is the Kingis mynd that the said forest be sett in few ferme'.[8] Within a matter of decades, a new breed of occupier (many by the name of Scott)[9] had become established in the forest, one whose horizons were set by the profits of sheep rather than the pleasures of the chase.

By the sixteenth century, then, the farm pattern of the Southern Uplands had filled out completely, with subsequent changes stemming only from splitting and amalgamation, not from any further pioneering. Nor can there be much doubt that once this point had been reached, sheep production on some scale had spread to all parts of the region. In 1578, Bishop Leslie wrote of Tweeddale that in 'this cuntrie . . . evin as with thair nychbouris, that sum of thame ar knawen to have four or fyve hundir, utheris agane aucht or nyne hundir, and sum tyme thay ar knawen to have a thousand scheip'.[10] Evidently, the sheep flocks carried by Border farms during the sixteenth century were sufficient to excite comment from contemporaries.

Sheep Production v Subsistence, 1600–1720

By the seventeenth century, the fuller documentation that now becomes available enables us to see the developing character of local sheep farming in some detail. It reveals an industry that was unquestionably large-scale in operation and commercial in orientation. However, it also suggests that the subsistence needs of the local community may have been a check on its continuing growth: the interests of the two sectors standing in conflict with each other.

The scale of sheep farming can be gleaned from data for farm size and from stocking figures. Those for farm size are the less satisfactory. There are no seventeenth century surveys. The earliest is a survey of the vast Buccleuch estate drawn up in 1718.[11] With over 140 farms in Ettrick, Teviotdale, Liddesdale, Ewesdale and Eskdalemuir, it provides a fair sample of farm size in the region. Two classes of holding emerge from it. Where low ground was available in some quantity, as in Canonby parish, farm size was generally under 200 acres and holdings of only 30–50 acres were quite common. However, as the valley ground narrowed and as farms comprised more and more hill ground, farm sizes of around 500–1000 acres became the norm. In fact, the increasing habit amongst tenants of leasing two or more farms meant that average working units were commonly in excess of 1000 acres.

The main source of data for stocking is again provided by the Buccleuch estate. During the early 1680s, southern Scotland was badly affected by a succession of severe winters. Not only did thousands of sheep perish but tradition has it that as many as thirteen shepherds died on Eskdalemuir in one storm alone. Tenants throughout the Southern Uplands found great difficulty in paying their rent. Set down in the very heart of the Southern Uplands, the Buccleuch estate were more deeply affected by this natural disaster than other estates, and were forced to implement a policy of extensive rent abatements. As part of their calculation of what each tenant should be allowed, they carried out a survey of all their upland farms.[12] Tenants were required to furnish information on how many sheep and cattle had been carried by their farms in 1681, 1682 and 1683, and how many had perished during each winter. For reasons not disclosed, some farms are ascribed information for only one or two years. However, this defect apart, the census still provides a perspective usually lacking for pre-Improvement Scottish agriculture. Out of 148 farms given a stocking figure for 1681, 20 had over 1000 sheep and 47 over 500. In 1683, 146 were included in the census, of which 26 had over 1000 sheep and 58 over 500. The largest flocks — or those on farms like Eltrieve, Wester Doloraine, Garwald and Linhope — were to be found in the higher, remoter districts: Ettrick, Teviotdalehead, Ewesdale and upper Liddesdale. Conversely, the smallest flocks were those on low-ground farms, such as in Canonby parish, where the broader valley bottoms offered more scope for arable.

The patently commercial character of sheep farming by the seventeenth century is emphasised by one further parameter, or the extent to which rents were computed in cash rather than kind. Cash rents were being levied as early as the sixteenth century, with early Crown rentals for Ettrick showing all its stedes as contracted primarily for cash, supplemented by only a few sheep.[13] By the time rentals for other estates are to hand (1640+), they also tend to show cash as the prevailing rent form. This was certainly true for upland farms on the Buccleuch,[14] Roxburgh[15] and

Lauderdale[16] estates. In terms of gross rental yield, an estate like Buccleuch was already drawing over £80,000 Scots from its upland farms by 1664. The growth of its income from such farms can be traced at regular intervals thereafter. In the case of Ettrick, the perspective is even longer, with a series of rental statements — all in cash — from the late fifteenth century onwards.[17] The massive rise in rent which they display can, of course, be put down to the *general* inflation of prices rather than the enhanced profitability of sheep farming in particular, though the latter may have played a small part.

The payment of cash rents did not necessarily denote a background of conversion. The majority of tenures burdened by cash rents had been formed out of ex-monastic or ex-forest land at a relatively late date and naturally reflect the social and economic conditions under which they were first defined. By the same argument, it was amongst *old*-established settlement that one was most likely to find the exceptions, or farms that paid rents in kind. The farms making up the Barony of Lyne (Peeblesshire) fell into this category, a rental of 1591 showing fairly sizeable payments of grain as rent.[18] Also exempt from the widespread pattern of cash rents were those estates that operated a system of thirders and teinders. Thirders represented a form of steelbow tenure, with tenants paying a third of their produce in return for provision of seed and stock by the landowner. It was an arrangement that seems to have been significant only in Roxburghshire, where it can be documented for the Minto estate[19] as well as for one or two led farms on the higher ground.[20] The payment of teind was another means by which produce could be abstracted from the peasant economy. By the seventeenth century, its collection in many parts of the Southern Uplands had passed into the hands of the large estates. The Buccleuch estate especially commandeered substantial amounts of both grain and stock (lambs, stirks) as teind, the full details being entered in a series of lists for areas like Ettrick and Liddesdale and headed 'The Riding of Teinds'.[21]

Whereas their predecessors had been concerned first and foremost with the marketing of wool, upland farmers of the seventeenth and early eighteenth centuries set themselves a broader range of objectives. Sheep were now reared as much for their meat as for their wool, with lamb production assuming more and more importance in the marketing strategy of farms as time went by. When Pennecuick wrote about the higher ground of Peeblesshire c.1715, what seemed to matter most to him was that the local sheep were 'small, yet very sweet and delicious'.[22] A discussion of how the rent of Anglehope (Ettrick) was devised in 1718 described the farm as producing 'fatt lambs' and went on to say that it 'keeps all old sheep', with no mention of wool as a prime source of income.[23] Where the income spread of upland farms can actually be analysed, as in the case of Broadlie beside Hermitage Water, it confirms that the value of wool and skin sales was far outweighed by the combined sales of lamb, hogs and cast ewes.[24] The main source of demand for this expanding trade in mutton and lamb was the north-east coalfield and, to a lesser extent, central Scotland. A local commentator on farming once dismissed the Cheviot, the Border's most successful breed, as 'fit only to glide down the throat of a Newcastle coalheaver'.[25] His remark was ill-considered, for it was really the appetite of the Newcastle coalheaver that sustained the early growth of the sheep and lamb trade. The brief run of figures published by D. Woodward for the 1680s gives some scale to the cross-Border trade in sheep and lambs.[26]

However, sheep and lamb production had yet to become the exclusive goal of the upland farmer. Alongside it, there still existed another, equally vital objective: subsistence. To understand the role of subsistence from 1600 to 1720, we must answer two questions. First, there is the question of how many people were directly dependent on the upland farm economy. Secondly, there is the question of how much land was cultivated and to what purpose.

Inevitably, farming in the Southern Uplands was greatly affected by its proximity to the Border with the auld enemy. Apart from the ravages of invading armies and the cattle rieving carried out by groups like the Armstrongs of upper Liddesdale[27] — both severely disruptive of the farm economy — the unsettled conditions along the Border had their most significant impact on landholding. In such a troubled area, advancement for any family depended as much on the support of a loyal and numerous following as on the procurement of a sizeable estate. The fairly late rise of both the Scotts of Buccleuch and the Kerrs of Cessford was certainly buttressed by both. When the former acquired holdings in Eskdale and Ettrick over the sixteenth century, Scotts were soon infiltrated into the landholding pattern.[28] Similarly, an eighteenth-century document tells how the latter implanted kinsmen on their Cheviot properties over the fifteenth and sixteenth centuries.[29] Even in the late seventeenth century, such force of kinship still mattered. When the Buccleuch estate surveyed the damage caused by the appalling stock losses of the early 1680s, it was specifically agreed that the assessors for each district should be Scotts.[30] This concern for a large and loyal following probably created its own pressures on landholding. So long as the Borders remained a troubled area, then large, strategic estates would have been tolerant of a numerous tenantry. Only during the seventeenth century, with the Border problem settled, would a different attitude have taken root. Even then, adjustments would have needed time to take effect.

Rentals for the latter part of the seventeenth and opening decades of the eighteenth centuries enable the pattern of landholding to be reconstructed in some depth. Those for the Buccleuch[31] and Roxburgh[32] estates — the two largest in the region — show that farms held by more than one tenant (= multiple tenancy) were in the majority, if not overwhelmingly so. There are signs that single tenancy may have been on the increase by the late seventeenth century, though the clarity of any such trend is obscured a little by the small handful of farms (i.e. in Ettrick) which, somewhat perversely, moved back into multiple tenancy at this point.[33] But whilst there were noticeably more single-tenant farms than in lowland areas, including some exceptionally large gerss farms held by only one tenant, nevertheless the conclusion must be that upland farms were, as a whole, heavily weighted with tenants. Some farms also carried sub-tenants, whose existence would normally be concealed by a rental. This is borne out by the earlier-mentioned survey of stock losses on the Buccleuch estate which was compiled in the early 1680s. In order to arrive at an equitable allocation of rent abatements, the state enquired into those farms that were 'sett to several subtennents' or were 'sett in subtennandrie'. The number of farms involved, though, was not high.[34] Adding more substantially to farm population was the range of hired labour required by upland farms: ploughmen, shepherds, shearers, websters, house servants, led-farm managers, etc. Two of the more explicit sources, both farm day or account books, suggest that the contractual relationship between tenants and their hired labour was of a different sort to that of tenants and landowners, with wages in kind figuring prominently.[35]

Given their limited opportunity for arable cropping, it follows that even a modest farm population would have found it difficult to subsist entirely on what the farm itself could provide. Yet what data can be mustered on this suggest that upland farms maintained a surprisingly high arable acreage during the seventeenth and early eighteenth centuries. Three types of evidence support this conclusion. First, there is the amount of arable implied by the payment of grain as teind. To some extent, this is the least satisfactory of the data available but it does offer a commentary on the problem as early as the 1630s. As a measure of its value, Eskdalemuir paid over 25 bolls of corn as teind in 1652, suggesting a total crop for this high, exposed area of over 250 bolls.[36] At a rough estimate of two or three bolls yield per acre, this would indicate an arable acreage for the area of around 100 acres. The Buccleuch farms in the Baronies of Branxholm and Wilton (Teviotdale) paid 434 bolls of grain as teind,[37] making later claims that most hillsides in Wilton parish had once (or c.1700) been cultivated quite credible. The second type of evidence is that provided by surveys, the earliest and most useful being that drawn up for the Buccleuch estate in 1718.[38] If those sections dealing with the more remote or higher ground are inspected, such as those covering Westerkirk or Ewes parishes (Dumfriesshire), there appears no lack of corn ground, with some hill farms reportedly having over 200 acres of cultivated land. The third type of evidence is the most telling. It consists of late eighteenth and early nineteenth-century commentators who look back to before the mid-eighteenth century and draw attention to the amount of land which had formerly been cultivated. As I propose to look at this evidence more fully in the following section, one illustration will suffice here. It is taken from the *New Statistical Account* report for Hutton and Corrie parish (Dumfriesshire). Penned in 1834, its author observed that 'at an earlier period, and before the middle of the last century, cultivation had been extended considerably further than it has been latterly . . . and the marks of plough are visible on many places which have long been under sheep pasture'.[39]

So long as the upland farm economy had a strong subsistence element to it, then the full potential of sheep farming could not be realised. Early sheep farmers faced the inescapable fact that the summer carrying capacity of their hill pastures was determined in large measure by how many sheep could be over-wintered on the farm. The expensive buying-in of fodder was absent at this stage. The seasonal movement of stock between upland and lowland farms was present, but only on a small scale.[40] Most upland farms had to live within their resources. For this reason, the cultivation of so much land in upland areas — the very land needed for the wintering of sheep and on which the best pasture could have been established — was a major restriction on how many sheep could be carried by upland farms at this point. By about 1700, though, it must have been apparent to the more commercially minded farmers that, by reducing their arable, the size of their flocks and lambing rates could be increased. But in order to reduce arable, the subsistence needs of the farm had to be reduced. This, in turn, meant that tenant numbers had to be reduced and larger, more commercially viable units established. There are signs that this sort of strategy was being pursued by some estates from the early eighteenth century onwards.

Sheep Farming on the Eve of the Improvers' Movement, 1720–80

The gradual reduction of tenant numbers and farm population generally can be vouched for by both rentals and contemporary comment. The former show that most of the multiple tenancies still remaining by the opening years of the eighteenth century were systematically removed over the next five or six decades. On the Roxburgh estate, for instance, no upland farm appears to have had multiple tenants by the 1750s,[41] whilst on the Buccleuch estate only about one third had multiple tenants left by 1766 and only about one tenth by 1792.[42] Typical of this shift into single tenancy is the experience of Linhope, one of the largest farms on the Buccleuch estate. Its tenurial history is laid bare in a farm day book maintained by Robert Grieve, one of its occupiers during the eighteenth century. When Grieve first entered the farm in 1729, it had four tenants, three of whom (including Grieve) held a sixth share and the fourth tenant, a half. After acquiring the other two-sixth parts in 1737 and 1738, Grieve finally took possession of the entire farm in 1753.[43] Contemporary reviews of landholding corroborate this fall in tenant numbers over the early and middle decades of the century, some coupling it to a further trend or the leasing of more than one farm by individual tenants,[44] so that not only were more single tenants taking charge of upland farms but the operational size of the latter was being dramatically enlarged. Both the *Old* (= *OSA*) and the *New* (= *NSA*) *Statistical Accounts* are replete with relevant comment. The parish of Hownam in the Cheviots, for instance, was said in its *OSA* report to have had three or four times more tenants back in the opening decades of the century compared with the number left by the 1790s.[45] The parish of Cranshaws on the edge of the Lammermuirs recorded a decrease from 16 to only three tenants over the same period.[46] In Tweedsmuir parish (Peeblesshire) the same trend was expressed in a slightly different form, its *OSA* reporter describing how the number of farms had declined from 24 to 16 and the number of tenants by an even greater amount owing to the practice of some tenants now leasing more than one farm and others not residing in the parish.[47] Appended to many of these references to tenant reduction and the conjoining of farms were critical comments on the sharp decline which had also occurred in the number of cottagers since the early eighteenth century. Overall, the impression given is one of a rural community being slowly thinned. Indeed, in some cases whole settlements disappeared. Ettrick village in Selkirkshire was said to have been lived in by no less than 32 families, yet it was only a memory by the 1790s.[48] A similar fate seems to have befallen Old Thornylees in Peeblesshire.[49] The obvious analogy here is with the Highland clearances. Tenurial contraction was probably on a smaller scale and at a more gradual pace in the Southern Uplands, but it was still a replacement of people with sheep.

Complementary to this progressive decline in tenant numbers was a sharp decrease in the amount of arable on upland farms. The *NSA* reports for the parishes of Castleton, Oxnam, Wilton and Ashkirk in Roxburghshire all refer to the extensive signs of former cultivation to be seen on their hillsides.[50] So too do the reports for parishes in north-east Dumfriesshire, like those for Applegarth or for Hutton and Corrie.[51] Where they are specific, such reports date these visible signs of former land pressure to the pre-1750 period. The reporter for Southdean parish in Roxburghshire tried to be even more exact. After citing the survey of the Forest portion of the Buccleuch estate that was compiled in 1718, he estimated that its 4000 or so acres of cultivated land had shrunk to barely 500 acres by the 1790s.[52] Figures given in the *NSA* reports for various Berwickshire parishes (such as Longformacus and Abbey St Bathans),[53] as well as figures supplied by local *General Views* for the parishes of Cranshaws, Bunckle and Preston, Westruther, Hownam, Linton, Roberton and Ashkirk all indicate a contraction of arable.[54] Comparison of estate surveys, such as those for the Cheviot farms of the Roxburgh estate, can yield further proof of a decline.[55] Nor, it seems, was the self-evident shrinkage of arable over the eighteenth century lost on travellers through the region. Robert Heron's description of Roberton parish (upper Clydesdale) in 1793 reads like a page out of nineteenth-century Highland history. 'Every where,' he wrote, 'as I proceeded up this vale, I could discover by certain marks, that it had anciently been a scene of agricultural industry, and a seat of no inconsiderable population. The houses were only cottages. But, in many instances, the walls of these cottages seemed of very ancient erection.'[56]

The *NSA* reporter for the parish of Castleton in Roxburghshire explained the massive shift from arable to grass as due to the high price of sheep and wool.[57] A tack issued in 1740 for the farm of Grubbet in the Cheviots confirms this connection, for it required the tenant to make the lands 'more convenient for the Breeding of Stock and for bringing them up thereof than it has formerly been or now is And for that purpose Shall soon as may be Reduce the Tillage into pasture ground'.[58] Tacks issued by other estates, such as those of the Roxburgh,[59] Lothian[60] and Marchmont[61] estates, were equally restrictive of how much land could be tilled on upland farms by the 1740s. Stocking capacities must have increased dramatically as a result.[62]

To argue that the farming community of upland areas suffered a marked regression over the eighteenth century, as upland farm resources were directed more exclusively to the sustenance of sheep rather than people, begs the question of what happened to those displaced from the land or at least from the farming ladder. Did hardship and poverty increase? Were supplementary forms of income introduced to offset the declining opportunities for subsistence farming? I do not feel I can offer satisfactory answers to these questions. There are traces of poverty, but not on an exceptional scale or in a context which links it to the adverse side-effects of agricultural change. Thus, when Hawick was flooded with 'mendicating persons and familys' from the surrounding countryside in the 1690s, to the great detriment of the burgh's 'ancient poore', it was put down to 'this time of great scarcity, and extreme dearth'.[63] More revealing might be the small bequest by William Grieve of

Commonside in 1701 to 'poor broken tenents or other honest people within the parish that are blameless in their walk, unable to worke, and not by prodigalitie nor sloth, but by Providence, reduct to povertie'.[64]

The possibility that families impoverished by the expansion of sheep farming turned to some form of domestic industry receives stronger support. In his study of the Border textile industry, Gulvin fixed the chronology of its large-scale growth at c.1780 onwards, but acknowledged that this particular phase was prefaced by one in which production was organised on a small-scale domestic basis and integrated with the tasks of husbandry.[65] In fact, activities like spinning, weaving or handknitting were being exploited as prime or supplementary sources of income by the late seventeenth century. By its very nature, domestic industry did not generate a great deal of documentation. Burgh or town records offer the best chance of documenting its early growth in the region. At Hawick, for example, there was a dispute involving local websters in 1643, twenty-three years before it became a burgh for the 'buying and selling of bestiall, victuall and other commodities'.[66] The websters, it seems, had refused some of the town's work. By 1685, the weavers and cordiners of the new burgh were sufficiently organised to have been incorporated.[67] A list of inhabitants in the burgh who had stented themselves for the casting of a new bell in the 1690s included no fewer than twenty-three weavers.[68] Shoemakers, too, are mentioned frequently in Hawick's records.[69] Nor was Hawick alone in making capital out of the resources of its hinterland. Weaving was said to be the main activity of Moffat, even by 1750, 'chiefly owing to the activity of strangers'.[70] Elsewhere, towns like Selkirk had its shoemakers, Melrose its linen weavers and Denholm its stocking knitters, all before the late eighteenth century. David Loch's tour through the region in 1778 offers a view of how much industrial activity had taken root prior to the take-off of the textile trades in the closing decades of the eighteenth century. His list is notable not only for its range of different textile or wool-based trades (including the manufacture of tapes, shalloons, blankets, duffles, serges, plaids, carpets, linen, napkins and stockings) but also for the number of centres involved (i.e. Selkirk, Hawick, Peebles, Melrose, Duns, Kelso, Jedburgh, Dryburgh, Moffat, Carnwath, Dumfries and Sanquhar).[71]

Naturally, the countryside was not insulated from this activity. As early as c.1700, a description of Selkirkshire credited it with producing 'great plenty of well spun worset, which is sold and carried for the most part into forreign Nations'.[72] Most of this yarn would have come from the landward part of the county rather than from Selkirk or Galashiels. This was later confirmed by Andrew Wight. When he toured the country districts around Selkirk and Peebles in the 1770s, he found that the spinning of yarn was the staple employment amongst the women. They were 'fully employed by the English manufacturers of woollen cloth, who find their account in it, by having their wool spun cheaper there than at home'.[73] Loch too confirmed the survival of this particular trade well into the late eighteenth century, with wool being brought from England to Selkirk by a regular traffic of waggons, carded and spun locally, then returned southwards.[74] Local weaving centres, like Hawick and Moffat, would have been equally reliant on wool carded and spun in the surrounding countryside. Offering a glimpse of this trade at its source are two farm account books, one for the 1690s and the other for the 1740s, both of which reveal spinning as an on-the-farm activity.[75]

As the comment by Wight implied, domestic industry flourished best where labour was both cheap and plentiful. Arguably, the removal of so many rungs on the farming ladder and the conversion of so much arable to grass would have created an ideal social environment in the Southern Uplands. For those whose livelihood was squeezed by such trends, the adoption of some form of domestic industry would have been part of their strategy for survival. The same verdict might be passed on the relationship contracted between hired labour and upland farmers, at least where it involved a high proportion of factor payments (i.e. grain, sheep, cattle grazings, old clothes, footwear, etc.): clearly, in such instances, the labourer secured some of his basic necessities directly through his wage contract. Such conditions must have contrasted sharply with those opening up before the large, commercial sheep farmer. Tentatively, I would suggest that from the late seventeenth down to the late eighteenth centuries, or from when landholding began to shed its surplus tenants and smallholders down to the large-scale growth of industry in centres like Galashiels and Hawick, we can best structure this contrast in the rural economy of the Southern Uplands by construing it in the form of a dual economy. On the one hand, there existed an expanding sector that was committed to commercial sheep production and characterised by large units of operation, cash rents and market responsiveness. On the other hand, there was the household economy of diverse cottagers, labourers and landless, an economy characterised by increasing numbers but declining opportunities, by payments in kind, by a trading in use rather than exchange values, and by an overriding concern for subsistence and survival: the principles which shaped the economy of such households may have been those of supply rather than demand economics, with employment not profit being paramount.

Conclusion

I have tried to show that when the so-called new husbandry began to be diffused from lowland areas like the Merse into the Southern Uplands during the 1780s and '90s, it signalled only a fresh direction for change rather than the advent of change. Far from being dormant, or a laggard sector, the Southern Uplands already had a century of change and adjustment behind it. At the centre of this change was the growing ascendency of large-scale commercial sheep farming. Although firmly established by the start of the seventeenth century, the needs of sheep farming came into conflict with what appears to have been a fairly substantial subsistence sector. Slowly over the late seventeenth and early eighteenth centuries, this conflict was resolved in the interests of the former. As the size of holdings and sheep flocks was enlarged, the number of landholders and the amount of arable underwent a corresponding decrease. Farm resources became devoted more exclusively to sheep. I feel the passing analogy which I drew with the Highland clearances is both fair and apt. Admittedly, the scale on which landholders were squeezed off the land was probably less than in the Highlands. Moreover, it did not involve any forceful clearance of farms. To this extent, there was less social drama about it. However, it was still a process capable of profound social disruption, one that reduced many communities in the Southern Uplands to the status of single farms. If it was a social change that appears to have had few publicists, it was not necessarily because it was a social change without tears. Arguably, part of the reason why these events in the Southern Uplands have received relatively little attention lies in the role played by the growth of domestic industry and alternative employment. If tenant reduction and the shift towards a farm economy geared more wholeheartedly for sheep caused a massive displacement from the land, domestic industry might possibly have prevented this massive displacement being turned into an equally massive migration out of the region. Perhaps by not exporting its problem, by devising a local solution in the form of the textile trades, the Southern Uplands was seen by social commentators of the time as having coped well with the sorts of change which I have tried to describe.

REFERENCES

1. C. Fox, *The Personality of Britain* (Cardiff, 4th edition, 1959).

2. E. J. T. Collins, *The Economy of Upland Britain, 1750-1950* (Centre for Agricultural Strategy, University of Reading, 1978), p. 13.

3. J. Thirsk, 'The Farming Regions of England', in J. Thirsk, ed., *The Agrarian History of England and Wales, vol. IV* (Cambridge, 1967), pp. 1-160.

4. T. Bedford Franklin, *A History of Scottish Farming* (Edinburgh, 1952), Chapters VIII and X; R. A. Dodgshon, *Land and Society in Early Scotland* (Oxford, 1981), pp. 120-4.

5. Typical of this material is the rental reprinted in *Liber S. Marie de Calchou 1113-1567* (Bannatyne Club, Edinburgh, 1846), vol. 1, p. 489 *et seq.*

6. *Registrum Honoris de Morton* (Bannatyne Club, Edinburgh, 1853), vol. 1, p. xlvii *et seq.*

7. G. Burnett, ed., *The Exchequer Rolls of Scotland, vol. XI, A.D. 1497-1501* (Edinburgh, 1888), p. 395.

8. G. Burnett, ed., *The Exchequer Rolls of Scotland, vol. XII, A.D. 1502-1507* (Edinburgh, 1889), p. 659.

9. See, for example, G. P. M'Neill, ed., *The Exchequer Rolls of Scotland, vol. XVII, A.D. 1537-1542* (Edinburgh, 1901), pp. 707-8.

10. P. H. Brown, *Scotland Before 1700 from Contemporary Documents* (Edinburgh, 1893), p. 122.

11. S.R.O., RHP9429.

12. S.R.O., GD224/243/7.

13. Burnett, ed., *Exchequer Rolls of Scotland 1497-1501*, p. 402.

14. S.R.O., GD224/283/1, General Rental Book 1661; GD224/937/15, Rental of Forest, 1650.

15. Roxburgh MSS, Floors Castle, Rentals 1680-1, particularly entries dealing with farms beside Bowmont and Kale Waters.

16. See examples given in R. Romanes and J. Curle, 'Letter to the Secretary, Presenting the Silver Chain Known as "Midside Maggie's Girdle" to the National Museum of Antiquities; with Notes Upon the Story of the Girdle and Its Owner', *Proceedings Soc. of Antiquaries of Scotland*, XXXII (1897-8), p. 199.

17. Its gross rental was:
    1499 £469 12s 5d Scots
    1586 £2763 16s 8d Scots
    1650 £22,760 Scots
    1696 £23,148 19s 2d Scots
    1718 £2017 13s 2d English
    1766 £2247 1s 8d English

18. C. C. H. Harvey and J. Macleod, eds., *Calendar of Writs Preserved at Yester House 1166–1625* (Scottish Record Society, Edinburgh), 1930, p. 242.

19. National Library of Scotland, Minto MSS, Box 18/124 Farming Accounts for 1692.

20. Anon., 'On the Ancient Husbandry of Roxburghshire', *Farmer's Magazine*, VIII (1807), pp. 166–7.

21. S.R.O. GD224/393/6/15, 10/2 and 10/10 are typical.

22. J. W. Buchan and H. Paton, *A History of Peebles-shire* (Glasgow, 1927), vol. III, p. 363.

23. S.R.O. GD224/243/5, Ettrick Forest Rental 1718.

24. Wilton Lodge Museum, Hawick, The Broadlie Day Book 1748–55, provides a range of figures which suggest that wool provided only about 25% of the farm's income, the rest coming mainly from the sale of sheep for mutton or lamb with a small proportion from skins, stirks and cheese.

25. *The Farmer's Magazine*, IV (1803), p. 377.

26. D. Woodward, 'A Comparative Study of the Irish and Scottish Livestock Trades in the Seventeenth Century', in L. M. Cullen and T. C. Smout, eds., *Comparative Aspects of Scottish and Irish Economic and Social History 1600–1900* (Edinburgh, 1977), pp. 159–60.

27. J. Raine, ed., *The History and Antiquities of North Durham* (London, 1852), pp. xiv–xvii.

28. There is a useful summary of the Scotts' expansion in *Royal Comm. Ancient Monuments, Selkirkshire* (Edinburgh, 1957), pp. 9–10.

29. Roxburgh MSS, Floors Castle, Representation for William Ker and Davidson of Summerdean Against Pringle of Cliftoun 1713.

30. S.R.O. GD224/291/1.

31. S.R.O. GD224/243/7 is presented in the form of a rental for 1681–4.

32. Roxburgh MSS, Floors Castle, Rental and Tacks for 1680–1.

33. See, for example, the references to Ettrick farms in S.R.O., GD224/280/1 and 280/2.

34. S.R.O. GD224/939/28.

35. Wilton Lodge Museum, Hawick, The Broadlie Day Book, 1752, April 27th is typical of a number of sections dealing with the hiring of labour; A. O. Curle, 'Some Notes on the Account-Book of Dame Magdalen Nicholson, Widow of Sir Gilbert Elliot, First Baronet of Stobs, 1671–1693', *Proc. Soc. Antiq. Scot.* XXXIX (1904–5), pp. 127–8 (this shows a greater proportion of cash wages, but payments in kind are still present). See also, Anon., 'Ancient Husbandry of Roxburghshire', pp. 166–7.

36. S.R.O. GD224/937/15.

37. Ibid.

38. S.R.O. RHP9429.

39. *New Statistical Account* (NSA) *Dumfries-shire*, IV (Edinburgh, 1854), pp. 539–40.

40. *Ibid.* Eskdalemuir parish, pp. 410–1 suggests that sheep were droved to the lower dale ground during exceptional storms.

41. This statement is based on tacks for farms along Bowmont and Kale Waters in the Roxburgh collection.

42. For 1766, see S.R.O., GD224/281. For 1792, see Rental of His Grace The Duke of Buccleuch's Estates in the Counties of Roxburgh, Selkirk and Peebles 1792–3.

43. Wilton Lodge Museum, Hawick, The Broadlie Day Book, 1748–55.

44. The Buccleuch rentals afford many instances of this practice. See, for instance, S.R.O., GD224/243/7.

45. *Old Statistical Account* (OSA), I, pp. 51–2.

46. *Ibid*, V, p. 436.

47. *Ibid*, VIII, p. 88.

48. *NSA, Selkirkshire*, III (1845), p. 76.

49. *Royal Comm. Ancient Monuments, Peebles-shire*, Edinburgh, 1967, Vol. II, pp. 359-62.

50. *NSA, Roxburghshire*, 20 (1845), pp. 28, 78, 94, 276 and 373.

51. *NSA Dumfries-shire*, IV (1845), pp. 189 and 539-40.

52. *OSA*, XII, p. 67.

53. *NSA, Berwickshire*, I (1845), p. 142.

54. A. Bruce, *Appendix to the General View of the Agriculture of Berwick* (Edinburgh, 1794), pp. 110-11; R. Douglas, *General View of the Agriculture of the County of Roxburgh and Selkirk* (Edinburgh, 1794), p. 126.

55. Roxburgh MSS, Floors Castle, Note of the Contents of Lands Adjacent to the Waters of Bowmont and Kaill belonging to His Grace The Duke of Roxburgh, Dec. 1769 and Report of the Farms of Hownam and Kirkraw Let in Tack as One Farm and Sharplaw and Bearhope Let in the Same Manner, 1806.

56. R. Heron, *Observations Made in a Journey Through the Western Counties of Scotland* (Perth, 1793), vol. II, p. 32.

57. *NSA, Roxburghshire*, p. 78.

58. S.R.O. GD6/1601/3.

59. Roxburgh MSS, Floors Castle, Tack for Southcoat 1746 is typical of the restrictive tacks which the Roxburgh estate began to issue from the mid-eighteenth century onwards.

60. S.R.O. GD237/66.

61. Berwickshire County Library, Duns, Marchmont Folio, Folder 11.

62. Wilton Lodge Museum, Hawick, The Broadlie Day Book, 1748-55 provides figures which, when used in conjunction with figures from S.R.O., GD224/243/7 and GD224/935/15, suggest stocking levels rose as arable acreages fell. See also, R.A. Dodgshon, 'The Economics of Sheep Farming in the Southern Uplands During the Age of Improvement, 1750-1833', *Economic History Rev.*, 2nd Series, XXIX (1976), pp. 559-60.

63. J. Wilson, ed., *Annals of Hawick A.D. 1214-1814* (Edinburgh, 1850), pp. 105-6.

64. J. J. Vernon, 'Extracts from the Kirk Sessions of Hawick, 1700-1704', *Hawick Archaeological Society*, 1909, p. 31.

65. C. Gulvin, *The Tweedmakers: A History of the Scottish Fancy Woollen Industry 1600-1914*, (Newton Abbot, 1973), especially pp. 38-69.

66. *Acts of the Privy Council*, VII, p. 661; Wilson, *Annals of Hawick*, p. 51.

67. *Ibid*, p. 89.

68. *Ibid*, pp. 96-102.

69. *Ibid*.

70. W. Robertson Turnbull, *History of Moffat* (Edinburgh, 1871), pp. 109-10.

71. Sir Arthur Mitchell, 'David Loch's Tour in Scotland in 1778', *Proc. Soc. Antiq. Scot.*, XXXII (1897-98), pp. 25-8.

72. *Geographical Collections Relating to Scotland Made by W. Macfarlane*, vol. III, (Scottish History Society, LIII), p. 168.

73. A. Wight, *Present State of Husbandry in Scotland* (Edinburgh, 1784), vol. III, part i, pp. 20-1, tour dated 1777.

74. Mitchell, 'Loch's Tour', p. 25.

75. Curle, 'Letter to the Secretary', p. 131; Wilton Lodge Museum, Hawick, The Broadlie Day Book, 1748-1755, 1752, April 27th.

5

Ulster as a Mirror of the Two Societies

W. H. Crawford

IN approaching a comparison of economic and social change in Scotland and Ireland there is always the temptation to identify in the more successful economy certain virtues consistent with the gospel of economic progress. The comments may be modified with the admission that these economic changes were occurring within two distinct countries that differed fundamentally in cultural history and natural endowments. Yet one Irish province, Ulster, did contain a significant colony descended from Scottish immigrants, so that it should be possible to observe the contrasting cultures and analyse their performances in coping with the same environment. The major snag is that neither the Irish nor the Scots in Ulster can be considered as representative of their respective peoples. The Irish in Ulster were more traditional and conservative than the Leinster Irish, for example, mainly because they had not had to adapt to the changes in social organisation, landholding, and farming practices introduced by the Anglo-Normans. The Scottish colonists, for their part, although drawn from a broad spectrum of Scottish society, should be viewed as displaced people superfluous to the economic and social needs of the colonising society. First to settle were the Highlanders whom their fellow countrymen contemptuously termed 'Irish', and they were succeeded by Lowlanders, Borderers and, more especially, by people from the south-west of Scotland.

With this proviso, that neither the Irish nor the Scots in Ulster accurately reflect the qualities of their people, it is still a valuable exercise to analyse the behaviour of the two groups in Ulster. Although both were subject to the Dublin government and suffered religious disabilities, the Scots ended the seventeenth century in possession of good leases of the better quality land. Together with the descendants of English immigrants, they almost monopolised Ulster's trade, leaving the Irish to pick up the crumbs. Nevertheless, neither the Irish nor the Scots could escape the tremendous impact of the expansion of the domestic linen industry on the economy of the province. A society of small tenant farmers and a population explosion converted Ulster into a province where, even as late as 1926, the average area of land per farm was smaller than in any other political division of the British Isles after more than half a century of consolidation.[1] In 1821 the population of Ulster stood at 1,998,494, equivalent to just over ninety-five per cent of Scottish population at that stage. Although the agricultural system was considered backward, it was able to feed the Ulster populace and to send large quantities of butter, grain and pork to both Scotland and England after the 1770s.

I

Without the succession of King James VI of Scotland to the throne of England, it is unlikely that Scots would have been able to colonise any significant districts of Ireland. Although the Macdonnells of Islay had already established themselves on the moorlands and rocky coasts of north-west Antrim, there can be little doubt that any English successor to Elizabeth's crown would have prevented substantial Lowland Settlement in Ulster. James encouraged the Scots to join the English in exploiting Irish lands in the vacuum created by the overthrow of the traditional structure of power in Ulster. He provided the Scots with a timely opportunity to speculate in colonisation with some prospects of success: they had not earned the privilege. They were to prove more fortunate in Ulster than in their own contemporary colonies established at Lochaber, Lewis and Kintyre (from which some settlers moved on to County Antrim). In Ulster, Scots were given a good share of the Crown grants of newly created, compact manors.[2] Although tenants were attracted from both England and Scotland by cheap land on good terms, the seventeenth century was to elapse before there were sufficient British farmers in Ulster to generate significant competition for land. By then the Scots occupied much of the north and east coasts of the province along with the river valleys of the Main, Lower Bann, Foyle and Erne, while English settlers were most numerous in the Lagan, Upper Bann and Blackwater valleys and around much of the shoreline of Lough Neagh. In all spheres of Ulster life the Scots were very prominent: with Belfast and Londonderry as their chief ports, they almost monopolised trade and were strongly represented on the municipal corporations.

Yet by the early eighteenth century the Scots in Ulster had good reason to feel dissatisfied with their situation. Whereas the Glorious Revolution had given the established Church of Scotland a Presbyterian government, it had confirmed the episcopalian structure of the Church of Ireland. The Anglo-Irish in Dublin, intent on securing their grip on Irish government, were not prepared to concede any power to the Presbyterians in Ulster, especially since new congregations were still being established in the south of that province. Therefore this new Protestant ascendancy resisted all attempts by the Presbyterians to secure religious equality, and it managed to confirm itself in power with the extension to Ireland of the sacramental test in 1704. This enacted that any person holding any position, civil or military, under the crown had not only to take certain oaths and declarations but also to produce a certificate of having received the sacrament in the Church of Ireland. As a result many Presbyterians were compelled to resign from the municipal corporations and were effectively excluded from local government. They resented also interference by the ecclesiastical courts in their family settlements on the pretext that marriages performed by anyone but a Church of Ireland priest were invalid: this annoyance was ended with the passage of a relief act of 1737.[3] They still had to pay parish cess or rates to the Established Church, and like everyone else were liable for tithes for the upkeep of its clergy. In short, although the Scots in Ulster enjoyed security in their property, they exercised very little political influence on laws that were made by the Anglo-Irish in Dublin and administered within the English legal framework. It should always be remembered, however, that in the other three provinces of Ireland the numbers of Scottish Presbyterians were insignificant.

Although the Scots might justly resent their exclusion from Irish political life, they were in a much more fortunate position in Ulster than the native Irish, whose leaders had been deprived of their lands, and who had suffered a colonial assault on their society and its traditional way of life. In much of the north and east of the province the Irish were swamped by repeated incursions of colonists throughout the seventeenth century: their only options were to adapt to the British way of life, often assuming a British variant of their surnames, or to leave their homes. In the south and west of the province, however, where the British were less densely settled, Irish society was not so seriously affected: although the remnants of the old Gaelic aristocracy were swept away by the Williamite Wars, their functions were assumed by families of the second rank who were more likely than the old rulers to adapt to changing economic and social circumstances. These descendants of cadet branches, of sub-chieftains, and of *erenagh* families obtained leases from the new British landlords on the grounds that they could and would exercise control over their people. They did assume responsibility for the welfare of their clients, and from their families came the priests who ministered to the people. In those districts where the Irish survived the seventeenth-century invasions but saw their lands let to Protestant British farmers, they were often prepared to remain on the land as sub-tenants without leases and to pay higher rents.[4]

The wide variation in the nature and depth of the disturbance of native society and economy by the British settlers is of fundamental importance to any understanding of Ulster society. In many districts of south and west Ulster, Irish society not only remained intact but, by retaining its economy, ensured the survival of many of its traditional practices, concepts and values. For the native inhabitants there was no incentive to change and every reason to maintain the Gaelic way of life. With their own language and their own religion the Irish in Ulster were able to insulate themselves against the newcomers. But at what cost to their future prospects? A commentator at the close of the eighteenth century reckoned that the Irish entered the commercial linen industry late because 'they considered it as a manufacture introduced by the Protestants or Huguenots tending to change their religion and they preferred for many years being labourers to that of being weavers'.[5]

II

The most distinctive Ulster characteristic in comparison either with the rest of Ireland or with Scotland in the eighteenth century was the evolution of a society of small tenant farmers. This was not an inevitable development, since in the early decades of the century farms were quite substantial. Their owners were protected against the appetites of their landlords as well as the ambitions of their undertenants by their leases. The balance between landlords and tenants was reflected in the widespread recognition not only of the right of a tenant to sell his lease to another person without undue interference from the landlord, but even of the justice of his claim to renewal of the lease at its expiry on offering to pay the current value of the farm in increased rent. In the improving economic climate after 1740 many of these leaseholders began to prosper at the expense of their undertenants: there was more profit in subletting to weavers than in farming. In the districts where the domestic industry of weaving fine linens was spreading through the countryside, landlords were jealous of the profits made by many farmers in subletting holdings to weavers on short leases. Whenever these head leases fell due for renewal, landlords insisted on renewing to the farmers only the holdings they actually occupied and on letting the properties that the farmers had sublet, directly to the weavers who lived on them. This measure destroyed the farmer class in these districts, and the weavers' holdings continued to subdivide so that by the end of the century the average size of holdings in County Armagh was little more than five acres. Contemporaries pointed out that it was not possible for a family to make a good living from these small holdings, but that in order to retain a secure stake in the land weavers were prepared to offset farming losses against their earnings in the domestic linen industry. The industry was responsible for the backwardness of agriculture in Ulster for the reason that weavers could not concentrate both on farming and the weaving of fine linens, if only because of the condition of their hands.[6]

Outside those districts specialising in the weaving of fine linens, landlords might approve of this policy of encouraging sub-tenants to become leaseholders, but in practice they had to take care that they did not grant leases to men who could not afford the regular payment of considerable rents. The result was that substantial farmers continued to thrive on the better farming lands, especially in County Down and the main river valleys. In contrast, on the poorer lands in mid- and west Ulster many small farms were created by the enclosure and cultivation of marginal lands as population continued to spread up the many tributary valleys in search of turf for fuel and ground for planting potatoes. Because the inheritance customs of both Scots and Irish provided for all the family on such a farm, these holdings were usually farmed in common until an active landlord helped the family members to agree on subdivision into compact farms that made them more competitive in the market.

The corollary of the great increase in the number of small leaseholders was aggravation of the problems of man management for the landlords. The displacement of substantial farmers and middlemen compelled the landlord and his agent to deal directly with larger numbers of tenants so that there was less emphasis on trying to induce tenants to improve their farming methods and more on maintaining law and order on the estate. It is this duty of exercising social control that many critics of Irish agents have overlooked: to be effective, an agent had to know the estate intimately. Neglected tenants devised their own customs, converted concessions into precedents, and were able to make it very difficult for any newcomer, either landlord or agent, to formulate any effective solutions to their backwardness. Indeed these expressions of their strong convictions of natural justice provided the excuse for agrarian disturbances attributed in the early 1760s to the Hearts of Oak and in the early 1770s to the Hearts of Steel.[7]

Another major reason for these disturbances was the structural change in the economy produced by the expansion of the domestic linen industry. It is important to try to assess the significance of this industry for the wealth of the province. As early as 1728 linen cloth and yarn comprised over sixty per cent of the total value of Irish exports to Britain, and this share rose to a peak of eighty per cent by 1758; even by the close of the century linen cloth was still responsible for more than one half of the total value of Irish exports to Britain at a time of rapidly increasing exports of agricultural produce.[8] Throughout the century more than three-quarters of all Irish linens were woven in Ulster by a population of between one quarter and one third of the population of all Ireland. There must therefore have been periods, especially in the middle of the century, when income per head in Ulster was running at more than twice that of the rest of Ireland. This wealth did not disappear immediately into the pockets of a small proportion of the population. In the linen industry the raw materials could not be cornered by middlemen to organise a 'putting out' system, because most of the yarn was spun from flax grown locally by small farmers. Annual sales of linen by independent weavers in the cloth markets (always conducted in cash because banknotes were not taken) were estimated to be worth more than £2.17 millions as late as 1803.[9] This cash percolated throughout the whole economic network by way of the weavers, the spinners, the petty yarn dealers and farmers. As demand for linens increased, it was these people in rural Ulster who exploited the poorer class of cottiers by putting out work to them. As long as income from the linen industry continued to be substantial, the ability of many rural families to improve and secure their economic and social status proved cardinal to their subsequent fortunes. Their chief weapon was security of tenure: whereas landlords had conceded to tenants a claim to renewal of leases at their expiry, these same tenants granted no such concession to either undertenants or cottiers.

By the close of the century changes in the textile industries were accentuating certain regional distinctions within the province. The weavers in and around Belfast transferred from linen to cotton because for a while it paid twice as well; many of them moved to Belfast where their wives and children could find employment in the spinning-mills from which they themselves obtained their yarn. Elsewhere new machines invented in Britain to spin cotton yarn strong enough for warp threads were severely damaging the livelihood of many spinners of linen yarn. Most seriously affected were those of north-west Ulster, especially around the port of Londonderry, which had traditionally supplied Lancashire with the linen yarn used for warps. Exports of yarn from Londonderry (responsible for almost half of total Irish linen yarn exports) were more than halved in the early 1790s and never recovered.[10] It is significant that about this time migration from the Londonderry region to Scotland that had been seasonal, began to assume a more permanent character. This phenomenon appeared also in the south of the province because the income from linen sales could no longer be supplemented by increased agricultural production: although agriculture had become very intensive, there were too many mouths to feed.[11]

It was not to agriculture but to trade and commerce that the eighteenth century left its most valuable legacy, the capital to generate new industry. Most of this capital in Ulster was in the hands of the Protestants. In the linen industry, according to a commentator in 1795,

> It is worth notice that few, if any Roman Catholics are head bleachers in the North, and still more extraordinary on looking into this great manufacture in Ulster, which occupies at least three millions sterling to carry it on, that it is almost every shilling in the hands of Protestants, as it is believed there are not four bleach yards in the hands of Roman Catholics and those of little consequence when compared with the extensive works in their neighbourhood. Strange as it may appear, it will bear examination.[12]

The predominance of the Protestants in the linen finishing trades was based on their success in devising new mechanical bleaching techniques in the 1730s. To exploit these techniques the bleachers required water power, and so they set out to lease the water rights of all the best sites for bleaching throughout the province. Latecomers could not offset such advantages, nor could they compete successfully with experienced bleachers at a time when the skill of bleaching owed more to observation and ingenuity than to science. A bleacher whose reputation depended on skills acquired during and since his apprenticeship was unlikely to impart them to newcomers and potential competitors.[13] In the ports Irish merchants found it almost as difficult to establish themselves. Scottish merchants had settled in Belfast in the seventeenth century, and their strength both there and in Londonderry was a thorn in the side of the establishment. The Irish were few in the Belfast region: in 1708 it was reported of Belfast to the Dublin government that there were not 'within the town above seven Papists and by the return made by the High Constable there is (*sic*) not above 150 Papists in the whole barony'.[14] It is significant that the Catholic merchants began to appear in the south of the province. They acquired capital by dealing initially in oatmeal or yarn and later in linens; this provided them with experience and opportunities in the growing provision trade and the distilling and brewing industries. Denis Caulfied, the most successful merchant in Newry between 1790 and 1818, owned both of the large distilleries in the town.[15]

III

The rise of a Catholic merchant class in the late eighteenth century was only one sign of a resurgence of native society throughout Ireland that affected the Ulster Irish. Another was the erection of many mass-houses that symbolised the new vitality of the Catholic church. The success of the Catholic church in maintaining its support in Gaelic Ireland (but not in Gaelic Scotland) had been ensured in the seventeenth century by the success of its policy of maintaining a supply of priests for every parish. During the penal period the clergy depended for their livelihood and support on the more influential local families whose members, in return, provided many of the clergy. By means of the penal laws which sought the total exclusion of the hierarchy and the regular clergy, the government had planned to undermine the structure of the church, but parish priests who registered officially were permitted to continue their ministry. In consequence, the parish priest became an integral part of Irish life and played a vital role in creating the character of Ulster Catholicism. Throughout the eighteenth century the Ulster priest experienced the tensions in Catholic life caused by the attempt to impose more modern doctrines and observances which were being introduced from the continent in place of the more discreditable and primitive beliefs and practices of the Gaelic church and its adherents, especially those concerned with waking the dead and seeking for cures at holy wells. For their part the bishops, generally in residence once again in Ulster by the mid-1730s in spite of the penal prohibitions, found great difficulty in enforcing clerical discipline in the face of opposition that was often local in extent and personal in character. By the close of the century, however, it seemed that they had established their authority with the aid of a new class of clergy who were less dependent on the old local families and better trained and educated than their predecessors. The Church was well organised to support the political emancipation movement that would restore to Catholics their full civic rights in the early nineteenth century.[16]

While the Catholic Church was busy consolidating its authority and influence among the Ulster Irish, the Scots in Ulster were indulging themselves in various theological controversies that split the Presbyterian church into several independent and often unfriendly groups. The most important issue concerned subscription to the Westminster Confession. Between 1719 and 1726 raged the first controversy over the need for every minister to subscribe. The 'non-subscribers' were in the minority, and they decided to set up a separate non-subscribing body, the Presbytery of Antrim, autonomous from the official Synod of Ulster. The other issue concerned the 'Regium Donum', the royal grant paid to the Presbyterian Church to supplement the incomes of the clergy. The failure of their negotiators to obtain in 1729 an increase commensurate with the increasing numbers of congregations compelled both bodies to stipulate certain minimum requirements before a new congregation could receive a grant towards its minister's stipend. The next applicants who met with refusal thereupon sent to Scotland for assistance from the Seceders in the immediate aftermath of the Scottish expulsions of 1740: as a result Ulster imported both Burgher and Anti-Burgher clergy who erected synods in 1779 and 1788 respectively. From south-west Scotland, the home of the Cameronian sect, came the first minister to represent the Reformed Presbyterian Church, in 1761. By 1792 there were 185 congregations in the General Synod of Ulster and the Presbytery of Antrim together, twenty-eight congregations of Burghers, eighteen of Anti-Burghers, and fewer than ten of Covenanters. Many of these congregations were themselves the products of disputes within congregations, sometimes on doctrinal grounds but often for personal reasons. Because the clergy were dependent for their incomes on their congregations and not on patrons, there was tension between the clergy and the elders of each congregation and many opportunities for mutual criticism and recriminations. Perhaps the vigour of theological controversy was a measure of the health of the church's religious life, but it was divisive and weakened the potential political influence of the Presbyterian church.[17]

The Presbyterian love of controversy was founded on the premise that every individual should have a personal knowledge of the Scriptures. Therefore the Presbyterian Church in Scotland since its foundation had always stressed the right of the individual to education, and this principle was carried to Ulster. There, however, education was controlled by the Episcopalians, and by an act of 1665 all teachers had to be licensed by the bishops of each diocese. By the eighteenth century interference by the Ascendancy in the work of Presbyterian schoolmasters must have lapsed, since it had disappeared from the grievances listed in Presbyterian petitions. The Scots taught mainly in private schools, although local congregations usually supported an elementary school. There was no shortage of schoolmasters, many of them trained in the Scottish universities, especially Glasgow. Their need for pupils ensured their readiness to adapt their curricula to the needs of their pupils. There is evidence that even in the smaller provincial towns it was possible by the mid-century to obtain instruction in the practical application of mathematics, such as land-surveying, book-keeping and navigation. By 1785 the first of the Ulster academies, on the Scottish model, was opened at Strabane and it was soon followed by one in Belfast. The intellectuals in Ulster were confident of their ability to provide education to university level, and they were aware of the importance of teaching science and mathematics. Their efforts were rewarded in 1814 with the opening of the Belfast Academical Institution, with professors in mathematics, natural philosophy, and anatomy and physiology before 1820.[18]

Attitudes to education among the Ulster Irish were much more diverse. Before the Plantations, learning among the laity in any district had been the preserve of certain families who received privileges in return for services to their chief as bards or brehon lawyers. Churchmen had been educated at universities in Britain and Europe, and so the closing to them of the British universities, as a consequence of the Reformation settlements in England and Scotland, compelled Irish scholars to seek learning on the Continent.[19] This more expensive education had to be sponsored by Church bursaries and it tended to be confined to the more influential families. In Ulster itself the Church did not make provision for the training of its priests until late in the eighteenth century, and there were no diocesan policies for educating the mass of its people. In default, many leading men picked up a basic education as they went about their business, a growing acquaintance with the spoken English language and the ability to count money, but they were illiterate and unable to write. As the century passed, those who wanted more education repaired to private, or 'hedge', schools run often by successors of the old bardic families who could no longer rely for their living on patronage.[20] It was to regularise this haphazard pattern of education that the British government introduced a national system of education in Ireland in the 1830s.

IV

This paper has attempted a broad survey of the major influences in Ulster economy, society and culture that affected both the Scots and the Irish throughout the period. To evaluate their relative success it is necessary to consider what various groups in Ulster society would have regarded as success. The capitalist tradition in Ulster did not have deep roots: many business families had made their capital only in the eighteenth century. The Protestant merchants and linen drapers were still ambitious to extend their range of activities and interests. On the other hand, opportunities outside the family business for surplus sons were rapidly improving. On the land, substantial Protestant leaseholders dreamt of establishing their sons in prosperous farms not far from the home farm: surplus sons could be provided for in religion, medicine, education or an apprenticeship. Lower down the social scale among the group that comprised very many small farmers, both Catholic and Protestant, there had been a strong urge to maintain the family circle either by preserving the farm intact or by parcelling it out among all the family, especially when domestic handloom weaving was still providing a major supplementary source of income. The collapse of domestic weaving in the first half of the nineteenth century would make this the more dangerous option because the owner of such a share in the family farm could realise his share's value by selling it to an outsider. To maintain the farm intact, and with it the family's social position, it would become necessary either to find opportunities for the children away from the land or to leave them to the care of the son who received the entire farm under his father's will. At the lowest social level in the countryside were landless labourers. They had made ends meet with employment by the farmers or linen manufacturers (a term applied to master weavers): in the nineteenth century their livelihood would become much more precarious and they would be forced off the land by famine and lack of employment. In all these matters an unprejudiced contemporary observer could not have distinguished differences in response attributable to cultural or religious factors.

REFERENCES

1. *The Marketing of Northern Ireland Agricultural Produce*, 1932 [N.I. Ministry of Agriculture], p. 4.
2. M. Perceval-Maxwell, *The Scottish Migration to Ulster in the Reign of James I* (London, 1973), pp. 10–18.
3. J. C. Beckett, *Protestant Dissent in Ireland 1687–1780* (London, 1948), pp. 43–50, 89, 120–3.
4. W. H. Crawford, 'The Ulster Irish in the Eighteenth Century', *Ulster Folklife*, 28 (1982).
5. Public Record Office of Northern Ireland, Massereene-Foster MS, D.562/1270, 'Scheme of Robert Stevenson 1795'.
6. W. H. Crawford, 'Landlord-Tenant Relations in Ulster 1690–1820', *Irish Economic and Social History*, II (1975), pp. 10–15; Royal Irish Academy, Haliday Pamphlet 377, *Serious Considerations on the Present Alarming State of Agriculture and the Linen Trade* (Dublin, 1773), pp. 9–23.

7. W. H. Crawford and B. Trainor, eds., *Aspects of Irish Social History 1750-1800* (Belfast, 1969), pp. 35, 38.

8. L. M. Cullen, *Anglo-Irish Trade 1660-1800* (Manchester, 1968), Table 13 on p. 50; L. M. Cullen and T. C. Smout, eds., *Comparative Aspects of Scottish and Irish Economic and Social History 1600-1900* (Edinburgh, 1977), p. 5.

9. W. H. Crawford, *Domestic Industry in Ireland: the Experience of the Linen Industry* (Dublin, 1972), p. 80, based on Public Record Office of Northern Ireland, Massereene-Foster MS, D.562/6225.

10. T. F. Colby, ed., *The Ordnance Survey Memoir of the City and North-Western Liberties of Londonderry, Parish of Templemore* (Dublin, 1837), pp. 254-93.

11. B. Collins, 'Aspects of Irish Immigration into Two Scottish Towns during the Mid-Nineteenth Century' (unpublished M.Phil. thesis, University of Edinburgh, 1978); S. H. Cousens, 'The Regional Variation in Emigration from Ireland between 1821 and 1841', *Transactions of the Institute of British Geographers,* 37 (1965), p. 17.

12. 'Scheme of Robert Stevenson 1795'.

13. W. H. Crawford, 'Drapers and Bleachers in the Early Ulster Linen Industry', in L. M. Cullen and P. Butel, eds., *Négoce et Industrie en France et en Irlande aux XVIIIe et XIXe Siècles* (Paris, 1980), pp. 113-8.

14. George Macartney, Belfast to Joshua Dawson, Dublin, 24 March 1707/8, quoted in G. Benn, *A History of the Town of Belfast* (London, 1877), pp. 416-7.

15. A. Marmion, *The Ancient and Modern History of the Maritime Ports of Ireland* (London, 1855), pp. 308, 313.

16. Crawford, 'Ulster Irish in the Eighteenth Century'.

17. J. L. M. Haire, ed., *Challenge and Conflict: Essays in Irish Presbyterian History and Doctrine* (Antrim, 1981); J. S. Reid, *History of the Presbyterian Church in Ireland* (Belfast, 1867).

18. D. Kennedy, 'The Ulster Academies and the Teaching of Science (1785-1835)', *Irish Ecclesiastical Record,* 63 (1944), pp. 30-7.

19. *Ibid.,* p. 26.

20. L. M. Cullen, 'The Social and Cultural Modernisation of Rural Ireland, 1600-1900', in L. M. Cullen and F. Furet, eds., *Ireland and France 17th-20th Centuries: Towards a Comparative Study of Rural History* (Paris, 1980), pp. 208-9.

F

6

Agricultural Productivity and Economic Development in Ireland and Scotland in the Early Nineteenth Century

Peter M. Solar

Whatever the reason, the fact that agriculture was being transformed in Scotland but not in Ireland at the end of the eighteenth century was a critical difference between the two countries, probably the most critical of all . . . No country has ever been transformed into a modern economy without a successful agricultural revolution preceding or coinciding with industrialisation: Ireland could not be an exception to that rule.

L. M. Cullen and T. C. Smout[1]

IT is ironic that in the same year in which the above bold statement of the importance of agriculture in economic development was published, the *Economic History Review* carried a review essay by P. K. O'Brien which returned a rather sceptical verdict on the claims made for English agriculture during the Industrial Revolution.[2] O'Brien found that systematic quantitative evidence concerning changes in agricultural output and productivity was wanting and that the evidence which did exist had not been very effectively deployed in the analysis of the interactions between agricultural and industrial development. These judgements apply with equal or greater force to Scots and Irish agriculture. Much of what is known about agricultural change depends heavily on the writings of contemporary observers who were often advocates or adherents of certain notions of improvement. Much of what is said about the impetus given to industrial development by agricultural change is based upon the activities of landowners who often had limited contact with farming as such and who were also owners of mineral resources and urban property and beneficiaries of office and patronage. The weaknesses of these sources are known, but, with a few exceptions, research on Scottish and Irish agriculture in the early nineteenth century has not gone much beyond them.[3] Irish agricultural history, as distinct from Irish agrarian history, has received little attention for the period before the Agricultural Statistics begin in 1847. Scottish agricultural historians, by contrast, seem to have been surfeited by the riches of the *Old Statistical Account*. Cullen and Smout, despite their confident pronouncement, do recognise these deficiencies and place agriculture at the top of their agenda for further research.[4]

Here, in what is necessarily a limited contribution, it will be argued that Cullen and Smout overrate the importance of the agricultural sector in explaining the divergent development of Scotland and Ireland. Irish agriculture was by no means so backward or susceptible to improvement as contemporaries and subsequent writers have thought, and many of its characteristics and some of its problems are better seen as consequences of the exceptionally rapid growth of Ireland's population and of developments elsewhere in the economy of the United Kingdom. We shall proceed in three steps. First, we shall look at some indicators of the performance of Irish agriculture vis-a-vis Scottish agriculture and suggest why Ireland shows up quite well in certain respects (Sections I and II). Then, we shall ask why, in the light of these results, contemporary and modern opinion on early nineteenth-century Irish agriculture has been so dismal (Section III). Finally, we shall consider briefly the implications of a more optimistic view of Irish agricultural performance for the analysis of industrialisation in Scotland and Ireland (Section IV).

I

There are few estimates of agricultural output for Scotland and Ireland which permit comparison. McCulloch, always willing to try his hand, gave figures for gross agricultural output in 1846 of £28m for Scotland and £48m for Ireland, but these are merely guesses.[5] Ó Gráda, in an unpublished paper, has made detailed estimates of gross value added in Irish agriculture for several years in the mid- to late nineteenth century. He arrived at £39.3m for 1840/5 and £43.0m for 1854, both in current prices.[6] Ó Gráda compared these figures to Deane and Cole's estimates of agricultural income in Great Britain; however, there is no very satisfactory way to extract the Scottish element from the British totals. Here we shall make some rough but truly comparable estimates of net agricultural output in Scotland and Ireland for the years 1855–57. This is admittedly ten years or so too late, coming after the appearance of the potato blight and the repeal of the Corn Laws, but the estimates reveal certain features of agriculture in the two countries and give a better vantage point on the statistical void of the early nineteenth century.

The choice of years was dictated by the availability of fairly comprehensive statistics for Scotland, those collected unofficially by the Highland and Agricultural Society. These statistics are probably reasonably accurate, though they understate Scottish crop acreages and livestock numbers slightly because of the exclusion of small holdings. Irish agricultural statistics were collected annually from 1847 and were considered to be reliable.[7] The estimates of output required a number of technical coefficients, such as the shares which constituted net output for different crops; milk and wool yields for dairy cattle and sheep, respectively; and rates of turnover and average sale weights for cattle, sheep and pigs. The choice of coefficients has been based upon a rather better knowledge of Irish agriculture than Scottish. Some contemporary syntheses, such as Youatt's books on cattle, sheep and swine, have been helpful.[8] The turnover rates for livestock are consistent with the replacement rates implicit in the agricultural statistics. In general, the coefficients chosen will tend to overstate Scottish output relative to Irish. This was done to compensate for some underenumeration in the Scottish statistics and as part of a general strategy of biasing the results against Ireland. Total ouput was arrived at by weighting the different products by a common set of prices more or less representative of the mid-1850s. The same prices were used on the assumption that actual price differences between countries reflected locational factors rather than differences in product quality. The result is a quantity index of agricultural output in one country relative to the other. It should be emphasised that these estimates are not intended to be definitive measures of the volume or value of agricultural output in either Scotland or Ireland.

The results of this exercise are shown in Table 1. Irish agricultural output in the mid-1850s was a little over two and a half times that of Scotland. The most startling feature of the estimates is the almost identical partition of output between crops and animal products in the two countries. The importance of livestock husbandry is evident, with the relative emphases on sheep in Scotland and dairying and swine in Ireland showing up clearly. The importance of tillage is somewhat understated because the value of fodder crops is included in the value of the meat, milk and wool produced. Among the non-fodder crops the distributions of output are quite similar. The relative importance of the three cereals is the same, although, taken together, cereals were somewhat less important in Ireland than in Scotland. Potatoes were, of course, more important in Ireland, as was flax.

With these estimates we shall hazard a comparison of agricultural productivity for Scotland and Ireland in the mid-1850s. Such exercises are strewn with conceptual and practical snares capable of catching the great and the small, so the results must be treated with extreme caution.[9] Some pitfalls will be avoided because of the similarities in the composition of output in Scotland and Ireland and because the experience of several years (which unfortunately include the Crimean War) has been used. Measurement of the inputs, however, poses some difficulties, so we shall adopt the strategy of tilting the scales against Ireland when uncertainties arise. Thus the estimate should exaggerate the relative inefficiency of Irish agriculture.

For the labour input we rely on the occupational distributions in the censuses of 1861. These show 238,000 persons (205,000 men and 33,000 women) occupied in Scottish agriculture and 928,000 individuals (844,000 men and 84,000 women) in Irish agriculture.[10] It is necessary, however, to adjust these totals for seasonal migration. Ó Gráda argues that post-famine harvest migration remained at pre-famine levels until the 1860s, which would suggest a downward adjustment of around 60,000 to the Irish total. If the distribution of Irish migrants between England and Scotland was unchanged, an upward adjustment of 25,000 to the Scottish total would also be called for. Another 10,000 might be added to allow for seasonal migration to agriculture within Scotland.[11] The result of these adjustments is an index for Irish labour input in terms of Scottish of 318. Using the 1851 census

TABLE 1. *Net Agricultural Output, Scotland and Ireland, 1855-7*

| | Scotland | | Ireland | |
	£000s	%	£000s	%
Wheat	2115	13.2	4405	10.9
Oats	3017	18.9	7230	17.9
Barley	1064	6.7	1262	3.1
Potatoes	709	4.4	3538	8.8
Flax	24	0.2	808	2.0
Crops subtotal	6929	43.4	17243	42.7
Dairy	1805	11.3	9492	23.5
Beef	2510	15.7	7079	17.5
Mutton	3300	20.7	2097	5.2
Wool	960	6.0	610	1.5
Pork	467	2.9	3840	9.5
Animal Subtotal	9042	56.6	23118	57.3
Total	15971	100.0	40361	100.0
Index (Scotland = 100)	100		253	

Sources: The calculations which produced these estimates are described in the Appendix.

Note: These estimates were made as a comparative exercise and should be used with great caution in other contexts. They are not intended to be definitive estimates of the current value of output in either country and cannot be because a common set of prices has been used for aggregation.

would have produced a much higher figure, but the 1861 estimate is more appropriate to the years 1855–7, given the massive emigration from Ireland in the early 1850s. To be on the safe side we shall take the index of relative Irish labour input to be 340. There are other problems in defining and measuring the labour input, but we shall return to these later.

Both Scotland and Ireland are characterised by great variations in soil quality, and both contain large areas of low-grade land. One way to arrive at an estimate of relative land input in the face of these difficulties is to use total rentals. Stamp's estimates from the income tax returns (Schedule A) give an index of 150 for Irish relative land input in the mid-1850s.[12] However, the use of rents is not entirely satisfactory, in part because it incorporates locational elements and in part because it also includes some of the value of improvements, which is better classified under capital. Both of these factors will tend to understate the Irish input of pure land relative to the Scottish. An alternative indicator of effective land input is the relative area under crops (excluding grasses), which for the mid-1850s gives an index of 193.[13] We shall use a value closer to this measure and take the relative land input to be 180.

Comprehensive estimates of agricultural capital are not available for either country, but we can make a rough approach to the relative magnitudes by following the procedures employed by Feinstein in his work on British capital formation.[14] Working capital (the value of standing and stored crops, livestock and horses) can be estimated from the information in the agricultural statistics. If we use Feinstein's adjustments and valuations, for want of detailed information on Scotland and Ireland, then the result for relative working capital almost replicates the output index. This is due to the similarities in the structure of output. However, Irish working capital is almost certainly overstated by this procedure because Irish farmers tended to sell their crops very shortly after the harvest, whilst Scottish farmers were better placed to hold stocks for more favourable market conditions. We shall take relative Irish working capital to be 205. Fixed capital can be approached through investment, again following Feinstein. He estimates that total investment by landlords and tenants in Great Britain came to 15 per cent of gross rental. We shall assume that the British figure was also true of Scotland as a region. Ó Gráda has suggested that Irish landlords invested only 4–5 per cent of gross rental in this period.[15] If we take tenant investment in Ireland to have equalled landlord investment, then total investment can be taken, rather generously, to be 10 per cent of gross rental. Given the rentals of the two countries, these percentages imply that annual fixed capital formation in agriculture was the same in Scotland and Ireland. If we take the relative levels of fixed capital formation to have been long-standing, then similar fixed capital stocks are suggested. We shall take relative fixed capital to be 100. Combining the indices for fixed and working capital according to their shares in British agricultural capital gives the Irish agricultural capital stock relative to the Scottish as 138.[16]

Two matters remain before we can make the productivity calculations. First, we need to allow for the exclusion of small holdings from the Scottish agricultural statistics, since our input indices effectively include these holdings.[17] We shall take Irish output relative to Scottish to be 230, instead of 250. Second, we need coefficients with which to weight the inputs. Estimates of total rental and the current value of agricultural output suggest that the share of rent in Ireland was between 20 and 25 per cent. The problem is to know what part of rent and what part of the residual were really returns to capital. We do not know, but take the coefficients of labour, land and capital to be 0.7, 0.2 and 0.1 respectively. These values probably give too high a weight to labour, which will tend to overstate the relative inefficiency of Irish agriculture, in line with our general strategy. As an alternative set of coefficients, we use Ó Gráda's values for Great Britain in 1870/72 (though he has taken all rents to be returns to land).[18]

The calculations of total factor productivity are summarised in Table 2. They show that, if we have produced estimates truly biased against Irish agriculture, it was at worst 16 per cent less efficient than Scottish agriculture. That Irish agriculture was less efficient is not surprising; the slenderness of the Scottish advantage may be. At an agricultural productivity growth rate of .5 per cent, the gap we have found suggests that Irish agriculture was at most 24 years behind Scottish.[19] It should be emphasised again that the estimates made here of output, inputs and productivity are very rough and not to be regarded as definitive. However, they fit in with other evidence, to be discussed in the succeeding sections, which suggests that Irish agriculture was not so backward as its reputation would lead one to believe.

TABLE 2.*Total Factor Productivity, Scotland and Ireland, mid–1850s*

Input Coefficients			Irish Total Factor Productivity (Scotland = 100)
Labour	*Land*	*Capital*	
0.70	0.20	0.10	84
0.63	0.23	0.13	88

Sources: see text.
Note: The input and output indices used in these calculations are, with Scotland = 100:

Labour	340
Land	180
Capital	138
Output	230

The pre-famine difference in productivity was of course likely to have been greater because the Irish labour force had been reduced drastically by the famine and emigration. Yet there are reasons to think that the labour input to Irish agriculture is overstated before the famine, and to a lesser degree after the famine as well. These are important because the productivity calculations are quite sensitive to changes in the labour input. An accomplished statistician of Irish agriculture warned in 1846: 'In every comparison instituted between the productiveness of British and Irish agricultural labour, it has been assumed that the rural labourers of Ireland are agricultural labourers only. This is a mistake, similar in kind to that which would classify the colliers with the farm servants of England.' Irish labourers were 'the fuel providers for a nation' (a task which he estimated might occupy 240,000 men full-time) and 'the builders of all the mud-cabins, farm-houses, cow-houses, and stables in Ireland'.[20] Much of this work must have been done during lulls in the agricultural year, but it does suggest that by comparison to Scotland, where rural occupational specialisation was more pronounced and where agricultural labourers were often hired for long periods, the labour input to Irish agriculture is exaggerated by calculation in man-years rather than man-days.[21] Also, if we take seriously the claims for Scottish education, it might be argued that the agricultural labour force in efficiency terms would be relatively larger in Scotland. The overall labour intensity of Irish agriculture is also somewhat misleading because labour was often concentrated away from important producing areas. Rural population densities were lowest in the fertile east and south. Even within these areas concentrations of population and small holdings existed in or near the mountains and bogs which pock the Irish landscape.[22] Farmers did draw upon these pools of labour, particularly at harvest time. However, the lack of correlation between fertile land and labour suggests the possibility that though marginal returns to labour may have been equalised, average returns differed systematically across and within regions. Which is only to say that certain regions were more productive than others, which is true for Scotland as well as Ireland. Comparative research using broad regions of the two countries might reward the effort, though it would be complicated by the need to come up with regional technical coefficients and by inter-regional movements of labour and livestock.

II

Whatever Scotland's advantage in productivity was, it did not manifest itself in terms of higher returns from the land. Per acre output was higher in Ireland on all three measures of the land inputs and was likely to have been significantly higher before the famine. Crop yields were greater in Ireland on all three measures of the land input and were likely to have been even higher before the famine. Crop yields in Ireland generally exceeded those in Scotland. In the mid-1850s barley yields were on average higher than turnips.[23] Milk yields were probably higher in Ireland, especially if only the south of Ireland is considered.[24] The turnover rates of the beef herds and sheep flocks were similar, which suggests some Irish advantage because Scotland was relatively more involved in the trade in store, as opposed to fat, animals. Stocking densities were also higher in Ireland, a result which persists when Lowland Scotland is compared to the provinces of Leinster and Munster.[25] Ireland's superiority in these respects probably existed during the immediate pre-famine period as well. Bourke's careful study of crop yields suggests that pre-famine cereal yields had already reached post-famine levels and that potato yields were, of course, much higher.[26]

Labour intensity is one explanation for these high returns, but recent work by Chorley suggests another.[27] First, it is necessary to recognise that Irish yields, like English and Scottish, were high by European standards. Mid-century Irish yields were 10–40 per cent higher than the figures Chorley gives for north-western Europe around 1880, and two to three times greater than his estimates of European yields c.1800. Chorley argues quite persuasively that the increase in northern European yields, and by implication the earlier increase in British yields, was due primarily to improved nitrogen supplies resulting from the generalisation of leguminous crops. Labour does enter the story, for the cultivation of root crops cleaned and prepared the soil, and liming and marling prevented valuable nutrients from being leached away. However, the major change was apparently managerial.

Chorley's explanation is easily believable of Scotland, but did Ireland undergo an early leguminous revolution? It will be argued here that Irish agriculture in the eighteenth and early nineteenth centuries developed under conditions which obviated the need for one and which, if anything, presented dangers of regression. The key elements in producing high Irish yields were, on an interpretation which follows Chorley, the relatively large share of the land kept under grass, the use of rotations which frequently broke up these pastures, and the fact that clover grew naturally and abundantly in much of Ireland. The pastoral orientation of Irish agriculture was evident, even on the eve of the famine. Bourke's estimates of land use c.1845 show that more than half the land (excluding waste) was under grass.[28] Some of this grassland was rough grazing which had never been cultivated, but most of it would have been broken up at one time or another under the system, or rather lack of system, of agriculture repeatedly condemned by contemporaries. A representative judgement, made by a Scottish land agent, was that 'the farmers in the south of Ireland have very little skill in agriculture; after a field or garden is put in fair condition they continue cropping it until it will not yield the seed again, and then they let it go to grass naturally'.[29] The speed with which Irish pastures regenerated themselves was also remarked by contemporaries, but what is crucial for this argument is the sort of plant which reappeared. Arthur Young was astonished by 'the quantity of spontaneous white clover (*trifolium repens*) in almost all the fields, which much exceeds any thing we know in England'.[30] Thompson, in his *Statistical Survey of Meath*, observed that 'the nice, dry, warm, gravelly soils of the county throw up a luxuriant coat of white clover, even though there may not have been any seed sown, and grounds rather inclined to clay, when drained and manured with limestone ground, often show a disposition to it also'.[31] Periodic grass-clover leys would have fortified the nitrogen content of Irish soil and permitted the perpetuation of a ruinous system of cropping which never seemed to lead to ruin.

This system of agriculture, the heritage of a sparsely populated pastoral economy and a benign environment, could have been put under pressure by the demographic expansion of the late eighteenth and early nineteenth centuries. Had tillage encroached too far upon pasture, yields might have suffered. One reason that it did not was simply the value of Irish grass in the production of butter and meat for the growing British market. That cereal cultivation grew as it did was probably due as much to the growth of British demand during the wars and under the Corn Laws as it was to the growth of Irish demand.[32] Irishmen would gladly have eaten more bread, if they could have afforded it, and would have grown more wheat and oats, if they had had control of the land to do so. However, their demand was largely ineffective. Labourers' incomes remained low or fell under the pressure of numbers. Despite the great numbers of small holdings, most of the land, especially the good land in the south of Ireland, remained in the hands of commercial farmers.

Farms of several hundred acres, like those found in eastern Scotland, were rare in Ireland. More common were farms of thirty to two hundred acres, which in 1854 occupied at least 53 per cent of the non-waste land, as compared to at most 31 per cent for farms with less than thirty acres. These figures mask marked regional differences. The Ireland of the small farm was the north, where more than half the land was taken up by farms of less than thirty acres. South of a line between Westport and Drogheda such farms rarely controlled more than 15–20 per cent of the profitable acreage.[33] These conclusions hold with almost equal force for the immediate pre-famine period. Estimates using data in the Devon Commission Report of 1845 indicate that generally in the south of Ireland more than half the land was held on farms of more than fifty acres.[34] Moreover, as a few detailed studies have shown, small farms in the south tended to be in less fertile areas and had often been reclaimed from waste by their occupants.[35] Farms of thirty acres or so — 'snug farms', as one writer called them — were realistic by early nineteenth-century standards, particularly in pastoral regions. Farms in south-western Scotland were probably somewhat larger, but not significantly so.[36]

Irish farmers with twenty to thirty acres or more could and did keep much of their land under grass, thus helping to maintain its fertility. Subdivision was not allowed to proceed too far on the good lands. Farmers also resisted, more or less successfully, the pressure from labourers to keep more land in tillage. Tenures for a single potato crop, called con-acre, were an important element in the rural economy, providing the farmer with the labour necessary to prepare pasture land for cereal crops and the labourer with the means of subsistence.[37] Attempts to reduce the supply of potato ground often caused agrarian unrest, but it is not known to what extent unrest or the threat of unrest prevented farmers from reacting to market pressures by altering their product mix. In the face of a rapidly increasing population, landlords and farmers did generally maintain control of the fertile lowlands, by force and by letting live in the uplands.[38]

The interpretation of Irish agriculture along these lines suggests that it was rich, not because of abundant labour, but in spite of it. Since the labour was available and cheap, farmers used it in spade husbandry and in liming and manuring. These practices were important in maintaining returns which were already high because of Ireland's rich, nitrogen-producing grasslands. The intense exertions of labourers trying to eke out subsistence on relatively marginal lands only confuse the picture. The implication of this interpretation for the Scottish comparison is that industrious improvers were required if Scotland, with its less favourable environment, was to be brought up to Irish standards.

III

Were contemporary observers, who almost universally condemned Irish agriculture as backward and in want of improvement, simply wrong? Irish agriculture had a very bad press in this period and Scottish agriculture a very good one. However, it is important to recognise that the printed page was one of Scottish agriculture's most important products. Scotland's renown in agriculture's pre-scientific era owed much to its abundant supply of confident and energetic publicists, led by the prolific Sir John Sinclair.[39] By contrast, the contemporaries to whom we owe much of our knowledge of Irish agriculture were more or less sympathetic English and Scots visitors, such as Young, Wakefield, the English assistant Poor Law Commissioners, and the anonymous 'D' of the *Quarterly Journal of Agriculture*.[40] Or they were men of the Protestant Ascendancy in Ireland, a class which was generally eager to follow British models. For example, the Rev. H. Townsend, an astute agricultural observer from Cork, observed that 'Between Ireland and Scotland there appears to me to be more congeniality than between the former and England, as well in the general nature of the soil as in the manners and habits of the people . . . In the excellent husbandry of East Lothian, I saw nothing which might not be easily and safely brought within the compass of Hibernian management . . .'.[41] Here we shall make a *tour d'horizon* of Scottish improvement and try to assess whether it was indeed relevant to Ireland.

One important element of Scottish improvement was the betterment of soil quality, often associated with the reclamation of waste land. Bringing new land into use figures prominently in Sir John Sinclair's account of the achievements of 'those distinguished patriots to whom the agricultural improvement of Scotland is principally to be attributed'.[42] The application of marl and lime played a key role in reclamation and in general improvement of soil quality.[43] These nutrients, particularly lime, were also used widely and intensively in Ireland. From the time of Arthur Young there are reports from different parts of the country of lime and sea sand being carted ten to twenty miles in cases where local deposits were unavailable.[44] It has even been suggested that overliming may have impaired production in the early nineteenth century.[45] Reclamation also proceeded rapidly in the late eighteenth and early nineteenth centuries before levelling off in the 1830s and 1840s, when it may have reached its practical limits.[46] By contrast with Scotland, the principal agents of reclamation were small holders, who would hardly have been called distinguished patriots. Irish landlords were exhorted to drain and reclaim on a grand scale, but it is doubtful that their failure to do so (or their occasional costly failures in trying) set back the expansion of the profitable land area.

Enclosure was another essential ingredient of Scottish improvement. Here it is useful to distinguish three aspects of enclosure: (1) the definition of property rights; (2) the fencing of unenclosed land; and (3) the rationalisation and consolidation of fields and farms. The elimination of commons and run-riggs had no parallel in Ireland because property rights had been effectively settled as a result of the turmoil of the seventeenth century. Recent research on hedged enclosures suggests that they were spreading rapidly from the better lands into the uplands in the late eighteenth and early nineteenth centuries.[47] Irish fences and hedges were frequently criticised for being poorly built and kept, but it is possible that high population density kept down the damage threatened by inadequate enclosures. A related, and highly visible, element of Scottish improvement was the planting of trees as windbreaks. These offered protection to cereal crops and to animals which may have been less necessary in Ireland's milder climate. As for the rationalisation and consolidation of farms, we have already observed that in the south of Ireland medium-sized farms prevailed in terms of area. However, there were still large numbers of small farmers and cottiers who did prove difficult to displace. As one observer put it: 'Were there not serious impediments to a consolidation of farms on a more extended scale, arising from the unpopularity of such a measure, and the certainty in some counties of agrarian outrages to a frightful extent, the class of small holders would disappear . . .'[48] This small farm sector may have restrained improvement.

The problem of feeding livestock, especially over the winter, gave rise to the cultivation of sown grasses and turnips in Scotland. In Ireland winter feeding was much less of a problem. In Clare, for example, 'the graziers say, that the perpetual verdure of their land, especially on calcareous soils, precludes the necessity of providing either hay or any cultivated green food'.[49] Over much of Ireland the period of little or no grass growth lasts only three and a half months on average.[50] Even so, clover and other grasses were being sown in the eastern Lowlands in the late eighteenth century, and their use spread during the early nineteenth century.[51]

Turnips were rarely cultivated in pre-famine Ireland. Potatoes were preferred because they could be used as human or animal food, and because relative yields of potatoes were higher in Ireland than in Scotland, if post-famine statistics give any indication of pre-blight conditions. Potatoes took the place of turnips as a cleansing root crop and as animal fodder. Bourke estimates that about 40 per cent of net potato output was fed to livestock, mostly to pigs but also to cattle during the winter months.[52] Some visitors recognised that potatoes played much the same role in Irish agriculture as turnips did in Scottish, but most were obsessed with the need for turnip cultivation.

Improvements in livestock by breeding or better feeding were particularly important for pastoral economies like Scotland and Ireland. The value of these improvements is difficult to assess because the performance of different breeds depended on specific conditions of soil, climate, and feeding and because changes often involved trade-offs between characteristics, for example between mutton and wool or beef and milk. Scottish improvers were active breeders, with a few distinctive and popular breeds to their credit. Animals in Ireland usually went under the designation 'Irish'; however, from the late eighteenth century, and particularly in the early nineteenth century, English and Scottish breeds were introduced and generally crossbred with native Irish animals. Wholesale adoption of British breeds of cattle seems to have been resisted, probably because most of these animals had been bred for meat. Beef production in Ireland was principally a byproduct of dairying. Irish cows were recognised as good milkers, though there were efforts to improve them by crosses with Ayrshire and Devon cattle. There is little evidence on the trend in milk yields, but weights of cows when fattened seem to have been drifting upward from as early as the 1790s.[53] The principal stimulus for the improvement of the meat-producing characteristics of Irish cattle (and sheep) seems to have been, as in parts of Scotland, better access to markets. 'The increase of livestock in Ireland in numbers, weight and quality, since steam navigation opened the English markets, is already unprecedented in the annals of any other nation.' Thus did a writer in the *Quarterly Journal of Agriculture* try to impress upon Scottish farmers the value of emulating Ireland's rapid adoption of the steamship for transporting fat animals.[54]

We have considered, rather summarily, some tenets of the Scottish improving faith as they bore on Irish agricultural conditions and practice. Some, such as the definition of property rights and the use of turnips and sown grasses for winter feeding, were of less relevance to Ireland. With respect to others, it has been suggested that Irish farmers were humble believers. They zealously limed and reclaimed, and they adopted and adapted breeds of livestock suitable to Irish conditions. There were other elements of the faith, notably the use of improved implements and machinery, which were probably inappropriate to Irish labour supply conditions. All in all, Irish agriculturalists were eclectics. They resisted repeated entreaties to conform and so earned the condemnation of the true believers. This is not to say that all was well with Irish agriculture (the evident weediness of pastures and fields is perplexing, given the lavish applications of labour elsewhere). Nor is it to say that Irish agriculture might not have done better by more strenuous adherence to certain elements of the creed. It is merely to suggest that contemporary judgements on Irish agriculture may have been unduly harsh and may mislead the scholar into thinking of it as stagnant and unproductive.

IV

A more optimistic view of Irish agricultural performance suggests that we reconsider the role of the agricultural sectors in Scottish and Irish economic development. Agriculture is supposed to supply food and raw materials, labour, and capital to the non-agricultural sectors of an economy in transition. Irish agriculture was clearly capable of producing a substantial surplus. On the eve of the famine it was supporting an urban population which was relatively large by European standards and still exporting roughly a quarter of its output to Britain.[55] Scotland had a considerably larger urban population, but had already become a net importer of cereals and probably of dairy products.[56] The Scots were better fed than the Irish by contemporary standards (though perhaps not so clearly on modern nutritional criteria).[57] However, it should be recognised that Irish food exports could have supported, at British consumption levels, another $1-1\frac{1}{4}$ million people in Ireland.[58] An augmentation of this magnitude would have pushed the share of the urban population in Ireland up toward that in Scotland.

Instead Irish agricultural exports sustained workers and their families in Britain, many of whom were of Irish origin. The Irish agricultural sector released large amounts of labour to industry in Britain and America, and it is arguable that limitations on the potential migrant's capital and on employment opportunities elsewhere, rather than any attachment to the soil in Ireland, prevented even more extensive emigration before the famine.[59] As Cobden observed in the 1830s: 'great as this evil has hitherto been, it is only a subject of astonishment to us that the immigration of the Irish people into this portion of the empire has not been more extensive'.[60] The cost of getting to Britain was relatively low, but once there, the Irishmen often faced the hostility of British workers and poor law authorities, particularly in times of industrial depression. The problems of getting established in Britain may have discouraged migration by the class of Irishman who could not finance a move to North America. This class of marginal workers, who inhabited the mountains and bogs and begged along the roads and in the towns, was a product of Ireland's extraordinarily high rate of population growth. In comparing Scotland and Ireland, it should be kept firmly in mind that during the late eighteenth and early nineteenth centuries the Irish population may have been growing nearly twice as fast as the Scottish.[61] Ireland thus faced much larger problems of labour transfer than did Scotland.

Finally, with respect to the contribution of the agricultural sector to non-agricultural capital formation, Irish agriculture generated a large rent to landowners and reasonable returns to those who occupied sufficient amounts of land. Capital was readily forthcoming for the development of agricultural processing industries, such as corn milling and bacon curing, and for the introduction of steam navigation in the Irish Sea. In the absence of detailed work on capital formation, we can best agree with Cullen's conclusions that 'Ireland did not seriously suffer from a shortage of capital', that 'the real problem was one of finding remunerative investment outlets', and that, in the early nineteenth century, 'lacking outlets in Ireland, Irish capital was beginning to flow to England'.[62]

The Irish agricultural sector was thus a ready source of food, labour and capital. It seems difficult to sustain the belief that the absence of an agricultural transformation was crucial to understanding Ireland's poor industrial performance relative to Scotland's. It might be better to ask what implications commercial and industrial prosperity, whatever its sources may have been, had for agricultural development in these two countries. One benefit to Scottish farmers was their proximity to one of the growing markets for food. As prices in the north of England and Scotland converged with those in London, holders of land in these areas benefited from the higher prices, from lower transportation costs, and from opportunities for specialisation in products, such as fat cattle and sheep, which lost value in transit.[63] Irish agriculturists also benefited from this northward movement, especially with the introduction of steam navigation, but their gains from indigenous industrial development would have been even greater.

Competition from industry for labour also affected nearby agriculture. As Kane observed on the eve of the famine:

> Large farm cultivation is possible only in countries possessing thin and scattered population, or else in countries where the existence of extensive manufacturing employment removes the inhabitants of the agricultural districts to other places. Thus certain Scotch counties had actually a smaller population in 1841 than in 1831, owing to the migration of labourers to the manufacturing districts. In such counties the tendency must be to increase the size of farms, and to introduce, as far as possible, mechanical substitutes for labour . . . In Ireland, however, the circumstances are widely different, a large population is totally dependent on the land for its subsistence.[64]

A tighter labour market also encouraged Scottish farmers to use labour more efficiently across the agricultural year. The availability of constant employment for those who stayed in agriculture and of opportunities for those who left are the factors to which Devine has attributed the remarkable stability of the Scottish countryside in the early nineteenth century.[65] His investigation was prompted by the contrast with unrest in southern England, but it is even more striking with respect to Ireland, where irregular employment was the root of Irish land hunger and hence of much agrarian unrest.

There is no denying that there were enormous social and economic problems in the Irish economy of the early nineteenth century. What we have tried to argue is that their sources did not originate in a failure to modernise agriculture along Scottish lines. Indeed, given that the failure of industry to develop was not for lack of a productive agricultural sector, it would have been socially disastrous for Irish agriculture to adhere to the creed of Scottish improvement. Much research remains to be done on Irish and Scottish agriculture in the early nineteenth century;

however, we do not believe that this research will answer the question of why Scotland industrialised and Ireland did not.

Appendix

Since these estimates are not intended to be definitive, we shall not document and defend all of the technical coefficients or methods of estimation. Here we shall show the calculations for those who are interested.

I. CROPS

	Gross Output	Net Output Share	Price (s.)	Value of Net Output (£000s)
Ireland				
Wheat	1,604,570 qtrs	0.90	61.0	4,405
Oats	9,466,189 qtrs	0.65	23.5	7,320
Barley	901,317 qtrs	0.80	35.0	1,262
Potatoes	4,717,723 tons	0.50	30.0	3,538
Flax	18,898 tons	0.90	950.0	808
Total				17,243
Scotland				
Wheat	770,375 qtrs	0.90	61.0	2,115
Oats	3,949,937 qtrs	0.65	23.5	3,017
Barley	759,974 qtrs	0.80	35.0	1,064
Potatoes	525,509	0.90	30.0	709
Flax	550 tons*	0.90	950.0	24
Total				6,929

*The flax output for Scotland is 2,920 acres at the Irish yield.

II. ANIMAL PRODUCTS

A. *Dairy*

	Milk Cows	Butter Yield	Price	Value
Ireland	1,582,058	1 cwt	120 s.	9,492
Scotland	300,778	1 cwt	120 s.	1,805

B. *Beef*

		Milk	Cows	Other	Cattle	Meat Output (1,000 cwt)	Price	Value
	Cattle > 2 yrs	Share Sold	Weight	Share Sold	Weight			
Ireland	778,557	0.167	400 lbs	0.427	550 lbs	2,574	55 s.	7,079
Scotland	285,944	0.167	400 lbs	0.479	600 lbs	913	55 s.	2,510

Other cattle > 2 yrs was derived for Scotland by subtracting 0.94 times the number of calves recorded.

C. *Sheep*

	Total − Lambs	Share Sold	Weight	Meat Output (1,000 cwt)	Price	Value
Ireland	2,439,955	0.5	70 lbs	762	55 s.	2,097
Scotland	3,840,421	0.5	70 lbs	1,200	55 s.	3,300

D. *Wool*

	Fleece Weight	Output (1,000 lbs)	Price (s.)	Value
Ireland	4 lbs	9,760	1/3	610
Scotland	4 lbs	15,362	1/3	960

E. *Pork*

	Pigs	Share Sold	Yield	Meat Output (1,000 cwt)	Price	Value
Ireland	1,117,105	1.0	1.25 cwt	1,396	55 s.	3,840
Scotland	135,876	1.0	1.25 cwt	170	55 s.	467

REFERENCES

1. L. M. Cullen and T. C. Smout, 'Economic Growth in Ireland and Scotland', in L. M. Cullen and T. C. Smout, eds., *Comparative Aspects of Scottish and Irish Economic and Social History, 1600–1900* (Edinburgh, 1977), p. 10.

2. P. K. O'Brien, 'Agriculture and the Industrial Revolution', *Econ. Hist. Rev.*, 2nd ser., 30 (1977), pp. 166–181.

3. On the Irish side, the work of R. Crotty and P. M. A. Bourke (neither of whom is an economic historian by training) stands out. On the Scottish side, eighteenth-century agriculture has been well served, but the literature on the early nineteenth century is sparse. An important exception is M. Gray, 'Scottish Emigration: The Social Impact of Agrarian Change in the Rural Lowlands, 1775–1875', *Perspectives in American History*, 7 (1973), pp. 95–714.

4. Cullen and Smout, *Comparative Aspects*, p. 16.

5. M. G. Mulhall, *Dictionary of Statistics* (London, 1892), p. 16.

6. C. Ó Gráda, 'On Some Aspects of Productivity Change in Irish Agriculture, 1845–1926', paper presented at the Seventh International Economic History Conference, Edinburgh, 1978, p. 2.

7. The Scottish statistics come from *Agricultural Statistics (Scotland)*, 1855 (*P.P.* 1856, LIX); 1856 (*P.P.* 1857, XV); 1857 (*P.P.* 1857–8, LVI). On the reliability of these statistics, see J. T. Coppock, 'The Statistical Assessment of British Agriculture', *Agricultural Hist. Rev.*, 4 (1956), 14. The Irish statistics are in the *Returns of Agricultural Produce in Ireland,* 1855 (*P.P.* 1857, XV); 1856 (*P.P.* 1857–58, LVI); 1857 (*P.P.* 1859 (1), XXVI). On the reliability of these returns, see testimony in the *Report from the Select Committee . . . [on] Agricultural Statistics* (*P.P.* 1854–5, VIII), pp. 96–101.

8. W. Youatt, *Cattle* (London, 1834), *Sheep* (London, 1837), *The Complete Grazier* (London, 1846), *The Pig* (London, 1847); R. Herbert, 'Statistics of Livestock and Dead Meat for Consumption in the Metropolis', *Journal of the Royal Agricultural Society of England*, 20 (1859), pp. 473–81; D. Low, *Breeds of Domestic Animals* (London, 1842).

9. Many of the dangers are discussed in the debate over the relative efficiency of southern agriculture in the antebellum United States (R. W. Fogel and S. Engerman, 'Explaining the Relative Efficiency of Slave Agriculture in the Antebellum South', *American Economic Review*, 67 (1977), pp. 275–96; comments by P. A. David and P. Temin, R. Schaefer and M. Schmitz, and G. Wright, *Amer. Econ. Rev.*, 69 (1979), pp. 208–26; and a rejoinder by Fogel and Engerman, *Amer. Econ. Rev.*, 70 (1980), pp. 272–90.

10. These calculations skirt the problem of the way in which the census treats women's work and occupations. We have excluded from the Scottish figures those women classed as 'farmers' wives' and 'farmers' daughters', etc.' because the Irish statistics do not include these categories. The general assumption that we are making is that women's participation in the agricultural labour force was not markedly different in the two countries.

11. C. Ó Gráda, 'Seasonal Migration and Post-Famine Adjustment in the West of Ireland', *Studia Hibernia*, 13 (1973), pp. 49–56; T. M. Devine, 'Temporary Migration and the Scottish Highlands in the Nineteenth Century', *Econ. Hist. Rev.*, 2nd ser., 32 (1979), pp. 344–59.

12. J. Stamp, *British Incomes and Property* (London, 1928), p. 49.

13. The total acreages under crops (excluding grass and meadow) in the mid-1850s were 4.44m acres in Ireland and 2.30m acres in Scotland. Non-waste land accounted for 15.28m acres and 11.42m acres, respectively.

14. C. H. Feinstein, 'Capital Formation in Great Britain', in P. Mathias and M. M. Postan, eds., *Cambridge Economic History of Europe* (Cambridge, 1978), VII, Pt. I, pp. 48–50, 69–71.

15. C. Ó Gráda, 'The Investment Behaviour of Irish Landlords, 1850–75', *Agricultural History Review*, 23 (1975), p. 151.

16. The shares of fixed and working capital were .64 and .36, respectively (Feinstein, 'Capital Formation'). The assumption is that these shares characterised Scotland as an element in Great Britain. Then the calculation is:

$$\frac{I_F + I_W}{S_F + S_W} = \frac{I_F}{S_F}\frac{S_F}{S_F + S_W} + \frac{I_W}{S_W}\frac{S_W}{S_F + S_W}$$
$$= 100(.64) + 205(.36)$$
$$= 138.$$

17. A supplementary return to the 1854 Scottish agricultural statistics suggests that the omissions accounted for less than 10 per cent of the arable, somewhat more than 10 per cent of cattle and swine, and a trivial share of the sheep (*Returns Relating to Small Holdings* (*P.P.* 1854-5, XLVII), p. 2).

18. C. Ó Gráda, 'Agricultural Decline, 1860–1914', in R. Floud and D. McCloskey, eds., *The Economic History of Britain since 1700* (Cambridge, 1981), II, p. 179.

19. Estimates for agricultural productivity growth in the United Kingdom in the nineteenth century fall on both sides of this figure, with British rates at or below it and Irish rates above it (*ibid.*, 178; G. Hueckel, 'Agriculture during Industrialisation', in Floud and McCloskey, *Economic History of Britain*, I, p. 192; Ó Gráda, unpublished work on Ireland).

20. 'Statistics of Irish Agriculture', *Dublin Evening Herald*, 24 Nov. 1846.

21. On Scottish agricultural labour, see T. M. Devine, 'Social Stability and Agrarian Change in the Eastern Lowlands of Scotland, 1810-1840', *Social History*, 3 (1978), pp. 334-8; on Irish occupational specialisation, there is an interesting unpublished paper by E. L. Almquist, 'Labour Specialization and the Irish Economy in 1841: An Aggregate Occupational Analysis' (1980).

22. J. H. Andrews, 'Changes in the Rural Landscape of Late Eighteenth- and Early Nineteenth-Century Ireland: An Example from County Waterford', paper presented to the Institute of British Geographers, Belfast, 1970; W. J. Smyth, 'Land Values, Landownership and Population Patterns in Co. Tipperary for 1641/60 and 1841/50: Some Comparisons', and J. H. Andrews, 'Limits of Agricultural Settlement in Pre-Famine Ireland', in L. M. Cullen and F. Furet, eds., *Ireland and France 17th-20th Centuries: Towards a Comparative Study of Rural History* (Paris, 1980), pp. 47-55.

23. These comparisons are based on the yields implied by the statistics of acreage and production for Scotland and Ireland (see n. 7 above).

24. In the 1830s average butter yields were given as 1–1¼ cwt in the south of Ireland and somewhat less than a hundredweight in the north (see the evidence in the *First Report of Inquiry into the Condition of the Poorer Classes in Ireland* (*P.P.* 1836, XXXIII), Appendix F). The numbers of milk cows in the two regions suggest a national average of one hundredweight of butter, which would have required 320–336 gallons of milk. Figures for Scotland are less easy to come by. Annual cheese output per cow was given for several parishes in the *New Statistical Account* of Ayrshire at about 3 cwt, which implies a milk yield of 340–400 gallons per annum (*N.S.A.*, V, pp. 226, 300, 590, 767). Yields in Ayrshire, a prime dairying area, were likely to have been above average. For comparison, D. Taylor's best estimate for the average milk yield in England in the 1860s and 1870s is 350 gallons ('The English Dairying Industry, 1860-1930', *Econ. Hist. Rev.*, 2nd ser., 29 (1976), p. 589).

25. This statement is based upon calculations of livestock units per acre of non-waste land. The animal numbers from the agricultural statistics of the mid-1850s were combined, using both modern sets of weights and weights derived from contemporary measures of stocking capacity, such as collops and soums. The result is relatively insensitive to the set of weights employed.

26. P. M. A. Bourke, 'The Average Yields of Food Crops on the Eve of the Great Famine', *Irish Department of Agriculture and Fisheries Journal*, 66 (1969), pp. 3–16.

27. G. P. H. Chorley, 'The Agricultural Revolution in Northern Europe, 1750–1880: Nitrogen, Legumes, and Crop Productivity', *Econ. Hist. Rev.*, 34 (1981), pp. 71–93.

28. P. M. A. Bourke, 'The Potato, Blight, Weather, and the Irish Famine', (Ph.D. thesis, National University of Ireland, 1965), Appendix 4.

29. *Report of the Select Committee on Agriculture (P.P.* 1833, V), Minutes of Evidence, Q. 300.

30. A. Young, *A Tour in Ireland 1776–1779*, A. W. Hutton, ed. (London, 1892), II, 49–50. There is also an interesting unpublished paper by P. M. A. Bourke, 'Grass and the Irish Climate', which was given at the National Conference on Grass Conservation, Dublin, 1963.

31. R. Thompson, *Statistical Survey of the County of Meath* (Dublin, 1802), p. 210.

32. For example, wheat and flour exports, which on the eve of the famine were roughly 40 per cent of net output, had grown at the rate of more than 4 per cent per annum during the previous half-century. Dublin flour sales, by contrast, had grown by about 1 per cent per annum.

33. *Returns of Agricultural Produce in Ireland,* 1854 (*P.P.* 1856, LIII), p. viii. County estimates have been made by multiplying the number of holdings in each class by the average size of holding in the class, beginning with the smallest holdings. Since the county holding size distributions include waste land, an upper bound estimate for the share of non-waste land on farms of *less* than a given acreage results from using county non-waste acreage as the divisor.

34. *Report . . . [on] the Occupation of the Land in Ireland* (*P.P.* 1845, XXII), Appendix No. 94. Estimates were made along the lines described in the preceding note, but the classification of holdings does not permit an estimate of the share of the land on farms of more than thirty acres.

35. Andrews, 'Limits of Agricultural Settlement . . .'

36. In Ayrshire average farm size was given variously as 60, 80 and 90 acres in the *New Statistical Account* (V, 767, 758–9, 827).

37. Interestingly, a good description of con-acre, though not under that name, appears in the statistical account of the parish of Longforgan on the border between Perth and Angus: 'the practice [cultivation of potatoes] is promoted by the master farmers who occupy the rich brae land in the neighbourhood, letting out small portions of it which they mean to be wheat, at perhaps the rate of four guineas or more per acre. The farmer ploughs and prepares the land, and each man plants or dibbles his measured portion with potatoes . . . during the whole progress of the plants coming forward, they make it their business to clean the ground perfectly by hand-hoeing, which prepares it for the succeeding crop' (J. Sinclair, ed., *The Statistical Account of Scotland, 1791–1799* new ed. (Wakefield, 1976), XI, 386–7). For descriptions of this practice in Ireland, see J. F. Burgoyne, *Ireland in 1831* (London, 1831), p. 14, and the evidence in the Irish Poor Law Report.

38. J. J. Lee, 'The Ribbonmen', in T. D. Williams, ed., *Secret Societies In Ireland* (Dublin, 1973), pp. 26–35; Andrews, 'Changes in the Rural Landscape'.

39. J. E. Handley, *The Agricultural Revolution in Scotland* (Glasgow, 1963), ch. 4.

40. The last published a series of 13 articles on the agriculture of various Irish counties from 1832 to 1845. A general survey appeared in 1837 ('On Ireland', *Quarterly Journal of Agriculture*, 8 (1837–8), pp. 127–53).

41. H. Townsend, 'Remarks on the Agriculture of Ireland', *Quarterly Journal of Agriculture*, 1 (1828–9), pp. 71–2.

42. J. Sinclair, *Analysis of the Statistical Account of Scotland* (Edinburgh, 1825), I, 237–43.

43. R. A. Dodgshon, 'Land Improvement in Scottish Farming: Marl and Lime in Roxburghshire and Berwickshire in the Eighteenth Century', *Agricultural Hist. Rev.*, 26 (1978), pp. 1–14.

44. A. Young, *Tour in Ireland*, II, 93–4.

45. T. Walsh, P. F. Ryan and J. Kilroy, 'A Half Century of Fertiliser and Lime Use in Ireland', *Journal of the Statistical and Social Inquiry Society of Ireland*, 19, pt. 5 (1956–57), p. 106.

46. K. H. Connell, 'The Colonization of Waste Land in Ireland, 1780–1845', *Econ. Hist. Rev.*, 2nd ser., 3 (1951), pp. 44–71; P. M. A. Bourke, 'The Agricultural Statistics of the 1841 Census of Ireland: A Critical Review', *Econ. Hist. Rev.*, 2nd ser., 18 (1965), pp. 382–91; Andrews, 'Limits of Agricultural Settlement . . .'

47. P. Robinson, 'The Spread of Hedged Enclosure in Ulster', *Ulster Folklife*, 23 (1977), 57–69.

48. D., 'On Ireland', p. 130.

49. H. Dutton, *Statistical Survey of the County of Clare* (Dublin, 1808), p. 73.

50. P. M. A. Bourke, 'Grass and the Irish Climate', p. 2.

51. Thompson, *Statistical Survey*, 155; D., 'On Ireland', p. 139.

52. P. M. A. Bourke, 'The Use of the Potato Crop in Pre-Famine Ireland', *Journal of the Statistical and Social Inquiry Society of Ireland*, 21, pt. 6 (1967–68), pp. 72–96.

53. This statement is based upon analysis of the ranges of cow weights for which prices were quoted in Cork newspapers.

54. Anon., 'On the Preparation of Live-Stock and Meat in Reference to their Exportation by Steam-Vessels', *Quarterly Journal of Agriculture*, 8 (1837–8), p. 244. On Scotland, see I. Carter, *Farmlife in Northeast Scotland, 1840–1914* (Edinburgh, 1979), pp. 35–6.

55. My unpublished estimates of Irish agricultural trade show that the value of net exports in the early 1840s was around £10m. Ó Gráda has estimated agricultural output at £39.3m (see note 6 above).

56. Scotland's need for grain imports can be deduced from figures for trade among England, Scotland, and Ireland for the years 1836–8, *Accounts of Grain, Malt and Flour . . .* (*P.P.* 1840, XLIII), p. 81.

57. On the nutritional merits of the Irish diet, see E. M. Crawford, 'A Nutritional Analysis of Diets in Ireland's Workhouses', unpublished paper, 1978.

58. This estimate is based on the share of Irish imports in total consumption of agricultural products in Great Britain, the sum of Irish and foreign imports and Dean and Cole's estimate of agricultural output in 1841.

59. This argument is elaborated in my unpublished paper on poor relief in Britain and Ireland.

60. R. Cobden, *England, Ireland and America* (1835), p. 72.

61. From 1755 to 1821 Scotland's population grew at 0.77 per cent per annum. Daultrey, Dickson, and Ó Gráda, 'Eighteenth-Century Irish Population: Old Sources and New Speculations', *Journal of Economic History*, 41 (1981), pp. 601–28 suggest that the Irish population may have grown at a rate of 1.5 per cent per annum or more over a similar period.

62. L. M. Cullen, *An Economic History of Ireland since 1660* (London, 1972), p. 129.

63. On price movements, see T. Gourvish, 'A Note on Bread Prices in London and Glasgow, 1788–1815', *Journal of Economic History*, 30 (1970), 854–60.

64. R. Kane, *The Industrial Resources of Ireland* (Dublin, 1845), pp. 307–8.

65. Devine, 'Social Stability . . .'

7
*Uncertainty and Prefamine Irish Agriculture**

Joel Mokyr

1. Introduction

THE Irish economy on the eve of the Famine was one of the most agrarian in Europe. The 1841 Census reported that 66.1 per cent in Irish families were 'chiefly employed' in agriculture and that 74.2 per cent of the employed males were classified as 'ministering to food'. The physical and social forces underlying the agrarian economy will thus by necessity form the backbone of any analysis of prefamine poverty and backwardness in Ireland.

In the past decade, economists and economic historians have tended to emphasize increasingly the role of risk and uncertainty in agriculture.[1] It is felt that an appreciation of the role of uncertainty is quite essential to an understanding of the institutional structure and the microeconomic behaviour characteristic of many agrarian societies, especially very poor ones in which minor fluctuations in output can lead to widespread starvation. Uncertainty has been said to have determined the composition of output in some economies, and has been held responsible for the persistence of scattered open fields and the ubiquity of sharecropping arrangements. What follows is a few notes and ideas which attempt to apply some of the work in the economics of uncertainty to the Irish economy. These notes are unashamedly tentative, but it is to be hoped that they will induce future historians of Irish agriculture to pay more attention to risk and uncertainty.

It is useful to distinguish between two kinds of uncertainty. One kind is the traditional notion of uncertainty: factors beyond the farmer's control which cause output to fluctuate. Weather, pests, and market conditions belong to this category. A second kind of uncertainty is associated with the information flowing between the participants in the production process. For instance, the landlord may try to stipulate that the tenant weed, fertilize, and drain the soil regularly. In practice, however, it is difficult (i.e., costly) for him to check whether the tenant actually does so. This problem is sometimes referred to by economists as the 'principal-agent' problem, and has been applied in a wide variety of contexts.[2] As we shall see, the solutions to the two problems are mutually dependent, which complicates real-

*The comments and suggestions of Louis Cain, Stefano Fenoaltea, Elizabeth Hoffman, Cormac Ó Gráda, and Evelyne Seebauer are gratefuly acknowledged.

world situations and thus reduces our ability to analyze them with simple tools. In what follows, the terms risk and uncertainty will be used interchangeably.

2. *Uncertainty and Economic Arrangements in Prefamine Ireland*

Economic agents typically dislike risk-taking. While this view is more often asserted than demonstrated, it is an assumption which we will make throughout this paper. Suppose that we are dealing with an agricultural economy in which there are two economic agents, landlords and tenants. The two agents each contribute an amount of productive resources (land or labour) and the product is distributed between them. The contractual arrangement between them determines not only the distribution of output but also the distribution of risk. To illustrate this point, consider three pure types of agricultural organization. First, there is pure demesne (wage labour) farming in which the landlord absorbs all the risk and the labour is paid a predetermined wage which is independent of the success of the harvest. Second, there is the case of fixed rent tenancy, in which the landlord receives a predetermined payment, so that the tenant appears to absorb all the risk. Third, there is sharecropping, in which landlord and tenant share the risk in some contracted proportion.

Prefamine Ireland was, on the surface at least, a classic example of 'pure tenancy'. Sharecropping seems to have been completely absent. Demesne farming, in which the landlord (or a quasi landlord such as a middleman who sublet the land to a lower 'layer' of tenants) actively ran the operation in the manner of central European *Gutsherrschaft*, can be found, but clearly it was the exception rather than the rule. Tenants, it seems, bore most of the risk in the prefamine economy, but in actuality the situation was a bit more complex than that. The calculus of risk-bearing is confounded by the possibility of defaults or arrears. For instance, if the tenant paid his fixed rent as long as conditions were favourable but fell in arrears when harvests failed or prices declined, the landlord was left in a situation in which an unusually good season was beneficial to the tenant but a disastrous one was bad for both.[3] Moreover, the landlord enjoyed a risk-free income only if the rental contract was fixed in real rather than in money terms. Since this was never the case, landlords' real income fluctuated with the price level in the fifty years before the Famine.

In spite of these qualifications, it seems that as far as risk-taking is concerned, the formal arrangements favoured the landlord. If harvests were poor, the peasants starved. If harvests were plentiful or prices high (as they were in the first decade of the nineteenth century), the tenants prospered. In a way the arrangement seems odd, since the tenants do not seem to have been in a better position than the landlords to bear risk.[4] Risk aversion on the part of the tenants implies that they would have preferred a safer (or less volatile) income. Is it possible to explain why Irish agriculture was based on family-farm tenants rather than on agricultural labourers and labour-employing tenants (as in England) or on sharecroppers (as in parts of France, Italy, and elsewhere)?

One possible answer, I suggest, lies in the realm of information flows between landlord and tenant. If the Irish landlord was to share in some of the risk, he would have to obtain some information to distinguish 'real' (i.e. exogenous) sources of output fluctuations from those which depended on the tenant's input. In order to distinguish effectively between 'luck' and laziness or incompetence, the landlord would have to receive a systematic flow of information from the field.[5] In other words, he would have to supervise the labour or hire somebody trustworthy to do it for him. In Ireland, especially in the regions in which unmechanized arable farming was the mainstay of the population, such information was very costly.

In order to absorb some risk without being cheated, the landlord had to be more than a *rentier:* he had to be something of a manager of his estate. Strict residency was neither a necessary nor a sufficient condition for the landlords to be successful managers. In a number of cases, the landlords could 'replace themselves' by good land-agents, though these were rare birds in prefamine Ireland. On the other hand, it often happened that resident gentlemen ignored their estates or concentrated on a tiny portion of it where they carried out experiments and improvements.[6] Residency, nevertheless, was of the utmost importance, because of the way it affected the cost of information flowing from the estate to the landlord. Absenteeism by its very nature raised that cost, although it was neither zero for residents nor infinite for absentees.[7]

A further question which demands some treatment is why the Irish did not sharecrop. Mill's and Marshall's strictures notwithstanding, economists have increasingly come to realize that sharecropping represents an attractive solution to the 'principal-agent' problem. The landlord does not have to worry about how hard the tenant works since the tenant's effort can be measured by the quantity of the output, while there is an incentive for the tenant to work since his income is proportional to output. The absence of sharecroping in Ireland can be in part explained by the behaviour of Irish landlords. Since landlords supplied neither capital nor expertise, there was little to be gained from sharecropping. The main advantage of sharecropping is precisely to provide the landlords with an incentive to make an effort in supplying factors other than land, and to aid and advise the worker.[8] Moreover, sharecropping involes some monitoring of labour (though less so than wage labour), and this was something Irish landlords — with some exceptions — were neither willing nor able to do.

Furthermore, although regional variations were considerable, much of the Irish agrarian economy can be roughly described as follows: the typical Irish rural household constituted a miniature 'dual economy'. It contained two sectors, a subsistence sector and a cash sector. The subsistence sector consisted of the production of potatoes and peat, while cash was obtained from a variety of sources including oats, wheat, cattle, pigs, cottage industry, dairy products, and seasonal wage labour. Since landlords usually had little or no use for the goods produced by the subsistence sectors, and since these goods were not easily converted into cash, they had no use for a share in these crops.[9] The tenant bore the entire risk of the subsistence crop. The rent was paid out of the proceeds of the cash crops, and the risk associated with those crops was absorbed by him only insofar as he met his rent payments scrupulously. When the subsistence crop failed, many tenants made supreme efforts to continue to pay their rents, a phenomenon which has amazed observers of the Great Famine ever since. In some sense, this duality can be regarded as replacing sharecropping. The dichotomy between the cash and the subsistence crop, however, eliminated most of the advantages of the sharecropping system. The reality in Ireland was that the tenant absorbed most of the risk. Almost the only way in which the landlord could be made to bear the risk was by the tenant defaulting on his rental commitments, i.e., falling into arrears. Arrears were a common enough phenomenon before the famine, but it is far from clear whether it seriously relieved the tenant from the concern and hardship caused by factors beyond his control which caused his output to fluctuate.

3. Potatoes and Risk

The role of the potato in the prefamine economy is undisputed, at least as the main staple food of the population. Did the potato increase or decrease the riskiness of Irish economic life? At first glance, the answer to this question seems self-evident. After all, the Great Famine seems to prove *ex post facto* that the potato was unreliable. In some sense, however, the potato failure represents a dilemma to the economist, because it was unanticipated; that is, before the Famine people assigned a very low probability to a disaster of such magnitude.[10] To put the matter differently, if one had annual data for potato yields between 1800 and 1850, and one computed the variance of the yields as a measure of the riskiness of output, the figure for 1800–1850 would be much higher than the figure for 1800–1845. If we were to find that the variance for the years 1800–45 was very small, growing potatoes would be 'correct' from a risk-behaviour point of view, and thus in a sense the potato would create a less risky economy.

The matter is more complex than that, however. The potato was never a monoculture in Ireland. Of the 6.5 million acres under arable cultivation on the eve of the Famine, only about 2.1 million were under potatoes.[11] This proportion is less than that under wheat in contemporary south-west France, which approximated 50 per cent. As far as the value of output is concerned, Ó Gráda has assessed the value of the potato crop at 20 per cent of the value of agricultural output in Ireland, and less than 10 per cent of national income.[12] It would seem, therefore, that lack of diversification was surely not the Achilles heel of the Irish economy. Some doubts linger on, however. It is striking that in an economy in which there was so much diversification in *production*, there was so little diversification in *consumption*.[13] Moreover, as shown in detail elsewhere, those features of the potato which made it into a subsistence crop were expensive transportation and the difficulties in carrying over buffer stock. These same features tended to increase the riskiness of consumption by making each tenant depend entirely on that year's crop.[14]

Contrary to some opinions, it is by no means true that growing a cash crop which is wholly exchanged at the market is riskier than growing a subsistence food crop.[15] While it is true that the commercial farmer encounters uncertainty both with respect to quantity and to price, movements in the two tend to go in opposite directions, as it were neutralizing each other. We cannot be completely certain that subsistence farming is more vulnerable than commercial farming. The formal conditions under which this is so can be computed, and they seem to cover most of the realistic situations.[16] The subsistence farmer must rely on his home-grown food supply — the commercial farmer can always hope to buy food elsewhere.

In order to say anything more definitive about the riskiness of the Irish potato economy, it is necessary to look at the year to year variability of potato yields compared to those of other crops. For Ireland, unfortunately, no times series are available. Qualitative evidence suggests that between 1750 and 1810, few major crop failures occurred. K. H. Connell referred to this period as the 'gap in famines'. In the decade around Waterloo the potato seems to have reached a turning point, and gradually lost some of its reliability. William Wilde's account of pre-1845 famines indicates that the season of 1813/14 may have been the turning point.[17] In 1830, James Bicheno told a Parliamentary Committee that the potato was more liable to failure than grains.[18] It is therefore not far-fetched to hypothesize that, even without considering the Great Famine, the risk-reducing effects of the potato were not very impressive.

For more quantitative evidence we have to turn, *faute de mieux*, to the annual crop statistics for France.[19] From these statistics, indices of riskiness have been computed and are presented in Table 1. The indices were defined as the coefficient of variation if no statistically significant trend was present in the series, and the coefficient of variation of the de-trended data if the trend was significant at the 1 per cent level for the period 1829–45. The areas utilized were regions I and II, the North-West (nine *départements*), and the North (eleven *départements*). In addition data were collected for a sample of eight *départements*, selected because they all had a higher than average acreage under potatoes and because the data in these *départements* looked relatively reliable.[20]

Table 1 shows that the variability of potato crops and yields was not usually lower and in most cases significantly higher than the variability of cereals. If we expand the sample period to 1829–1855, this difference is much increased. If Ireland was at

TABLE 1. *Riskiness of alternative crops: yields and total products:*
France 1829–45

	Potatoes yield	output	Wheat yield	output	Oats yield	output
Regions						
North-West	0.184*	0.171*	0.072*	0.067*	0.084*	0.097*
North	0.136	0.126*	0.108	0.112	0.096*	0.095*
Départements						
Cotes du Nord	0.247	0.350*	0.106	0.107*	0.167	0.165
Nord	0.113	0.103*	0.090	0.104	0.072*	0.089*
Bas Rhin	0.147*	0.186*	0.200	0.198	0.205	0.211
Moselle	0.215	0.194*	0.155	0.157	0.157	0.175
Vosges	0.199	0.217	0.170	0.187	0.177	0.256
Aveyron	0.314	0.372*	0.193	0.230	0.280	0.282
Loire	0.525*	0.3110	0.252	0.220*	0.257	0.294
Jura	0.315	0.292	0.191	0.223	0.190	0.255
Average of eight depts.	0.232	0.253	0.170	0.178	0.188	0.216

Asterisked (*) figures were obtained after detrending.
Source: Computed from Ministère d'Agriculture, *Récoltes des Céréales et des Pommes de Terre* (Paris, 1913), *passim.*

all similar to France in this respect, potatoes in all likelihood made the Irish food supply more volatile.

It might be objected that even if the variability of the potato crop was higher than cereals, the potato enabled the Irish economy to diversify and thus to reduce the overall variability of the combined output of potatoes and cereal crops. Some computations using the arithmetic of variances show that if the variance of the potato crop was twice as high as that of oats, the correlation between the two crops was .260 (which is the mean of the correlation coefficients of the eight *départements*), and if potatoes occupied a third of the arable land, the total variance would be 18 per cent less than if oats alone were grown and 51 per cent less than if potatoes alone had been cultivated. It is important to remember, however, that this 'portfolio effect' was not directly relevant to the majority of Irish peasants who relied almost exclusively on (mostly home-grown) potatoes for their daily food.

To be sure, the French statistics of crops and yields are of poor quality, and there is no compelling reason to believe that the Irish situation was all that similar to the French. Nonetheless, it seems reasonable to conclude from this evidence that it is quite likely that even before the Great Famine, the potato increased rather than reduced the riskiness of the economic environment in Ireland.

4. Uncertainty and Tenant-Right

One phenomenon which has captured the interest of historians and played a central role in the historiography of Irish agriculture is the 'Ulster Custom', centering around the free sale of 'tenant-right'. Briefly, tenant-right referred to the right of undisturbed possession, as long as rent was paid. As Solow has pointed out, this right means little as long as rents can be raised freely. More must therefore have been involved, since on the eve of the Famine tenant-right was sold and bought all over Ireland, although most frequently in Ulster. This sale involved the payment of a lump sum by an incoming tenant to a departing tenant. Tenant-right, then, was a form of property right: giving up a tenancy entitled the tenant to compensation.[21] And yet even in Ulster there was never any formal claim of the tenant to proprietorship. Consequently contemporaries complained that 'tenant right confuses the rights of the landlord and tenant and is an undue interference with the interests of the proprietor'.[22] What, then, was the payment for? Contemporaries usually pointed out that the incoming tenant bought the 'goodwill' of the outgoing tenant (or his relatives) so that the neighbouring peasants would permit him 'peaceable possession'. These explanations point to an informal set of property rights, enforced extra-legally but effectively. But property rights in what exactly?

The two most widespread explanations for the phenomenon are the 'Key Money Hypothesis' (KMH) and the 'Unexhausted Improvements Hypothesis' (UIH). The KMH, especially espoused by Solow, maintained that for some reason the landlords charged the tenant a rent which was lower than the competitive rent. Tenant-right was then sold at a competitive price equal to the present value of the expected difference between the actual rent and the maximum rent the market could bear. While logically attractive, there is not much hard evidence for 'rent control' in the prefamine Irish economy.[23] Although there may have been *some* landlords who because of existing contracts, fear, incompetence, or humaneness refrained from charging the maximum rent, it is hard to believe that they were as widespread as the universality of the sale of tenant-right suggests.

The UIH is equally straightforward, and is based on the notion that tenant-right was a way in which the outgoing tenant was compensated for capital investment which he could not take along. Although of some importance, the UIH cannot account for the entire phenomenon either. The *Devon Commission Digest* pointed out that 'tenant-right is seldom sold by improving tenants . . . even if the price of tenant-right be at all affected by the improvements made on the farm (a fact doubted by some witnesses) it is not so influenced in proportion to the value of the improvements'.[24]

The KMH and the UIH are both reasonable explanations and have some support in the evidence. The support is not strong enough, however, to consider them, even jointly, as exhaustive. Both the KMH and the UIH implicitly assume that output is constant, perfectly known in advance, and not a function of anything either landlord or tenant does subsequent to the contract. It is this assumption that I wish to relax. Uncertainty can lead to phenomena like tenant-right through a number of mechanisms. The most obvious is that holding a farm may have been regarded as safer than the next best alternative, even if holding a farm meant absorbing all the risk.[25] In Ireland the alternative to holding a farm was becoming a landless labourer subsisting often on conacre land, widely denounced as risky.[26] Even those tenants who could find a new landlord after losing their lease would incur search — and other transaction costs. 'Security of tenure', therefore, has economic significance independent of and in addition to the processes implied by the KMH and the UIH. Tenant-right was a payment for the right to hold land; but from an economic point of view it has, in part, the character of an insurance premium.

It could be argued that if the holding of land provided a further service as 'insurance' in addition to its usual use, such services ought to have been incorporated in the rent. Assuming there was no 'rent control', therefore, the more security a plot provided, the higher the rent would be. Matters were, however, a bit more complex than that; the amount of security that a plot of land provided depended among other things on the personality and management practices of the landlord. If he was willing to absorb part of the risk by foregoing part of the rent or allowing the tenant to fall in arrears, holding land from him would be desirable and thus more valuable.

Consider the hypothetical example of two neighbouring landowners, Lord Squeezum and Sir Bigheart. In normal years, both charge the same rent. A failure in the cash crop, or a sharp decline in its price, forces them to make some choices. Sir Bigheart, living on the estate and perceiving that the failure of the harvest was due to frost and hail, absorbs part of the loss by allowing the arrears to accumulate to be paid back later (perhaps). Lord Squeezum, from his vantage point in the French Riviera, thinks his tenants are cheating him and insists on payment in full. The collection of rents owed usually involved the seizure or distraint of the tenant's crop and livestock. Or Lord Squeezum may compel his tenants to seek outside employment coming at the expense of, say, maintenance of drainage works. In any of these alternatives, the actions of the landlord may reduce the flow of future rents. In addition, his actions may increase the 'turbulence' among his tenants, which means that he is more likely to encounter situations in the future in which tenants experience or feign difficulties in rent payment. If he is not successful, he may have to evict the tenant, but that may lead to further difficulties and costs.[27] On the other hand, Sir Bigheart can expect some of the arrears to be repaid from the proceeds of the tenant-right. In short, the expected (or average) value of the rental income of the two estates is not necessarily different, but Sir Bigheart allows his tenants to 'roll with the punch' and, by so doing, creates a value important enough to have a market.

Not every resident landlord reduced the riskiness of farming for his tenants and not every absentee increased it. Tight-fisted, tyrannical resident gentlemen who insisted upon payment and threatened eviction were less desirable than absentee rentiers, minors, or lunatics who may have lacked the means to enforce rent payments in bad years. In other words, a poorly informed landlord also could be a valuable asset to his tenant, which would be reflected in the value of tenant-right. Here the 'uncertainty hypothesis' merges with the KMH, since the tenant, using as an excuse factors beyond his control, cheats his poorly informed landlord out of part of the rent.

Still, why should a landlord like Sir Bigheart not be able to charge a higher average rent, especially in view of the fact that his rental income was more irregular? If the 'insurance' that he provided to his tenants was so valuable to them, could it not permit him to charge a higher rent so that there would be no room for tenant-right? It is quite possible that some 'good' landlords were able to translate their 'magnanimity' into higher rents, but unless they were able to expropriate the *entire* gain in the tenant's welfare due to their more liberal management practice, the gains were shared by the two. Tenant-right then simply reflected the tenant's share. Many landlords were of course not so much 'liberal' as incompetent, weak, or uninterested; these landlords may very well have provided insurance without realizing it.

Moreover, the existence of high information costs implies that it was not always optimal for the landlord to charge the maximum rent the market would bear. As every land agent knew, there were 'good' tenants and 'bad' tenants. Good tenants were less likely to default, to misrepresent laziness and incompetence as natural disasters, or to harm the soil. It was not easy, however, to distinguish between the two kinds in practice. Once a tenant was recognized as 'good', it was in the landlord's interest to charge him a lower rent, since losing him would incur the cost of evaluating his successors. Once such a tenant left by his free will (most frequently to emigrate), he attempted to transfer his 'label' as a good tenant (or goodwill) to the incoming tenant. The difficulties arose when the landlords or their agents insisted on ascertaining the qualities of the incoming tenant. The KMH is thus correct but incomplete; uncertainty and information costs provide a logical explanation why some tenants paid a lower rent than the maximum the market could bear. Repeated complaints that some landlords charged rents which were 'too high' and were ruining their estates indicates that not all landlords followed this policy.[28]

Evidence on the operation of tenant-right in the prefamine decades is very sporadic. There is not much evidence that its sale was very widely practised before 1815. Neither Arthur Young nor Edward Wakefield in their massive works on Ireland make any reference to it. The *Parochial Surveys* edited by W. S. Mason contain one single reference to it.[29] William Greig, in his *Report* on the Gosford Estates in Co. Armagh, spends one paragraph on the issue, pointing out the peculiarity of the custom of tenant-right 'where no lease exists and no improvements have been made'.[30] G. V. Sampson in his *Survey* of Co. Londonderry mentions the custom, but the statistical notes contained in the *Ordnance Survey Memoirs* for the county compiled in the 1830s seem often at odds with the existence of tenant-right, complaining that tenants refuse to introduce improvements out of fear of losing the value of the investment upon departure.[31] By the time the Devon Commission started its huge project on the state of the law and practice of land occupation in Ireland (1844), the sale of tenant-right was occurring much more frequently. This increase was doubtless associated with the rise in emigration, which caused tenants to give up possession voluntarily.[32] The recovery of agricultural prices in the 1840s may also have added to the importance of tenant-right, if rents lagged behind.

In what follows, I shall use the testimonies given by Devon Commission witnesses to try to provide backing for the various hypotheses put forward to explain tenant-right. The use of this procedure is anything but straightforward. Not all witnesses expressed their opinion on all aspects of the custom, so that even though there were 453 witnesses who had at least something to say on the tenant-right issue, for most questions there are far fewer testimonies that can be used. Selectivity biases of various kinds obviously contaminate this 'sample'. Furthermore, the testimonies are highly contradictory, and it is possible to support *any* explanation by a careful choice of witnesses. The only way to circumvent, at least in part, the inconsistency of the evidence is to *count* the number of witnesses expressing each view, in the hope of isolating some form of consensus.[33]

First, how prevalent was the sale of tenant-right on the eve of the Famine and to what extent was it recognized by landlords? A distinction should be made between formal or informal recognition of the sale by landlords and their specific control over the incoming tenant. Table 2 presents a summary of the Devon testimonies.

Table 2 suggests that 'Ulster Custom' is something of a misnomer, although the practice was indeed most prevalent in the North. Nor was it in Ulster only that the sale was sanctioned by the landlords.[34] It seems that wherever tenant-right was sold, landlords tried to control the phenomenon, reserving the right to select or approve the incoming tenant. It would seem that if the KMH was the only explanation, there is no reason why the landlords would wish to keep such tight control over the process.

The witnesses were not asked point blank how they explained the existence of the custom in the first place. A few related questions can, however, shed some indirect light on the problem. The issue of unexhausted improvements did come up, though the analysis of the Devon witnesses cannot be regarded as a fair test of the UIH. In all, 46 witnesses said that the value of tenant-right was associated with

TABLE 2. *Tenant right before the famine*

	Ulster	Leinster	Munster	Connaught	Ireland
Index of Prevalence	1.81	1.19	1.10	1.44	1.44
No. of witnesses used in prevalence index	157	85	60	48	350
Landlord recognizes?					
Yes (no. of witnesses)	135	26	22	21	204
No	9	6	6	7	28
Landlord controls?					
Yes	81	27	11	12	131
No	29	5	4	6	44

Note: Index of prevalence is computed on a range between zero (no tenant-right sold) to 2 (prevalent).
Source: Devon Commission Report, *passim.*

improvements, while 17 said that it was not. Interestingly, 13 witnesses denied explicitly that the payment for tenant-right fully equalled the value of the unexhausted improvements, while only two witnesses said it did. Another question that arose was the extent to which tenant-right depended on whether the outgoing tenant had a lease, presumably transferable to the buyer. Of the witnesses addressing this question, 47 affirmed that the value of tenant-right was a function of the mode of tenure, while 49 denied it. However, when asked whether the tenant-right was paid even in the absence of leases, 119 witnesses answered in the affirmative and 14 in the negative. The KMH finds some support in the 23 witnesses who noted that the value of tenant-right depended on the rent. But almost twice as many (44) pointed to the importance of 'confidence in the landlord' or 'character of the landlord' as factors determining the value of tenant-right.[35] If rents were the only thing that mattered, why did the witnesses not draw the connexion directly more often?

The search for 'security' cut both ways, as is confirmed by the large number of witnesses confirming that landlords actively sought control over the sale of tenant-right. The relation between tenant-right and arrears is of importance to the argument, and it is thus interesting to note that everywhere witnesses confirmed that the proceeds from the sale of tenant-right were used for arrears: 73 witnesses, among them 24 from Munster and Leinster (where the sale of tenant-right was more limited) confirmed that this was the case. The use of arrears indicates that some of those landlords who were willing to permit arrears to accumulate, i.e. to absorb some part of the risk, were ultimately repaid, at least in part.

5. *Conclusion*

It is by no means the intention here to argue that the explicit consideration of uncertainty in the economic analysis of prefamine agriculture will necessarily lead to a radical revision of the conventional wisdom. It is likely, however, to enrich the analysis by the introduction of novel lines of thinking about the issues, which may help to account for phenomena thus far only partially understood, and focus the attention of scholars on new questions. Agricultural production is inherently risky, and the separation between cultivation and ownership led to 'principal-agent' relations everywhere in Europe. Security and reliable information were then, as they are now, commodities most people were willing to pay for. The market for these goods, however, is usually fraught with failures and traps, which affect the entire operation of the economy. In spite of its many peculiarities, the Irish economy does not seem an exception to that rule.

REFERENCES

1. For some examples, see James A. Roumasset and Jean-Marc Boussard, eds., *Risk, Uncertainty, and Agricultural Development* (College Laguna, 1979); Donald N. McCloskey, 'English Open Fields as a Behavior Toward Risk', *Research in Economic History*, I (1976), 124–170; Gavin Wright and Howard Kunreuther, 'Cotton, Corn, and Risk in the Nineteenth Century', *Journal of Economic History*, XXXV (1975), 526–551; Robert McGuire, 'A Portfolio Analysis of Crop Diversification and Risk in the Cotton South', *Explorations in Economic History*, XVII (Oct. 1980), 342–371.

2. See for instance Stephen A. Ross, 'The Economic Theory of Agency: the Principal's Problem', *American Economic Review*, XIII (May, 1973), 134–139; Steven Shavell, 'Risk Sharing and Incentives in the Principal and Agent Relationship', *Bell Journal of Economics and Management Science*, X (Spring 1979), 55–73. For a brilliant application of these models to economic history, see Stefano Fenoaltea, 'Authority, Efficiency, and Agricultural Organization in Medieval England and Beyond: a Hypothesis', *Journal of Economic History*, XXXV (December 1975), 693–718; *id.*, 'Risk, Transaction Costs, and the Organization of Medieval Agriculture', *Explorations in Economic History*, XIII (April 1976), 129–151.

3. A classic exposition of the landlord's dilemma was given by Daniel O'Connell in his testimony before the Devon Commission (*Parliamentary Papers*, 1845, XXI, 933).

4. It might be argued that the landlords were more risk-averse than their tenants because of their substantial fixed liabilities (e.g. interest charges, family settlements). The tenants were, however, much poorer and had less access to capital market to help them weather the storms or poor harvests. In any event, it will readily be recognized that if both sides are averse to risk, it is likely (though not certain) that they will try to share the risk.

5. The problem the landlord faces is analogous to the 'moral hazard' problem faced by insurers.

6. J. P. Kennedy, *Instruct, Employ, Don't Hang Them: Ireland Tranquilized Without Soldiers and Without English Capital* (London, 1835), 81.

7. For a more complete exposition of the absenteeism problem, see Joel Mokyr, *Why Ireland Starved: A Quantitative and Analytical History of the Irish Economy, 1800–1850* (London, 1982), ch. VII; A. P. W. Malcomson, 'Absenteeism in Eighteenth-Century Ireland', *Irish Economic and Social History*, I (1974), 15–35.

8. Joseph D. Reid, 'Sharecropping and Agricultural Uncertainty', *Economic Development and Cultural Change*, XXIV (April 1976), 549–576; *id.*, 'Sharecropping in History and Theory', *Agricultural History*, XLIX (April 1975), 426–440.

9. For a more complete description and analysis of this 'dualism' see Mokyr, *Why Ireland Starved*, ch. II, and Elizabeth Hoffman and Joel Mokyr, 'Peasants, Poverty, and Potatoes: Transactions Costs in Prefamine Ireland', Northwestern University Center for Mathematical Studies in Economics and Management Science, Discussion Paper no. 474 (April 1981).

10. Experimental economists and psychologists have long recognized that the evaluation of events with extremely low probabilities leads to apparently irrational and inconsistent behaviour. People buy tickets for 'unfair' lotteries and refuse to buy subsidized flood insurance although maximizing behaviour suggests that they should. See Daniel Kahneman and Amos Tversky, 'Prospect Theory: An Analysis of Decision under Risk', *Econometrica*, XLVII (March 1979), esp. 282–283. For a summary of the experimental literature and some puzzled reflections, see David Grether and Charles R. Plott, 'Economic Theory and the Preference Reversal Function', *American Economic Review*, LXIX Sept. 1979, 623–38.

11. The potato acreage estimate is based on calculations presented in Joel Mokyr, 'Irish History with the Potato', *Irish Economic and Social History*, VIII (1981), 8–29. The arable acreage is based on estimations using the earliest post-famine agricultural censuses for all other crops and adjusting for potato acreage.

12. Cormac Ó Gráda, 'Irish Agriculture Before and After the Famine' (unpublished manuscript, June 1980).

13. The monotony of the potato diet among cottiers and smallholders was a major complaint raised by the witnesses before the Poor Law Commission (*Parliamentary Papers*, 1836, XXXII, 1–37).

14. Hoffman and Mokyr, 'Peasants, Poverty, and Potatoes'.

15. See for example Howard Kunreuther and Gavin Wright, 'Safety First, Gambling, and the Subsistence Farmer', in Roumasset and Bousard, eds., *Risk, Uncertainty, and Agricultural Development*, 217.

16. The algebraic demonstration of these conditions is presented in Hoffman and Mokyr, 'Peasants, Poverty, and Potatoes'.

17. *Parliamentary Papers*, 1856, XXIX, 50206.

18. *Parliamentary Papers*, 1830, VII, 378.

19. Ministère d'Agriculture, *Récoltes des Céréales et des Pommes de Terre* (Paris, 1913). A description and evaluation of this source can be found in William H. Newell, 'The Agricultural Revolution in Nineteenth-Century France', *Journal of Economic History*, XXXIII (Dec. 1973), 697–731. I am indebted to Professors William Newell and George Grantham for their co-operation which enabled me to use this source.

20. The data were collected by each *département*, and there is clearly much variation in their quality. Aggregation thus involves combining high quality with low quality figures. By selecting some individual *départements*, the most plausible series could be chosen.

21. Originally, tenant-right meant the right to priority in negotiating a new lease upon expiry. In the eighteenth century what was sold was considered the 'interest' which included also the value of term remaining in the lease, and the 'goodwill'. In practice this value was determined by supply and demand. For the eighteenth-century origins of the Ulster Custom, see W. H. Crawford, 'Landlord-Tenant Relations in Ulster, 1609–1820', *Irish Economic and Social History*, II (1975), 5–21. For the nineteenth century see, for example, John E. Pomfret, *The Struggle for Land in Ireland, 1800–1923* (Princeton, 1930), 51; Barbara Solow, *The Land Question and the Irish Economy 1870–1913* (Cambridge, Mass., 1971), 26–30.

22. J. P. Kennedy, *Digest of Evidence Taken . . .* (before the Devon Commission), (Dublin, 1847), 290.

23. For details see Mokyr, *Why Ireland Starved*, ch. V. The Devon Commission *Report* noted that the tenant-right was sold 'not only when the rent is considered low, but when it is fully equal to the value' (*Parliamentary Papers*, 1845, XIX, 14).

24. Kennedy, *Devon Commission Digest*, 291. Crawford in 'Landlord-Tenant Relations', 20, suggests that the payment for improvements was to some extent a legal fiction. The law could recognize only payment for a yet unexpired lease or payment for unexhausted improvements. When tenancy became gradually more and more 'at will', this was the only way of formalizing a payment for property rights in something the law had difficulty in dealing with.

25. See, for instance, *Parliamentary Papers*, 1836, XXXII, 91, 200; *Parliamentary Papers*, 1825, VIII, 318. For a similar argument made for French peasants, see George Grantham,

'Scale and Organization in French Farming, 1840–1880', in William N. Parker and Eric L. Jones, eds., *European Peasants and Their Markets* (Princeton, 1975), 310.

26. Kennedy, *Devon Commission Digest*, 522.

27. W. H. Crawford, 'The Influence of the Landlord in Eighteenth-Century Ulster', in L. M. Cullen and T. C. Smout, eds., *Comparative Aspects of Scottish and Irish Economic and Social History, 1600–1900* (Edinburgh, 1977), 197.

28. See for instance John Wiggins, *The 'Monster' Misery of Ireland: A Practical Treatise on the Relation of Landlord and Tenant* (London, 1844), 47–59; Horatio Townsend, *A General and Statistical Survey of the County of Cork*, 2nd ed. (Cork, 1815), II, 53.

29. William S. Mason, *A Statistical Account or Parochial Survey of Ireland* (Dublin, 1814–19), II, 262, pertaining to the parishes of Glenavy, Camplin, and Tullyrush, Co. Antrim. See also Robert Fraser, *General View of the County Wicklow* (Dublin, 1801), 118–119.

30. William Greig, *General Report on the Gosford Estates in County Armagh, 1821*, ed. with an introduction by F. M. L. Thompson and D. Tierney (Belfast, 1976), 169.

31. G. V. Sampson, *Statistical Survey of the County of Londonderry* (Dublin, 1802), 253; Ordnance Survey Memoirs (Royal Irish Academy, Dublin) Box 45, file I (Magherafelt) and Box 39, file II (Dungiven).

32. The decline in agricultural prices in the thirty years after Waterloo would lead us to expect a decline in the value of tenant-right, an expectation confirmed by the Devon Commission witnesses of whom 68 said that the value of tenant-right had been falling lately, as against 28 who said that it had been rising and nine claiming that it had been constant.

33. Obviously, this methodology can be criticized on a number of grounds. For a defence of the procedure and a description of the Devon Commission witnesses, see Mokyr, *Why Ireland Starved*, ch. IV.

34. George O'Brien, *The Economic History of Ireland from the Union to the Famine* (London, 1921), 111; Pomfret, *The Struggle for Land in Ireland*, 53; Brian A. Kennedy, 'Tenant-Right Before 1870', in T. W. Moody and J. C. Beckett, eds., *Ulster Since 1800: A Political and Economic Survey* (London, 1954), 39–49.

35. For some examples of such statements for counties as different as Londonderry, Louth, and Sligo, see *Parliamentary Papers*, 1845, XIX, 703, q. 19; XIX, 418, q. 101; XX, 190, q. 20.

H

Part III

Migration

8

Migration in the Rural Lowlands of Scotland, 1750–1850

Malcolm Gray

OVER the past two centuries the Scots have shown themselves to be a singularly mobile people; indeed there are probably few Scottish families which have not produced at least some migrant members. It is the movement from the Highlands and Islands which, whether from bitterness or — on the part of Lowlanders — guilt, has remained most strongly in the folk memory but the people of the Lowlands have participated no less, and probably more willingly. Considerable numbers from the Lowlands as from the Highlands have gone overseas but far more numerous have been those who have shifted home within the country. Such movement has been inevitably less documented than the more emotive severance from the homeland and has left comparatively little record except in the severe pages of census and parliamentary reports. For our period such accounts became gradually more detailed and reliable, particularly after the first official census in 1801, until the census of 1851 with its enumeration of the birth-places of the people, arranged by county and principal towns, uncovers a most intricate pattern, traced out presumably over the previous fifty years. Every county of lowland Scotland had evidently been sending its migrants to every other part of the country, and every county received some from sources just as widespread. Our concern is with the lowland area, that is all the counties of Scotland except those making up the Western Highlands and the Islands (Argyll, Inverness, Ross and Cromarty, Sutherland, Caithness and Orkney and Shetland).

To judge by the birth-place evidence summarised in the 1871 census report — which is the first to allow such calculation — a fair proportion of these movements consisted simply of the exchange of population between adjacent rural areas without change in the relative population sizes.[1] Rural movements can be identified most clearly in the three north-eastern counties of Aberdeen, Kincardine and Banff (Table 1). Within this group, outside the city of Aberdeen there was almost no urban growth, at least beyond what might be expected from natural increase; since the city can be separately identified in the census tables both as to the origins of its inhabitants and as to the destination of its out-migrants, movements into and out of rural areas can also be adequately established. Thus, of those born in rural Aberdeenshire, 7026 are recorded as resident in Banffshire; the lack of towns growing at beyond their rate of natural increase in the latter suggests that this was largely a move into the rural areas. This migration, moreover, was matched by a move of very slightly greater scale into the land-ward, and overwhelmingly rural, areas of Aberdeenshire. Similar balancing movements are found between Aberdeenshire and Kincardineshire. Indeed, throughout Scotland, wherever statistical isolation of areas of little urban growth is possible, these matching rural flows between adjacent areas are to be found — between Dumfries and Kirkcudbright, or Peebles and Berwick, or Kinross and Perth.

This is evidence from a time of record beyond the end of our period but presumably it reflects movements that had been taking place for some time before 1850. There is, indeed, no reason to suppose that there was anything new about the shifts of rural population that come to light in 1871. Widespread movements, not connected with any trend in social or industrial development, or with any overall shift of population, were probably an underlying feature of long standing. Even the record of 1871, showing, as it does, mainly the movements between counties, must very much understate the true volume of such migration, particularly in large counties such as Aberdeen, Perth or Dumfries. Thus, it is not impossible that the commonest type of migration was between farms or between rural communities, even in the full flood of industrialisation. Still, in itself, the census record suggests that the balancing moves between the rural sectors of adjacent counties were fewer than the moves out of these areas, all of which were showing big net losses at least from 1800 onwards. Thus, rural Aberdeenshire, while losing migrants into nearby non-urbanised counties, also sent more than three times as many to the city of Aberdeen and to more distant, and mainly urban, destinations. Loss of population from most agricultural parishes is evident between 1755 and 1801 with actual decline of population very common in the northern part of the country and only along the southern tier of counties from Berwick westwards to Wigton was there an increase of rural population that anything like matched the presumed addition by natural increase.[2] From 1801 to 1851, most areas and most agricultural parishes showed increases of population well below any credible rate of natural increase, with the counties of the far South-West standing out as an exception.[3] In all, outside these south-western areas only 19 out of 220 agricultural parishes showed increases amounting to more than 10 per cent per decade.[4]

Rural losses, then, were general and large but destinations can be only approximately estimated. There was the possibility of an overseas emigration which would be lost from the census record. It is true that numbers of emigrants from the country as a whole have been estimated, but what proportions of this somewhat notional total came from towns, from lowland rural districts and from the Highlands can scarcely even be guessed.[5] It is clear beyond doubt, however, that great numbers were moving out of rural parishes into other areas of the Lowlands and more particularly to urban areas. The 1851 census finds considerable proportions of the native-born of mainly rural counties scattered over Scotland, many of them in towns.[6] For example, 8 per cent of those born in Kincardine were in the city of Aberdeen and a similar proportion in the urbanising county of Angus. Similarly, Peeblesshire had 15 per cent in Edinburgh. On the other hand, the

TABLE 1. *Migration from and within the County of Aberdeen*

Migrants from landward areas of county[1] 43,143			% of Total
Of this there went to:	Aberdeen city	19,166	44
	adjacent agricul-		
	tural counties	10,885	25
	distant parts	13,092	30
		43,143	
	Further there went to the cities of:		
	Dundee	1,029	2
	Glasgow	1,634	4
	Edinburgh	1,699	4
		4,362	10
	the counties of:		
	Forfar[2]	2,865	7
	Lanark[2]	2,334	5
	Edinburgh[2]	2,473	6
	Renfrew	343	
	Ayr	176	
		8,191	19

1. Evidence of migration is a difference between place of residence
   in 1871 and place of birth.
2. Includes cities of Dundee, Glasgow and Edinburgh.
   63% of migrants to distant parts are found in the industrial counties
   of Edinburgh, Lanark, Renfrew, Ayr.

Source: 1871 Census, Birth-Places of the People.

---

enumeration of the birth-places of the residents of the main towns shows the scale of
recruitment from lowland rural areas. Glasgow took 53 per cent of those not born in
the city from lowland sources, Edinburgh 66 per cent, Dundee 60 and Aberdeen
80.[7]

The figures for the birth-places of the town residents also show, not
unexpectedly, large numbers coming from immediate hinterlands. But also there
was a considerable volume of long-distance movement. The people of rural
Aberdeenshire had the opportunity of shifting to a nearby and rapidly growing
town, but still many chose a longer move to the south; we find that, in 1871, 30,051
have gone to nearby and 13,092 to more distant destinations. Altogether
movements beyond the immediately adjacent centres of growth helped to produce a
steady swing in population balance from the outer areas into the Central Belt and
particularly into the four industrial counties of the west of Scotland. In 1755 these

held 18 per cent of the population of the Lowlands, while for 1801 and 1851 the figures were 25 and 37 per cent. The proportion on the eastern side of the belt, steady between 1755 and 1801, also increased, if slightly, between 1801 and 1851.

These intertwining flows — from country to town and from north and south into the Central Belt — were a crucial part of the process of industrialisation. On the one hand a high rate of migration was sustained by the demand for industrial and general urban labour; on the other, industrialisation was helped by ease of migration. To find causes, then, we have to look both to the rural and to the urban spheres. But since it is mainly a movement of rural people that we are observing, surely we might expect to find the major impulses in the stirrings of the rural community.

From some time in the second half of the eighteenth century rural arrangements were threatened by a rising rate of natural increase. Other factors might supervene and conceal the tendency — indeed rural population might actually decline — but accommodation or dispersal of growing numbers was unavoidable. It is not clear when the pressure began to build up, but by the early 1800s rural communities everywhere were facing the possibility that their numbers might grow by more than 10 per cent in every decade.[8]

A rural community experiencing even the rates of increase typical of the late eighteenth century was bound to either readjust its internal structure or to lose its surplus by migration, and the nature of its response can be seen as critical for the economic growth of the whole country. One possible outcome is for the increased population to be absorbed in the rural economy. But unless there are extensive reserves of good but unused land, the likely outcome then is subdivision of holdings or underemployment, with a fall in productivity per head; more seriously it may mean the closing of the agrarian trap where insufficient supplies of surplus food are produced to support the excess of numbers outside the agricultural sector, and with the rural population thus tied down, productivities continue to decline. The danger may be moderated by more efficient use of land, even land arranged in small holdings, say by the adoption of a new crop such as the potato. Forms of rural industrialisation, too, may sustain incomes. But there appear generally to have been limits to sustaining the productivity per head of a congested rural population.

The other main possibility is for the rural community to shed some of its growing population, thus allowing an agrarian adaptation that helps to raise the output of those who remain on the land sufficiently to give a surplus to sustain a growing urban population swelled by the immigrants from the rural areas. This was clearly the outcome in lowland Scotland, although not in the Highlands and probably not in many parts of Ireland.

How, then, did the rural Lowlands, in face of a potential local increase of population, achieve the balance of land and population in which productivities could be raised? There was indeed some increase of the areas of cultivation through the later eighteenth century and up to 1815, or possibly even 1830.[9] The replanning of estates and farms, coupled with determined efforts at drainage, had taken in many corners unused under the older more haphazard systems and there were broader moors to be tackled with the plough. But even in this phase the margin of cultivation was in some upland places drawing in. After 1815 the extension of arable area continued in only a few areas, most notably in the North-East, where as late as 1870 upland moors were still being settled by small holders.[10] On the whole, however, the increase in cultivated land could nothing like match the potential increase of population. It was mainly by migration that the required balance of land and population was kept.

Part of the reason that the increasing population produced migration rather than congestion lay in the nature of the lowland agrarian and farming system. The structure of land rights coupled with the forms of employment offered to agricultural labourers welded a strong instrument for excluding unwanted members from any share in local society. Only in a belt running across the country from Fife to Ayrshire was any significant proportion of the land owned by the working farmers, and in no part were the owner-occupiers dominant; mainly, then, the land was arranged in medium- or large-size estates which were divided into individual farms to be let to the working farmers.[11] On such land the size of the holdings could be effectively controlled to give units on which a reasonable standard of cultivation might be reached. From the middle of the eighteenth century onwards the stress was all on increasing the size of holdings even as population was tending to increase. It is true that it took some time to consolidate the numerous holdings which had existed earlier in the eighteenth century to reach a size now coming to be regarded as minimal. Equally there had been large numbers of subtenancies that could not be suddenly abolished. But the tendency was in that direction and by 1830 the greater part of the recognised farms were of viable size while subtenancy had almost disappeared.[12] In most areas there could be little thought of additional tenancies. In some districts the move towards viable farming units meant the complete prodominance of large farms, with a typical holding of, say, 200 arable acres (a unit on which there might be six men in full-time employment). But more generally there would be a variety of farm sizes with numerous family-sized farms, which could be cultivated with one plough-team and where at most there would be one servant.[13] Such a mixture of farm sizes, with at leat a fair sprinkling of large units, was the aim of most landlords. And when the land was so divided it gave no scope for an increase of tenant numbers beyond the levels of the mid-eighteenth century; the tendency would be rather to diminish than to increase the numbers on the rent-roll.

There were, it is true, areas where this strategy of putting the land exclusively under units of efficient farming size, sufficient to give a full livelihood, did not entirely prevail. In the more northern parts of the country, and particularly in the North-East, there could be numerous 'croft' holdings which would give neither full-time employment nor a complete livelihood. In Aberdeenshire, indeed, the crofts form a majority of all holdings.[14] They were, moreover, becoming more numerous even while other farms were being enlarged and tenants dispossessed. There can be little doubt that, on balance, tenant numbers increased in Aberdeenshire and Banffshire over the period 1800 to 1850. While this may be an exception to the strategy of enlargement of tenancies, it did not necessarily conflict with the aim of keeping the rural population at a level necessary for the efficient use of the land.

Formation of farms was kept strictly under the control of landlords who were thinking carefully about how their land should be utilised to give maximum return. Small-holdings were the chosen means for bringing land into cultivation with little expenditure of capital, and the increase in the number of holdings was no more than commensurate with the increase in improved land. But the usefulness of creating small-holdings did not end there. For crofts were regarded as providers of labour for the large farms in the form both of young lads to be hired as servants and of members of the occupying families who could provide seasonal help on a day labour basis. Further they might provide an ultimate home and livelihood for some of the servants who lost their employment on marriage.[15] They did not make for an ineffective use of land in the farming system as a whole or for overcrowding beyond the requirements for the productive use of land.

The labour force attached to farming also was kept much to the minimum by the prevailing system of hiring. Most of the work on Scottish farms was reputedly done by 'servants' who were hired for at least six months at a time to be then at the disposal of the one master.[16] Having thus to pay a full wage to every man in his employ, a farmer was unlikely to hire more men than was absolutely necessary; in fact the size of his labour force was finely conditioned by the number of plough-teams needed to get through the farm work; full value also had to be obtained from the horses.[17] The dominance of the long hire in the system, well documented in literary evidence, is illustrated by the figures collected for the census of 1861.[18] In mainland rural areas, in the male labour force men apparently on long hire outnumbered day labourers by about two to one. But the work-force included also farmers, bailiffs (or grieves) and collateral or younger members of farmers' families In this whole work-force day labourers made up 24 per cent. It is not a negligible figure but it is probable that it would include a number of skilled men such as dykers who worked around the farms on a day-labour basis and certainly the prospect of work as a day labourer could not keep many on the land who had failed to find permanent employment let alone a holding of their own. The exclusiveness of farm organisation made itself felt at this end of the scale as well as among the claimants for land.[19]

It is true that many farm tasks were seasonal additions to the steady burden of work undertaken by horsemen, cattlemen and other full-time employees. Such aid came from various quarters. In the northern areas crofting families met the need both at harvest and for the summer tasks in the fields. Further south there was migrant Irish labour for the harvest, while the families of the ploughmen, housed in the farm cottages, would help where it was customary to hire married men for full-time service. Weaving villages, too, were a source of seasonal help, for whole families might turn over to agricultural work on occasion. In the Lothians girls from the Highlands were hired for a season's work, being housed in bothies on the farms. By these various devices dependence on agricultural day labourers who would get only uncertain and irregular work on farms was avoided.[20]

The structure of rural society, the customs of hiring and disciplining labour, and the drive of the men in control tended to keep down the rural population to a level which would no more than supply the need for the full but not overcrowded occupation of the land and for its working by full-time employees and their families. Such rural pressures operating on their own would tend to hold wages at a low level, if not even to drive them down, as dispossessed or frustrated tenants or semi-employed small-holders struggled to find full-time work. And we might expect that with the tendency to depend upon full-time employees, heavy and full-time unemployment would grow. But neither of these signs is evident.[21] Agricultural wages rose sharply, admittedly from very low levels, in the period to 1815. There followed a period of some hesitation, but between the 1830s and the 1860s there was further considerable increase, and while it is difficult to find data for mid-century, it appears likely that the rise was well started by 1850. Also there was little sign of unemployment in rural parishes, even in the depressed years of the early 1840s. The explanation must be either a high propensity to migrate in search of better conditions even when the local situation was not worsening, or a particularly strong pull to the towns in the context of a geography which opened rural areas to strong urban influence.[22] In any case the gap between rural and urban wages became narrower in Scotland than, for example, in southern England — a fact which suggests ease of movement from country to town however it might be caused.[23]

The evidence on the propensity to migrate, stemming as it does from mental attitude and the hold of custom, must necessarily be limited, but there are some stray indicators of favourable attitudes in Scotland. The involvement of Scots in overseas affairs both in Europe and in America is well known and of long standing, and although it may have sprung from the restricted opportunities in their own country, a habit of migrating and seeking opportunity wherever it might be found must have grown and become almost hereditary. Within the period of our discussion there is much clearer evidence that the rural population was well accustomed to move about the countryside. Farm servants, in spite of the long period of hire, were notoriously restless, with even married men making move after move without change in the nature of their employment. Thus the successive sons and daughters of individual farm servants can be shown as being born often in a series of different parishes, tracing at least some of the moves of the parents.[24] The movements cannot be so precisely identified for earlier periods but the habit was probably traditional, and in the nineteenth century it is an obvious and ever-present basis for more fundamental shifts into new environments and jobs. Further, the normal sequences of the farm servant's life might well precipitate such decisive changes. Where the main body of the farm labour force was composed of unmarried men, an unshakable and widespread custom in some districts, the intention of marriage might well mean not only loss of the farm servant's immediate job but also of his whole position as a skilled man in the local society.[25] It seems that, failing to get full-time jobs, such men might well neither become day labourers nor take over a croft, but move to a town perhaps to become carters, an occupation in which their acquired skills were not wasted.

The strength of the pull to the towns can in no way be measured and indeed joined the rural stirrings in an indivisible momentum; but it may be judged by certain objective signs — by the size, by the variety and number of jobs, by the level of wages, by the proximity of rural sources of labour. Here we confine ourselves to size and speed of growth.

Towns, indeed, were very unevenly distributed over the country, and just because of geographical position we would expect rural communities to be somewhat differently sensitive to their attractions. A first crude estimate of relative pull may be made by plotting the increase of urban population in different parts of the country (Table 2). It is then found that even in the eighteenth century the western Lowlands were growing disproportionately: 51 per cent of the total urban increase (towns being defined as units which had more than 2000 inhabitants in 1801) came in the four industrial counties of the west.[26] Other important urban growth areas were the eastern industrial counties of Stirling, Clackmannan, West Lothian and Mid Lothian, with 21 per cent of the urban increase, and Angus with 12 per cent.

The actual intake of migrants needed to sustain the total increase of urban population depends upon the prevailing rate of natural increase in the recipient towns. Until 1861, this is a largely unknown factor, but at least from 1801 to 1851 the assumption of a rate of 10 per cent per decade probably gives a more accurate picture of the net intake of migrants than do simple figures of actual increase. Using this measure, we find four main areas of urban attraction, corresponding to the four main cities and therefore widely distributed over the Lowlands.[27] Between them these areas accounted for 94 per cent of urban growth above the assumed natural increase. Each centred on a dominant city but otherwise were of very differing urban constitution and there were great differences in the numbers of immigrants they had evidently attracted. In the Glasgow area, there were two other major and fast-growing centres, Paisley and Greenock, and some forty-eight towns of lesser size together making a considerable call on the migrant streams. Altogether the area accounted for 67 per cent of the excess urban growth. The Edinburgh area, with 12 per cent, was of much less consequence, and indeed growth almost entirely centred on the one city (Leith being considered as part of Edinburgh). Dundee was not far behind with 8 per cent, and the strength of the pull of the area partly derived from the four lesser towns in which linen was still a growing industry. Aberdeen, like Edinburgh, stood very much on its own, but was still very close to the Dundee or Angus level of attraction.

These figures, at best fragile estimates, need some broad qualification. They represent in each case net figures of intake, and since all towns had some outward as well as inward migration, the gross numbers entering a town might well considerably exceed this net increase; moreover this factor alters the relative scale of migration into the main areas. Thus, in 1851 the cities of Edinburgh and Aberdeen had proportionately a much greater number of their native-born in other parts of Scotland than did either Glasgow or Dundee.[28] Another factor altering the estimate of relative pull is the extent to which towns or regions might depend on non-lowland sources for their immigrants; in particular the Highlands and Ireland might make important contributions. This gives an additional reason for downgrading the pull by the West of Scotland on lowland sources and for upgrading Edinburgh and, even more, Aberdeen. In 1851 in Glasgow, 47 per cent of those not born in the city

TABLE 2. *Increase of Population of Urban Parishes*

Region	Actual Increase 1755–1801	Per cent of Total	Actual Increase 1801–1851	Per cent of Total	Excess Growth (beyond Natural Increase)*	Per cent of Total
1. North-East	13,848	6	70,069	8	40,793	7
2. Angus	24,999	12	76,123	8	44,781	8
3. North-Central	11,370	5	51,158	6	12,769	2
4. South-Central	6,226	3	39,971	43	16,492	3
5. West-Central	109,234	51	533,398	57	378,708	67
6. Lothians	45,554	21	131,589	14	65,741	12
7. East Borders	88	—	13,814	1	4,833	1
8. South-West	2,771	1	18,384	2	4,316	1
	214,090	99	934,506	100	568,433	101

Sources: Kyd, *Population Statistics;*
1851 Census, Number of the
Inhabitants.

* Assumed to be 10 per cent per decade.
1. Counties of Nairn, Moray, Banff, Aberdeen, Kincardine.
2. Angus.
3. Fife, Perth, Kinross.
4. Stirling, Clackmannan.
5. Lanark, Renfrew, Ayr, Dunbarton.
6. West Lothian, Mid Lothian, East Lothian.
7. Berwick, Roxburgh, Selkirk, Peebles.
8. Dumfries, Kirkcudbright, Wigton.

came from distant sources; in Edinburgh, drawing less on Ireland and the Highlands, the proportion was 34 per cent, but in Dundee, with its substantial Irish component, it was 40. Aberdeen, of all major urban centres, was the most dependent on purely local and lowland sources and drew only 20 per cent of its immigrants from elsewhere.

In all, then, there were four main types of influence likely to affect the scale of migration out of specific areas — the rate of natural increase, the degree of proximity to growing towns, the nature of agricultural development, and the survival or growth of non-agricultural employment. Population figures from the different areas, with parishes grouped according to their predominant form of employment, give indications sometimes of strength in one or other of these factors but not so as to suggest one generally prevailing predominant force, while very often the evidence is completely ambiguous (Table 3).

The analysis may be helped by distinguishing parishes which through the whole hundred years remained purely rural (that is, they neither contained a substantial industrial population nor did they have more than a third of their people in villages when these were enumerated in the 1861 census); those with appreciable village growth; and those where weaving was important.[29] Fishing and mining villages have been entirely omitted from these calculations.

The actual rate of population increase is a crude measure of the scale of migration but must be used when, as between 1755 and 1801, there can be no meaningful estimate of rates of natural increase. However, in this period there were clear regional differences in actual rates of increase, and these give some indications of the forces at work without offering any easy general explanation. The agricultural parts of the most southerly tier of counties from Berwickshire westwards to Wigton mostly show increases well up to the average rate of growth for the country as a whole, and there may well have been little migration from them, possibly since, of all the Lowlands, this is the area most remote from growing towns. The belt just to the north from Ayrshire across to Fife, traversing the main urbanising sector, would be more closely affected by urban pull, and it is not surprising to find a decrease of population which must, however we may guess at natural increase, indicate a strong migration. These decreases were quite dramatic in the counties of Stirling and East Lothian. The decrease in East Lothian may be significant, for it was a county developing in the same manner and at least as fast as Berwickshire. Perhaps proximity to Edinburgh accounts for its different demographic trend; there was much concentration of farms in the county but intensive cropping was well developed, with, in some parts, the growth of turnip husbandry.[30] Further north again, beyond the Tay, there is certainly evidence of heavy migration, for the picture in rural areas is generally of declining population. Possibly the explanation of decline in these areas, many of which were fairly remote from growing towns — particularly since Aberdeen was in a period of slow growth — was that agrarian change had started, with some consolidation of farms and removal of subtenants, but had not progressed far enough to bring with it the new intensive forms of cropping; the first change on the old methods of cultivation was generally to introduce a succession of sown grasses into the still experimental rotations, while

TABLE 3. *Percentage Change of Population in Rural Parishes*

County	1755-1801			1801-1851			Natural increase 1861-71 %
	Agricultural Parishes	Weaving Parishes	Weaving Villages	Agricultural Parishes	Weaving Parishes	Weaving Villages	
Banff							
Lower	-10			+29			17
Mountain	-13			+33			
Aberdeen							
Lower	-2			+43			
Upland	-27			+39			19
Mountain	-27			+18			
Kincardine	-1			+26			16
Angus							
Coast	+18	+32		+1	+8		
Inland	-14			+5	+27	+41	15
Mountain	-35		+8	-2			
Perth							
Lower	-12	+4	+17	-9	+1	+26	
Carse of Gowrie	+11	+17	-9	-1			10
Mountain	-9			-22			
Stirling	-17			-3			11
Fife	-8	+5	+12	+18	+28	+54	12
West Lothian	-3			+14			19
Mid Lothian	+18			+39			21
East Lothian	-18			+20			14
Berwick	+26			+13			15
Roxburgh	+7			+13			15
Peebles	+18			+15			17
Lanark	+2			+18			17
Dumfries	+19			+22			13
Kirkcudbright	+24			+38			12
Wigton	+41			+87			16
Ayr	+7			+66			16

Sources: Kyd, *Scottish Population Statistics; 1851 Census Great Britain,* Numbers of the Inhabitants.

turnips which were later to be so important in the area had made little progress by the end of the century. The purely agricultural parishes which showed increase were mainly areas of heavy soil whose improvement was early in starting and where intensive wheat-growing became the rule. In addition, not surprisingly, parishes where weaving was a main occupation, although losing some of their natural increase, were also showing some tendency to increase.

The half-century from 1800 brought considerable change in rates of increase of rural population in the one area relative to the other. In terms simply of actual increase of population, there were now four quite clearly distinguishable blocks of counties, or sections of counties, within each of which rural parishes showed demographic similarity. Firstly, there were two areas characterised by considerable increases in the individual parishes: the one in the South-West where, in the counties of Kirkcudbright, Wigton and Ayr, the growth of rural population may well have matched the rate of natural increase; the other in the North-East where growth was considerable, if below natural increase. At the other end of the scale, areas of particularly slow increase, or of actual decline, are found in a belt running southwards from Angus through Perthshire — always outstandingly an area of population loss — into Stirling. Mountain parishes, too, a westerly fringe to several counties, were characterised by loss of population or by increase at notably lower rates than adjacent lowland parishes. The last zone stretched from Fife southwards over the Lothians and into the Borders in a belt broadening to include the westerly counties of Lanark and Dumfries; here, except in Mid Lothian which had considerable growth, were to be found modest or moderate rates of increase ranging between 13 and 22 per cent for the fifty-year period — obviously well below their natural increase.

Evidently no single type of influence explains these differences or the implicitly differing rates of migration. If the rates of natural increase pertaining to specific areas after 1861 are applied to the relevant areas in the period before 1850, there were two areas where high or low rates might explain correspondingly high or low rates of actual increase. The North-East had a high rate of natural increase corresponding to a high actual increase; in Perthshire on the other hand both types of rate were low. It may be that in these two cases the rates of migration were somewhat similar despite the glaring difference in population trend. But such a relationship did not prevail generally. Rates of natural increase were not particularly high in the South-West, whereas they were high in Lanark, where actual increases were moderate. Rates of migration, then, must have varied considerably. Such differences might be explained by varying degrees of proximity to growing urban areas; yet no such clear association appears. Lanarkshire and East Lothian, well situated to meet urban needs, show normal increases of population while Mid Lothian and Ayrshire had high rates of increase in their rural parishes. The last form of explanation might be the autonomous force of agricultural development with the consequent labour needs. The North-East offers a clear example of population trend responding to agricultural needs and opportunities. The expansion of arable acreage continued there till well after 1850, a change that was only possible because of a clearly independent factor, the large reserve of under-utilised land that was available to be opened up for cultivation at the beginning of the period; factors of price and changing agricultural techniques also played their part. The declines or relatively slow increase of the parishes of the mountain fringe had also a clear connection with the development of land usage, although the rage for sheep-farming was felt mainly before 1801. The agricultural spurt in the North-East after 1800 might also be explained as a delayed phase of agricultural improvement, and in general there are suggestions here and there of an alternation in the figures which correspond to different phasing of the move to agricultural re-organisation. The North-East itself swings from decline in the eighteenth century to high rates of increase, while the early-improved areas of the Carse of Gowrie and the coastal strip of Angus swing to low increase after 1800. But again it is not a pattern that can be generalised into an over-all explanation. Over the greater part of the country detailed differences between types of farming — such as cropping, cattle raising, and dairying — do not at all fit the differences of population trend; nor can the timing of improvement be made to fit.

The migrations that we have been examining were a necessary part of a very complete and swift transformation in Scottish society. The rise of Scottish industry, the most obvious aspect of this transformation, was in part sustained, it has recently been argued, by the low cost of labour.[31] Relatively low wages were, in turn, ensured partly by the influx to the industrial areas of migrants from Ireland and from the Highlands. But even greater was the flow from the Lowlands and particularly from the rural Lowlands. The readiness of the rural population to move into industrial work and into towns was surely a prime factor in industrialisation. It cannot, we have seen, be simply explained by any single peculiarity of the Scottish scene. The accidents of geography which set the rising industry so close to substantial rural populations, the semi-rural nature at least of early Scottish factory industry, the underlying propensity to seek for better jobs, the unskilled nature of much of the labour force, resource factors that, as technology developed, created sudden opportunities: all played a part. But also the imminent developments on the countryside as well as the structure of rural society and the pressure of growing population were also surely potent in their influence.

REFERENCES

1. *1871 Census Scotland* (P.P. 1871, lxviii), XIII, Birth-Places of the People, pp. 176–89.

2. Figures for 1755 from J. G. Kyd, *Scottish Population Statistics* (Scottish History Society, 1952), 3rd ser. 44 (Dr. Webster's); for 1801 from *1851 Census Great Britain* (P.P. 1852–3, lxxxvi), Numbers of the Inhabitants.

3. *1851 Census.*

4. *1851 Census.* For the definition and selection of agricultural parishes see below.

5. M. Flinn, ed., *Scottish Population History* (Cambridge, 1976), pp. 441–8. On emigration surveyed at the points of origin see Ian Levitt and Christopher Smout, *The State of the Working Class in Scotland in 1843* (Edinburgh, 1979), pp. 236–49. It is clear at least that the Highlands and Islands were contributing disproportionately large numbers to the emigrant total. Parish details can be traced in *R. C. on the Poor Law* (P'P. 1844, xxiii–xxiv), Answers to Questionnaire, Q.30, which Levitt and Smout have analysed.

6. *1851 Census* (P.P. 1952–3, lxxxviii), Birth-Places of the People.

7. *1851 Census.*

8. M. Flinn, *Scottish Population History*, pp. 14–16.

9. M. L. Parry, 'Changes in the Extent of Improved Farmland', in M. L. Parry and T. R. Slater, eds., *The Making of the Scottish Countryside* (London, 1980), pp. 177–99; I. Carter, *Farm Life in Northeast Scotland* (Edinburgh, 1979), pp. 52–4; M. Gray, 'North-East Agriculture and the Labour Force, 1790–1875', in A. Allan Maclaren, ed., *Social Class in Scotland* (Edinburgh, 1976), p. 94.

10. I. Carter, *Farm Life*, pp. 52-4; M. Gray, 'North-East Agriculture'; M. Gray, 'Scottish Emigration', pp. 148-9.

11. L. R. Timperley, 'Landholding in Eighteenth Century Scotland' in Parry and Slater, *Making of the Scottish Countryside*, pp. 137-52; L. R. Timperley, *A Dictionary of Landownership in Scotland c.1770* (Scottish Record Society, 1976), new series, 5; L. R. Timperley, 'Landownership in Scotland in the 18th Century' (unpublished Ph.D. thesis, University of Edinburgh, 1977).

12. Gray, 'North-East Agriculture', pp. 92-3; *Fourth Report on the Employment of Children, Young Persons and Women*, (P.P. 1870, xiii), App. Pt. 1.

13. L. J. Saunders, *Scottish Democracy* (Edinburgh, 1950), pp. 36-75; Gray, 'Scottish Emigration', pp. 126-7.

14. Carter, *Farm Life*, pp. 28-31; Gray, 'North-East Agriculture', p. 92.

15. Carter, *Farm Life*, pp. 56-60; Gray, 'North-East Agriculture', pp. 93-5; Gray, 'Scottish Emigration', pp. 167-8.

16. *R. C. on Labour* (P.P. 1893-4, xxxvi). The Agricultural Labourer. Scotland, 14-9, 43-122. 288; *Report on the Employment of Children*, App. Pt. 1, 34, 47, 84; T. M. Devine, 'Social Stability in the Eastern Lowlands of Scotland during the Agricultural Revolution, 1780-1830', in T. M. Devine, ed., *Lairds and Improvement in the Scotland of the Enlightenment* (Glasgow, 1979), pp. 62-4.

17. Gray, 'Scottish Emigration', pp. 139-42.

18. *1861 Census Scotland* (P.P. 1864, li), Occupation of the People, 124. But also, for regional variations, see Levitt and Smout, *State of the Scottish Working Class*, p. 76; Devine, 'Social Stability', pp. 64-4.

19. See particularly, *Report on the Employment of Children*, App. Pt' 1, 47, para. 11.

20. T. M. Devine, 'Temporary Migration and the Scottish Higlands in the Nineteenth Century', *Econ Hist Rev*, 2nd Series, xxxii, no. 3, pp. 344-59; Devine, 'Social Stability', pp. 61-4; Gray, 'Sottish Emigration', pp. 141-2.

21. V. Morgan, 'Agricultural Wage Rates in Late Eighteenth Centruy Scotland', *Econ Hist Rev*, 2nd Series, 24 (1971), pp. 181-201; Gray, 'Scottish Emigration', pp. 141-3, 154-5; Devine, 'Social Stability', p. 64.

22. Devine, 'Social Stability', p. 65.

23. See also Levitt and Smout, *State of the Scottish Working Class*, p. 79.

24. Gray, 'Scottish Emigration', p. 161.

25. For local variations in the conditions of hire of farm labour see the answers to Q.22 in *R.C. on the Poor Law*. Levitt and Smout summarise and analyse this information in *State of the Scottish Working Class*, pp. 70-5. See also Devine, 'Social Stability', pp. 61-4; Gray, 'Scottish Emigration', p. 170.

26. Kyd, *Scottish Population; 1851 Census*, Numbers of the Inhabitants.

27. The towns used for this calculation are those listed as such (being 2000 inhabitants or more) in the 1861 census. Throughout it has been necessary to use the total populations of urban parishes.

28. *1851 Census*, Birth-Places of the People.

29. The judgement on what constitutes a weaving parish is necessarily somewhat subjective and liable to error, but none have been placed in the category without fairly strong evidence that weaving was an important occupation. The occupation descriptions given in answer to Q.14, 17 of the *R.C. on the Poor Law* have been particularly helpful. For the agricultural category where there was some doubt as to whether a parish was overwhelmingly agricultural, the policy has been to exclude.

30. T. C. Smout, 'Introduction' to Sir John Sinclair, ed., *The Statistical Account of Scotland, 1791-1799* (Reprint Ed., Wakefield, 1975), Vol. II, pp. ix-xxxvi; T. I. Rae, 'Introduction' in Sinclair, ed., *Statistical Account*, Vol. III, pp. xi-xlv.

31. R. H. Campbell, *The Rise and Fall of Scottish Industry* (Edinburgh, 1980), pp. 15-17.

9

Across the Briny Ocean: Some Thoughts on Irish Emigration to America, 1800–1850

Cormac Ó Gráda

THAT emigration from Ireland was already substantial in the years between Waterloo and the Great Famine is nowadays universally conceded. Then, as later, it was the most favoured means of population control. But the contrast with the post-Famine record, however, the reluctance or inability of the Irish to move in still greater numbers to distant lands, remains an important historiographical theme.[1] The image of peasant multitudes clinging to home, 'like sailors to the mast or hull of a wreck',[2] is given point by the million or more fatalities of the Famine. It must not be forgotten, though, how small overall emigration from Europe was before 1845. Between the Discoveries and that date it is estimated that no more than five million or so Europeans settled in the New World, half of them after 1815.[3] Of the latter, Ireland supplied one-third, ten times more than her population share. No other country contributed as much. In addition, perhaps another six hundred thousand Irish made Great Britain their home between 1815 and 1845.[4] These numbers go a long way towards accounting for the apparently low level of permanent migration *within* Ireland before 1845. Though post-Famine rates put earlier emigrations in the shade, by contemporary standards the pre-Famine Irish must be characterized as 'highly mobile' rather than *adscriptus glebae*.[5]

The extent, nature, and consequences of the pre-Famine outflow have been discussed and debated over the years by Adams, Cousens, Jones, MacDonagh, and others.[6] For such a historically significant phenomenon, the literature is small although of a high quality. From the standpoint of this essay, the general emphasis on the distinctive regional character and social composition of the pre-Famine emigration, and on the tendency of families rather than individuals to dominate, is most relevant. The claim that Catholic emigrants were disproportionately few early in the century, and Adams' point that the outflow was becoming both larger and more proletarian on the eve of the Famine, are also important. My main purpose here is to establish a somewhat clearer profile of the pre-Famine emigrant through the use of contemporary passenger lists and allied material (Part I), and to review some economic aspects of the emigration in light of the data (Part II).

I. 'Who were the Irish emigrants to America before 1845?'[7]

The data base for this paper is information on the age, sex, occupation (usually), and regional origin (sometimes) of over thirty thousand pre-Famine emigrants. The passenger lists used are as follows:[8]

Year	Destination	Source	Number of Emigrants
1803–6	North America	(1)	3603
1819–20	U.S.A.	(2)	1423
1830–9	North America	(3)	1834
1822–39	Boston	(4)	7000
1820–48	New York	(4)	30534

(1) Public Record Office, London
(2) United States Congressional Papers
(3) Ordnance Survey Memoirs (R.I.A., Dublin)
(4) United States Immigration Archives

The 1819–48 United States lists used here all have their origin in the same administrative concern: safeguarding the lives and welfare of the passengers who made the crossing. An act of 2 March, 1819 required the master of a vessel arriving at any U.S. port from another country to present a list of passengers to the collector of the local customs district. The master was supposed to swear to the veracity of the list in the collectors' presence.[9] The 1830–6 lists are a byproduct of legislation to reduce emigration during the Napoleonic Wars.[10] The 1830s Ordnance Survey Memoirs data refer to one northern Irish county only: they were collected as part of a scheme — abortive as it turned out — to accompany the survey with detailed socio-economic and antiquarian reports for each area.[11] While probably incomplete in their coverage, in no case is there a presumption that these data are grossly misleading.

Computer frequency counts and cross-tabulations produced the results summarized in Tables 1–8, which form the basis of our discussion. Let us review the more important findings.

(I) All lists imply that proportionately *more children* and over-35s emigrated before 1845 than later in the century. Overall, fewer women left than men, but for those who travelled unaccompanied, the male concentration is rather remarkable. The number of unaccompanied men exceeded women by two-to-one among the Boston and New York immigrants of the 1820s and 1830s, but the ratio was almost four-to-one in 1819–20 and nine-to-one in 1803–6. This pattern evidently contrasts sharply with the post-Famine picture, but is quite in line with the nineteenth-century norm for other European nationalities. The factors which held down the emigration of Irishwomen early on in the century, and made it blossom later on, are imperfectly understood; however, possible explanations include the relatively harsh life of women in post-Famine Ireland, the increasing demand for domestic servants in America during the second half of the century, and the vast size of the emigration itself.[12] Finally, the data illustrate a feature seemingly common to all Irish nineteenth-century emigrations across the Atlantic: unaccompanied women left at an earlier age than unaccompanied men, many of them in their late teens.[13]

(II) According to Adams, 'the Irish preferred to emigrate in families when they could'. In the case of all groups examined here, 'family' emigrants, in the sense of people of the same surname travelling together, outnumbered unaccompanied emigrants, although the lists imply a stronger unaccompanied element than might be inferred from a reading of the existing literature. Nor were the family units that left typical: on average they were smaller than the average family in the population at large. Some were big, but a substantial majority was of two or three people. The lists show that even in 1803–6 almost seventy per cent of all emigrants left singly, or in parties of two to three people, while seventy-five per cent of the Boston emigrants travelled in parties of three or less. Moreover, the lopsided sex-ratio of the outflow indicates that only a minority of those unaccompanied can have paved the way for the rest of their households. Finally, the prevalence of units of one to three *may* suggest that the majority of emigrants came from a poorer background, but only if Adams' unsupported assertion about preferences holds.[14]

(III) The lists produce a large and, at first bewildering, catalogue of occupations, which I have reduced to six broad categories (Tables 3 and 4). The results should be interpreted with caution: the 1803–6 data are particularly suspect, and probably a goodly proportion of those described therein as 'labourers' were in fact semi-skilled or skilled artisans. For the rest, it is likely that some of those termed 'farmers' in the lists were simply labourers, though I have not attempted to adjust for this. A cautious guess, then, is that perhaps about a third of the men who left before 1820 were farmers or farmers' sons, about a tenth white-collar (gentlemen, merchants, etc.) and the remainder about equally divided between labourers and artisans. The Boston and New York immigrants were less skilled, and only a small proportion of them listed as farmers.[15]

In all lists, artisans are more heavily represented among emigrants than in the population as a whole. This, on the face of it, may look like a 'human capital' or 'skill' drain, a possibility which worried some contemporary critics of pre-Famine emigration. Quick conclusions from the data are not warranted, however, since presumably *some* proportion of these artisans — particularly in the textile sector — were structurally unemployed, and their specific skills were therefore rendered worthless. This after all was an era of unprecedented structural transformation in both Britain and Ireland.[16] In the Boston lists, though not in the others, artisans outside the textile sector tended to be concentrated in the older age-groups, an indication, perhaps, of redundant skills. Interestingly, a few former employers are to be found in the lists. The Boston data, for instance, give one 'ironfounder', four 'manufacturers', twenty-seven 'merchants', and seven 'brewers' and 'distillers'.

(IV) The Derry Ordnance Survey Memoirs are silent on some of the issues discussed so far, but are alone in containing the religious affiliations of emigrants. They indicate that during the 1830s Presbyterians and other Dissenters left in greater numbers than their share in the population would predict, and Catholics and Established Church members less. The same pattern was found for neighbouring Antrim by Adams.[17] The lists also prompt a look at differences in destination across religious affiliation, controlling for area of origin within the county. To avoid the problem of empty or very small cells, I have grouped all parishes providing data into three areas (Table 7). A common pattern within any area might then be regarded as evidence that people of all creeds used the same information flow about the New World in choosing their destination. However, at this level of disaggregation the differences are significant on standard statistical criteria.

(V) The 1803–6 lists also provide details on port of destination. Cross-tabulations by province of origin yield no interesting patterns in this case, but the data suggest that unaccompanied emigrants were rather more prone to go to New York, and families to the more traditional ports such as Baltimore and Philadelphia. Further, as Maldwyn Jones has already pointed out,[18] the lists show that New York had already become the main port of disembarkation for Irish immigrants by the 1800s. During the 1820s and 1830s New York handled at least thirty times as many Irish immigrants as Boston.

The Boston lists show that the great majority of its Irish arrivals proceeded not directly from Ireland, but via the Canadian Maritime ports.[19] Of seven thousand emigrants, over 5,400 took the Canadian route, arriving for the most part in dribs and drabs by smaller ships, some of which seem to have specialised in the traffic. Only 216 arrived directly from Ireland. The Canadian crossing was the third-class route of the day.[20] The role it played in the Boston immigration may mean that the Irish who went there were of a lower socio-economic status than those who preceded them to the States in the 1800s and the 1810s, if not also those who were travelling to New York in the 1820s and 1830s.

(VI) Tables 6a and 6b provide some insight into the changing composition of the Atlantic emigration over time. The New York and other lists suggest that the unaccompanied component, and the female proportion of it, were increasing; the occupational data suggest a rising proportion of labourers, and fewer artisanal and textile workers. Overall the data confirm Adams' claim of a lowering of the socio-economic status of the emigrants after 1835 or so.[21]

(VII) Adams and Cousens have highlighted the Ulster element in pre-Famine emigration.[22] Only the 1803–6 lists provide comprehensive county-of-origin data: they confirm Ulster's pre-eminence at that juncture, with, interestingly enough, the western counties of Donegal and Tyrone to the fore in relative terms. Of the 3215 whose county origins can be traced, almost four-fifths came from Ulster, and another twelve per cent from Leinster. Only Sligo of the Connacht or Munster counties supplied an appreciable number of emigrants, though Sligo was arguably within the west Ulster orbit.

The New York lists (Table 5b) give the county origins of some eleven thousand emigrants. Ulster's share turns out to have still been disproportionately large, but had fallen to only thirty-seven per cent in the period 1820–46. Connacht's share, though always small, rose over time.

II. *Some economic implications*

(I) A comparison of the usual cost of a passage — £4 to £8 — and the annual earnings of a pre-Famine labourer — £10 to £15 — explains the resilience of the hypothesis that a 'poverty trap' prevented the poorest in Ireland from leaving in those years. The 1803–6 data are at least consistent with this: Ulster, the richest of the four provinces, accounted for the lion's share of the emigrants, and non-labourers comfortably outnumbered labourers. The New York data too suggest that Ireland's poorer districts yielded disproportionately small pre-Famine emigrant flows. Qualitative evidence arguing in the same direction is plentiful. Nevertheless the 'poverty trap' hypothesis needs more careful definition, since it was not merely the fare but — more importantly — other transactions, costs of the move and the poorer prospects facing Irish-speaking peasants from the south and west in America that kept down the numbers wanting to leave.[23] A comparison with contemporary European data indicates that not only the Famine, but greatly reduced travel and job-search time, altered the balance after mid-century.[24]

(II) The passenger lists give no straightforward answer to the question, 'Were the emigrants the most talented and ambitious?' As we have just seen, they are elusive even on the simpler problem of determining the outflow of useful skills and training. *A priori* reasoning is of little help in predicting who emigrated. On the one hand, insofar as people who were relatively productive in Ireland in agriculture and other sectors earned incomes related to their specific complementarities with respect to other inputs, there is some theoretical presumption that they would stay. On the other, if emigration is regarded as a lottery, wherein the 'best' leave because the odds of their improving their lot are better, the outcome is reversed.

Our data provide the raw material for one crude test of the educational or literacy level of the emigrants relative to the population as a whole — not exactly what we want, yet relevant nevertheless. Demographers have long noted the association between economic backwardness and illiteracy on the one hand, and 'age-heaping' in censal returns on the other. In poorer countries a disproportionately large number of people give their ages rounded to the nearest zero or five. The Irish census of 1841, the first to publish year-by-year age information, suffers from notoriously extreme age-heaping.[25] A comparison of the 1841 data and those taken from the emigrant lists should, by extension, tell us whether those who left were more or less 'backward' than the average. Many measures of age-heaping have been proposed,[26] but we simply define **I** here as a relative age-heaping index, where

$$\mathbf{I} = \frac{\Sigma \; w_i \; \pi_i}{\Sigma \; w_i \; \pi^{\star}_i}$$

Here w_i equals the share of emigrants aged i in the emigrant flow, and π_i and $\pi^{\star}_i$ the proportion of those in age-bracket i (e.g. 20–4 years) who reported their age as a multiple of ten (e.g. 20) in the lists and the census, respectively. When **I** is unity the population at large and the emigrants age-heaped equally; if **I** is greater than one, the emigrants heaped more.

The results, calculated from the data in Table 8, give $\mathbf{I}_{1803-6} = 1.06$, $\mathbf{I}_{1819-20} = 0.99$, $\mathbf{I}_{1822-39} = 1.11$, and $\mathbf{I}_{1820-46} = 1.13$. No comfort here, then, for the 'brain drain' argument. It might be countered that the lists reflect the ship master's carelessness rather than the passengers' lack of numeracy. Certainly a perusal of some of the lists would give some support to this view, but a comparison with the Swedish pre-1850 data, culled from the same source as some of the Irish lists, suggests that the passengers' numerical ability was indeed being captured.[27]

(III) From an economic standpoint, the notion that emigration was beneficial in the long run, since those who left eventually did well, and the law of diminishing returns worked in favour of those who stayed, is an appealing one. For the pre-Famine period in particular, the argument has a plausible ring to it. Nevertheless, emigration has had its cogent critics, and one of their strongest points is that the self-selected character of the outflow could have hurt the stay-at-homes. There are two main reasons for this, the first of which was discussed above. The second source of putative loss, stemming from the unbalanced age-structure of the emigration, can only be considered briefly here.[28]

Just as the arrival of 'ready-made' workers conferred a human capital boon on nineteenth-century America,[29] it has long been recognised by European writers that the age-selectivity of emigration could simultaneously injure the sending country. The 'loss' follows from the emigrant often spending his unproductive years at home running up debts against family and fellow citizens, but supplying credits in turn under another flag. Whether remittances provide adequate compensation is an open question.[30] We may assume that the average emigrant who left before the age of thirty or thirty-five years had not fully repaid his debts. Full calculations of the loss from this source require assumptions about consumption and earnings at different points over the life cycle, and about remittances. They also require somewhat restrictive assumptions about the nature of the intergenerational transfers that took place. Preliminary estimates of the loss, taking account also of emigration to places other than the United States, range from 0.5 to 2 per cent of contemporary national income. Not a large proportion, certainly, but appreciable in a faltering economy.

(IV) The profile of the New York emigrants of 1847 and 1848 reported in Tables 1, 2, and 3b differs less markedly from those who preceded them in the late 1830s and early 1840s than might be expected. True, they were somewhat more likely to be under fifteen or over thirty-five years of age, and less likely to travel alone; they may also have been less skilled. Moreover, a full sample of Famine emigrants may accentuate the differences. But if these results provide even an approximate description of the outflow, they add an intriguing insight to our understanding of the workings of the Famine. For if the emigrants continued to be disproportionately male and young, the structure of the surviving population implies that the excess deaths of the Famine years were more likely to have been the women, the very young, and the elderly. It is possible, too, that the age and sex structure of the Famine emigration, by leaving behind those most at risk, increased the human toll of those years.[31]

TABLE 1. *Age of Distribution of Irish Emigrants to America, 1800–1900* (in percentage)

Age	1803–5 [1]	1819–20 [2]	1820–46 [3]	1822–39 [4]	1847–8 [3]	1865 [2]	1900 [2]	1841 Population
0–14	13.4	27.8	18.4	19.5	20.5	16.9	8.6	32.8
15–19	11.3	9.6	15.6	11.7	15.1	45.1	50.0	10.8
20–24	25.3	21.9	31.1	28.0	30.2			9.6
25–34	30.6	25.1	24.8	31.1	21.2	25.7	25.2	14.5
35–44	11.4	8.1	5.7	6.3	8.0	7.2	5.4	11.0
45 +	8.1	7.4	4.6	3.4	5.0	5.1	3.8	21.3

Sources: see text
[1] North America
[2] United States
[3] New York
[4] Boston

TABLE 2. Emigrants' Age and Sex, 1800–1850

| | 1803–5 | | | | 1819–20 | | | | 1822–39 | | | | 1820–46 | | | | 1847–48 | | | |
| | Unaccompanied | | Family | | Unaccompanied | | Family | | Unaccompanied | | Family | | Unaccompanied | | Family | | Unaccompanied | | Family | |
Age	M	F	M	F	M	F	M	F	M	F	M	F	M	F	M	F	M	F	M	F
0–14	15	8	214	185	19	7	114	104	60	43	598	573	260	257	1985	1986	72	60	585	544
15–19	154	24	112	100	39	25	37	55	184	299	104	205	936	1178	642	987	208	235	221	269
20–24	432	60	207	174	144	42	82	89	810	407	303	376	3188	1650	1303	1437	628	398	379	396
25–34	424	54	337	241	182	36	101	91	867	235	541	462	2470	794	1473	1308	469	182	361	294
35–44	124	12	148	107	55	12	63	70	153	32	134	111	477	111	420	388	124	57	148	161
45 +	54	12	124	90	5	4	30	14	49	34	69	78	212	128	389	393	51	41	116	101
	1023	172	1142	897	444	127	427	423	2123	1050	1749	1805	7543	4118	6212	6499	1112	973	1810	1765

TABLE 3. *Occupation and Emigrants' Family Status, 1803-5, 1819-20, 1822-39 and 1820-46*

Occupational Category	1803-5 (U.S.)		1819-20 (U.S.)	
	U	F	U	F
1	626 (45.6)	378 (28.1)	124 (31.7)	60 (20.5)
2	88 (6.4)	379 (28.2)	49 (12.3)	54 (18.5)
3	433 (31.6)	516 (38.3)	105 (26.3)	129 (44.2)
4	17 (1.2)	11 (0.8)	52 (13.0)	27 (9.2)
5	206 (15.0)	61 (4.3)	66 (16.5)	22 (7.5)
6	2 (0.0)	1 (0.0)	3 (0.8)	0 (0.0)
	1372 (100.0)	1346 (100.0)	399 (100.0)	292 (100.0)

Occupational Category	1822-39 (Boston)		1820-46 (New York)	
	U	F	U	F
1	1191 (60.0)	840 (66.6)	5554 (60.7)	3499 (52.5)
2	125 (6.3)	107 (8.5)	977 (10.7)	847 (12.7)
3	150 (7.6)	109 (8.6)	1093 (11.9)	1056 (15.8)
4	435 (21.9)	184 (14.6)	1181 (12.9)	1042 (15.6)
5	82 (4.1)	22 (1.7)	193 (2.1)	136 (2.0)
6	3 (0.2)	1 (0.1)	151 (1.7)	83 (1.2)
	1926 (100.0)	1261 (100.0)	9149 (100.0)	6663 (100.0)

1 = labourers, servants
2 = textile workers
3 = farmers
4 = other artisans
5 = white collar
6 = other

TABLE 4. *Occupations of Irish Emigrants to Boston and New York, Compared to the Census Data 1841*
(Percentages)

Occupa-tional Category	Boston		New York		Census 1841	
	Male	*Female*	*Male*	*Female*	*Male*	*Female*
1	62.7	78.6	60.5	63.3	55.4	33.7
2	3.5	11.1	7.0	24.4	7.1	59.3
3	10.4	0.5	15.7	9.2	20.7	1.9
4	20.5	8.1	13.3	2.3	10.5	0.7
5	2.7	1.0	3.6	0.8	4.9	3.4
6	0.2	0.7	—	—	1.5	0.4

TABLE 5A. *Emigrants' Province of Origin, 1803–5*

	Unaccompanied	Family	Total
Leinster	217	185	402
Munster	35	48	83
Ulster	936	1612	2548
Connacht	100	82	182
	1288	1927	3215

TABLE 5B. *New York Emigrants' Province of Origins, 1820–1848*

	1820–34	1835–1846	1847–8
Leinster	897 (38.8)	2361 (38.8)	590 (21.5)
Munster	357 (15.4)	706 (11.6)	375 (13.7)
Ulster	904 (39.1)	2237 (36.7)	1114 (40.6)
Connacht	156 (6.7)	787 (12.9)	663 (24.2)
	2314	6091	2742

TABLE 6A. *The Changing Composition of Emigration Over Time: Sex and Family Status, New York 1820–48*

Period	Unaccompanied		Total	
	Male	Female	Male	Female
1820–9	870 (77.2)	257 (22.8)	1586 (62.2)	963 (37.8)
1830–4	1306 (69.7)	567 (30.3)	2344 (59.1)	1623 (40.9)
1835–9	2177 (64.4)	1206 (35.6)	3936 (57.0)	2968 (43.0)
1840–6	3196 (60.5)	2088 (39.5)	5894 (53.8)	5063 (46.2)
1847–8	1612 (62.4)	973 (37.6)	3422 (55.6)	2738 (44.4)

TABLE 6B. *Occupations, New York 1820–48*

Occupation	1820–34	1835–46	1847–48
1	1956 (48.0)	7097 (60.4)	2719 (60.2)
2	352 (13.5)	1272 (10.8)	591 (13.1)
3	687 (16.9)	1472 (12.5)	506 (11.2)
4	691 (16.9)	1532 (13.0)	580 (12.8)
5	117 (2.9)	212 (1.8)	70 (1.6)
6	74 (1.8)	160 (1.4)	49 (1.1)

TABLE 7. *The Destination of Co. Derry Emigrants of 1835–8 by Religion*
(in percentages)

Destination	Diss.	R.C.	E.C.
A. *West Derry*			
New York	19.3	28.3	14.3
Philadelphia	43.7	16.2	9.5
Quebec	25.3	40.3	47.6
St. Johns	11.7	14.9	28.6

	R.C.	Other
B. *South Derry*		
New York	45.8	20.4
Philadelphia	14.7	18.3
Quebec	32.4	45.5
Other	7.1	15.8
C. *East Derry*		
New York	15.6	11.0
Philadelphia	7.8	27.0
Quebec	55.8	51.6
Other	20.8	10.4

Source: see text.

TABLE 8. *Values of π from Irish passenger lists 1803–1839, the 1841 and 1851 censuses, and Swedish passenger lists 1820–1850*

Ireland 1803–6

Age	π	n
20 – 4	.260	874
30 – 4	.631	374
40 – 4	.690	158
50 – 4	.716	95

Ireland 1819–20

20 – 4	.212	358
30 – 4	.697	132
40 – 4	.704	54
50 – 4	.611	36

Ireland 1822–39

20 – 4	.269	1910
30 – 4	.672	772
40 – 4	.829	199
50 – 4	.771	83

Irish Census 1841, 1851

	$\pi^\star$ 1841	$\pi^\star$ 1851
20 – 4	.308	.338
30 – 4	.498	.517
40 – 4	.576	.661
50 – 4	.617	.604

Sweden 1820–50

	π	n
20 – 4	.261	471
30 – 4	.341	422
40 – 4	.465	243
50 – 4	.380	100

REFERENCES

1. For a quick introduction to the subject, see G. Ó Tuathaigh, *Ireland before the Famine 1798–1848* (Dublin, 1972), pp. 140–2. On the inability/unwillingness to emigrate, e.g. J. C. Beckett, *The Making of Modern Ireland 1603–1923* (London, 1966), p. 344; O. MacDonagh, *A Pattern of Government Growth 1800–60: The Passenger Acts and their Enforcement* (London, 1961), pp. 24–7; P. Taylor, *The Distant Magnet: European Migration to the United States* (London, 1971), pp. 34–5. The comments and advice of Joel Mokyr, Philip Neher and Peter Solar are gratefully acknowledged.

2. MacDonagh, *Pattern of Government Growth*, p. 25, quoting William Cobbett.

3. C. McEvedy and R. Jones, *Atlas of World Population History* (Harmondsworth, 1978), pp. 30–1.

4. Compare Ó Tuathaigh, *Ireland before the Famine*.

5. J. K. Ingram, 'Considerations on the State of Ireland', *Journal of the Statistical and Social Inquiry Society of Ireland*, IV, part xxvi (1864), 14.

6. W. F. Adams, *Ireland and Irish Emigration to the New World from 1815 to the Famine* (New Haven, 1932); S. H. Cousens, 'The Regional Variation in Emigration from Ireland between 1821 and 1841', *Institute of British Geographers, Transactions and Papers*, 37 (1965), pp. 15–30; M. Jones, 'Irish Emigration 1783–1815', in E. R. R. Green, ed., *Essays in Scotch-Irish History* (London, 1969), pp. 48–68; MacDonagh, *Pattern of Government Growth*.

7. Compare C. Erickson's well-known 'Who Were the Emigrants from England and Scotland in the Late Nineteenth Century?', in D. V. Glass and R. Revelle, eds., *Population and Social Change* (London, 1972).

8. The 1803–6 lists come from British Library, Additional Ms. 35932, 'Passengers from Ireland to America'. The 1819–20 lists were published in 1821 in United States State Department, *Letter from the Secretary of State, with a Transcript of the List of Passengers Who Arrived in the United States from 10/1/19 to 9/30/20* (Washington, 1821). The other U.S. lists are deposited in the United States National Immigration Archives, Temple University, Philadelphia; the National Library, Dublin, has microfilm copies. The Ordnance Survey Memoirs are held in the Royal Irish Academy, Dublin.

Brian Trainor, Director of the Public Record Office of Northern Ireland, kindly provided me with the 1803–6 and 1822–39 data in typed, easily codable, form. Joel Mokyr allowed me to use his New York emigrants file (fully explained in his *Why Ireland Starved: A Quantitative and Analytical History of the Irish Economy 1800–1850* (London, 1982, ch. 7). My thanks to them both.

9. The legislation and its background are explained in United States Immigration Commission, *Abstracts of Reports*, vol. 2 (Washington, 1911), pp. 589–91.

10. Jones, 'Irish Emigration'.

11. J. H. Andrews, *A Paper Landscape: The Ordnance Survey in Nineteenth-Century Ireland* (Oxford, 1975), pp. 144–79.

12. R. E. Kennedy, Jr., *The Irish: Emigration, Marriage, and Fertility* (Berkeley, 1973), pp. 66–85; J. J. Lee, 'Women and the Church since the Famine', in M. MacCurtain and D. Ó Corráin, eds., *Women in Irish Society: The Historical Dimension* (Westport, Conn., 1979), pp. 37–45.

13. On the age and sex of European emigrants to the Americas during the nineteenth century, cf. United States Immigration Commission, pp. 5–8; I. Ferenczi, *International Migrations: Statistics* (New York, 1929).

14. The average size of the emigrating Boston 'family', for instance, was just over three. Compare F. J. Carney, 'Aspects of Pre-Famine Irish Household Size: Composition and Differentials', in L. M. Cullen and T. C. Smout, eds., *Comparative Aspects of Scottish and Irish Economic and Social History 1600–1900* (Edinburgh, 1977), pp. 32–46. An exception to the pattern outlined here is provided by Peter Robinson's planned emigration of 1823–5, which carried about three thousand Irish, mainly from Cork, to Upper Canada. This emigration was overwhelmingly a family emigration, for reasons clearly explained in W. Cameron, 'Selecting Peter Robinson's Irish Emigrants', *Social History/Histoire Sociale*, IX no. 17 (1976), 29–46. This latter emigration, it might be noted, much more closely resembled contemporary Scottish Highland emigration than the usual Irish pattern. My cursory inspection of Scottish passenger lists suggests more young people and women, and a higher proportion of family emigrants. See e.g. Home Office, London, 102/18 (lists of passengers aboard the *Sarah* and *Dove* bound for Pictou, Nova Scotia in 1801); Public Archives, Canada, MG 40 C 10 (lists of passengers aboard the *Commerce* out of Greenock in 1820). Scottish emigration is discussed at some length in M. Flinn, ed., *Scottish Population History* (Cambridge, 1977), pp. 93–6, 435, 443–7, but more relevant to the present discussion is M. Flinn, 'Malthus, Emigration and Potatoes in the Scottish North-west, 1770–1870', in L. M. Cullen and T. C. Smout, eds., *Comparative Aspects*, especially pp. 57–8.

15. On difficulties with interpreting the 1803–6 lists, see Jones, 'Irish Emigration'.

16. The disastrous effect on Irish industry and proto-industrial employment may be gauged from a comparison of the occupational details given in the censuses of 1821 and 1841. See C. Ó Gráda, 'Demographic Adjustment and Seasonal Migration in Nineteenth-century Ireland' in L. M. Cullen and F. Furet, eds., *Ireland and France: Towards a Comparative Study of Rural History* (Paris, 1981).

17. Adams, *Ireland and Irish Emigration;* J. H. Johnson, 'Population Movements in County Derry during a Pre-Famine Year', *Proceedings of the Royal Irish Academy,* 60, Section C (1959), pp. 141–62, O.S.M. data are used to answer several related questions.

18. Jones, 'Irish Emigration', p. 60.

19. On the role of the Maritime ports in Irish immigration, see J. S. Martell, *Immigration to and Emigration from Nova Scotia 1815–38* (Halifax, 1942); H. Cowan, *British Emigration to British North America* (Toronto, 1928).

20. There was a fourth-class route to Boston: an indeterminate number made their way there from the Maritimes by foot. See O. Handlin, *The Uprooted* (New York, 1951), pp. 59–60.

21. Adams, *Ireland and Irish Emigration,* ch. 5.

22. *Ibid.,* pp. 118–20, 188, 221; Cousens, 'Regional Variation in Emigration'.

23. On the implausibility of the 'poverty trap' argument after 1850 see C. Ó Gráda, 'On Some Aspects of Nineteenth-century Irish Emigration', in L. M. Cullen and T. C. Smout, eds., *Comparative Aspects.* The importance of seasonal migration from the west and south before 1845 means that the passage money alone — for single young men at least — was no insuperable obstacle to emigration.

24. The huge rise in emigration from England, Germany, and the Scandinavian countries in the 1850s is documented in I. Ferenczi, *International Migrations,* pp. 377–80.

25. As noted by the census commissioners themselves, and discussed in J. Lee, 'Marriage and Population in pre-Famine Ireland', *Economic History Review,* 21 (1968), pp. 289–90.

26. S. Shrycock and J. S. Siegel, *The Methods and Materials of Demography* (Washington, 1973), pp. 700–4. For further analysis along the same lines, using other measures, see J. Mokyr and C. Ó Gráda, 'Emigration and Irish Poverty before 1845' (paper in progress, Northwestern University, Sept. 1981).

27. The Swedish data are taken from N. W. Olsson, *Swedish Passenger Arrivals in New York* (Chicago, 1967).

28. It is discussed in more detail in J. Mokyr, *Why Ireland Starved,* ch. 7; C. Ó Gráda, 'On Some Economic Aspects of Pre-Famine Emigration' (unpublished paper, February 1981); J. Mokyr and C. Ó Gráda, 'Emigration and Irish Poverty'.

29. L. Neal and P. J. Uselding, 'Immigration, a Neglected Source of American Economic Growth: 1790 to 1912', *Oxford Economic Papers,* 24 (1972), pp. 68–88; P. J. Hill, *The Economic Consequences of Immigration into the United States* (New York, 1975).

30. W. Farr, *Vital Statistics* (London, 1885), pp. 59–64; A. Marshall, *Principles of Economics,* Variorum Edition (London, 1961), II, p. 622; F. Kapp, *Immigration and the Commissioners of Emigration* (New York, 1870), pp. 144–7.

31. The author is currently engaged in a study of these issues with Phelim Boyle of the University of British Columbia.

Part IV

Markets and Trade

10

Planned Village Development in Scotland and Ireland, 1700–1850

D. G. Lockhart

THE small towns and villages of both Ireland and Scotland owe much of their early development to landowners who from medieval times until the early twentieth century promoted settlement on their estates. Burghs of barony, plantation towns and villages, and coastal resorts were among the types of settlement that were shaped by landed society.[1] However, the period between 1700 and 1850 was particularly important since it saw the founding of about 600 planned villages which were closely associated with the reorganisation of agriculture, the development of domestic textile industries, spinning mills and bleachfields, the rationalisation of local markets and fairs, and developments in overland transport and harbour construction.[2] It would be expected, therefore, that planned villages were a very diverse type of settlement, and examples of the major categories are shown in Table 1.

TABLE 1. *Types of planned village in Ireland and Scotland*

Agricultural	Non-agricultural
Enclosure and resettling surplus farm population (Lewiston, Inverness-shire)	Textile industries: linen (Glenboy, Leitrim)
Replacement of an existing village as a result of changes to the mansion (demesne) and policy (Adare, Limerick)	Textile industries: woollen Barnbarroch, Kirkcudbrightshire)
	Textile industries: cotton (Linwood, Renfrewshire)
The improvement and cultivation of wasteland (New Pitsligo, Aberdeenshire)	Canal port (Robertstown, Kildare)
Housing estate workers (Seaforde, Down)	Coal port (Troon, Ayrshire)
The management of the forfeited estates in Scotland (Strelitz, Perthshire)	New fishing harbour (Roundstone, Galway)
Sale of agricultural land owned by burgh, guildry and incorporated trades organisations in Scotland (Guildtown, Perthshire)	General cargo port (Westport, Mayo)
	Minor port (Carsethorn, Kirkcudbrightshire)
Markets and fairs (Cornhill, Banffshire)	Adjacent railway station (Ardler, Perthshire)
	Roadside locations attractive to tradesmen (Carrutherstown, Dumfriesshire)
	Residential suburb of an existing town or village (Harryville, Antrim)
	Religious minorities (Gracehill, Antrim)

Some were specialist communities such as fishing and factory villages, while employment in others embraced a range of labouring, craft and textile occupations. Every village, however, was characterised by a carefully regulated layout of streets, building plots and fields, and it was a condition of settlement that each householder adhered to the building and land use regulations contained in his title deeds.

I

Using variations in the motivation for building and the geographical distribution of new foundations, it is possible to divide the period from 1700 to 1850 into four separate phases. As Table 2 shows, planned villages tended to be founded at an earlier date in Ireland, though from the late eighteenth century the number of villages being built in Scotland was much greater.

TABLE 2. *The chronology of village planning in Scotland and Ireland, 1700-1850*

	SCOTLAND				
Region		Period			Total
	1725–69	1770–99	1800–19	1820–50	
Highlands and Islands	5	33	42	11	91
North-East	26	32	42	30	130
East Central	6	19	4	6	35
West Central	10	36	11	2	59
Dumfries and Galloway	7	30	18	3	58
Borders	1	14	2	3	20
	55	164	119	55	393

	IRELAND				
Region		Period			Total
	1700–69	1770–99	1800–19	1820–50	
Ulster	27	15	12	5	59
Munster	16	11	7	7	41
Connaught	14	9	6	4	33
Leinster	17	19	15	4	55
	74	54	40	20	188

Note: These figures are incomplete and recent research by L. M. Cullen on Irish villages suggests that the Irish estimates need to be increased considerably, see Cullen, *Emergence of Modern Ireland,* pp.61–2.
Sources: IRELAND
D. G. Lockhart, 'The Advertising of Towns and Villages in the *Belfast News Letter,* 1738–1825', *Ulster Folklife* XXII (1976), pp. 91–3; *idem.,* 'The Linen Industry and the Advertising of Towns and Villages in Ireland, 1700–1750', *Textile History* VIII, pp. 163–6; S. Lewis, *A topographical dictionary of Ireland* (Port Washington, N.Y. reprint edition, 1970); Cullen, *Emergence of Modern Ireland,* pp. 61–82.
SCOTLAND
D. G. Lockhart, *The planned villages of Scotland 1700–1900* (forthcoming, Edinburgh) and the references cited therein.

The first villages were built in south-east Ireland (Cork and Waterford), Ulster (Down and Tyrone) and in East Lothian, Perthshire and the North-East.[3] In both countries, they were associated with estate improvement, and the growth of the linen industry within existing areas of production as well as in new areas. The founders of these villages were among the most progressive landowners of the time (Cox of Dunmanway, Cork; Cumine of Auchry, Aberdeenshire), and in Scotland several were members of policy-making bodies such as the Board of Trustees for Manufactures and Fisheries (John Mackenzie of Delvine, Perthshire) or were Commissioners of the Forfeited Annexed Estates (Lord Deskford, Banffshire) which provided opportunities to discuss and diffuse knowledge of economic development.[4] It is interesting to note that the success of the early villages led to neighbouring landowners founding villages as well (Villierstown, Waterford; New Byth, Aberdeenshire). Towards the end of the period, the first villages were being built in areas that had experienced little activity (Leitrim, Cavan, Western Isles).

1770–1799

The financial crisis of 1772–3 led to a downturn in village development that lasted almost ten years. The revival of planning in the 1780s in Scotland was largely dependent on the cotton industry, which replaced linen as the major textile in the west-central and Dumfries and Galloway regions.[5] In both areas, the erection of new water-powered spinning mills and bleachfields was accompanied by planned villages (Houston, Renfrewshire; Dalbeattie, Kirkcudbrightshire).[6] This form of development and small cotton weavers' villages (Springfield, Dumfriesshire) account for the majority of places built throughout the South-West.

Fishing villages were the second major innovation in this phase. Most were established in the Highlands and Islands in the years following the founding of the British Fisheries Society (1786). The Society was responsible for Ullapool (Ross and Cromarty), Stein (Inverness-shire) and Tobermory (Argyllshire)[7] while Aultbea (Ross and Cromarty), Dervaig (Argyllshire) and a number of others were begun by private landowners.[8] In other regions, new villages were less numerous, except in the North-East where second villages were built on a number of estates to accommodate displaced tenants (New Leeds, Aberdeenshire).[9]

The functions of villages in Ireland were similar, though in this period the scale of development was much less impressive. The less rapid growth in the fortunes of the linen industry after 1773 meant that few villages were built. However, some landowners chose to encourage alternative manufacturing enterprises such as wool (Ballymurray, Roscommon; Blarney, Cork), cotton (Prosperous, Kildare) and agricultural processing (Fermoy, Cork).[10] Unlike the Scottish cotton industry, cotton manufacturing had a very limited impact upon village development because it was concentrated in existing towns in Ulster, Louth and Dublin.

Relatively few maritime villages were built in the period too but, as in Scotland, harbour development on the west coast led to the founding of villages, and examples of corporate endeavour (Innismacadurn, Sligo) and individual enterprise (Westport and Binghamstown, Mayo) can be found. Development in the West during this phase can best be described as modest due to a lack of adequate roads and the limited funds available for harbour works.[11]

1800–1819

The early decades of the nineteenth century were characterised by a continuation and for a time an intensification of effort in remote areas. Village planning can be explained by clearance of minor tenants from inland areas of Sutherland and their resettlement on the east coast (Brora, Portgower, Helmsdale), large-scale harbour construction in the Moray Firth (Burghead, Morayshire; Cullen, Banffshire)[12] and further maritime villages on the west coasts built to provide alternative employment that would reduce emigration (Clifden, Galway).[13]

Inland villages continued to be founded. Tradesman settlements and agricultural service centres predominate (Springholm, Kirkcudbrightshire; Dufftown, Banffshire; Strokestown, Roscommon). Tradesmen and labourers found work on neighbouring farms, while larger villages provided a wide range of services, including markets, for their hinterland.[14]

1820–1850

By 1820 the development of new villages had begun to slacken. Only in north-east Scotland did vigorous planning persist down to c.1840, while in Ireland, apart from the physical replanning of earlier villages (Abbeyleix, Queen's; Draperstown and Moneymore, Londonderry), new foundations also become infrequent. The Scottish villages fall into three categories: small fishing villages which were founded largely in the North-East (Sandhaven and Burnhaven, Aberdeenshire), weavers' villages dependent for employment on the towns (Padanaram and Newtyle, Angus), and residential villages built on high amenity value coast and countryside sites (Newton of Panbride, Angus; Bridge of Earn, Perthshire).[15]

Ireland's village development followed a parallel course. Maritime villages were found throughout the West and South-West and reflected private enterprise and the support given by the Commissioners of the Irish Fisheries. Residential development occurred on the coast near Dublin (Newtownsmythe) and in east Ulster (Dundrum, Down). The textile villages were built on a much larger scale than previously (Portlaw, Waterford; Sion Mills, Tyrone; Bessbrook, Armagh). Each was associated with a large integrated factory complex and was also intended to satisfy the philanthropic ideals of its founder by providing the workforce with factory employment and a high standard of housing in a pleasant environment.[16]

The development of planned villages ceased after 1850 simply because many of the economic conditions that had favoured their building had diminished in importance. Surplus farm labour could be accommodated in existing villages and in the expansion of larger towns, the scope for building new harbours was largely exhausted, and textile manufacturing was contracting in rural areas. On the other hand, transport development reduced the isolation of rural communities, allowed the penetration of urban manufactured goods and eroded the volume of transactions at village markets and fairs. Landowners presented with conditions which were unfavourable to village development encouraged high status housing in places served by railways (Banchory, Kincardineshire; Bangor, Down) and organised the layout of new streets in existing towns and villages (Buckie, Banffshire). This trend continued down to the First World War, after which time the declining power of the landed aristocracy allowed the initiative to pass to artisan builders.[17]

II

Although planned villages were founded over a period of 150 years and were associated with different types of economic stimuli, the physical planning processes remained little changed throughout. The selection of a suitable site was the most important decision in the early stages of planning. Two major criteria, access and suitable land which was out of lease, influenced site selection. The latter was rarely a hindrance since founding usually coincided with changes in landholdings, and in practice the choice of site was influenced by access to major roads and a water supply, and the existence of fairly level ground. Wherever possible, villages were located on the poorest agricultural land which would yield a high return when used for building. The site was surveyed and a plan of the building plots was made. Recruitment of settlers could then begin. The most widely used method to people a village was the newspaper advertisement, which had the advantage of a wide circulation and the facility to be reprinted in the form of handbills for distribution at markets and churches. A typical advertisement is that of Fuerty (Roscommon):

> THOMAS MITCHELL, of Castlestrange, in the County of Roscommon, Esq; will give great Encouragement to common Weavers to come and settle in the Town of Fuerty, where he has built a Number of good Houses, and intends building more this Summer, which he will give Free, with good Plots, with other Advantages; and constant Work, and the highest Price given in the Kingdom. He has also a great Number of choice Looms already made, which he will also give Free.
> — N.B. great Convenience of Fire and Water to the Town of Fuerty, and in the midst of a fine, plentiful Country.					Feb 20, 1762[18]

Advertising was used to attract substantial numbers of settlers to large villages as well as skilled labour such as weavers. Subsequently, settlers purchased building land at a roup held on the site or by private agreement with estate management.[19] Landowners also relied on friends to help with recruitment by making known the names of interested parties and by recommending textile manufacturers. The choice of manufacturers was one of the most difficult issues to resolve. It was important to ensure that only competent persons began manufacturing since grants and loans were usually provided by the landowner to help industry establish itself. In contrast, active recruitment was sometimes unnecessary, for instance when a planned village replaced an existing village that was being cleared to make way for landscaped policies around a mansion.

Responsibility for building was divided between the landowner and the inhabitants, though the proportions varied considerably from one community to the next. As a rule landowners built houses to attract skilled labour and to provide accommodation for estate workers. In most places, landowners provided only the public buildings — a church, an inn, and in Ireland a market hall — and the inhabitants engaged masons or built their own housing.

Once building arrangements were finalised, settlers were able to migrate. Migration patterns have been analysed in detail for north-east Scotland and indicate that at least 90 per cent of migrants were drawn from distances of less than ten miles and that many had originated in the estate or from adjacent estates.[20] The main exceptions to such a short distance pattern were fishermen, senior textile manufacturers who were encouraged to set up small factories in areas remote from major manufacturing centres, and experienced Ulster weavers who were attracted by advertisements of cheap land offered by southern landowners.

Planned villages were populated by labourers, craftsmen and maritime and textile workers. Analysis of employment suggests that the majority of planned villages can be assigned to one of three contrasting structures:

(i) the tradesmen-agricultural type peopled by labourers, craftsmen, merchants and textile workers.

(ii) the maritime type in which fishermen and ship masters were the most common occupations.

(iii) mill settlements inhabited by textile workers.

Examples of each type of employment structure are shown in Table 3.

TABLE 3. *Employment of male household heads in selected planned villages*

	Rathfriland, Down 1819	Cairneyhill, Fife 1797	Hopeman, Morayshire 1814	Glencaple, Dumfriess-shire (new feus) 1812	New Lanark, Lanarkshire 1810	Houston, Renf'wshire 1785
Agricultural	4.4	21.7	5.0	—	—	21.4
Maritime	—	—	48.3	43.8	—	3.6
Crafts (including textiles)	46.0	73.9	41.7	31.2	97.3 (71.8)	60.7
Manu-facturers	0.7	—	—	—	—	—
Shops, Inns	32.8	—	1.7	12.5	1.2	3.6
Professional	8.8	4.4	—	12.5	1.5	10.7
Miscellan-eous	7.3	—	3.3	—	—	—

Notes:(1) The classification is that given by M. C. Storrie, 'Landholdings and population on Arran from the late eighteenth century', *Scottish Studies* XI (1967), p. 70.
(2) The data for New Lanark include all adult males. The percentage figure in brackets is for employment in the mills.

Sources:
Public Record Office of Northern Ireland, McCracken Mss T 1181/2, The general directory of Newry and Armagh . . . for 1820 (Newry, 1819); Scottish Record Office, Particular Register of Sasines (Fife), county abridgement, 1781–1820; Wink and Mackenzie, Solicitors, Elgin, Hopeman estate book, no. 1, 1807–1854; Dumfries Town Council A4/2, Charter Book 1801–1829; University of Glasgow, papers of Gourock Ropework Company UGD 42/31/7, New Lanark population statistics; Scottish Record Office, Particular Register of Sasines (Renfrewshire) county abridgement, 1781–1820.

Full-time employment was available only for fishermen and the workforce of factory villages built in the 1780s in Scotland and during the early nineteenth century in Ireland. Tradesmen and labourers, however, relied on subsistence gardening and part-time farming to supplement their earnings. Inland villages had large kitchen gardens, and the adjacent fields (lotted lands) were subdivided into rectangular lots rented by the inhabitants. The villagers kept horses, cattle and sheep and grew fodder crops and vegetables on these lands. A typical example was Stuartfield (Aberdeenshire) in which the average holding was 6.3 acres, while the mean area of lotted lands in a sample of fourteen villages in north-east Scotland during the early nineteenth century was 174.8 acres.[21] Lotted lands covered a much smaller area in fishing villages where only the craftsmen were part-time cultivators, and were absent in factory villages.[22]

Apart from part-time farming, perhaps the most important economic activity was domestic spinning and weaving undertaken for urban manufacturers whose agents supplied raw materials and collected finished products. Thus William Pirie and Company of Aberdeen had agencies in several centrally located villages (New Deer and Strichen, Aberdeenshire). A similar dependency on urban manufacturers existed in Strathmore during the 1820s and 1830s when the growth and diversity of alternative employment in Dundee led to a shortage of labour in the physically demanding coarse sector. Manufacturers recruited weavers from among lower income groups in rural areas, and by 1833 it was estimated that two-thirds of Dundee manufacturers' coarse linen cloth was woven outside the city. The small planned villages built at this time (Padanaram and Newtyle) were founded specifically to accommodate weavers.[23]

Another type of textile organisation was the small factory established by the landowner and managed by a resident manufacturer who employed village weavers. Small factories were begun in newly built villages located in districts where there was little tradition of commercial manufacturing and were intended to generate employment. Unfortunately, production in such locations was isolated from the source of supplies and the market. Further, uncertain trading conditions discouraged experienced manufacturers and, instead, senior journeymen wanting to begin business or speculators hoping to secure sufficient credit to permit a period of profitable manufacturing tended to gravitate to new villages.

Records of the linen industry of Archiestown (Morayshire) have survived and provide evidence of the difficulties of establishing industry. A journeyman with previous employment experience at Mungo Rannie's bleachfield in Cullen was recruited in 1761 and was joined two years later by three weavers from Huntly (Aberdeenshire), another established centre of the linen industry. Loans amounting to £300 were granted by Sir Archibald Grant; however, by 1765 annual losses were running at about £200. Problems such as high transport and production costs and the indifferent quality of the brown cloth put the industry at an immediate disadvantage. Sir Archibald arranged for William Sandeman of Perth to act as consultant, which led to an improvement in quality, ironically just as the market became depressed. By 1769, the journeyman pleaded bankruptcy and shortly afterwards emigrated to the West Indies. Commercial production of linen cloth ceased after his departure and Sandeman, aware of the impracticability of a revival, urged reclamation of the moss that surrounded the village as the best method of employing the population.[24] A similar fate seems to have befallen many other schemes underwritten by landowners (Dunmanway; Grantown-on-Spey, Morayshire).[25]

Landowners were also partners in small manufacturing companies in which the initial investment was shared among a group of landowning friends, merchants and manufacturers. The introduction of partners may have spread risks and assisted in marketing, but death and disputes among the partners and difficult trading conditions allied to lack of vertical integration, which manifested itself in the inability of some companies to train their own apprentices and the absence of a lint mill or bleachfield at the village, meant that such ventures too were usually short-lived (New Byth and Cuminestown, Aberdeenshire).[26]

The failure of small-scale manufacturing together with the increasing scale and complexity of the textile industry after 1780 gradually led to disillusionment among landowners. Instead landowners chose simply to provide the site for industry while manufacturers, merchants and artisans invested in plant and machinery (Friockheim, Angus).[27] On coastal estates, harbour construction was a major exception to the declining investment role of the landowner in industry during the nineteenth century. Here, unlike the inland village where textile manufacturing had at best been a support measure for the local economy, success in attracting fishermen was directly related to the provision of an adequate harbour infrastructure. We can now turn to the question of the level of investment required to build villages and to deal with the profits which a landowner might expect from having a village on his estate.

III

A large volume of evidence has survived which indicates that landowners regarded the founding of planned villages as a reliable method of increasing the rental of their estates.[28] The evidence of contemporary writers, too, points to much higher rents being obtained from building plots and land adjacent to small towns and villages than from land let to farmers.[29] It is more difficult, however, to calculate precisely the profitability of planned villages or to compare their performance with other outlets for landed investment on the estate such as the improvement of wasteland.[30] Data for expenditure and income were only available for approximately 10 per cent of the villages, and even among this sample there are gaps for particular cost elements. All that one can hope to do is to indicate the costs of planning and the income derived from a cross-section of villages representative in terms of their size and type of economic activities. Expenditure took three forms. The first type of cost was related to recruitment and included newspaper advertising, fees paid to display handbills and entertainment at auctions of building plots. Each of these activities absorbed relatively small sums of money, and total expenditure rarely exceeded £30.00.[31] Second, the creation of the infrastructure, comprising surveyors' fees, laying out the streets, providing the water supply, erecting public buildings, and in some places the provision of houses, accounted for a larger percentage of total costs. The third element of expenditure was costs incurred in the formation of industrial development and harbours, and although occurring in a minority of villages, they were nevertheless particularly expensive projects to fund.

Support for textile industries varied considerably. On the one hand, initial equipment grants to weavers rarely exceeded £100 per person, and the funding of small weaving companies could be achieved with investments of about £300 (Grantown-on-Spey); however, the scale of investment sharply increased in those settlements where factories were built; thus £3000 was spent at Spinningdale (Sutherland) and £8000 at Douglastown (Angus) on a mill and workers' housing.[32] The greatest investments were made in the factory villages of central Scotland, and in 1838 the works, machinery and housing at Catrine (Ayrshire) and Deanston (Perthshire) were valued at £101,263.24 and £178,720.34.[33] Such levels of investment were atypical and were achieved primarily by the input of merchant and manufacturers' capital.[34] Harbours on the other hand continued to attract landed investment throughout the nineteenth century. The initial costs were rarely very high due to repairs and extension schemes being used to accommodate the increasing size of fishing fleets. There is much evidence to suggest that harbour construction was a considerable strain on landowners' resources. The construction of a new harbour at Burghead (Morayshire) proved too expensive for Sir Archibald Dunbar of Northfield, and instead a consortium of local lairds were responsible for raising more than £11,000 towards the total cost of £14,000, the balance being paid by the government, while many other landowners sought assistance from the Board of Fisheries and the Commissioners of the Irish Fisheries.[35]

The majority of villages, then, were not endowed with large-scale manufacturing or maritime enterprises, and costs can fairly be described as modest. Least cost locations, such as those alongside an existing road or a small grid-iron plan on a flat site, could be developed c.1800 for a few hundred pounds (Cummingstown, Morayshire).[36] On a slightly larger scale a fishing village comprising a street of houses and harbour improvements was completed at Sarclet (Caithness) at a cost of £950.[37] Even the largest villages of the North-East could be built during the late eighteenth century for less than £5000. Grantown-on-Spey cost Sir James Grant about £3000 between 1765 and 1792, and the principal recruitment and infrastructure costs of founding New Pitsligo (Aberdeenshire) are known to have been less than £3500.[38]

Income came from feu-duties and rents of building plots, rent of fields and peat diggings, and harbour dues. Profits arose from the fact that building plots contributed a greater rent than an identical acreage leased to a farmer. A similar argument applied to the lotted lands which were always rented at higher rates than farm fields. In addition, fields that were reclaimed from wasteland, although initially rent-free to encourage improvement, subsequently contributed to the rental. The rent of such land rose rapidly after improvement; for instance at Hopeman an increase from £0.12 to £3.00 per acre was recorded over a five-year period.[39]

TABLE 4. *Income from building plots and lotted lands on selected planned villages*

Village	date	feu-duty (and number of building plots)	rent (and acreage of lotted lands)
Burghead, Morayshire	1827	£2.40 (268)	none
Cummingstown, Morayshire	1829	£0.50 (36)	£1.25 (103)
New Pitsligo, Aberdeenshire	1807	£0.50 (166)	£1.36 initially rent free (234)
Pitcairngreen, Perthshire	1798	£1.00–£1.25 (20)	£1.75 (144.5)
Gasstown, Dumfriesshire	1812	£0.50–£1.55 (33)	none
Dundrum, Down	1836	£2.00 minimum (20)	no information
Glenavy, Antrim	1749	£0.60 (24)	£0.30 (192)

Sources:
S.R.O., Particular Register of Sasines RS 29/18 p. 270; National Library of Scotland (N.L.S.), Gordon Cumming Papers, Deposit 175, box 132, Land out of lease at Port Cumming Whitsunday 1829; N.L.S., Fettercairn Papers Acc 4796 (first deposit), box 31, Draft notes for a memorial regarding the land rights of the feuars of New Pitsligo, 30 November 1870; N.L.S., Lynedoch Papers Acc 2540, box 3 bundle 4, Missives of offer for Pitcairngreen pendicles, 1798–99; Dumfries Town Council A 4/2, Charter book, 1801–1829; Public Record Office of Northern Ireland, Downshire Papers, D 671/C/45/26, Advertisement for building houses at Dundrum, 1811; ibid., D 671/L5/3, Dundrum leases, 1819–36; *Belfast Newsletter,* 5 January, 1749; Public Record Office of N. Ireland, D 491/8, Indenture, Lord Conway and Andrew Hare.

By comparison, harbour revenue was relatively small and insufficient to compensate for high construction costs. Landowners could reduce their outlay by petitioning the Board of Fisheries for financial assistance, but acceptance of a grant led to disqualification from levying tolls on fishing vessels using a grant-aided harbour.[40] Sandhaven (Aberdeenshire) illustrates the financial problems associated with harbour construction (see Table 5), and although the statistics are incomplete, they indicate nevertheless that construction costs were never recovered. On the other hand some indirect benefits would arise, such as savings on the transport of coal, lime and agricultural produce, and good harbour facilities would make a village more attractive to settlers.[41] Moreover, revenue from feu-duties in large maritime villages was sufficient to offset harbour construction and maintenance costs.

It is difficult to calculate the exact amount of profit which individual villages yielded or the number of years which elapsed before a profit was recorded. The incomplete survival of accounts and rentals and differing regulations which incorporated concessionary rents during the initial years of settlement make forecasting hazardous. What one can suggest is that during the early years of a village's existence, costs exceeded revenue. Thereafter, however, the balance shifted steadily towards higher rents as the population increased and land was improved, and lower costs once the infrastructure had been completed. In the long term, the

TABLE 5. *Harbour expenditure and revenue at Sandhaven, Aberdeenshire, 1838–1936*

Year	expenditure (£)	revenue (£)	comments
1838–40	4205.00	none	Board and landowner shared costs in the ratio 3:1
1841–8	70.54	56.22	
1866–71	721.00	267.00	
1873	not available	59.00	
1876–85	22716.00	609.00	dues for 1885 only
June 1906– May 1936	395.40	576.48	

Sources:
N.L.S., Fettercairn Papers, Acc 4796 (first deposit) box 43, Memorandum as to the harbour of Sandhaven and Pitullie; S.R.O., Records of the Board of Agriculture and Fisheries AF 7/12, Harbours — General Account and Index, f. 16; *Banffshire Journal,* 19 October 1886; Middlemuir Farm Office, Strichen, Sandhaven Harbour Master's cash book from June 1906.

rise in rent which occurred was often spectacular, especially where lotted lands were cultivated by the villagers.[42]

IV

It has been shown that planned villages were a feature of the development of the economies of both countries. Recent research by Cullen has suggested that some 500 villages were founded in Ireland.[43] A similar figure could be presented for Scotland if burghs of barony, which commonly show planned characteristics, are added to the planned villages built between 1725 and 1850. A second attribute of Scottish and Irish villages was the similarity of the planning methods which resulted in the creation of improved standards of housing, regular street plans and large central squares, many of which are still prominent features of the landscape. Thirdly, the villages have been shown to have played a key role in social and economic changes in the countryside, notably through easing the redistribution of labour after enclosure, the promotion of textile and fishing industries, and the relocation of markets and fairs. The pattern of village founding suggests that economic development in the Irish and Scottish countryside was superficially similar during much of the eighteenth century when a majority of villages were peopled by part-time farmers, craftsmen and domestic textile workers and had local market functions. There is, however, some evidence of divergence by 1800. Relatively few maritime villages were founded in Ireland, due mainly to the failure to develop west-coast fishing harbours. Differences in the scale of manufacturing between the two economies become apparent after 1790 and are reflected in the greater number of factory and printfield villages being built throughout central Scotland. The period of divergence continued during the early nineteenth century, but by the 1830s the rate of planned village founding was in decline in both countries. Factors such as the stagnation of rural industries, the decline of the influence of landowners on the course of economic growth, improved overland transport, and the large number of existing towns and villages, greatly reduced opportunities for further planning. Planned villages were no longer related to the growth sectors of the economy, and further planning lingered down to the 1850s only in a few remote areas and in suburban locations which were attractive to those employed in the professions.[44]

REFERENCES

1. G. S. Pryde, *The Burghs of Scotland* (Glasgow, 1965); *idem.*, 'The Scottish burgh of barony in decline 1707-1908', *Proceedings of the Royal Philosophical Society of Glasgow* LXXIII (1948-9), pp. 43-64; G. Camblin, *The Town in Ulster* (Belfast, 1951); R. A. Butlin, *The development of the Irish town* (London, 1977).

2. Previous publications on planned villages include: J. M. Houston, 'Village planning in Scotland: 1745-1845', *Advancement of Science* V (1948), pp. 129-32; T. C. Smout, 'The landowner and the planned village in Scotland, 1730-1830', in N. T. Phillipson and R. Mitchison, eds., *Scotland in the age of improvement* (Edinburgh, 1970), pp. 73-106; D. G. Lockhart, 'The planned villages', in M. L. Parry and T. R. Slater, eds., *The making of the Scottish countryside* (London, 1980), pp. 249-70; L. M. Cullen, *The emergence of modern Ireland 1600-1900* (London, 1981), pp. 61-82.

3. D. G. Lockhart, 'Select documents XXXIII: Dunanway, Co. Cork 1746-9', *Irish Historical Studies* XX (1976), p. 171; C. Gill, *The rise of the Irish Linen industry* (Oxford, 1925); D. G. Lockhart, 'The evolution of the planned villages of north-east Scotland, c.1700-c.1900' (unpublished Ph.D. thesis, University of Dundee, 1974), vol. 1, pp. 37-42.

4. Lockhart, 'Evolution of planned villages', vol. 1, pp. 29-31.

5. J. P. Shaw, 'The new rural industries: water power and textiles', in Parry and Slater, eds., *Making of the Scottish countryside*, pp. 298-9.

6. *Glasgow Mercury*, 4 January 1781; *Old Statistical Account* XI (1794), p. 73; G. Crawford, *The history of the shire of Renfrew . . . continued to the present period by William Semple* (Paisley, 1782), pp. 106, 145, 170-2, 257-61.

7. *Caledonian Mercury*, 8 March 1788; 22 June 1789; J. Dunlop, *The British Fisheries Society 1786-1893* (Edinburgh, 1978). A further village was built by the Society at Pulteneytown near Wick in 1808.

8. *Edinburgh Evening Courant*, 3 December 1789; 2 March 1799; J. Macdonald, *General view of the agriculture of the Hebrides* (Edinburgh, 1811), pp. 684-5.

9. *Aberdeen Journal*, 27 March 1798.

10. *Belfast Newsletter*, 9-13 July 1784; A. Young, *Tour in Ireland, 1776-1779* (London, 1892), pp. 313-4; Gill, *op.cit.*, pp. 229-31; Rev. H. Townsend, *Statistical survey of the county of Cork* (Dublin, 1810), pp. 490-4.

11. P.P., 1823 (383) X, Fourth report of the Commissioners of the Irish fisheries, 1822, p. 26; J. McParlan, *Statistical survey of the county of Mayo* (Dublin, 1802), p. 85; P. Knight, *Erris in the 'Irish Highlands'* (Dublin, 1836), pp. 68-71.

12. R. J. Adam, ed., *Papers on Sutherland estate management 1802-16* (Scottish History Society, 4th series, 8 & 9); *Inverness Journal*, 20 May 1808; Lockhart, 'Evolution of Planned Villages', vol. 1, pp. 236-46.

13. H. Dutton, *A statistical and agricultural survey of the county of Galway* (Dublin, 1824), p. 339; P.P. 1827 (487) LI, Eighth report of the Commissioners of the Irish fisheries for the year ended 5th April 1827, p. 37.

14. D. Frew, *The parish of Urr: a history* (Dalbeattie, 1909), pp. 89-90, 101, 106; *Aberdeen Journal*, 22 January 1817; I. Weld, *Statistical survey of the county of Roscommon* (Dublin, 1832), pp. 319-27.

15. Lockhart, 'Evolution of Planned Villages', vol. 2; *Perth Courier*, 23 May 1823.

16. D. Dickson, 'Aspects of the Irish cotton industry', in L. M. Cullen and T. C. Smout, eds., *Comparative aspects of Scottish and Irish economic and social history 1600-1900*

(Edinburgh, 1977), p. 111; S. C. Hall, *Ireland, its scenery, character, etc* (London, 1841–3), I, pp. 309–10; III, pp. 43–5; Camblin, *The Town in Ulster*, pp. 99–101.

17. *Belfast Newsletter*, 16 July 1833 (Holywood, Down); Macdonald Collection, Department of Geography, University of Aberdeen, plans of Aboyne and Crathes estates; Lockhart, 'Evolution of Planned Villages', vol. 1, pp. 320–3.

18. *Dublin Journal*, 20–23 February 1762. For a comment on the linen industry of Fuerty, see R. Stephenson, *Reports and observations 1760-61* (Dublin, 1762), p. 61.

19. W. and J. Cook, W.S., Edinburgh, Chartulary of the Brucklay Estates (1844), pp. 12–18.

20. D. G. Lockhart, 'Sources for studies of migration to estate villages in north-east Scotland, 1750-1850' *The Local Historian* XIV (1980), pp. 35–43.

21. D. G. Lockhart, 'Evolution of Planned Villages', p. 150 and pp. 155–6; National Library of Scotland (N.L.S.), Lynedoch Papers Acc 2540 box 3 indicates that the villagers of Pitcairngreen, Perthshire had lots of two or four acres and a cow pasture. For an account of holdings in the lotted lands of Rathfriland, Down, see P.P. XXIII 1840, Reports from Assistant Commissioners on the condition of the Handloom Weavers, pp. 635–6.

22. Scottish Record Office (S.R.O.), British Fisheries Society Papers, GD 9/366/2, Hints and observations regarding fishers and fishing villages . . . March 1808; see Young, *Tour in Ireland*, p. 226 for the case against weavers being allowed large gardens and lotted lands; *New Statistical Account* V (1845), p. 138 (Catrine, Ayrshire).

23. Lockhart, 'Evolution of Planned Villages', vol. 1, pp. 200–02.

24. Ibid., pp. 203–207.

25. Ibid., pp. 207–208; Sir R. Cox, *A letter from Sir Richard Cox, Bart to Thomas Prior, Esq.* (Dublin, 1749), pp. 15–6.

26. Lockhart, 'Evolution of Planned Villages', vol. 2, p. 212: National Register of Archives, Scotland (N.R.A.), Grant of Monymusk Papers, 099, uniform box G, bundle 29. Thomas Anderson to Sir Archibald Grant, Archiestown, 26 January 1768; ibid., Copy of the expence Thos Anderson is at in sending two weavers to be instructed by Messrs Biggars 1765. (Since research was completed the Grant of Monymusk Papers have been deposited in the S.R.O., reference GD 345).

27. Lockhart, 'Evolution of Planned Villages', vol. 2, pp. 103–4; Shaw, 'New Rural Industries', pp. 294–7.

28. N.R.A., Grant of Monymusk Papers, uniform box H, bundle 15, Sir Archibald Grant to Archibald Grant, 29 December 1762; Sheffield Central Library, Wharncliffe Muniments, Wh.M. 277, Andrew Dalgairns to Lord Wharncliffe, 3 January 1832.

29. G. S. Mackenzie, *A survey of the counties of Ross and Cromarty* (London, 1810), p. 249; D. Ure, *General View of the agriculture of the county of Kinross* (Edinburgh, 1979), p. 23; P. Graham, *Agricultural survey of Kinross-shire* (Edinburgh, 1814), p. 146; W. Singer, *General View of the agriculture of Dumfries* (Edinburgh, 1812), p. 596.

30. Lockhart, 'Evolution of Planned Villages', vol. 1, pp. 291–3.

31. N.L.S. Fettercairn Papers (first deposit), box 37, Discharged account, Jas Chalmers & Coy advertisements anent New pitsligo, 11 July 1796; ibid. box 36, Discharged account, Sir Wm Forbes to Joseph Hendry for advertising New pitsligo Markets at difft Parish Kirks, 10 March 1798; N.L.S. Gordon Cumming Papers, deposit 175, box 125, Receipt, John Young for advertising Rose Isle, Dollas Ec & Fues, 1811.

32. N.R.A., Grant of Monymusk Papers, uniform box G, bundle 24, Accot. of feus sett in Archiestown and the money given by Sir Archd Grant . . . 15 Septr 1764; S.R.O. Seafield Papers GD 248/443, Scroll contract of copartnery. The Grantown Linen Coy, October 1769; *OSA* VIII (1793), p. 377; *Dundee Advertiser*, 3 November 1809.

33. University of Glasgow Archives, Papers of James Finlay & Co., Ltd., UGD 91/76. Statements and calculations for works at Ballindalloch, Deanston and Catrine, 1835-57.

34. T. M. Devine, 'An eighteenth-century business élite: Glasgow West India merchants, c.1750-1815', *Scottish Historical Review* LVII (1978), pp. 45–6.

35. *Aberdeen Journal,* 9 September 1801; N.R.A., Dunbar of Northfield Papers 065, box 15b, Archibald Dunbar W.S. to Sir Archibald Dunbar, 9 December 1802; *Caledonian Mercury,* 13 January 1803; S.R.O., Seafield Papers GD 248/623, Copys of Conveyances and Deeds Ec. relative to the Town and Harbour of Burgh-head, 1808.

36. N.L.S., Gordon Cumming Papers, box 155, State of Payments on (Accot) of Port Cumming, Donald Smith's Account Book, p. 78.

37. J. Henderson, *General View of the agriculture of Caithness* (London, 1812), appendix, p. 54.

38. S.R.O., Seafield Papers, GD 248/25/2/3, notes c.1792. These indicate that Grantown-on-Spey cost Sir James Grant £3000 'to establish forward and encourage the village and its industries in the period 1765 to 1792'; N.L.S., Fettercairn Papers, second deposit, box 73, Scroll account of agricultural improvements in Buchan . . . 1784 to 1800; ibid., first deposit, box 40. Account of estimated sums for building and other operations carried on at New Pitsligo, 1806.

39. Adam, ed., *Sutherland Estate Management,* p. 18.

40. N.L.S., Fettercairn Papers, first deposit, box 43, Bond by Sir John Stuart Forbes . . . in favour of Commissioners of the white herring fishery c.1838.

41. S.R.O., North West Securities Ltd., Papers of William Mackenzie W.S., GD 271/50/27, William Young to William Mackenzie, 25 May 1829; ibid., GD 271/114/32, Sir J. W. Mackenzie to William Mackenzie, 25 April 1832.

42. N.L.S., Gordon Cumming Papers, box 62, Plan of part of the village of Cummingstown by George Johnstone, 1809; ibid., box 132. Land out of lease at Port Cumming Whitsunday 1829; P.P. 1894 (238) XI, Report from the Select Committee on Feus and Leases (Scotland), 1894, pp. 17–18 and p. 29; Young, *Tour in Ireland,* pp. 314-5.

43. Cullen, *The emergence of modern Ireland,* pp. 61–82.

44. *Ibid.,* pp. 80–1; examples of Scottish villages can be located in: Lockhart, 'Evolution of Planned Villages', vol. 2.

11

Settlement Development and Trading in Ireland, 1600–1800: A Preliminary Investigation

Patrick O'Flanagan

THE significance of trading activity as a stimulus to the growth of new settlement and indeed to the expansion of existing settlement has been recognised as crucial in many societies, past and present.[1] But in Ireland little or no attention has been paid to trading activity as a catalyst of urban or proto-urban evolution.[2] The study of settlement form rather than of settlement function has acted as the focus of most rural settlement studies in Ireland, and hence the analysis of generative processes has been relatively neglected. Recently Irish settlement studies have become more broadly based, with a wider range of investigative approaches being applied,[3] and results from some of these approaches are revealing the existence of much more complex and varied conditions affecting settlement trends, with massive and profound changes even in the most recent past. Our task here in this preliminary review is relatively simple; it is to suggest that an examination of the changing patterns of market location may provide a general pointer to shifts in regional economic performance over time; secondly, we wish to make an initial exploration of the general impact of market functions on settlements themselves.

As is the case for Scotland and indeed for most parts of Western Europe, the source materials detailing market foundation in Ireland are by no means comprehensive.[4] There are many gaps in the information set out in the 1853 Report on Irish fairs and markets, which is the most comprehensive compendium on the formal development of markets in Ireland.[5] This Report provides some general data on the site, licensee and patent date of each market, but little else. There was no systematic information gathered on the current or former activity at individual markets, which seriously qualified the Report's value. We have little information, there or elsewhere, on the degree to which specialised markets developed, or on the volume, type and nature of transactions. Few quantitative data are available in any form relating to tolls, fines, taxes, rents or turnover, especially during the seventeenth century, and it is difficult to reconstruct the networks and trade flows generated by such markets; changes in the hierarchy of market centres in Ireland over the past two hundred years must, as yet, remain elusive. We are left at present

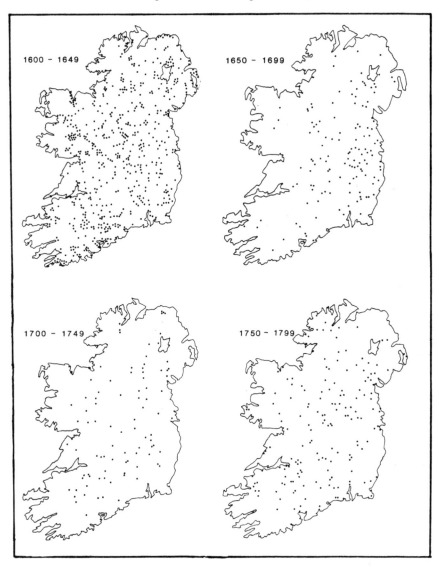

1600 – 1649

1650 – 1699

1700 – 1749

1750 – 1799

Dates of Market Foundation

with the fairly comprehensive evidence relating to the dates on which patents were granted for the holding of individual markets. The problem is of course that many market places were already in existence prior to being awarded a patent, so that the confirmation of a patent and the germination or growth of a settlement were by no means synchronous. There is the obvious temptation to assume some relationship between patent confirmation and urban growth when in fact it is often impossible to distinguish between cause-effect dichotomies. There is also the problem of estimating the number of unlicensed centres, seemingly quite large at least in the nineteenth century; furthermore, records rarely indicate when centres ceased to trade or when some of them came to be revived. With so little information to go on, we are by no means near a position where trading hinterlands since 1600 can be delineated with any degree of accuracy, nor can we at present judge how far the changing density of market centres may be used as a barometer of regional economic development. Legal, social and political considerations may have significantly influenced the timing of formal market creation, in some areas more than others.

The beginning of the seventeenth century did not of course witness the start of marketing at fixed, licensed centres in Ireland. The Anglo-Normans established, in some areas at least, a complex and dense network of market centres, where later hierarchical arrangements often became apparent.[6] Gaelic society had by this time also devised a series of trading institutions which in organisation may have been not unlike those observed in some so-called underdeveloped areas in Africa and elsewhere.[7] It would be an almost impossible task to ascertain how many of these medieval centres actually managed to retain market functions up to the seventeenth century, or even to Tudor times. Several of the centres recorded in the 1853 Report as being without patents were clearly market sites long before the beginning of the seventeenth century.[8]

When the Commissioners made their Report, there were only 349 market places functioning in Ireland; at the same time there were four times that number of fair sites in operation. Less than a dozen market places had been granted patents after 1800, which indicates that a phase of contraction in the number of market sites had begun by that date, due most likely to communications and other technological changes. It would seem from the Report that the rate of new market creation reached an all-time high during the first quarter of the seventeenth century, when more than five hundred centres were awarded patents. To this number must be added those medieval creations still active in the early seventeenth century, plus the illegal, unpatented centres which most likely sprang up in response to the relatively buoyant economic conditions at that period. This figure of five hundred 'new' market centres was at least three times the total number of pre-Tudor market patents. In England, by contrast, the peak of market density — as indicated by the recorded number of patents granted — was the Tudor period.[9] It has been suggested that the intense localism of the English agrarian economy at that stage helped to account for such a high number.[10] In Scotland the greatest flurry of market foundation was slightly later than in Ireland — in the post-Restoration period.[11] Can these periods of highest market-patent confirmation be regarded as critical stages in the economic development of their respective economies? There are problems of comparison: in England the average population of the market towns by the seventeenth century was in the order of 600 to 1000 people, whereas in Ireland and Scotland market settlements with over a hundred people were relatively rare.[12] Desertion of centres was commonplace in Scotland and England, and Everitt makes the point that the studies of deserted market centres may be as significant as those of other types of deserted settlements.[13] But in Ireland complete desertion of post-Elizabethan market centres was unusual (although it would be difficult to suggest a broadly acceptable definition of 'desertion'). However, this may not be so true of medieval and sixteenth-century creations; the study of market origins and development before the seventeenth century should help to indicate the degree to which the marketing and internal trading structure in Ireland of the post-plantation period was shaped by earlier events.

Certainly, by comparison with many other countries in Europe during the first quarter of the seventeenth century, market density in Ireland was relatively high, suggesting that many people were directly or indirectly participating in commercial economic activity with varying degrees of intensity. It is also true that, given the relatively high density of markets, the production of saleable surpluses must have been a constant rather than a sporadic occurrence, as few markets could have survived with an irregular supply of materials. Between 1600 and 1649 the 'turnover' rate of market sites seems to have been at its highest, helped perhaps by the economic and political instability at the end of this period: in Co. Mayo, for example, thirty-one of the forty-odd markets granted patents during this period had failed by the mid-nineteenth century. The Map for 1600–49 shows that the density of markets over the country at that stage was quite uneven — with some perplexing concentrations, notably in parts of the west of Ireland. Lower densities of markets in other areas were not necessarily a function of weaker trading organisation or institutions, for in some areas larger and more vigorous markets may have already eliminated local competition; in some districts unprocessed or semi-processed commodities may have been shipped directly overseas without passing through any market place.

Market foundation after 1650 was never to be as rapid or as spatially 'footloose' as before (see Maps). Few new market patents were granted in the very poorly served areas until after 1750. More often than not, centres in such 'disadvantaged' districts were located close to existing market places, and after a short career they seem to have been usually obliged to abandon their market functions, being unable to offer effective competition, Binghamstown's surrender to Belmullet (Co. Mayo) being a case in point. There can be little doubt that the intensity of market patent confirmation over time acts as a general indicator of the development of the national economy, but major regional and local processes are concealed by concentrating on national trends. Indeed it is the analysis of the changing regional incidence of market patent grants that offers some of the more tantalising challenges in this kind of study.

There remains the problem of what contribution these marketing activities made to the overall character of settlements in which they were sited. By comparison with other European countries, especially England, formally planned market towns seem to have been quite rare in Ireland. Market functions often developed long after the foundation of many settlements. Buildings directly associated with marketing activities are quite rare throughout Ireland, except in larger centres, but they are sometimes found in smaller, often landlord-developed villages or towns, Glanworth (Co. Cork), with its market-house overlooking a triangular green, being a good example.[14] Other marketing accoutrements such as pounds, fairgreens or fairgrounds are sited as a rule on the edge of, or at a small distance from the edge of, settlements. Rarely, as at Kilpatrick, Co. Cork, are fairgreens sited in a central position dominating the morphology of an entire settlement. In general the contribution of marketing activities to the formal layout of settlement has been slight, and as an influence such activity has tended to modify rather than reshape or re-organise the morphology of settlements. It is also of importance to note that in at least the counties of south Munster there is invariably a correspondence between civil parish centre (church, graveyard, etc.) and the market site, implying that here and probably elsewhere in Ireland many of these parish centres retained an important economic function to the end of the eighteenth century, serving as significant foci for many small communities, despite their religious background. Given the existence of close on five hundred market villages or towns in Ireland at the beginning of the nineteenth century, the view that there was a weak development of central places in pre-nineteenth century Ireland requires some modification.

REFERENCES

1. W. W. Parker and E. L. Jones, *European Peasants and their Markets* (Princeton, 1975), and M. Mirables Bedera and J. M. Casas Tomes, 'Mercados Periodicos de Galicia, Distribucion Espacial, Frequencia, Rango y Area de Influencia', *Consejo Superior de Investigaciones Cientificas* (Madrid, 1974).

2. See, for example, R. H. Buchanan, 'Rural Settlement in Ireland', in N. Stephens and R. E. Glascock, eds., *Irish Geographical Studies* (Belfast, 1970), pp. 146–161.

3. D. Harkness and M. O'Dowd, eds., *The Town in Ireland: Historical Studies XIV* (Belfast, 1981).

4. I. Whyte, *Agriculture and Society in Seventeenth-Century Scotland* (Edinburgh, 1979).

5. *Report of the Commissioners appointed to Inquire into the State of the Fairs and Markets in Ireland* (P.P. 1852–3, XLI).

6. B. J. Graham, *Medieval Irish Settlement,* Historical Geography Research Series, 3 (Norwich, 1980).

7. B. W. Hodder, 'Some Comments on the Origins of Traditional Markets in Africa', *Trans. Inst. Br. Geogr.* 36 (1965), pp. 97–105.

8. *Fairs and Markets Rep.* P.P. 1852–3, XLI.

9. *Ibid.*

10. A. Everitt, 'The Marketing of Agricultural Produce', in Joan Thirsk, ed., *The Agrarian History of England and Wales IV: 1500-1640* (Cambridge, 1967), pp. 466–594.

11. Whyte, *Agriculture and Society.*

12. A. Everitt, 'Marketing of Agricultural Produce', pp. 466–594.

13. T. Jones Hughes, 'Landlordism in the Mullet of Mayo', *Irish Geogr.* IV (1959–1960).

14. For a different view on certain aspects of rural settlement development over the same period, see L. M. Cullen, *The Emergence of Modern Ireland 1600-1900* (London, 1981), pp. 61–82.

12

Scottish–Irish Trade in the Eighteenth Century

Laura E. Cochran

ALTHOUGH the aim of this paper is to identify sources of growth for the Scottish and Irish economies in their mutual trade, it must be recognised from the outset that commerce between these two countries in the eighteenth century was not of major importance to either country. It is thus apparent that any sources of expansion in Scottish-Irish trade are unlikely to have had a major impact on the national economies of Scotland and Ireland. This discussion, therefore, will concentrate on the impact of Scottish-Irish trade on certain regions of Scotland and Ireland and on particular aspects of agriculture, industry and commerce.

In common with both the Irish and Scottish economies in the early eighteenth century, Scottish-Irish trade showed few signs of marked growth in the first three decades of the century.[1] From mid-century, however (when statistics are once again extant), until the end of the century, Scottish-Irish trade grew at 2.4 per cent per annum. A considerable part of this growth was, of course, a reflection of population increase and general economic development. Trade growth was also encouraged by the increasingly complementary nature of Scottish and Irish production and by the proximity of the two countries and their separation by sea which, in the eighteenth century, gave this commerce a marked cost advantage over land-based exchange. The general growth of trade within the British imperial territories, as well as the beneficial effects of certain pieces of commercial legislation — notably the Treaty of Union of 1707, the Linen Bounty Acts from 1742 onwards and the repeal of the Cattle Acts in 1758/9 — had identifiably positive effects on Scottish-Irish business relationships. Within this context four main issues will be considered: first, the additional or distinctive demands which Scottish-Irish trade placed on agriculture, industry and commerce in the two countries; second, the importance of the raw materials and foodstuffs which the trade provided; third, its significance in the development of ports and the shipping industry and, finally, the relationship of trade expansion to the evolution of the mercantile community.

I

Trade with Scotland placed few distinctive demands upon Irish agricultural and industrial production. Indeed, Irish trade with Scotland was so similar in composition to Anglo-Irish trade that it could be regarded as merely a minor branch of Ireland's 'British' commerce.[2] Also, while trade with Scotland placed additional demands on Irish production of grain, provisions and linen, the significance of these demands in quantitative terms was generally slight when compared with total Irish exports of these goods.

In regional terms, it is apparent that in the early decades of the century the export of oats, oatmeal and other provisions to Scotland from the north-east of Ireland was an important means by which local farmers marketed their agrarian surplus and boosted cash incomes. Similarly, the predominance of Belfast in the exportation of Irish linen to Scotland, again early in the century, possibly indicates a disproportionate concentration on production for the Scottish market in the north-east of Ireland. Throughout the century, however, the overwhelming predominance of the port of Dublin in shipping goods to Scotland obscures the origin of Irish goods and thus any evidence of local concentrations of production for the Scottish market.

Although in Scotland a similar situation prevailed, in that the Clyde ports handled most Scottish exports to Ireland, it is nonetheless apparent that the west of Scotland, particularly the west-central belt, was most involved in production for the Irish market with the major exception of exports of 'plain' linen produced in the east of Scotland. The Scottish industry which depended most heavily on Irish demand was the Ayrshire coal-mining industry. Increasing demand for coal in the Dublin market, in particular, provided the main motivation for the large-scale investment in Ayrshire mining in the late seventeenth and early eighteenth centuries, and it has been estimated that, throughout the eighteenth century, somewhere in the region of 50 per cent of Ayrshire coal production was exported to Ireland.[3] The link between local economic development in western Ayrshire in the eighteenth century and the coal trade to Ireland is therefore undisputed. Much capital and labour was channelled into mining and transportation and, as well as encouraging the growth of ancillary trades and other coal-burning industries in the area, this trade also provided additional demand for local agriculture. It must be emphasised, however, that the significance of Irish demand for Ayrshire coal was of limited national significance since the Ayrshire field is reckoned to have produced only 10 per cent of total Scottish coal production even at the end of the century.[4]

The main Scottish manufactured goods sent to Ireland were textiles and, latterly, glass, metal goods and chemicals. While the main difficulty in assessing the impact of Irish demand on the production of these goods is the lack of statistical data on total production levels, it can nevertheless be suggested that Ireland provided a considerable additional market for Scottish kentings (a type of fine linen),[5] carpets, glassware (mainly green-glass bottles and window glass) and certain chemicals used in the textile industry, notably sulphuric acid. These goods were almost all produced in west-central Scotland, mostly in and around Glasgow, and in themselves provide an interesting reflection of the increasing diversity of the late eighteenth-century economy of the west of Scotland.

For a large part of that century the most distinctive demand placed upon Scottish commerce by Ireland was her demand for large quantities of colonial goods. During the golden era of the Clyde's colonial commerce — the middle decades of the eighteenth century — Ireland was not the main market for Scottish re-exports of tobacco: continental Europe, and Holland and France in particular, retained that distinction.[6] With the outbreak of the American War of Independence, however, tobacco supplies from America were disrupted and Scotland's main continental markets were temporarily reduced. In this situation the Irish market not only remained open to Scottish re-exports of tobacco (it took almost all Scottish re-exports of tobacco during the war years) but also, by continuing to buy Scottish tobacco at greatly increased prices, allowed Glasgow merchants to cover their increased costs in importing tobacco and to realise an adequate return on accumulated stocks. After the war, however, continental markets once again dominated Scottish re-exports of tobacco.

Throughout the second half of the eighteenth century re-exports of muscovado sugar from Scotland to Ireland represented, on average, 20 per cent of the value of total Scottish exports to Ireland, and in the period from 1755 to 1779 Ireland took over 50 per cent of all the muscovado sugar imported into Scotland. Although legislative changes in 1780 — which allowed Ireland to trade directly with the British colonies in North America — caused considerable concern among Scottish colonial merchants, the subsequent decline in Scottish re-exports of tobacco and muscovado sugar to Ireland was not due to a sustained increase in Irish-American trade. Indeed, by the end of the century Ireland obtained most of her tobacco and muscovado sugar supplies via England. From the 1780s onwards, the increase in Scottish domestic demand for American products, notably muscovado sugar and cotton wool, seems to have ensured that Scottish merchants concentrated on supplying the domestic market at the expense of their previous dominance in the Irish market for such products. However, re-exports still remained a significant element in the value of Scottish exports to Ireland: in 1795, for example, representing 30 per cent of all goods.

Particularly in the middle decades of the eighteenth century, therefore, Ireland provided substantial additional demand for re-exports of tobacco and muscovado sugar from Scotland. While the significance of this demand for the general economic development of the west of Scotland largely depends on the significance granted to Scottish colonial commerce as a whole[7], it is apparent that these substantial and valuable re-exports from Scotland to Ireland gave Scotland a great measure of purchasing power in Ireland (and indirectly in London, through Irish bills on London) which could be used in the furtherance of Scottish commerce and the importation of raw materials and foodstuffs.

II

While Scotland provided a significant proportion of total Irish imports of fish, fine linens, tobacco and muscovado sugar, England also supplied Ireland with coal and most manufactured goods in far greater quantities than did Scotland. Ireland, on the other hand, was Scotland's major overseas source of grain, provisions, linen and raw hides and skins, and three of these imports, namely linen, linen yarn and hides/skins, made direct contributions to Scottish industry and commerce.

The bulk of Scottish imports of Irish linen were destined for the Scottish domestic market but, in the middle years of the century, a significant proportion of linen imports from Ireland was re-exported to America (in the two sample years, 1764 and 1774, about 50 and 75 per cent respectively), thus contributing to the expansion of Scottish colonial commerce. While the Scottish linen industry appears to have turned to Ireland for large supplies of linen yarn only when other sources failed, both in the 1780s and 1790s the disruption of normal sources due to war forced Scottish and English manufacturers to import greatly increased quantities of Irish linen yarn. The only other production goods imported into Scotland from Ireland in significant quantities were the hides and skins derived from the Irish cattle industry, which were subsequently used in the expanding Scottish tanning and leather-working manufacture.

Scottish imports of Irish foodstuffs made a rather less direct, but possibly more important, contribution to Scottish economic expansion. Throughout the eighteenth century Ireland was Scotland's largest and most reliable overseas supplier of oats and oatmeal, the staple grain foodstuff, and towards the end of the century increasingly large quantities of grain were imported into Scotland from Ireland. Rough estimates suggest that in the early decades of the eighteenth century Irish imports could have fed around 2,000 people per annum, or about 0.2 per cent of the Scottish population, and in the 1790s around 40,000 people per annum (2.5 per cent of the Scottish population).[8] However, the real influence of these food supplies was much greater than such estimates can suggest because the consumption of Irish supplies was concentrated in the west-central belt of Scotland, and trade was also mainly limited to late winter and spring when domestic supplies began to run out. Moreover, by generally reducing grain price increases in the west of Scotland and by possibly even preventing serious food shortage on occasion, these imports must have had a positive effect on the pace of economic development, industrialisation and urbanisation in that area.

Although imported in less impressive quantities than Irish grain, Irish salted provisions (mainly beef and pork) also made an important contribution to the Scottish food supply and, indirectly, to the vigour of the shipping industry. Irish salted provisions were used mainly as crews' stores on trading vessels operating out of the Clyde ports. As provisions represented a major element of the operating costs of trading vessels, their supply and cost was an important consideration in seaborne commerce, and in this way Irish provisions made a small, but recognisable, contribution to the success of western Scottish overseas trade.

III

The growth of Scottish-Irish trade had very limited effects on most of the ports through which it passed. At the major Irish ports of Dublin, Belfast and Cork, trade with Scotland was of relatively minor importance compared with English and more distant trades. Similarly, at Greenock and Port Glasgow trade with Ireland could have placed few additional demands on existing facilities. Three exceptions to this general conclusion must be mentioned, however, and these relate to the Ayrshire ports, the small ports of the north-east of Ireland and of the north-west of Scotland, and, finally, the 'transit' ports of Stranraer, Portpatrick, Donaghadee and Larne. In all three cases Scottish-Irish trade represented an exceptionally high proportion of all trade conducted.

While special facilities were provided at Ayrshire harbours for the more efficient handling of coal exports to Ireland, their only effect was on the coal trade, as little other trade passed through them. Similarly, at the 'transit' ports there appears to have been little opportunity for the local economies to take advantage, to any great extent, of the considerable amount of Scottish and Irish business, consisting mainly of livestock and textiles, passing through them. It could be argued that it was in the small ports around the north-east coast of Ireland and in those scattered around the fringes of the north-west Highlands and Islands that Scottish-Irish trade had its greatest impact. Often, for ports in the north-west of Scotland, the trade in fish to Ireland was one of their main sources of realisable income and a source of vital grain supplies. Small mixed cargoes of linen, linen yarn and foodstuffs from the north-eastern Irish ports to the Clyde were the bases of an interchange of local Irish surpluses and the acquisition of Scottish coal, fish and miscellaneous manufactured goods. The growth of Scottish-Irish trade at these tiny ports, however, had no significant ramifications for the national economies of Scotland and Ireland or for the development of other important trades or industries at these ports.

The effect on the shipping industry of growth in Scottish-Irish trade was rather more significant than its effect on the ports. The relatively bulky nature of many of the products traded between Scotland and Ireland meant that this trade occupied a disproportionate share of available shipping. In the 1770s and 1780s, for example, trade with Ireland occupied one-third of Scotland's total overseas shipping capacity while representing only one-fifth of the value of Scotland's overseas trade.[9] However, the average individual tonnage of ships trading between Scotland and Ireland was relatively small and does not appear to have increased significantly in the course of the century. In 1794, ships trading with Ireland and operating out of Greenock and Port Glasgow had an average tonnage of 72 tons, compared with 165 tons for those engaged in North American commerce and 145 tons for those trading with western Europe (excluding Ireland). Another estimate suggests an overall average of 40 tons for all ships trading between Scotland and Ireland towards the end of the century.[10] Since the average tonnage of ships in Scottish-Irish trade remained relatively low, their total number must have risen to accommodate the growth in trade. At the western Scottish ports the number of Irish entries and clearances, combined, amounted to 456 in 1744 and rose to 1,592 in 1794. Apart from the increased employment of seamen and the encouragement to shipbuilding and ancillary trades which this growth engendered, these small ships were used in alternative trades, notably in coastal commerce and in the 'buss' fishery. Occasionally the larger vessels used in Scottish-Irish trade made more distant voyages: for example, Ayrshire colliers occasionally went to the Baltic for timber. Alternatively, vessels designed for use in the transatlantic trades often made one or two late-season sailings between Scotland and Ireland, usually carrying goods derived from, or destined for, American markets.

A great deal of the volume of Scottish-Irish trade — and thus a great deal of the shipping engaged in the trade — sprang from the Ayrshire coal trade. In this trade, however, there existed a considerable capacity for lightweight goods to be exported along with coal to Ireland and, on the return voyage, a vast capacity in ballast. Only towards the end of the century were Scottish textiles exported to Ireland along with the coal and limestone imported in return: thus utilising a small part of this capacity.

IV

The preliminary conclusions of an ongoing study of the merchants involved in Scottish-Irish trade do not suggest that great fortunes were often made in this sector of commerce.[11] The majority of Scottish merchants involved in the trade were relatively modest men of business, and a great many others were closer to the level of enterprising ships' masters. A very small number of the Glasgow mercantile élite were involved: often only in the very specialised and presumably very profitable aspects of the trade such as the re-exportation of tobacco and muscovado sugar. By the end of the century it is apparent that manufacturers were becoming increasingly involved in the direct marketing of their products in Ireland and, although some of these men were of high standing in the west of Scotland business community, they were essentially producers turning to Scottish-Irish trade to assist their sales rather than traders becoming involved in Scottish manufacturing industry.

The typical merchant usually belonged to Greenock or Port Glasgow (not Glasgow) and often acted on behalf of larger Glasgow merchants. His prime interest was specifically in trade, and he combined his interest in Irish commerce with other coastal trades and the west-highland fishing industry. Some of these merchants were also engaged, in company with others, in business with the Continent — particularly northern Europe — and with America, though rarely to any great extent. Their industrial interests, from what evidence is available, were minimal, extending at most to shares in local 'works' or part-time involvement in ancillary trades such as coopering. The merchants of this class, identified as having been involved in Scottish-Irish trade at some point in the final three decades of the eighteenth century, showed few signs of marked advancement in wealth or diversification of interests over this period.

It is not entirely surprising that members of the Glasgow mercantile élite — that is, those identified as major tobacco and sugar importers in the middle decades of the century[12] — appear to have played a relatively small direct role in the re-export of tobacco to Ireland as, generally, the Irish market for tobacco was of secondary importance in the Scottish tobacco trade.[13] However, there was a marked contrast between the social and economic standing of the merchants dealing in tobacco re-exports to Ireland and those traders involved in the re-exportation of muscovado sugar. As the Irish market comprised the single largest external market for the Scottish muscovado sugar trade, the major merchants were inevitably heavily involved. In 1774, for example, Alexander Houston & Co. handled 24 per cent of all muscovado sugar re-exports from the Clyde to Ireland, and the firm of Connell &

Sommervell handled another 17 per cent, while in 1794 partnerships involving James McDowall, Robert Houston Rae, William Bell, Robert Dunmore and Patrick and Francis Murray handled 59 per cent of such re-exports.[14]

The letter and account books of Alexander Houston & Co., Glasgow form one of the best available sources of information on the operation of a Scottish firm engaged in West Indian and Irish trade in the final quarter of the eighteenth century.[15] Although the particular years, 1777–1778, covered by the letter book which contains information on Irish trade cannot be regarded as typical, due to the disruption to trade caused by the American War of Independence, it is reasonable to assume that the major importance of the Irish market in Alexander Houston & Co.'s considerations in these years was not entirely exceptional. This letter book reveals that although the firm had well-established links with Dublin and Belfast merchants and sugar-refiners, they rarely acted on their own account and more usually acted on commission for Irish merchants. As well as the stated $2\frac{1}{2}$ per cent commission on Irish transactions which was charged by Houston & Co., they also controlled the price paid to West Indian planters for whom they also acted on commission. From their relatively secure position as sizeable middlemen in the sugar trade, Houston & Co. (along with other similar firms) controlled the market without tying up their financial resources in stocks of West Indian products.

Throughout the second half of the century, textile manufacturers in the west of Scotland were directly involved in the marketing of their products in Ireland and in importing Irish linen to Scotland. Men such as Humphrey and John Barbour, John How and William Orr — all manufacturers in and around Paisley — and Alexander Speirs, who combined his manufacturing interests with a vast mercantile enterprise, not only acted as exporters and importers of textiles between Scotland and Ireland but also maintained shops or warehouses in Dublin city-centre. Although Alexander Speirs conducted a great deal of his trading business in the Clyde ports, both he and more particularly the Paisley manufacturers also used the Ayrshire port of Irvine extensively in the handling of their textile trade.[16] Similarly, towards the end of the century, the business interests of William Dixon of the Govan Colliery and John Dixon of the Dumbarton Glass Works Co. led them to send large joint cargoes of coal and glass from Port Glasgow to Ireland.[17]

The preliminary nature of this study of mercantile groups in Scottish-Irish trade means of course that those merchants engaged in other business activities, as well as Scottish-Irish trade, were relatively easier to identify than those merchants whose main livelihood was obtained in Scottish-Irish commerce. However, given that the main purpose of this paper is the identification of sources of growth in Scottish-Irish trade, the concentration on those with interests wider than this sector is not felt to be necessarily disadvantageous.[18]

V

Although the national impact of Scottish-Irish trade on both countries was small, it is clear that Irish commerce was of greater significance for Scotland than was Scottish trade for Ireland. This may be partly explained by the relative sizes of the

Scottish and Irish populations and by the lack of data on Anglo-Scottish trade, which possibly enhances the significance of Scottish overseas trade generally. It is nonetheless apparent that Irish commerce was not merely Scotland's second most valuable overseas trade, it was also an integral part of Scotland's external trading relations.

From the early decades of the eighteenth century until the 1780s the expansion of Scottish-Irish trade was largely dependent on the growth of Scottish colonial commerce as the re-export of colonial goods to Ireland and the Continent considerably extended Scotland's external purchasing power throughout the period. Although legislation favouring Scottish colonial commerce was important in fostering this trade, the notable success of Scottish merchants in this field was also related to their enterprise and skill, and to the development of an appropriate social and economic infrastructure in the west of Scotland. The apparent absence of such favourable factors in Ireland and the increasing English domination of the Irish economy meant that the removal of legislative barriers in 1780 did not engender a significant expansion in direct Irish-American commerce.

Moreover, the steady growth of trade with Ireland throughout the eighteenth century undoubtedly had a stabilising effect on Scottish overseas trade as a whole. This effect was particularly noticeable during the American War of Independence when many of Scotland's other trading areas in North America and continental Europe were disrupted and the Irish market temporarily absorbed a substantial amount of additional Scottish business.

While the role of American products in Scottish exports to Ireland is one of the most important findings to have emerged from this study of Scottish-Irish trade, the continuing Irish dependence on agriculture and the domestically organised linen industry for her exports to Scotland and the growing industrial diversity of Scottish exports to Ireland were also striking features. Although these factory-produced Scottish exports reflected the advance of manufacturing industry in that country, the increasing importation of grain from Ireland challenges any assumption that improvements in Scottish agriculture ensured the production of sufficient grain to feed the population in all but exceptionally poor years. Scotland's financial ability to import these large quantities of grain without provoking regular crises in the balance of payments did, however, reflect the increasing diversification of the Scottish economy and its ability to export colonial goods and, increasingly, manufactured goods in return for food and raw materials.

REFERENCES

1. Unless otherwise noted, the statistics referred to in this paper were derived from Public Record Office (P.R.O.) Scottish and Irish Ledgers of Imports and Exports, Customs 14 & 15 and Scottish Record Office (S.R.O.) Scottish Collectors' Quarterly Accounts, E 504. For a discussion of these statistics see L. E. Cochran, 'Scottish Trade with Ireland in the Eighteenth Century' (unpublished Ph.D. thesis, University of Stirling, 1980).
2. See L. M. Cullen, *Anglo-Irish Trade, 1660–1800* (Manchester, 1968).

3. C. Whatley, 'The Process of Industrialisation in Ayrshire, c.1707–1871' (unpublished Ph.D. thesis, University of Strathclyde, 1975), p. 56.

4. J. U. Nef, *The Rise of the British Coal Industry* (London, 1932), II, p. 355.

5. A. J. Durie, *The Scottish Linen Industry in the Eighteenth Century* (Edinburgh, 1979), p. 148.

6. T. M. Devine, *The Tobacco Lords* (Edinburgh, 1975), p. 65.

7. See T. M. Devine, 'Colonial Commerce and the Scottish Economy, 1730–1815', in L. M. Cullen and T. C. Smout, eds., *Comparative Aspects of Scottish and Irish Economic and Social History 1600–1900* (Edinburgh, 1977), pp. 177–190.

8. Estimates based on information contained in K. H. Connell, *The Population of Ireland 1750–1845* (Oxford, 1950), pp. 122–3, 139; *Fifth Annual Report of the Board of Supervision for the Relief of the Poor in Scotland* (P.P. 1851, XXVI), in R. H. Campbell and J. B. A. Dow, eds., *Source Book of Scottish Economic and Social History* (Oxford, 1968), pp. 181–2; W. Cobbett, *Tour in Scotland, 1832* (London, 1833), in Campbell and Dow, *Source Book,* pp. 215–7.

9. P.R.O. Numbers and tonnages of shipping at Scottish ports, 1771–5 and 1781–5, T. 64/251.

10. Ibid.

11. The following information is largely based on S.R.O. Scottish Collectors' Quarterly Accounts, E 504 and S.R.O. Unextracted Processes of the Court of Session, c.1760–1800.

12. Devine, *Tobacco Lords,* pp. 177–84.

13. It is possible that the role of the Glasgow élite has been underestimated by their use of agents in the lower Clyde ports, whose commissions were not always recorded in the port books of 1770s, or that the lower Clyde merchants re-exported these goods on the credit of the Glasgow merchants.

14. In 1774 re-exports of muscovado sugar to Ireland from Greenock and Port Glasgow amounted to 37438 cwt. and in 1794 to 24287 cwt. For details of these firms and personalities, see T. M. Devine, 'An Eighteenth Century Business Élite: Glasgow West India Merchants 1750–1815', *Scottish Historical Review,* LVII (1978), pp. 40–67.

15. National Library of Scotland, Alexander Houston & Co., Home Letter Book 1777–78, MS. 8795.

16. *Wilson's Dublin Directory* (Dublin, 1766; 1776; 1779; 1784; 1786 & 1798); Strathclyde Regional Archives (S.R.A.) Sederunt books of the Glasgow Chamber of Commerce, 1783–9, 1789–1803 (xerox copies), TD 76/1,2; S.R.A. Speirs papers (xerox copies), TD 131/1–5; T. M. Devine, 'A Glasgow Tobacco Merchant during the American War of Independence: Alexander Speirs of Elderslie, 1775 to 1781', *William and Mary Quarterly,* XXXIII (1976), pp. 501–13.

17. J. C. Logan, 'The Dumbarton Glass Works Company: A Study in Entrepreneurship', *Business History,* XIV (1972), p. 69; Senex, *Glasgow Past and Present* (Glasgow, 1856), II, pp. 20–1.

18. While information drawn from the Scottish port books forms the main basis of this study of merchants involved in Scottish-Irish trade, the resulting bias towards Scottish merchants is recognised but, to date, remains to be rectified. The evidence gleaned from an examination of some Irish merchants' papers and contemporary newspapers has proved too fragmentary to suggest any general conclusions at this stage. However, it remains a distinct possibility — given the relatively insignificant nature of Scottish trade in Irish overseas trade generally — that Irish merchants heavily involved in trade with Scotland cannot be identified. Many of the Scottish merchants who were most heavily involved in trade with Ireland are traceable only through the Scottish port books, as other sources fail to record their existence or else do so in an uninformative manner.

Part V

Urban and Financial Comparisons

13

The Social Composition of the Business Class in the Larger Scottish Towns, 1680–1740

T. M. Devine

IN his preface to a pioneering collection of essays on English urban history W. G. Hoskins remarked that an important and almost untilled field of study was the social composition of the town governing classes in the period before 1750.[1] Since Hoskins's comments were published in 1972, a number of investigations into London and some provincial centres have done much to extend understanding of both English towns in general and their élite groupings in particular.[2] In Scotland the field, though not entirely barren, is less fruitful. Only T. C. Smout's study of the seventeenth-century Glasgow merchant community offers a systematic attempt to probe the background of the men who controlled Scottish commerce in this period.[3] Older burghal histories, such as those by Mackenzie, Murray and Warden, were more concerned with the institutional framework of town government and less with the composition of the classes which comprised urban society.[4] Yet a discussion of town élites in this period is not simply an antiquarian exercise because it was from the merchant classes of the urban areas before 1750 that much of the business class which helped to guide economic expansion in the later eighteenth century derived. In studying the social composition of late seventeenth and early eighteenth-century merchant communities we are therefore focusing directly on the social roots of later enterprise.

The present essay is concerned with an analysis of the social composition of the Scottish merchant class between 1680 and 1740 because in this phase merchants dominated most of the major towns before industrialisation began to shift power slowly into the hands of manufacturers and professional groups. Was there a rigid hierarchy, founded on the self-perpetuating power of a handful of established families within the merchant communities, or was there a fair degree of mobility? If there was some social movement, what was the background of new recruits and what were the factors controlling entry into established circles? The evidence employed to try and answer these questions will be primarily derived from the larger Scottish towns of Edinburgh, Glasgow, Aberdeen and Dundee. Such an emphasis has two basic advantages. Firstly, the merchants of these towns were the decisive influences on Scottish commerce at this time. In 1705, for instance, the four towns accounted for about 64 per cent of total burghal taxation as measured by the stent rolls of the Convention of Royal Burghs, with Edinburgh and Glasgow alone contributing 35 per cent and 20 per cent respectively.[5] In the economically important central zone of the lowlands Edinburgh and Glasgow merchants also had a key role in the organisation of trade in many smaller urban centres which were essentially satellites of these larger burghs.[6] Secondly, the significant differences between the four towns in size, geographical location, trade connection and historical tradition mean that the danger of generalising from unrepresentative experience is reduced. All these burghs had important European links, but in this period Glasgow's external commerce diversified with the development of Irish trade and the growth of new relationships with the tobacco and sugar colonies. Dundee, on the other hand, was slipping down the burghal league table in the later seventeenth century with little basic alteration in the pattern of her traditional overseas trade. Edinburgh, despite the pace of Glasgow's development, remained the premier seat of commerce in Scotland, though the fortunes of the capital's merchant community remained firmly linked to historic ties with continental Europe. Finally, Aberdeen was an important centre of regional rather than national significance, with strong connections with Scandinavia and the Baltic countries.

I

It is important to recognise at the outset that the merchant communities of these towns were far from homogeneous. The point is immediately obvious if definition of the term 'merchant' in burghal tradition and practice is considered. As John Gibson, himself a trader of note, remarked in his *History of Glasgow* published in 1777: 'by merchants are to be understood all those who buy and sell'.[7] He implied a highly complex and diverse social grouping which included at one extreme the petty shopkeeper and packman, at the other the opulent merchant prince, and between a myriad army of men of varied social and material standing. Only bold simplification of these complexities allows the discussion to proceed beyond the level of description and impression. For the purposes of analysis therefore, three major categories have been established within the merchant class.

In the first place, there were those involved in trade who were not registered burgesses of a Scottish town. For much of the seventeenth century Scottish merchants functioned within an elaborate structure of protectionism. Commerce in the 'liberty' of the burghs was reserved for official burgesses of the towns. Only royal burghs until 1672 had the legal right to trade overseas. Entry both to the burgess class as a whole and to the merchant guild, the élite core of the business class, was jealously guarded, through admission fees and apprenticeship regulations, to benefit the kinsmen of established families. Yet, although in theory burgesses alone had the legal right to trade either in the burgh itself or within its hinterland, non-burgesses had always had a role to play and the evidence, such as it is, suggests that in the later seventeenth and early eighteenth centuries this unofficial sector was thriving as never before.

One indicator was the growth of commercial relationships between larger royal burghs and expanding 'unfree' towns and villages. In 1691 the Convention of Royal Burghs itself acknowledged that the burgesses of those towns who supposedly benefited from the old monopolies were in reality contributing to their rapid decay: 'It is resolved no longer to suffer the rights of royal burghs to be abused and encroached upon by there owne burgesses whoe be joining stocks with un-freemen inhabitants in the burghs of regalities and barronies and other unfree places bothe in point of trade and shipping.'[8] Significantly, a year after this resolution was passed Dundee admitted that it had trading links with at least fifteen 'unfree' towns and villages.[9] The slow decay of burgess regulation is another pointer to the growth of the 'unofficial' sector. As early as the 1680s the development of commerce around the burgh of Stirling was such as to render it increasingly difficult to retain the traditional monopolies. The merchant guild acknowledged this in 1686 when it agreed to permit non-burgesses to carry on trade within the town precinct after making a small annual payment without the need to register formally and pay the appropriate dues.[10] At both Aberdeen and Glasgow, too, by the 1720s, burgess-ship seems to have become regarded more as a mark of social distinction and less a necessary qualification for trade: several examples occur of individuals whose names appear in the burgess rolls after they had become established merchants.[11] What finally tends to suggest this decline in the protectionist system is the virtual absence of evidence of fining, after about 1710, in town guildry accounts as a punishment against those who had infringed the privileges of the burgess class.[12]

All this suggests the evolution of an economy in which the commercial enclave was becoming stronger. Greater economic maturity at once rendered protectionism less necessary and at the same time more difficult to enforce. From the middle decades of the seventeenth century the old rigidities of the Scottish domestic economy began partially to recede. The physical size of the larger towns grew. Burghs of barony, villages and fairs proliferated, and the increases in commodity exchange were further demonstrated by the conversion of rentals in kind into money and by the gradual disappearance of major regional price differentials for grain.[13] Legal controls had developed to suit the requirements of a society with a small, vulnerable and insecure commercial sector. They were increasingly inappropriate in the new context. Yet, it is not possible to carry the analysis of non-burgess merchants much further because they are naturally poorly documented in the apprenticeship and guild records which form the major sources for the present study. From the scattered references to their activities, however, it is tolerably clear that they were mainly men (and women) of relatively low status in the urban hierarchy, because even if burgess-ship was becoming less important in strictly economic terms, it still retained its value as a mark of significant social position. They plied the trades of small shopkeeper, pedlar, hawker and packman, and were unusually concerned with retail services in the burghs or in the buying of goods from greater wholesale merchants for distribution in the surrounding countryside.[14] The very fact that such a group existed outside the apparently exclusive framework of burgh and guild allowed those of humble origin to become involved in buying and selling to some extent.

M

The second and third groups within the merchant class were somewhat more important. Both consisted of registered burgesses of the four towns considered in this analysis. The burgesses can, however, be differentiated by the extent of their participation in foreign trade. Only a minority of all merchants had either the capital or the contacts to pursue this more lucrative type of commerce on a consistent basis. In Glasgow in the later seventeenth century less than a quarter of a merchant community of 400–500 strong were committed to the overseas sector, yet in Dundee the proportion of merchants with a stake in foreign trade was probably even less.[15] The distinction between the two forms of trade was, of course, not clear cut. Individuals who imported wines and brandies from France, like John Innes and William Caldwell of Edinburgh, were directly involved in selling them throughout Scotland and northern England.[16] Similarly, great overseas merchants such as John Steuart of Inverness and Walter Gibson of Glasgow both had interests in the domestic fisheries, exported herring to Europe and the New World and imported foreign commodities in return.[17] Such examples could be multiplied but they ought not to obscure the salient point that the inner core of the merchant community consisted mainly of the relatively small number of richer men with established foreign connections. The distinction became recognised in contemporary parlance which differentiated between ordinary traders and the 'merchant adventurers' or 'sea adventurers' and was embodied also in burghal law and tradition by the old regulation that, while all burgesses had the right to trade, only members of the merchant guild, entry to which was more costly and difficult than admission to the burgess class as a whole, had the legal right to trade abroad.[18] It follows, then, that an examination of the social composition of the merchant community involves two different but complementary tasks: first, to determine how easy or difficult it was to achieve entry into the burgess group and, second, to focus specifically on the business élites of the towns and examine the extent to which they drew on new blood from outside their own ranks.

II

There were certain obvious barriers to easy movement into the burgess class. Admission was unashamedly controlled to favour the kinsmen of established families for whom entry fees were lower and periods of apprenticeship shorter. It has already been argued that these controls were in decay at this time, but other obstacles remained. Merchant fathers commonly laid aside cash sums to enable their male offspring to set up business on their own account on attaining their majority and so perpetuate the prominence of the family into the next and succeeding generations.[19] Moreover, to a considerable extent, international trade was based on personal contacts and family links. The business world was a tight nexus in which a merchant's reputation and that of his family was his most precious asset. This was an era of developing but still unreliable communications, high risk and unsophisticated commercial law. It was therefore entirely sensible to favour dealing with one's kin and trusted acquaintances. Nepotism was not simply understandable but justifiable.[20]

In the light of this it is hardly suprising that merchants' sons formed the largest single category of new recruits to the burgess rank. From 1710 to 1730, 46 per cent of Edinburgh merchants became burgesses by right of their father, while at Dundee 48 per cent did so between 1705 and 1740, and 30 per cent at Aberdeen from 1707 to 1740.[21] Yet the majority of new entrants gained burgess status by marriage, apprenticeship, purchase or some other means. Moreover, the proportion of those obtaining burgess-ship by right of a father probably overestimates the number of merchants' sons who comprised the new generation of traders. An unknown number were simply awarded burgess status as infants or at their father's death in a formal sense, because entry fees for this group were entirely nominal, but they may never have practised as professional traders.

It remains to be determined whether there is evidence of similar movement among the inner élite of the merchant class. The social and financial barriers to upward mobility here were obviously greater than for the merchant community as a whole. Membership of the merchant guild was probably almost a prerequisite for membership of the élite, and attempts to control entry to it seem to have been maintained in our period. Thus, as late as 1751, the Guildry Court of Aberdeen resolved that 'when any persons apply to the Court for admission they resolved that none be found qualified unless they depon that they are worth one hundred and fifty pounds sterling of free stock and that they produced a certificate signed by two creditable burgesses attesting that the petitioner is of good character . . .'[22] At Glasgow in the late 1690s the property qualification for admission as a guild brother was about $3\frac{1}{2}$ times that for a mere burgess.[23] What may also have helped to perpetuate family power was the fact that the wealth of the greater merchants allowed them to diversify their assets, minimise the insecurities of trade, and so attempt to preserve their fortunes into the next and succeeding generations. The common pattern was to retain interests in a variety of different ventures both in overseas trade and in the domestic economy. Two examples must suffice to illustrate the point. Daniel Campbell, one of the greatest mercantile figures in early eighteenth-century Glasgow, was in association with two other merchants in a company with a total capital of £8,600 with trading interests in North America, the Caribbean and Europe. In addition, Campbell had acquired the estate of Shawfield at a price of £4000, had a major share in the Ropework Manufactory of Glasgow, and was lending substantial amounts on personal and heritable bond to a variety of kinsmen and associates.[24] A fellow Glasgow merchant, John Blackburn, had at his death, in 1737 a $\frac{3}{4}$ share in one ship importing salt and tobacco, $5/12$ in another valued at £240, $\frac{3}{8}$ part of a third worth £36 and $\frac{1}{4}$ of a fourth, valued at £200. Blackburn had also invested widely in house construction and in money-lending.[25]

Whether these factors were sufficient to stabilise membership of the mercantile élite can only be determined when the composition of the inner circle is examined over time. This can be done through a crude exercise in the comparison of surnames of those who controlled the key institutions of civic authority, namely the major offices of provost, baillie, dean of guild, and by an examination of the structure of the burgh council and the membership of the guildry court. A comparison of the dominant families of late seventeenth-century Glasgow with those of the mid-eighteenth suggests a relatively fluid pattern. The position of some families was indeed enduring. Such eminent colonial merchant families as the Bogles, Dunlops, Corbetts, Murdochs, Buchanans and Oswalds, who were all important in the tobacco trade in the 1760s, could trace their lineage back through two and three generations to late seventeenth-century burgess stock.[26] On the other hand the Glasgow élite was not an exclusive caste. In the later eighteenth century the city's American commerce was dominated by the great syndicates controlled by the Glassford, Speirs, Cunninghame and McDowall families. The heads of all these groupings were born outside the established circle and had managed to penetrate the very highest echelons of the élite within their own lifetime. John Glassford's father was a merchant burgess of Paisley; Alexander Speirs was the son of an Edinburgh merchant; William Cunninghame's father was a trader in Kilmarnock who belonged to a cadet branch of the Cunninghames of Caprington, lairds in Ayrshire; the McDowalls, who were the major partners in the giant West India house of Alexander Houston and Co, were the offspring of a Scots soldier who had made good in the Caribbean but traced his lineage back to landed stock in Wigtonshire.[27]

There is inevitably a danger in drawing general conclusions from the specific pattern revealed in the Glasgow case. The town's growth rate in the eighteenth century was exceptional and so also, it might be argued, was the turnover among its dominant merchant families. To determine how representative the Glasgow pattern was, the composition of the ruling families of Aberdeen and Dundee, two towns with a much less dramatic economic history, was studied. In both cases, however, similar evidence of steady movement among the élite can be identified. In the 1690s according to the poll tax records, there were 239 merchant burgesses in Aberdeen. The wealthiest elements, i.e. reckoned as those with stock valued at £530 sterling and above in the poll tax records, numbered about 27 in all and the majority belonged to the families of Mitchell, Skene, Johnston, Robertson and Gordon.[28] By the 1750s, on the other hand, little trace remained of any of these names in council and guildry records. Instead, a new grouping, built around the Youngs, Brebners, Auldjos, Mores and Leys, had emerged to dominate the political and economic life of the burgh.[29] The structure of authority in Dundee can be studied by examining the membership of the guildry court, the body concerned with the maintenance of the privileges of the greater merchants. Between 1683 and 1730, membership of the court fluctuated between 15 and 18. In 1681, seven of the names present in 1683 were still represented. By 1702 the number had dwindled to four, and all of them apparently were sons of the leading figures of the early 1680s. In 1708 only two names survived, and by 1720 there was no trace of any of the families who had served on the court three decades before.[30]

Inevitably, of course, surname comparison can only provide an impression of change rather than a systematic and precise account of its development. It is, for example, reasonable to suggest that the discontinuities revealed in the evidence are more apparent than real because family dominance could have been maintained through the female line and is therefore likely to escape notice by analysis on the simple basis of a surname check. On the other hand, changes in surnames are indeed a guide to the penetration of new men into the élite. In that sense they do suggest that the merchant communities, even in their highest echelons, were not closed oligarchies.

It is not possible to be wholly certain about the reasons for this turnover within the merchant community. Some contemporaries argued that it reflected the haemorrhage of men and money from town to country. So William Seton asserted in 1700 that, 'So soon as a merchant hath scraped together a piece of money . . . nothing will satisfy him but the laying of it upon a Land Estate, for having the Honour to make his son a Laird, that is, an idle person, who can find out as many methods in spending his father's money as he had of gaining it.'[31] That some merchants bought estates is indisputable, and several well-known instances are scattered throughout the secondary literature.[32] For a number of reasons, however, such examples can hardly in themselves explain social movement within the merchant community. First, only a handful of merchants had the resources to buy geographically compact estates of sufficient size to provide enough income to enable withdrawal from trade. Only seven of the 239 Aberdeen merchants of the 1690s seem to have owned country properties.[33] The Valuation Rolls suggest that almost all land purchasing in the period up to the early eighteenth century was carried out by established landed families rather than by new men from the towns.[34] According to the Register of the Great Seal for the period 1660 to 1668, merchants accounted for only 5.7 per cent of all recorded land transactions.[35] Only in the second half of the eighteenth century did townsmen begin to make an impact in any marked way on the land market.[36] Secondly, when most merchants did buy land they tended not to invest in geographically compact estates as a method of withdrawing from trade but in leases and mortgages both as means of diversifying their assets and increasing their income. Thus, of the 984 transactions recorded in the Register of the Great Seal over the period 1593 to 1660 involving non-landed groups, 300 were carried out as 'apprisings' by which the heritable rights of the debtor were sold for payment of the debt due to the appriser. The largest number of apprisings, about 68 per cent, were undertaken by merchants.[37] Thirdly, the ownership of estates, though uncommon before 1750 in the merchant community, did not in itself necessarily mean withdrawal from trade. There are some instances of this practice; for example, the Skenes of Rubieslaw, merchants of Aberdeen, in the later seventeenth century, and the Campbells of Shawfield, merchants of Glasgow, in the early eighteenth century.[38] On the other hand the normal pattern in both towns in the eighteenth century seems to have been for merchant-landowners to retain links in both land and commerce over several generations.[39]

A more significant cause of movement within the merchant class was probably the tendency of some merchant families to come to an end in the male line either through death or the habit of some sons opting for a career outside commerce. In Glasgow, for example, it was common for some at least of the male offspring of merchant families to enter the law or military service or to seek their fortunes overseas. This pattern, however, left daughters to provide opportunities for social movement through marriage.[40] In all the towns studied, entry to burgess-ship by right of marriage was second only to paternity as the most common means of registration. Of the 110 new merchant burgesses registered at Dundee between 1705 and 1740, 47 obtained entry by right of a father, 27 by marriage, 25 by purchase and 12 by apprenticeship. Similarly at Edinburgh from 1710 to 1720, 59 achieved burgess-ship by right of a father, 40 by marriage, 38 by purchase and 31 by apprenticeship.[41]

In addition, the period 1680 to 1740 was a phase of pronounced commercial expansion with a very significant growth in the internal trafficking of foods, raw materials, luxuries and crude manufactured goods and the development of Scottish external connections with the New World.[42] All this provided opportunity for the new generation of merchants and added to the influences generating social movement within the trading community. The risks of the commerce and the vicissitudes of business fortunes were also relevant. Social position in the merchant class was guaranteed not simply by blood and inheritance, as in landownership, or by institutional controls, as in the legal profession. It was based much more on a family's ability to survive the ebb and flow of competitive commercial pressures over successive generations. That some failed to do so, and that this left openings for newcomers, is made evident in the records of the merchant guilds. In 1736 the Aberdeen guild's finances became deficient because of the misfortunes that had recently overtaken some of its members, and 'the monies belonging to the Guild Box is not in a condition to support the poor decayed brethern of guild of this burgh and their widows and children'.[43] Again, in 1730, the funds of the Dundee guildry were deemed insufficient to meet the needs of families of insolvent members, and so entry and apprenticeship fees were raised to provide for them.[44] Ironically, the transience of commercial wealth was often most apparent in the lucrative colonial trades because there risks were maximised by communication difficulties, varying climatic conditions, war and fluctuating demand for colonial commodities. The succesful expansion of Scottish connections with North America and the Caribbean was punctuated by a series of spectacular bankruptcies among the Glasgow mercantile élite which eroded the possibilities of any enduring social monopoly.[45]

III

The fact of social *movement* both within the merchant communities and from the general body of merchants to the élite should not be taken to imply that there was extensive upward social *mobility* within these larger towns. Broadly, most newcomers to the merchant burgess class, when not sons of merchants, were born into broadly similar social backgrounds to those who were. While the upper echelons of the merchant community were therefore open-ended, they were not usually open to all ranks in society. Most new merchant burgesses were *petit bourgeois* in social origin. Twenty-seven merchant apprentices were registered in Aberdeen between 1709 and 1740. In the case of eight, the occupation of the father is unknown; of the remaining 19, eight were sons of small landowners, four of ministers of the church, two of tenant farmers, two of lawyers, two of craftsmen, and one was the son of a schoolmaster.[46] Between 1701 and 1730, 279 individuals were admitted to merchant apprenticeships in Edinburgh, 84 were the sons of small landowners or tenant farmers, 42 of professional families (including lawyers, schoolmasters and ministers), 37 of craftsmen and 30 of merchants in towns other than Edinburgh. The occupation of fathers of the remaining 48 is unknown.[47] Most 'craftsmen' fathers were goldsmiths, surgeons, maltsters, butchers and tailors and therefore were often of higher economic status than some within the merchant community itself. Indeed, the only significant differences between Aberdeen and Edinburgh lay in the overall number of apprentices and in their varying geographical origins. Aberdeen's area of recruitment was emphatically regional with all apprentices coming from the town itself, rural Aberdeenshire or the adjacent county of Kincardine. Edinburgh, however, attracted recruits over much longer distances, with a substantial minority of apprentices coming from outside the south-eastern lowlands.

Three factors help to explain the 'middling' class origin of merchant apprentices. It partly reflected the incidence of social pressures within the structure of landownership in lowland Scotland. A significant number of new apprentices were from small landed families, both in the burghs considered in this study and in other towns, such as Inverness and Dumbarton, where similar detailed evidence of merchant origins exists.[48] The Scottish pattern of landownership ensured a steady flow of sons of the minor landed classes into the professions and trade. In several areas, and especially in the western lowlands and east-central region, much territory was divided into relatively small estates, among a numerous laird class. Even in other parts of the lowlands where greater landowners of aristocratic rank held sway, the smaller men were still strong in numbers.[49] The practice of primogeniture among the lairds was a prime cause of the movement of sons off the land but, in addition, some properties probably yielded such marginal returns that even those who managed to gain an inheritance tended also to retain interests in commerce. Instances also exist, notably in the cases of the Burds of Foord and the Campbells of Cessnock, of eldest sons entering merchanting before their father's death and maintaining an active business role after they came into their inheritance.[50]

Needless to say, therefore, no gulfs of status or esteem separated land and commerce in Scotland. Indeed, the number of recruits from landed families into trade was augmented by the limited opportunities in alternative careers, itself a reflection of the relatively underdeveloped nature of the economy in the early eighteenth century. Recent work on eighteenth-century Scottish lawyers suggests that many Scottish landed gentlemen were principally interested in obtaining places for their sons in the law because it offered a more secure income and, in some of its branches, was more prestigious than trade. But entry to the powerful legal institutions of Writers to the Signet and the Faculty of Advocates was much more costly and difficult than obtaining a mercantile apprenticeship.[51] It may be, therefore, that the supply of new recruits to merchanting from the laird classes was maintained not simply because of the nature of the Scottish landed structure but because entry to the professions of the law and the ministry was more effectively regulated by institutional controls.

The system of patronage was a second factor reserving entry to the more lucrative types of merchanting principally to the sons of the 'middling' orders in society. The world of eighteenth-century commerce was no different from that of politics and the professions in this respect. Places were obtained through an informal system of clientage, connection and recommendation. Established merchants were regularly approached by close and distant kinsmen, friends and associates seeking to find opportunities for their sons in commercial careers. Once again this helped to perpetuate mercantile supremacy within a specific social stratum. Adam Montgomery, a Glasgow factor in Stockholm in the early eighteenth century, took on several young Scots as apprentices, but his letterbook indicates that they were invariably his kinsmen or sons of his personal friends.[52] Similarly, Alexander Shairp, an Edinburgh merchant resident in Amsterdam in 1717, supervised the training of the sons of a number of his Scottish friends in the commercial arts of book-keeping, writing, arithmetic and foreign languages.[53] In North America and the Caribbean young men who sought positions in Scottish stores or plantations were placed in exactly the same manner.[54]

Finally, the cost of training the new generation of overseas merchants merits consideration. Established merchants willing to take on new apprentices were probably in a buyer's market, especially since in foreign trade the formal experience of an apprenticeship or some less rigid form of training was a vital preparation for a business career. Only thus could the neophyte make the contacts, perfect the techniques and master the languages which would stand him in good stead in later years. Expenses, however, were often substantial. In a typical indenture in 1736 between William Middleton, merchant of Aberdeen, and John Forbes, Forbes's father was required to pay £60 sterling for his son's training over a three-year period and maintain him 'in backcloaths and all necessary abulziements for his body and a horse to ride to market'.[55] Costs were more onerous for overseas training. In the later seventeenth century many Scots enrolled in mercantile schools in the great European centres of Amsterdam, Rotterdam and Dort. When William Dunlop of Glasgow was in Dort in 1681, there were five fellow Scots from Edinburgh in his class but a significantly larger number under instruction in Rotterdam.[56] Normally, this kind of training involved supervision by a resident Scottish merchant, as when Adam Montgomery charged his friend Daniel Campbell of Shawfield £30 sterling in 1701 for a three-year apprenticeship for his son. But, as Montgomery pointed out, this was a personal favour because the going rate for similar services among other English and Scottish merchants in Stockholm at the time was between £100 and £200.[57]

IV

It is now possible to provide some tentative answers to the questions posed at the beginning of this essay. The merchant classes of the larger Scottish towns in this period were not rigid hierarchies with membership confined to sons of merchant burgesses and their immediate kin. There is much evidence that an 'unofficial' sector of trade existed and was expanding in the later seventeenth century. The elaborate structure of protectionism designed primarily to favour the kinsmen of established families was in decline. Social movement occurred within the middle and higher echelons of the merchant burgess class, with new men constantly being recruited to the élites from below, from other towns and from outside the merchant community. Movement, however, tended to take place within a relatively narrow social range. Newcomers to the rank of merchant burgess were recruited mainly from the middle strata of Scottish society and were sons of small landowners, tenant farmers, lawyers, teachers and ministers. Social relationships with the landed classes were particularly significant. In Scotland, the diffusion of small estates and traditions of primogeniture meant a constant flow of younger sons of the laird class into trade and the professions. This had two advantages for Scottish development in the eighteenth century. First, the smaller Scottish landowners, unlike some of the continental minor aristocracies, were not impoverished by demographic burdens. Second, the blood and marital links between merchants and landowners permitted the easy transfer of ideas, values and capital between town and country and were one reason why economic change in later eighteenth-century Scotland was not only accepted but vigorously promoted in unison by the representatives of ancient rural authority and new urban wealth.[58]

REFERENCES

1. Peter Clark and Paul Slack, eds., *Crisis and Order in English Towns, 1500-1700* (London, 1972), p. vii.

2. See *inter alia* Richard Grassby, 'The Personal Wealth of the Business Community in Seventeenth-century England', *Econ. Hist. Rev.*, 2nd ser., xxiii (1970); R. G. Lang, 'London's Aldermen in Business 1600-1625', *Guildhall Miscellany*, iii (1971); P. Clarke, *English Provincial Society: Religion, Politics and Society in Kent, 1500-1640* (Hassocks, 1976); P. Clarke and P. Slack, *English Towns in Transition, 1500-1700* (Oxford, 1976), pp. 97-125.

3. T. C. Smout, 'The Glasgow Merchant Community in the Seventeenth Century', *Scottish Historical Review*, XLVII (1968), pp. 53-68.

4. W. M. Mackenzie, *The Scottish Burghs* (Edinburgh, 1949); David Murray, *Early Burgh Organisation in Scotland* (Glasgow, 1924); A. J. Warden, *Burgh Laws of Dundee* (London, 1872).

5. J. D. Marwick, ed., *Extracts from the Records of the Convention of the Royal Burghs of Scotland, 1677-1711* (Edinburgh, 1880).

6. T. C. Smout, *Scottish Trade on the Eve of Union, 1660-1707* (Edinburgh, 1963), pp. 131-4, 144-6.

7. John Gibson, *The History of Glasgow from the Earliest accounts to the Present Time* (Glasgow, 1777), p. 113.

8. *Convention Records*, p. 133.

9. 'Register containing the State and Condition of every burgh within the Kingdome of Scotland in the year 1692', *Miscellany of the Scottish Burgh Records Society* (Edinburgh, 1881), p. 75.

10. David B. Morris, *The Stirling Merchant Guild and the Life of John Cowane* (Stirling, 1919), p. 73.

11. Aberdeen Town House, Charter Room (A.C.R.), Aberdeen Burgess Book, 1694-1760; Strathclyde Regional Archives (S.R.A.), T–MH/2, Minute Book of the Merchants' House of Glasgow, vol. 2, 1711-1754.

12. A.C.R. A.25/1, Aberdeen Guildry Minute Books; Dundee Archive and Record Centre (D.A.R.C.), GD/GRW/G1/2, Sederunt Book of Dundee Guild Court; GD/GRW/G3/1, Guildry Incorporation Account Book, 1696-1751.

13. For the increase in commercial activity in the later seventeenth century and early eighteenth century see I. D. Whyte, *Agriculture and Society in Seventeenth Century Scotland* (Edinburgh, 1979), pp. 222-245; *idem*, 'The growth of periodic market centres in Scotland, 1660-1707', *Scottish Geographical Magazine*, xcv (1979); G. D. Pryde, ed., *The Court Book of the Burgh of Kirkintilloch* (Edinburgh, 1963), p. lxxxi; Rosalind Mitchison, 'The Movement of Scottish Grain Prices in the Seventeenth and Eighteenth Centuries', *Econ. Hist. Rev.*, 2nd ser., xviii (1965).

14. References to them are to be found in the following: *Convention Records*, pp. 133, 209, 212; J. D. Marwick, *Edinburgh Guilds and Crafts* (Edinburgh, 1910), pp. 204-5; 'Register containing the state and condition of every burgh within the Kingdome of Scotland in the year 1692', *Miscellany of the Scottish Burgh Records Society* (Edinburgh, 1881), pp. 75, 81; D.A.R.C. GD/GRW/G1/2, Dundee Guild Court Sederunt Book, 6 July, 1728; A.C.R. A.25/1, Aberdeen Guildry Minute Book, 12 March, 1736.

15. Smout, 'Glasgow Merchant Community', pp. 61-2; D.A.R.C. Dundee Register of Ships, 1701-1713 demonstrates the coastal orientation of Dundee's trade.

16. Scottish Record Office (S.R.O.), RH15/147, Papers of John Innes, merchant in Edinburgh; RH15/126/1, Letters and other papers pertaining to W. Caldwell, merchant in Leith, 1720-34.

17. W. Mackay, ed., *The Letterbook of Baillie John Steuart of Inverness, 1715-1752* (Edinburgh, 1915); John McCure, *A View of the City of Glasgow*, (Glasgow, 1736), p. 169.

18. McCure, *City of Glasgow* p. 170; Robert Chambers, *Edinburgh Merchants and Merchandise in Old Times* (Edinburgh, 1899), p. 5.

19. There are abundant examples of this practice. See, for example, Mitchell Library, Glasgow (M.L.) MS120, Papers of the Dunlops of Garnkirk, Bond of Provision for James Dunlop, and the instances in A.C.R., A/31, Aberdeen Burgh Court Deeds Recorded, 1736-40.

20. Illustration of these points can be found in M.L. B325799, Letterbook of Adam Montgomery, Montgomery to R. Rodger, 10 May 1702; Dunlop of Garnkirk Papers, John Dunlop, 3, 24 March, 1683; National Library of Scotland (N.L.S.) MS1884, Letterbook of Alexander Shairp, merchant in Edinburgh, to W. Riddell, 17 August, 1714 and P. Aitkenhead, 26 October, 1714.

21. C.B.B. Watson, ed., *Roll of Edinburgh Burgesses and Guild Brethren, 1701-1760* (Edinburgh, 1930). Hereafter referred to as *Edinburgh Burgess Roll;* D.A.R.C. Lockit Book of Burgesses of Dundee, 1513-1973; A.C.R. Aberdeen Burgess Book, 1694-1760.

22. A.C.R. A.25/1, Aberdeen Guildry Minute Book, 29 June, 1751.

23. McCure, *City of Glasgow*, pp. 166 ff.

24. M. L. Campbell of Shawfield Papers, Boxes 1 and 2.

25. S.R.O. Commissariot of Glasgow Testaments, CC9/7/55/223, Testament of John Blackburn, 1737.

26. For the position of these families see McCure, *City of Glasgow*, p. 170; M. L. Bogle MSS, Genealogy of the Bogle family; Archibald Dunlop, *Memorabilia of the Family of Dunlop* (privately printed, n.d.); R. M. Buchanan, *Notes on the Members of the Buchanan Society 1725-1829* (Glasgow, 1931).

27. J. Gourlay, *A Glasgow Miscellany* (privately printed, n.d.), p. 43; S.R.A. Register of Deeds, B.10/15/8435, Settlement, Alexander Speirs, 16 December, 1782; S.R.O. GD247/10, Answers for W. Cunninghame . . .; S.R.O., GD237/139, Agreement between W. McDowall and J. Gordon, St. Kitts, 28 Dec. 1723; P. A. Ramsay, *Views in Renfrewshire with Historical and Descriptive Notices* (Edinburgh, 1839), p. 163.

28. J. Stuart, ed., *List of Pollable Persons within the Shire of Aberdeen in 1694* (Aberdeen, 1844). Hereafter referred to as *Aberdeen Poll List, 1694.*

29. A.C.R. A/5-6, Aberdeen Council Register, 1690-1750; A. Munro, *Memorials of the Aldermen, Provosts and Lord Provosts of Aberdeen* (Aberdeen, 1897), pp. 244-262. See also T. Donnelly, 'The Economic Activities of the Members of the Aberdeen Merchant Guild, 1750-1799', *Scottish Economic and Social History*, I (1981), pp. 25-41 for the structure of the town élite in the later eighteenth century.

30. D.A.R.C. GD/GRW/G1/1-2, Dundee Guildry Book, 1683-1720.

31. William Seton, *The Interest of Scotland* (1700), p. 75.

32. See, for example, Smout, *Scottish Trade*, pp. 78-79.

33. *Aberdeen Poll List, 1694.*

34. Loretta Timperley, 'The Pattern of Landholding in Eighteenth Century Scotland', in M. H. Parry and T. R. Slater, eds., *The Making of the Scottish Countryside* (London, 1980), pp. 137-154.

35. J. H. Stevenson, ed., *The Register of the Great Seal of Scotland, 1660-1668* (Edinburgh, 1914).

36. Timperley, 'Pattern of Landholding', pp. 137-154.

37. John di Folco, 'The Hopes of Craighall and Investment in Land in the Seventeenth Century', in T. M. Devine, ed., *Lairds and Improvement in the Scotland of the Enlightenment* (Glasgow, 1979), pp. 1-10.

38. W. T. Skene, *Memorials of the Family of Skene* (Aberdeen, 1887), p. 131; M. L. Campbell of Shawfield Papers.

39. These generalisations are based on T. M. Devine, *The Tobacco Lords: A Study of the Tobacco Merchants of Glasgow and their Trading Activities, 1740-1790* (Edinburgh, 1975), pp. 18-33; *idem*, 'Glasgow Colonial Merchants and Land, 1770-1815', in J. T. Ward and R. G. Wilson, eds., *Land and Industry*, pp. 205-244; Donnelly, 'Aberdeen Merchant Guild', pp. 35-38.

40. For examples, see W. J. Addison, ed., *The Matriculation Albums of the University of Glasgow, 1728-1858* (Glasgow, 1913); *A Roll of Graduates of the University of Glasgow* (Glasgow, 1898); Anon, *Old Glasgow Exhibition: Catalogue, Notes and Indexes* (Glasgow, 1894); R. M. Buchanan, *Notes on the Members of the Buchanan Society* (Glasgow, 1931); H. B. McCall, *Memoirs of My Ancestors* (Birmingham, 1884).

41. D.A.R.C. Lockit Book of Burgesses of Dundee, 1513-1973; *Edinburgh Burgess Roll,* 1710-20.

42. Rosalind Mitchison, *Life in Scotland* (London, 1978), pp. 75-94.

43. A.C.R., A.25/1, Aberdeen Guildry Minute Book, 19 February, 1736.

44. D.A.R.C., GD/GRW/G1/2, Sederunt Book of Dundee Guild Court, 30 January, 1730.

45. Devine, *Tobacco Lords*, pp. 7-8 and *idem*, 'An Eighteenth Century Business Élite', *Scottish Historical Review*, LVII (1978), p. 50.

46. A.C.R., A/21, Aberdeen Register of Indentures, 1701-1755.

47. C. B. Watson, ed., *Register of Edinburgh Apprentices, 1701-1755* (Edinburgh, 1929).

48. *Letterbook of Baillie John Steuart*, pp. viii-ix; Fergus Roberts, ed., *Roll of Dumbarton Burgesses and Guild Brethren, 1600-1846* (Edinburgh, 1937).

49. Sir John Sinclair, *General Report on the Agricultural State and Political Circumstances of Scotland* (Edinburgh, 1814), I, p. 89; Loretta Timperley, *A Directory of Landownership in Scotland c.1770* (Edinburgh, 1976).

50. S.R.O. RH15/54, Papers of Edward Burd, merchant in Edinburgh; N.L.S. MS3864, Campbell of Cessnock Papers, commission, Captain Hugh Campbell to Dougall and James Campbell, 1694.

51. John Shaw, 'Civic Leadership and the Edinburgh Lawyers in Eighteenth Century Scotland' (unpublished Stirling University Ph.D. thesis, 1979).

52. M.L. B325799, Adam Montgomery Letterbook, 1700-2.

53. N.L.S. MS1884, Letterbook of Alexander Shairp, merchant in Edinburgh, 1712-19.

54. N.L.S. MS5030, Charles Steuart Letterbooks, Thomas Riddoach to Charles Steuart, 5 January, 1777; S.R.O. Court of Session Unextracted Process, 1 Currie Mack, C/4/13, W. Cunninghame and Co. versus Craig (1777).

55. A.C.R. A/33, Aberdeen Burgh Court Deeds recorded, Indenture betwixt W. Middleton and J. Forbes, 1736.

56. M.L., MS120, Dunlop of Garnkirk Papers, William Dunlop to James Dunlop, 21 May, 1681.

57. M.L. B.325799, Adam Montgomery Letterbook, Montgomery to Daniel Campbell, 3 August, 1701.

58. The research for this essay was assisted by a grant from the Social Science Research Council. I am grateful to the Council for their generous support.

14

The Place of Dublin in the Eighteenth-Century Irish Economy

David Dickson

'Compare the improvements of Ireland and of Scotland [since 1707] . . . how much the former has been outstripped by the latter; but compare Dublin with Edinburgh and in the same time, the increase of the former will be found to have been fourfold of that of the latter . . .'

Reasons against an Union . . . (Dublin, 1798), p.19.

THE pre-eminence of Dublin as capital of Ireland and as second city of the king's dominions was so well-established by 1700[1] that subsequent changes in its position within the economy attracted relatively little attention in the course of the eighteenth century. Its claim to be the busiest port, and administrative, judicial and social centre was never in question, for its primacy seemed the logical consequence of topography, history and political geography. Visitors noted the dichotomy between capital and countryside in material standards, the contrast between the ostentatious social display of the city and the extreme backwardness of the countryside. Dublin's Neapolitan extravagance, its vulgar aping of London ways, invited Swiftian satire, and Swift had many imitators. There was also the occasionally expressed view that Dublin had become a monster, 'a head too big for the body', thanks to the influx of office-seeking gentry and the activities of building speculators.[2] But compared to the abuse heaped by some on London in its period of fastest pre-industrial growth, Dublin in fact escaped lightly. Commercial interests in the outports expressed no sustained grievance against Dublin, and the whole drift of parliamentary policy was to encourage, directly or indirectly, the capital's development. There was, of course, no general plan behind such encouragement, and no overall conception of the impact of Dublin's growth; but it would seem that to most who cared to consider the matter, the city's expansion was not perceived as a threat, but rather as a contribution to national improvement and as a reflection of it.

The first attempt at a comprehensive census of Dublin's population was not made until 1798,[3] so that eighteenth-century demographic trends must be somewhat speculatively based. Hearth-tax and other fiscal returns of houses inside the city's legal boundaries are available throughout the century, and while these are less unreliable than has usually been believed, there remains the acute problem of estimating mean household size. Dublin did not rival the population density of Edinburgh's Old Town, but household size was distinctly large by contemporary British standards — in the region of eight per house at the beginning of the century and over eleven at the end.[4] The city's population seems to have trebled over the century — from under 60,000 to rather over 180,000 — but it is most unlikely that there was a constant rate of growth across the century. Varying assumptions about household size and hearth-tax accuracy have given rise to very different estimates of the city's magnitude in the middle of the century; recent suggestions have ranged from 100,000 to 150,000.[5] The estimates provided in Table 1 are based on a refinement of the fragmentary data on household size in the city, and suggest stronger growth in the first two-thirds of the century than later. A comparison of these demographic estimates with statistical measures of the city's economic development strengthen their plausibility. Unfortunately, data on food and drink consumption are problematic, but fuel import returns are comprehensive for the period (see Table 2), and may legitimately be used to determine the timing, if not the dimensions, of growth: Dublin's almost complete dependence on British coal for household fuel was a fact of life throughout the century, despite vigorous parliamentary attempts to develop Irish coal supplies, and the growth of a trade in 'canal turf' at the end of the century. Nearly all the cross-channel coal brought to Dublin was used in domestic fireplaces, for industrial consumption (by breweries, sugar-houses, glass-works and salt pans) can at no stage have accounted for more than ten per cent of the coal landed, and there is little evidence of any large quantity of coal being forwarded from Dublin to other Irish destinations before the 1780s. However, the demographic value of the coal statistics is limited by the fact that *per capita* domestic consumption in Dublin was growing during the century (helped by the fall in real terms of coal prices). Dublin coal imports (as officially recorded) rose by rather more than fivefold over the century — a rate of growth considerably ahead of estimated population. The growth rate of coal imports in the first quarter of the century was however only about half that of population — a somewhat puzzling feature which cannot be easily explained — but over the rest of the century, coal import trends are not dissimilar from the suggested demographic pattern: pronounced expansion in the 1740s, 1750s and early 1760s, and a more modest advance in the last quarter of the century (see Table 3). Then in the early nineteenth century coal imports rose decidedly faster than urban population, but there are a number of possible non-demographic explanations for this.

The rapid growth of Dublin in the middle decades of the eighteenth century would appear to have been quite out of phase with national demographic trends, the rural mortality crises of the 1740s having no comparable impact on the metropolis. Dublin's share of national population (using the most recent re-estimates) would seem to have shifted markedly: from 3.3 per cent (1706) and 3.8 per cent (1725) to 5.3 per cent (1744) and 5.4 per cent (1760), gradually falling back to 4.4 per cent (1778), 3.6 per cent (1800) and 3.3 per cent again in 1821.[6] This suggests that Dublin's mid-century share of over five per cent was decidedly large by the standards of contemporary European capitals (although it was less than half of

London's share of English and Welsh population at that stage). However, given the tentative nature of the estimates of household size at both city and national levels, it is possible that future research may give a rather different picture of Dublin's changing share of national population.

A more direct measure of Dublin's economic activity in the eighteenth century is the customs series relating to ship tonnage invoiced (excluding vessels in the Irish coastal trade).[7] Between the first and last decades of the century ship tonnage grew between four- and fivefold, from about 58,000 tons p.a. to about 258,000 tons p.a., but colliers were a major element in this, rising from one-third of the city's total tonnage at the beginning of the century to about a half at its end;[8] tonnage of non-collier traffic rather more than trebled over the century. The aggregate tonnage returns (i.e. including colliers) suggest particularly high rates of growth at the beginning of the century and between the 1740s and the 1760s, with a much slacker performance in the following half-century (see Table 2). Dublin's share of national tonnage invoiced, slightly over half the total for most of the century, underlines the primacy of the port in Irish foreign trade, but here also there is a relative contraction in Dublin's position in the last three decades of the century.[9] Dublin's contribution to national customs receipts reveals a rather more stable pattern; Dublin's share remained at or above fifty per cent of the total throughout the eighteenth century.[10]

These general indices of growth give a fairly plausible statistical outline of Dublin's economic transformation, and while it is obvious that there was no revolutionary change in the relationship between the capital and the provinces during the century, the old assumption that the period of Dublin's greatest relative strength and prosperity coincided with 'Grattan's Parliament' in the last two decades of the century finds no support here.

The range of 'services' supplied by eighteenth-century Dublin was unusually wide by the standards of pre-industrial capitals. It was both 'court city', and market and financial centre, and in addition had a monopoly (within the country) in the provision of higher education. Only London, Amsterdam and Copenhagen among the leading cities of eighteenth-century Europe had as overarching a position within their respective countries as had the Irish capital.

TABLE 1. *Dublin Population Estimates, 1685–1821*

Year	Population
1685	45,000
1706	62,000
1725	92,000
1744	112,000
1760	140,000
1778	154,000
1800	182,000
1821 (census)	224,000

Sources: See Dickson, 'The Size of Eighteenth-Century Dublin' (unpublished paper).

In the commercial sphere, Dublin's most important function was as entry point for most primary and manufactured imports. A considerable part of this import trade was simply to satisfy Dublin's regular internal needs: coal, grain (from the 1720s), hops and much of the manufactured fineries, hardware and groceries were primarily for retail sale in Dublin, and the strength of the city's import traffic reflected the development of the metropolis as a place of seasonal and permanent resort for the Irish gentry and spending classes. However, quite apart from the rising level of demand within the metropolis, Dublin's wholesale hinterland within Ireland increased greatly during the century.

Trends in wine and sugar imports are indicative of the general pattern. In the late seventeenth century around half of the legally declared French wine entering Ireland had come via Dublin, and this share grew noticeably towards the middle of the eighteenth century. At the peak of the trade in the early 1760s, Irish imports were running at over 4,000 tons p.a., and Dublin merchants were handling little short of three-quarters of the total.[11] They maintained a large inland

TABLE 2. *Dublin Coal Imports and Non-Coastal Tonnage Invoiced, 1702/03-1820/21*

Years	Coal Imports: Annual Averages (Irish Tons)*	Coal: Annual Growth Rates (between decennial averages)	Non-Coastal Tonnage: Invoiced: Annual Averages	Tonnage: Annual Growth Rates (between decennial averages)
1702/03–1710/11	35932		57851	
		1.4		2.5
1711/12–1720/21	41100		73380**	
		1.3		2.3
1721/22–1730/31	46818		91819***	
		1.4		1.2
1731/32–1740/41	54019		103632	
		3.3		1.9
1741/42–1750/51	74775		124588	
		3.0		2.5
1751/52–1760/61	100095		160016	
		2.4		1.8
1761/62–1770/71	126420		192195	
		0.9		0.3
1771/72–1780/81	138902		198227	
		1.8		1.6
1781/82–1790/91	165995		231799	
		1.0		1.3
1791/92–1799/1800	183521		262799	
		2.1		1.1
1811/12–1820/21	282905		328233	

Sources: P.R.O. (London) Customs 15; N.L.I. Irish Customs Ledgers.
Notes:
   * The 'Irish ton' was a unit of measure; in the case of coal it weighed between 21 and 22 cwt. (cf. L. M. Cullen, *Anglo-Irish Trade 1660-1800* (Manchester, 1968) p.80).
   ** Tonnage date for 1715/16 unavailable.
*** The anomalous and apparently miscalculated tonnage figures for 1722/23 have not been used.

correspondence, consigning wines to the four provinces, and dealt direct with many of the country gentry.[12] Their control of the Irish trade continued through the period when wine imports from France (and elsewhere) were declining in the last decades of the century, as escalating import duties transformed the pattern of alcohol consumption.

Dublin's position in the sugar trade was even more striking. Before the tightening up of the Navigation Acts in 1685,[13] unrefined sugar had been imported directly into Ireland from the Caribbean on local account, and at that stage Dublin had shared the trade with Galway and the Munster ports, handling in the 1680s approximately one-third of Irish imports. But after the Williamite wars, when all colonial goods had to be imported indirectly,[14] Dublin's proportion of the traffic in sugar rose dramatically. National imports of unrefined sugar grew by a factor of eighteen between the 1700s and the 1790s (refined sugar imports were by comparison insignificant), and throughout this period the capital handled in excess of three-fifths of the total — 61 per cent in the first quarter of the century, 74 per cent in the second, 76 per cent in the third, falling back to 63 per cent in the final quarter.[15] The trade tied up a disproportionate amount of Dublin merchant capital, as in contrast to most other types of import lines, sugar continued to be imported on local account. Furthermore, until the rise of large-scale brewing and distilling at the end of the century, sugar-refining was the most important form of industrial capital investment in the city. Dublin's refined sugar sales were countrywide, reaching even the Munster ports whose sugar-houses had a much more precarious history.[16]

TABLE 3. *Rates of Growth of Dublin Population and Dublin Coal Imports, 1706–1821*

Years	Population Growth Rate (p.a.)	Coal Imports Growth Rate (p.a.)
1706–1725	2.1	1.3
1725–1744	1.0	2.3
1744–1760	1.4	2.6
1760–1778	0.5	1.5
1778–1800	0.8	0.9
1800–1821	1.0	2.6

Sources: As in Tables 1 and 2.
Note: The growth rate of coal imports is calculated here using the average imports for five years centred on each 'census' year; that for 1821 is calculated using the totals for 6 Jan. 1818–5 Jan. 1819 to 6 Jan. 1822–5 Jan. 1823.

The buoyancy of the metropolitan market and the greater financial resources of Dublin importers which enabled them to give longer credits than could the merchants of the outports[17] help to explain the capital's enhanced position in these and lesser import trades. But Dublin's ascendancy in this sphere was related to more fundamental processes within the economy in the late seventeenth and early eighteenth centuries — the marked concentration of all branches of foreign trade on four or five larger ports and a hastening of the process of national market integration.[18] Dublin was gaining both by the commercial eclipse of lesser east-coast ports, and by greater regional specialisation. In some sectors it became the centre of inter-regional trade — as an extension of its role as warehouse for much of the country's imports. The most valuable inter-regional trade throughout the eighteenth century was of course in cattle, and in this Dublin had relatively little direct role. But it does seem to have played a major part in redistributing regional grain surpluses between the 1720s and 1770s, usually from Munster to Ulster, for Dublin with its own massive appetite for grain was at this period the price and information centre of grain trading on the Irish Sea. Dublin's role as internal market centre was more clear-cut in the case of textiles: much of the linen yarn from the western and midlands counties reached Ulster weavers via Dublin, and northern linens reached consumers outside Ulster mainly through Dublin intermediaries. The woollen fabrics of Kilkenny and Carrick-on-Suir destined for northern markets were traded through Dublin.[19]

Dublin's emergence as a major manufacturing location was an extension of its commercial development. Most industrial activity in the eighteenth-century city involved the working up of domestic raw materials for the home market, woollen manufacture being the obvious example, although the processing of imported raw or semi-manufactured materials for metropolitan and country consumption was probably more capital intensive (in this category, in addition to sugar-baking, were the silk industry, the iron-founding and metal-finishing trades, furniture and glass manufacture and many lesser industries which depended primarily if not exclusively on domestic sales).

The growth of city manufacturing had been fairly rapid, in line with the seventeenth-century growth of urban population and the rising volume of seasonal visitors. Luxury goods manufacturers — gold- and silversmiths, jewellers, silk manufacturers — multiplied in Restoration Dublin, and the legal and political encouragement held out at that period to 'foreign Protestants' wishing to settle in the city facilitated the establishment of many English and Huguenot families. The silk industry was introduced *de novo*, and Old and New Draperies production was greatly extended. After a brief involvement in the cloth export trade before its closure in 1699, the Dublin industry adapted to an exclusive reliance on the home market: most of the broadcloths and silks worn in the country for the next sixty or seventy years were woven and finished within the neighbourhood of the city. At times there may well have been up to 10,000 men and women in and around Dublin engaged in the silk and woollen trades or in ancillary activities.[20] Increases in raw material costs and competition from England weakened the profitability of these industries in the 1760s and 1770s, and loom numbers fell sharply, but in the mid-1780s there appears to have been a marked recovery, helped by parliamentary backing, that lasted for at least a decade. Employment in New Draperies/worsted manufactures was probably never as important as in broadcloth, but it does not seem to have been affected by the setbacks of the '60s.

The city's involvement in the linen trade was of a different kind. From the first decade of the eighteenth century linen became the single most valuable export of the city, and this remained the case for over a hundred years, even though only a small fraction of the cloth was actually woven in the city. Linen was to be one of a small range of commodities for which Dublin became the main point of export. In the 1680s, when the manufacture of linen of export quality was still an infant industry, Dublin handled about one-third of national exports;[21] the main area of production was already south-east Ulster. By the end of the 1690s Dublin's share of linen exports had jumped to over 70 per cent, and this position was to remain unchallenged in the first four decades of the new century, when national exports rose from half a million yards p.a. to over five million. Dublin's share in the first quarter of the century was approximately 85 per cent of the national total and 76 per cent in the second quarter.[22] The bulk of the cloth came overland upwards of sixty miles from Ulster, already in a bleached state, to be purchased by wholesale linen drapers who either disposed of it within the country or consigned it to England.[23] The decision taken by the Linen Board Trustees in 1721 to build a White Linen Hall on the north side of the city, modelled on Blackwell Hall,[24] was a rational attempt to improve the facilities for existing dealers at a time of growing prosperity in the trade, but it also marked the Board's early commitment to develop Dublin as centre of the industry; in the '20s and '30s the Trustees gave subsidies to several bleaching and printing yards on the city's outskirts, and subsequently established a linen yarn hall, cotton hall and warehousing for imported flaxseed; there was a substantial body of linen weavers working in the city — upwards of 3,000 for much of the century — and a number of successful bleachyards carried on trade within a five-mile radius of the Linen Hall.[25] However, the two strategic contributions of Dublin to the industry lay firstly in the development of linen printing, and secondly in financing the rural industry.

Textile printing yards, working with linen and to a much lesser extent silk and mixed cloths, were established close to the city from the 1720s, and there were several very extensive concerns operating in the 1750s and 1760s, lubricated by parliamentary and Dublin Society grants.[26] They were producing strictly for the Irish market until the prohibition on the export of printed linens was lifted in 1779, and had few provincial competitors before the growth of the cotton printing in the 1780s. Even with the subsequent rise of Belfast and Cork printyards the Dublin firms retained their primacy well into the nineteenth century.[27]

The provision of seasonal credit to rural bleachers and dealers became a key element in economic relations between Dublin and the north before the middle of the century. Advances were made by Dublin dealers — increasingly they were specialised linen factors — to enable the Ulster bleachers to make their spring and summer purchases at the brown linen markets. The wholesale trade at the Hall became largely a commission one, but Dublin dealers' command over seasonal credit maintained the city's position in the export trade.[28] The volume of linen exported through the city rose to an all-time maximum of nearly 22,000,000 yards in the early 1790s, although the capital's *relative* importance was slipping from the '40s, as direct contact between Ulster bleachers and English linen merchants was built up through Newry and Belfast: Dublin's share of total exports fell to 57 per cent in the third quarter of the century and 47 per cent in the final quarter. Dublin of course remained the centre of the home market: at the end of the century about one-third of linen exposed for sale in the city was purchased for the home market.[29]

Apart from the profits of the factors and the shippers, Dublin's hold on the linen trade brought enormous indirect benefits: the ancillary employment in handling and packing the cloth was considerable, and the hundreds of inland carriers did not return northwards empty-handed. Dublin's chandlers were said to have regularly sold 100 tons of soap p.a. to bleachers,[30] and the dealers in unconnected trades doubtless thrived on Ulster custom.

Dublin's functions in the linen trade had some less conspicuous parallels. The city became the finishing centre and market place for Wicklow flannels, Queen's County stuffs and at the end of the century the handloom cottons of rural Leinster. And apart from textiles there was cattle processing: Dublin may have been eclipsed by the Munster ports in the export of butter, pork and (to a lesser extent) beef and tallow, but the city's tanners seem to have been more successful in developing overseas markets than their Cork counterparts. Helped by the local demand for harness and shoe leather, they maintained for most of the century a substantial trade with Spain that accounted for well over half of total Irish leather exports.[31]

Those engaged in the overseas trade of Dublin constituted a less than formidable group, for most British and foreign trade was done on English account, and this predominantly commission form of business weakened the corporate development of the merchant body and meant that the great commercial fortunes were made not in overseas trade *per se* but in sugar-baking, brewing, textile finishing, property development and banking.

In banking, Dublin firms were distinctly larger than most of their provincial counterparts. By the early eighteenth century a small number of leading traders had specialised in handling bills of exchange, supplying the facilities for the settlement of accounts between Dublin and London, providing a discounting service for those holding unexpired bills, and issuing promissory notes. A rudimentary inland bill trade had emerged before 1700 with Dublin in a pivotal position, given the flow of rents and exchequer remittances to the capital and Dublin's growing share of foreign trade. Cork alone among the outports developed an independent bill trade with London but, as L. M. Cullen has shown, the movement of Cork exchange rates came to reflect those of Dublin closely after the middle of the century.[32] Dublin's bankers' main profits came from their exchange and discounting activities, although some developed 'West End' characteristics, providing deposit and mortgage facilities to landowning clients.[33] Other financial services, such as insurance and stock trading, were slow to evolve. Dublin-based marine insurance hardly developed beyond the underwriting of coastal shipping; in this area London was capital.[34]

Aside from trade and banking, Dublin was the locus for a range of tertiary activities, political and administrative, cultural and social, that gave the city its metropolitan character. The importance of the law term and the sitting of parliament in the life of the city was evident even in the late 1630s,[35] and the business of parliament and the courts was greatly extended from the 1690s. The quickening of political life in the eighteenth century, the near-permanent residence of the Lord Lieutenant from the 1760s, the annual meeting of parliament from the mid-80s, and the enlarged number of positions in the civil and military establishments, meant that most country gentry felt the need to be in Dublin for a part of every year. The growth of the economy alone seems to have been responsible for the dramatic rise in legal business at the central Four Courts, and in the number of attornies based in the city. Over 700 attornies and 300 barristers had Dublin addresses in 1763, and there were half as many again by 1800.[36]

Apart from its lawyers, Dublin had a concentration of physicians and other medical specialists of sufficient repute to draw business to the city.[37] However, there was limited medical education available before the 1780s and no legal education. Dublin's lawyers were nearly all London-trained, while many of its doctors knew Edinburgh. The only institution of higher learning in the city, Trinity College, doubled its mainly genteel intake between mid-century and the 1790s, but contributed little to the development of professional education — other than preparing most of the future ordinands of the Church of Ireland; nevertheless, with its very considerable human and material resources the College provided a focus for the intelligentsia of the eighteenth-century city. Academies and private schools, offering a mainly classical syllabus for sons of the landed and professional classes, expanded noticeably in the second half of the century, although education in England and on the Continent remained the norm for the sons of the wealthiest.[38]

The most striking dimension of the city's cultural dominance was in the area of publishing. The Dublin book trade, outside the control of British copyright restrictions, thrived on its freedom to reprint London works and this gave it control of the home market and some scope for exports. There were about six master-booksellers and nine printers operating in the 1700s; by the 1780s there were 21 master-booksellers (plus about 30 less established dealers) with about 50 printers in business.[39] These included the newspaper publishers; from the news-sheets of the 1690s to the specialised journals of the 1760s, some 160 newspapers had begun publication in Dublin. Their format was similar to British counterparts, most coming to rely on commercial and property advertising for revenue, but their readership before 1750 was almost exclusively confined to Dublin. With improvements in the postal services and stage-coaching, their distribution in the country widened.[40] The book trade had more of a rural market from the beginning. Catholic booksellers pioneered a distinctive country trade, specialising in devotional works and chapbooks,[41] and the subscription lists of more ambitious publications often reveal strong provincial interest. But the publishing trade, like other craft and luxury manufactures, thrived on its doorstep market — the large number of literate upper- and middle-income households within the city, swollen every winter by the country influx.

Dublin's attractions to the educated and the propertied were sufficient to command the loyalties of all but the wealthiest and most ambitious over the more distant claims of London. The scope for entertainment and 'making connections' — at clubs and coffee-houses, public assemblies and balls, theatre and pleasure grounds — would have exceeded that of Edinburgh, and, if anything, this aspect of Dublin life was enhanced towards the end of the century with the greater number of permanently resident peers and gentry. In the 1790s about a hundred peers had

Dublin addresses, and their current expenditure in the city each year was estimated by contemporaries at around quarter of a million pounds; each M.P., according to one survey on the eve of the Union, spent on average over £1,400 p.a. in the city.[42]

The capital as a source of demand for food and fuel, labour and capital, had less drastic effects on its Irish hinterland before 1750 than its size might suggest, for there was some truth in Arthur Young's claim that until then Dublin had been 'in point of consumption more an English than an Irish city, in corn as much as in coals'.[43] Indeed its dependence on Britain had been wider; many of those who settled in the city in the seventeenth and early eighteenth centuries — skilled, capitalised or otherwise — were cross-channel migrants. As regards fuel, Cumbrian and Scottish pits, as we have seen, supplied the bulk of the city's fuel needs throughout the century, the Dublin market share held by the small Kilkenny and Ballycastle collieries — in spite of half a century of official encouragement — hardly amounting to more than two per cent in the 1790s.[44] Turf became more common as fuel for the poor in years of high coal prices after the opening of the Grand Canal, and an average of about 20,000 tons p.a. was brought in to the city in the later 1790s.[45] High canal tolls were blamed for its failure to become more than an auxiliary fuel.

The city's staple foodstuff was wheaten bread, and before about 1720 nearly all the city's needs were met by the farmers of Meath, north Dublin and Kildare. However, the traditional farming systems of Dublin's old granary districts began to be modified with the intensification of city demand, and in some neighbourhoods there was an early shift to dairying.[46] From the '20s Dublin came to depend for part of its cereal needs on much more distant sources; the city lacked a navigable river system to link it with inland Leinster, and the maritime districts north and south of Dublin had relatively poor soils. However, the coastal baronies of Down and Wexford were able to expand the cultivation of barley and oats for the Dublin market and, more importantly, wheat was available from the light soils and more efficient farming regions of southern and eastern England which underpriced inland Leinster grain, the English export bounty almost covering transport costs, risk and wastage. But between the 1720s and 1750s it was only in the years of serious domestic harvest failure that imports can have constituted much more than half of Dublin's wheat and flour needs.[47] Some of the old tillage districts within twenty-five miles continued to produce a large surplus. But Dublin demand does not appear at this stage to have had quite the fructifying effects on its surrounding region that Edinburgh had on Lothian agriculture. Admittedly mean farm size on good land in north Kildare and South-east Meath seems to have remained large, even by east Leinster standards, and clearly demand from Dublin markets was the key factor.[48] However, the evolution of this zone close to the city is not altogether clear; indeed the only identifiable agricultural innovations in the region before the late eighteenth-century advent of green crops were the more intensive use of lime, and the sub-letting of fallow for cottier potato cultivation.[49]

The potato was a regular element in the city dietary from at latest the early eighteenth century, and was a substitute food when bakers' bread was in short supply.[50] Proximity to water transport and marine fertilisers dictated the location of production, and from the beginning the supply area was the south Munster coast.[51] Potato consumption by the city's poor probably increased somewhat in the later years of the century, but around 1800 only about 10,000 tons p.a. were arriving by sea, canal and cart,[52] which implies a fairly modest place for the potato in city diets by comparison with the countryside.

The trade in wheat and flour remained Dublin's lifeline. Shortages in the mid-50s precipitated the parliamentary initiative of 1757/8 which established a bounty scheme, subsidising the carriage of grain and flour overland to Dublin; this was designed to stimulate inland tillage and to improve Dublin's supplies. The scheme lasted forty years, and underwent considerable adjustments, notably by the inclusion of coastal traffic.[53] Subsidies were sufficiently generous to cover transport costs from locations outside a ten-mile radius of Dublin. The following decades saw a substantial growth in wheat cultivation and rural flour-milling in inland Leinster[54] (paralleled by a considerable extension of oats and barley production), but it is hard to isolate the effects of the bounty legislation from the general impulse given to tillage by the upswing in cereal prices from the mid-60s. Contemporaries believed that the bounties had restored the Dublin market to Irish producers and given the capital cheap bread, although some negative consequences were recognised — the loss of comparative advantage of the old producers close to the city, and the exclusion of consumers elsewhere from its benefits.[55] Certainly in some years the quantity of grain reaching Dublin greatly exceeded the city's internal consumption, and it was re-routed (after the bounty was claimed), but the introduction in 1784 of a more attractive bounty on grain exported from any port except Dublin had a countervailing effect.[56] By the early 1790s the city was experiencing scarcities — or at least the fear of them — for the first time since the 1760s because of the periodic diversion of supplies to the booming cross-channel trade.[57] With the ending of the inland bounty (for financial reasons) in 1797, Dublin was brought in to the export bounty scheme, but by that stage Drogheda had become entrenched as the major east-coast port in the grain trade with Britain.

From the 1760s, then, there was a reorientation of Dublin's food supply-lines. English (and American) imports became a rarity, and first outer Leinster, notably Kilkenny, then Tipperary, Galway and Roscommon constituted the new supply region of the city.[58] Leinster counties received 86 per cent of inland bounty payments in the 1760s, 52 per cent by the 1790s, but these eastern counties remained dominant in the coastal trade throughout, thanks mainly to the great barley and malt trade from Wexford to Dublin.[59] The bounty scheme, whatever the frauds and inefficiencies, had the effect of hastening the intensification of tillage in the midlands and south-east, a region that in the early nineteenth century was to contribute a major share of Ireland's cereal exports to Britain.

Dublin's supplies of other foodstuffs with the exception of citrus fruits came from within the country, vegetables, eggs and milk from near at hand, fish and meat from the other provinces to some extent. It would seem that for all the importance of cattle processing in the life of the city, Dublin was more a mutton- and bacon-eating city than one dependent on beef; some parts of the country specialised in particular lines for the Dublin market, spring mutton in Tipperary, veal in Wicklow and

Kildare.[60] The opening of the first section of the Grand Canal into Kildare in 1779 and its link-up with the Barrow and the Shannon over the following twenty-five years strengthened Dublin's dependence on the midlands as a source of supply of food and fuel: 15 per cent of the 82,000 tons of freight arriving in Dublin in 1800/1 was flour, grain and potatoes, 31 per cent turf and 3 per cent coal. Of the much smaller freight despatched westwards, manure and dung formed two-fifths, a trade that improved environment and agriculture.[61]

The traffic in food to Dublin is easier to trace than the traffic in migrants. There is little doubt that the proportion of foreign-born residents in the city declined rapidly after the early decades, even though English craft workers, particularly in new industries, were quite numerous later on. Dublin employers in the 1780s and 1790s asserted that the inflow even of provincial craftsmen and apprentices had become severely regulated: 'about 1750 . . . the people of every part of Ireland could . . . get work freely in Dublin,' claimed a leading worsted manufacturer in 1782, 'people were often taught their trade for a sum of money, without serving at all';[62] but from the '60s combinations enforced limitations on recruitment. How far this put a brake on the growth of industrial employment and slowed Dublin's growth down is unclear; it undoubtedly stimulated manufacturers and later parliament to develop rural putting-out and the provincial relocation of certain industries.[63]

Assuming that the regional pattern of migration to Dublin recorded in the 1841 census bore some resemblance to earlier movements, it is likely that Leinster, especially the contiguous counties to Dublin, shouldered most of the burden of peopling the city. Eighteenth-century county house returns would seem to confirm this, for growth in the rural Leinster counties was slowest of the four provinces;[64] some districts close to the capital may have surrendered all their natural increases to Dublin.[65] One shift that confirms the changing demographic character of the eighteenth-century city was the disappearance of a Protestant majority; religious returns indicated that there was still a predominance of Protestant households in 1732,[66] but all later informal estimates assumed a Catholic majority. The eclipse of English migration and the great mid-century expansion of the city were responsible for creating a Catholic majority, a change which profoundly affected the city's view of itself.

Dublin by the 1790s was in some respects entering a period of awkward adaptation. The relative decline of its commercial position was in large part a consequence of the maturation of the economy as a whole: first, there was the growing economic independence of Ulster, as Dublin finance became less crucial and as direct links with British dealers and manufacturers strengthened; Belfast was (at last) emerging as a distinct regional capital.[67] Second, changes in the character of Irish foreign trade, notably the increased relative importance of Anglo-Irish trade and the establishment of correspondence between English manufacturers and inland wholesalers weakened the port merchants and specialist importers. This contributed after the turn of the century to the modification of Dublin's financial role within the economy as a settlement centre for inland trade.[68] These trends were hardly visible in the 1790s, and indeed in the industrial sphere Dublin's position seemed stronger than before. With a handloom cotton manufacture developing on the foundation of the old linen trade, a resurgent woollen industry thriving on war contracts, and the brewing and distilling industries being transformed in scale by legislative cosseting and new technology, the industrial prospects of Dublin in the 1790s seemed encouraging. However, as it turned out, Dublin — no more than the British ports — managed to hold its manufacturing base intact in the early nineteenth century; the comprehensive collapse of employment in textiles and in a number of other handicraft trades in the 1820s and 1830s was however to be unusually traumatic, thanks in part to the manner in which industrial protection was dismantled.[69] But the overall contraction of luxury manufactures was the result of a combination of factors: the dislocating effects of the Industrial Revolution and the somewhat less conspicuous consumption of the new élite of post-Union Dublin. The aristocratic withdrawal from the city in the wake of the Union is not completely a myth, although the growth of absenteeism was greatly exaggerated. But as Edinburgh had done, so Dublin adapted to the decline of its 'West End' element and became more of a professional city. The civilian bureaucracy expanded, the legal profession's growth rate was at least maintained, and educational institutions at all levels multiplied.

There were perhaps two distinctive characteristics of Dublin's role as capital in the period considered here. First, the eighteenth century was to be the only time Dublin was the unrivalled social and economic centre for the whole island. The dependence of Ulster, the most vigorous regional economy of eighteenth-century Ireland, on Dublin as market-place, financial centre and (for the Anglican landed classes at least) cultural capital was decisive in powering the city's growth. It was however a short-lived supremacy, as Ulster was to develop stronger cross-channel economic links and, subsequently, Belfast was to become a largely autonomous regional capital — the latter process being only completed in the Victorian age, with Belfast emerging as a real challenge to Dublin's commercial primacy. The second distinctive aspect of eighteenth-century Dublin's relationship with the country was the very concentration of so many economic and social functions in one city; one answer to the pamphleteer who in 1798 claimed that Dublin had thrived over the previous century when Edinburgh had hardly grown, is simply that Dublin had combined the functions of *both* Edinburgh and Glasgow — even if some aspects of foreign trade, notably provisions exports, were left to the Munster ports.[70]

Dublin's multi-faceted primacy was less enduring than that of London or the other major pre-industrial port-capitals, because its evolution as a capital was very much shaped by the political economy of the country. Its hegemony occurred during, and was a function of a transitional phase in, the integration of the Irish economy into the widening British system. Thus, in retrospect, the eighteenth-century city was far more important in determining Irish social and political development than in influencing the national economy. As the transmitter of new fashions and new ideas, derived usually from Britain, it set the tone for contemporary Anglo-Ireland. But it was also the locus for the formation of dissenting organisations; nearly all the opposition movements during the century crystallised in the city: the Patriot movement in the 1740s, the Catholic Committee in the 1750s, craft and industrial combinations in the 1760s, Whig reformism in the

1780s and, with Belfast, the United Irish Movement in the 1790s. Dublin provided the occasion and, in some cases, the necessary cover for association and organisation, as well as the means of propagation through the easy availability of the printing press. Of all these groups the Catholic Committee, maturing in the 1790s, was perhaps the one shaped most by its Dublin environment; the 'eminent' Catholic sugar-bakers and booksellers, lawyers and physicians provided the basic administrative energy and resources that their provincial counterparts either could not or would not commit. Insofar as eighteenth-century Dublin was a source of 'modernisation', the development of Catholic constitutional aspirations was its most fundamental contribution to this process.

REFERENCES

1. See John Dunton's comments on Dublin in 1698: E. MacLysaght, *Irish Life in the Seventeenth Century* (Shannon, 1969), pp. 377–90. I am grateful to L. M. Cullen, Arnold Horner and Peter M. Solar for helpful comments on an earlier draft of this paper.

2. *Dublin Weekly Journal*, 16 Aug. 1729, quoted in J. U. Nef, *The Rise of the British Coal Industry* (London, 1932), I, p. 91; 'Maxims Controlled in Ireland', in Jonathan Swift, *Irish Tracts, 1728–33*, ed. Herbert Davis (Oxford, 1971), p. 135.

3. Rev. J. Whitelaw, *An Essay on the Population of Dublin* (Dublin, 1805).

4. These and subsequent remarks on Dublin population are elaborated in my unpublished paper, 'The Size of Eighteenth-Century Dublin' (1982).

5. D. F. Ó Gráda, 'Dublin 1730–1850: The Origin and Early Growth of Suburban Development' (unpublished M.Sc. thesis, University of Dublin, 1979), pp. 6, 9; J. S. Price, 'Dublin 1750 to 1850: Spatial Distribution and Organisation of Economic Activity' (unpublished M.Sc. thesis, University of Dublin, 1980), p. 51.

6. The national population estimates used in this paper are derived from Stuart Daultrey, David Dickson and Cormac Ó Gráda, 'Eighteenth-Century Irish Population: New Perspectives from Old Sources', *Journal of Economic History*, xli, 3 (Sept. 1981), p. 624.

7. P.R.O. (London), Customs 15.

8. L. M. Cullen, *Anglo-Irish Trade 1660–1800* (Manchester, 1968), p. 78.

9. P.R.O. (London), Customs 15. Dublin's share of national tonnage averaged 55 per cent in the first quarter of the century, 54 per cent in the second, 55 per cent in the third and 40 per cent in the fourth. In the 1810s it had fallen further to about 35 per cent.

10. P.R.O. (London), Customs 15.

11. Ibid.

12. See Dillon Correspondence, 1730–55, National Library of Ireland, Mic. p. 2762; Reports on the Trades and Manufactures of Dublin *c*.1834, Haliday MSS, Royal Irish Academy MS 4. B. 31, I, pp. 66–7 (hereafter cited as Haliday Reports). I am grateful to John McHugh for bringing this remarkable document to my attention.

13. Cullen, *Anglo-Irish Trade*, p. 38.

14. Cullen, *An Economic History of Ireland since 1660* (London, 1972), pp. 37–9.

15. P.R.O. (London), Customs 15.

16. Cullen, *Anglo-Irish Trade*, p. 14; Dickson, 'An Economic History of the Cork Region in the Eighteenth Century' (unpublished Ph.D. thesis, University of Dublin, 1977), pp. 495–7.

17. Cullen, *Anglo-Irish Trade*, p. 15.

18. Cullen, *Anglo-Irish Trade*, pp. 11–16. Cf. Dickson, 'Cork', pp. 420–6.

19. *The Reports and Observations of Robert Stephenson to the . . . Trustees of the Linen Manufacture for the years 1760 and 1761* (Dublin, 1762), pp. 102–3; *To the . . . Trustees of the Linen Board the Report of John Arbuthnot Esq.* (n.p.[1783]), pp. 51–2.

20. Report from the Committee appointed to enquire into the state of the Manufactures of this Kingdom, 5 March 1784, *Journals of the House of Commons of Ireland*, XI, appendix pp. cxliii, cliii; J. Warburton, J. Whitelaw and R. Walsh, *History of the City of Dublin* (London, 1818), II, pp. 983–5.

21. Returns of Irish Imports and Exports 1682/3 — 1685/6, B.L. Add. MS 4759.

22. P.R.O. (London), Customs 15.

23. Cullen, *Anglo-Irish Trade*, pp. 95–6.

24. Conrad Gill, *The Rise of the Irish Linen Industry* (Oxford, 1925), pp. 79–80.

25. *Stephenson Reports, 1760 and 1761*, pp. 102–3; Report from the Grand Committee for Trade, 3 March 1782, *J.H.C.I.* X, appendix p. cxi; Gill, *Linen*, pp. 297–8.

26. Twelve printing-yard sites close to the city have been identified: A. K. Longfield, 'History of the Irish Linen and Cotton Printing Industry in the Eighteenth Century', *Journal of the Royal Society of Antiquaries of Ireland*, lxvii (1937), pp. 26–56.

27. David Dickson, 'Aspects of the Rise and Decline of the Irish Cotton Industry', in L. M. Cullen and T. C. Smout, eds., *Comparative Aspects of Scottish and Irish Economic and Social History 1600-1900* (Edinburgh, 1977), pp. 104, 106, 109–10.

28. Gill, *Linen*, pp. 80–1; Cullen, *Anglo-Irish Trade*, pp. 95–7, 103.

29. P.R.O. (London), Customs 15; Joseph Archer, *Statistical Survey of the County of Dublin* (Dublin, 1801), pp. 82, 84. Dublin also maintained a commanding position in overseas exports, although direct exports were very small by comparison with the British trade.

30. Haliday Reports, I, p. 89.

31. The trade peaked in the early '60s and fell away after the mid-70s: P.R.O. (London), Customs 15.

32. Cullen, *Anglo-Irish Trade*, ch. ix, esp. pp. 168–9.

33. Constantia Maxwell, *Dublin under the Georges* (London, 1936), pp. 245–6.

34. Warburton *et al.*, *Dublin*, II, pp. 987–8; Cullen, *Anglo-Irish Trade*, p. 138.

35. D. R. Hainsworth, 'Christopher Lowther's Canary Adventure: A Merchant Venturer in Dublin 1632-3', *Irish Economic and Social History*, ii (1975), pp. 27–8. Cf. *London Gazette*, 10 Feb. 1666 [17].

36. *Wilson's Dublin Directory for 1763; 1800*.

37. There were 94 physicians and surgeons in 1763, 138 twenty-five years later: *Dublin Directory, 1763; 1788*. Cf. R. B. McDowell, *Ireland in the Age of Imperialism and Revolution, 1760-1801* (Oxford, 1979), pp. 25–6.

38. McDowell, *Ireland in the Age of Imperialism*, pp. 84–92.

39. These are figures suggested in J. W. Phillips, 'A Bibliographical Inquiry into Printing and Bookselling in Dublin from 1670 to 1800' (unpublished Ph.D. thesis, University of Dublin, 1952), pp. 44, 66.

40. Robert Munter, *The History of the Irish Newspaper 1685-1760* (Cambridge, 1967), passim.

41. Phillips, 'Dublin Printing', pp. 48, 125–8.

42. Memorandum (printed) on Dublin's anticipated losses by the Union, 1800, P.R.O.N.I. Foster MSS, D207/10/9; Richard Jebb, *A Reply to a Pamphlet, Entitled Arguments for and against an Union*, 3rd ed. (Dublin, 1799), pp. 34–5; Maxwell, *Dublin*, pp. 245–6; McDowell, *Ireland in the Age of Imperialism*, pp. 24–5. Cf. *J.H.C.I.* IX, appendix p. cccxi.

43. Arthur Young, *A Tour in Ireland* . . . (Dublin, 1780), II, appendix p. 114.

44. *J.H.C.I.*, XVI, appendix pp. ccccxliii-iv; Hely Dutton, *Observations on Mr. Archer's Statistical Survey of the County of Dublin* (Dublin, 1802), p. 105; John Duboudieu, *Statistical Survey of the County of Antrim* (Dublin, 1812), pp. 79–84; Warburton *et al.*, *Dublin*, II, p. 1143n.

45. Dutton, *Observations*, p. 105. Cf. *Dublin Evening Post*, 1 April 1797.

46. Sam[uel] Pierson, *Farther Considerations for the Improvement of the Tillage of Ireland* . . . (Dublin, 1730), pp. 30–1.

47. Over the five years ending 25 March 1757 — a period of defective domestic harvests — Irish wheat brought to the market-house in Thomas St. formed only 40 per cent of the total legally declared wheat brought overland and imported into the city: *The Gentleman's and London Magazine*, xxvi (Dublin, 1757), p. 657.

48. Arnold Horner, 'Aspects of the Historical Geography of parts of the Duke of Leinster's Estates in Co. Kildare *c.*1750-1850' (unpublished B.A. thesis, Dept. of Geography, Trinity College, Dublin, 1968), pp. 37, 40, 73; Horner, 'Stability and Change in the Towns and Villages west of Dublin: An Investigation' (unpublished Ph.D. thesis, University of Dublin, 1974), p. 37; Peter Connell, 'An Economic Geography of Co. Meath, 1770-1870' (unpublished M.A. thesis, Maynooth College, 1979).

49. Young, *Tour*, I, pp. 9, 17-8, 25-6; Dutton, *Observations*, p. 26.

50. See *Dublin Gazette*, 17-21 Aug. 1736; 5-8 July 1740.

51. Dickson, 'Cork', pp. 328, 340-2, 466.

52. Account of Potatoes shipped Coastways to Dublin, 1798 and 1799, State Paper Office (Dublin), Official Papers 72/6; Ruth Delany, *The Grand Canal of Ireland* (Newton Abbot, 1973), p. 234.

53. K. H. Connell, *The Population of Ireland 1750-1845* (Oxford, 1950), pp. 270-1.

54. See L. M. Cullen, 'Eighteenth-Century Flour Milling in Ireland', *I.E.S.H.* iv (1977), pp. 5-25.

55. Observations on the Acts of Parliament of the 31st George II, c. 3 and of 33 George II, c. 12 (Dublin, 1768), pp. 1-2; Young, *Tour*, II, appendix pp. 114-44.

56. Connell, *Population*, pp. 109-12.

57. *J.H.C.I.* XIV, appendix pp. cccxii-xiv, cccxvii.

58. As the proportion of the bounty paid to non-Leinster counties rose in the 1780s, so did the relative importance of flour over unprocessed grain.

59. *J.H.C.I.* at large.

60. Young, *Tour*, I, p. 127, II, appendix p. 80; T. J. Rawson, *Statistical Survey of the County of Kildare* (Dublin, 1807), pp. 13-14; Warburton *et al.*, *Dublin*, II, pp. 1127n., 1129-30; Charles Varley, *The Unfortunate Husbandman*, ed. Desmond Clarke (London, 1964), pp. 70, 78-9.

61. Delany, *Grand Canal*, pp. 73, 234.

62. *J.H.C.I.* X, appendix p. cxv.

63. Cf. Dickson, 'Cotton Industry', pp. 101-2.

64. See Daultrey, Dickson and Ó Gráda, 'Irish Population', pp. 625-7.

65. Horner's findings indicate a long-term stagnation of house numbers in the manor of Maynooth: Horner, 'Duke of Leinster's Estates', pp. 35-6, 74-6. No attempt has as yet been made to calculate mortality levels for eighteenth-century Dublin, but judging by the pattern in comparable cities, it must be assumed that urban growth could only have been achieved by heavy immigration.

66. F. G. James, *Ireland in the Empire, 1688-1770* (Cambridge, Mass. 1973), pp. 315-6.

67. Cf. Maxwell, *Country and Town in Ireland under the Georges* (Dundalk, 1949), p. 234.

68. Cullen, *Anglo-Irish Trade*, pp. 203-4.

69. See Dickson, 'Cotton Industry', pp. 110-11.

70. See *Reasons against an Union: In which 'Arguments for and against an Union' supposed to have come from a Person in High Station, are particularly considered*, 2nd ed. (Dublin, 1798), pp. 19-20. The author himself believed that Edinburgh had 'remained nearly stationary, because it has ceased to be capital', and that Dublin's prosperity was precisely because of its capital function which would disappear in the event of a Union. This argument, in various forms, was a popular theme in anti-Union writings.

15

Belfast and Glasgow: Connections and Comparisons, 1790–1850

John Butt

ALTHOUGH clearly towns of developing economic and social significance in 1790, both Belfast and Glasgow, especially the former, were more likely to impress visitors with their amenity than their industry.[1] Undoubtedly, this impression would have been superficial, as most judgments by visitors tend to be, but their commercial élites were composed of merchants rather than industrialists, and the influence of some local landowners, the Campbells and the Maxwells in Glasgow and the Donegalls in Belfast, remained strong. By 1850 Belfast (which had a population of about 13,000 in 1790) had increased its population nearly eightfold (to 103,000 in 1851) and clearly become an industrial town — eleventh in British rankings, excluding London. Because Glasgow's growth in the eighteenth century had been more substantial, its population increase to 375,000 was less spectacular, in fact probably about fivefold.[2] However, both towns shared a common experience: they were products of, and contributors to, the process of industrialisation which had not merely widened their manufacturing structure, but also greatly extended their mercantile functions. Moreover the North Channel, which in earlier centuries had clearly separated Ulster from Scotland, was no impediment to social and economic interaction between the two towns, for the new steamboat technology nurtured on the Clyde in the first two decades of the nineteenth century greatly reduced transport costs and quickened journey times.

The cultural heritage was a unifying influence and had been so for at least two centuries. Ulstermen had made their way to the Scottish universities ever since the Plantation, and Scottish-trained ministers were constant bulwarks of Irish Presbyterianism. Migration and trade between the two communities via Belfast were well established by the late eighteenth century. Connections between the two towns were sometimes obviously direct and sometimes implicit and subtle. The same might be said of comparisons which can be made between them.

Although Belfast began to show obvious signs of physical expansion from the 1770s, Glasgow's development of new squares and streets was more marked until the 1830s. From the High Street and Trongate, the ancient centre of the town, new streets such as Buchanan Street and residential squares like St Enoch's Square and George Square attracted middle-class residents in great numbers; the movement westward had begun. Building companies and speculative partnerships responded to the demand for commercial and residential premises and also satisfied the often safer market for public buildings and utilities. Some of the latter were very significant employers of labour, including men from Ulster, for Glasgow interests inspired the Forth and Clyde and the Monkland Canals and later the first significant railways of Lanarkshire, the Monkland and Kirkintilloch (1826) and the Garnkirk and Glasgow (1831).[3]

Although the local building cycle still requires investigation, it is clear that Glasgow's building industry was very actively employed during the early years of the French Wars and in the 1820s and 1830s, with but relatively short intervals of crisis occasioned by sharp upward movements in interest rates. Experience in the 1840s was apparently much more mixed, although railway development in the latter years of the decade was a great stimulus. Inevitably, speculative builders, such as Dugald Bannatyne in the 1790s or William Harley in the period 1803-1814, symbolised both booms and depressions; their failures for very large sums of money did not demolish the streets and facilities which they had financed.[4] William and James Carsewell did not become bankrupt like Bannatyne and Harley, and they erected houses and business premises valued at £210,000 between 1807 and 1819.[5]

Belfast was much more under the control of the Donegall family, and its physical development, unlike Glasgow's, was at first largely dependent on an absentee landlord, the fifth earl, who spent most of his time in London or on his Staffordshire estate. Nonetheless, he was a great improver and townplanner, contributing substantially to the development of the town and adopting a liberal leasing policy. His son was a profligate who was compelled to reside in Belfast in the unsuccessful hope that he would thereby be free from his London creditors. He could not afford to act as a developer but equally he could not obstruct those who had the money and the ambition to speculate in urban development. Georgian Belfast came to be known, perhaps unkindly, as the 'Athens of Ireland' but, like Glasgow, it provided opportunities for local architects, such as Roger Mulholland, to demonstrate their genius.[6]

In both towns an energetic merchant class financed and controlled physical and economic expansion. There was some interchange between them and more intermarriage: the Gordons, Tennants, Connells and Montgomerys were represented in both élites before 1820, and the Barbours and Gemmills transferred their main operations to Belfast from Glasgow in the late eighteenth century. Both towns established their Chambers of Commerce in 1783, and both élites were tightly knit until the 1830s. Foreign and domestic trade was the main plank upon which the industrial structure rested in both towns. The merchant communities in Belfast and Glasgow performed essential economic functions for their hinterlands. They warehoused stock for a range of producers and served an extending geographical range of customers; they controlled the putting out system and transformed methods and organisation of production, making the evolution of the textile factory inevitable; they either financed or owned other industrial concerns such as grain mills, breweries, distilleries, glassworks, potteries, foundries and tanneries; they manipulated the supply of food to their towns and attempted to control their societies. Capital, land and labour were at their behest, and the inexorable laws of supply and demand were their shibboleths.

Glasgow was a much more significant centre of international trade than Belfast throughout this period. Even after the War of Independence Glasgow firms continued to control the American tobacco trade, although the end of the colonial connection made direct trade to the Continent the inevitable successor of what had been essentially a re-export activity. Trade with the West Indies was already well established by the middle of the eighteenth century, and after the American War began, increased its importance: sugar, rum and cotton replaced tobacco as leading imports, and in 1790 over 22 per cent of Scotland's imports came from these islands and 26 per cent of her exports went to them.[7]

Glasgow increased her trade with the Baltic after 1800, in particular sending greater quantities of cotton yarn to Germany and Russia from country mills such as New Lanark and Blantyre. Gradually, as the city became more industrial, its own cotton mills produced goods and yarn for a range of continental and Asiatic customers, India being a principal market from the 1830s.[8] As the iron industry of Lanarkshire developed in the 1830s and 1840s, pig iron and metalware became significant items in coastal and foreign trade.[9] From the industrial villages and towns of the Clyde basin, Glasgow merchants exported a range of commodities more varied than this brief discussion might suggest: glass from Dumbarton, sulphuric acid, bleaching powder and alkali from Dalmuir and Springburn, guns and shot from Carron and Calder, plantation tools from Port Dundas, beer and whisky from a range of suppliers along the banks of the Forth and Clyde Canal, coal and machinery to Dublin and Belfast.

Belfast's foreign trade was less substantial in volume and less diverse, although her industrial structure widened considerably in this period and provided an increasing range of products. Essentially, however, the basis of Belfast's trade was its increasing control over Irish linen exports, its development of food processing and the exports this activity engendered, and its imports of raw materials and a variety of industrial goods. By 1835 Belfast was, in terms of value of trade, the leading port of all Ireland, with £7.9 million against Dublin's £6.9 million.[10] The textile base had widened with the introduction of cotton in 1784, but over half of Belfast's exports were linen, with foodstuffs, including livestock, and cotton coming very much lower in the ranking order. Linen yarn was the leading import in 1835, followed by woollen goods, tea, cotton goods, clothing, sugar and coal.[11]

Belfast's port facilities were generally better than Glasgow's throughout the period under review. Reports in the eighteenth century by John Smeaton (1755 and 1758), John Golbourne (1768), and James Watt (1769) confirm the view that the Clyde at Glasgow was a shallow waterway which required extensive improvement before adequate docks could be built to handle the trade of the town. After 1790 John Rennie and Thomas Telford were merely the two most eminent civil engineers employed by the town of Glasgow to improve navigation and plan new docks. The process was continuous: in 1813 the length of the quay was only 941 feet, but dock space had been increased to 8,562 feet by 1848. Still the harbour was reported as overcrowded.[12]

Plans to improve the harbour at Belfast had been relatively numerous but abortive, and by 1785, when the Ballast Board was established to improve the port, the problems had been clearly diagnosed: inadequate quays, shallow water and a winding channel. Walker and Burges, the consulting engineers, later employed at Glasgow, produced the report in 1831 upon which improvement was based. A deep channel for the Lagan was begun in 1839, and by 1847, when the Belfast Harbour Commissioners replaced the Ballast Board, the basis for the development of the modern port had been laid.[13] Both towns improved their port facilities as a laggard response to the development of trade and local industry. But the ports were also great employers of labour: by 1815 over 10,000 men were at work on Glasgow-based ships, and this total excludes casual workers such as dockers.[14]

If the transport industries became great employers of labour in the first half of the nineteenth century, the production of fine linens such as lawns and cambrics had been Glasgow's principal economic activity from the mid-eighteenth century. This gave way after 1785 to cotton weaving, especially of fine muslins from yarn produced on mules, and of pullicate handkerchiefs. By 1850 the cotton industry was Glasgow's most important manufacturing industry in terms of capital and labour employed. That development was spectacular and rapid because it was possible for the new industry to attract capital, labour and enterprise from the fine linen industry.[15] However, the cotton spinning mills were new, although concentration of production in linen manufactories had been occurring in Glasgow from at least the 1750s. There were few unoccupied waterpower sites in the town, and therefore the Glasgow merchant community, including some of its foreign traders, invested in large country mills such as New Lanark, Catrine, Deanston and Stanley.[16] These ventures, in general, produced warp yarns using water frames, but from the late 1790s factory mule spinning became more common, and the principal development was in Glasgow itself. Improvements in Boulton and Watt engines — and the end of the patent in 1800 — contributed to this process.

The North Woodside mills were the first to be established in Glasgow in 1784; the site had previously been used for grain milling and malting.[17] At Springfield Robert Muir erected a steam engine in January 1792 at the new mill of Messrs. Scott and Stevenson.[18] Later, in the 1790s, there was much unpleasantness between Muir, his patron John Pattison and the firm of Boulton and Watt, the latter threatening legal action for piracy.[19] Most Glasgow cotton factories before 1800 were small affairs using hand-powered jennies or horse gins. A note made for the use of Boulton and Watt in August 1798 listed only four Glasgow mills using steampower and five with horse gins. Fire insurance records confirm the picture of a small 'Jennie cotton spinning house' as being most typical.[20]

Pattison and Henry Houldsworth — who had come to Glasgow from Nottingham to manage the North Woodside Mill and then gone independent — were the first to change this picture. They built large-scale steam-powered mills in Bridgeton and Anderston soon after 1800 and were aped by others such as the Dunlops, Oswalds, and Bartholomews. Cleland estimated that Glasgow manufacturers in 1818 owned 52 cotton mills, representing at least £1 million in capital investment and containing over half a million spindles.[21] At the census of 1831 Glasgow and its suburbs possessed 107 steam-driven cotton mills, including, of course, a number of power loom factories.[22] The increasing application of steampower to the mule and the increased spindleage which these machines had reached by 1840 further encouraged the concentration of the industry in Glasgow, where coal was cheap and engineering skills were developing rapidly.

Output naturally reflected these developments. In 1818, 105 million yards of cotton cloth were made in the Glasgow district worth £5.2 million, nearly half of which went for export. City enterprise controlled 16 weaving factories, 32,000 hand looms, 18 calico printing works and 19 calendar and lapping houses.[23] Some firms, notably James Finlay and Company and the Monteiths of Pollokshaws, pioneered the application of power looms within integrated factory complexes, but most were specialists in either spinning or weaving before 1850.[24]

The cotton industry, as already indicated, imparted an impetus to other industries, notably bleaching, dyeing and printing, not to mention machine-making and heavy chemicals. A wider momentum developed, despite the significance of the leading sector. For instance, Tennant, Knox and Company's St Rollox works at Springburn (established in 1799) at first concentrated on the production of bleaching materials for the cotton industry, particularly sulphuric acid, but this later formed the base for supplying a number of other industries, notably the soapmakers and the glass producers, with essential chemicals. The association with textiles was not merely profitable for the infant chemical industry; it also made possible the gradual assimilation of skill, if not genius, capable of producing a range of materials such as solvents, dyestuffs and mordants from which further technical progress was possible.[25]

Just as the chemical industry attracted incoming enterprise such as Tennant, the MacIntosh family, and P. J. Papillon and his sons from Rouen with the secret of turkey-red dyeing, so Glasgow gained expertise in machine-making.[26] As with chemicals, there was a local primitive engineering tradition which matured later in the nineteenth century. Archibald Buchanan, trained at Cromford, his nephew James Smith of Deanston and Robert Burns of Johnstone built and developed early textile machinery.[27] However, a reservoir of skilled craftsmen developed who could serve a wider range of industries. The Houldsworths added a foundry to their cotton empire and then an ironworks.[28] These incomers, like Robert Walsh of Halifax, who transferred his carding machinery business from Yorkshire to Glasgow in 1794, responded at first to the stimuli provided by the expansion of the cotton industry and then grafted onto this narrow base a variegated range of other engineering products.[29]

The small metalware trade was often the beginning of greater glory. Claud Girdwood, Stephen Miller and James Cook began businesses in the 1790s with the intention of supplying cast-iron household utensils and small malleable iron items such as files, locks, hinges and nails and soon responded to the boom in demand for textile machinery. In the Gorbals, gunsmiths were well established by the middle of the eighteenth century, and at Partick, Dalnottar and Springboig workshops existed for the production of edge tools. Population growth and urbanisation increased the demand for nails, pans, grates, fireplaces, railings, gutters and drainage pipes.

Growing civic sophistication was manifested in the demand for cisterns, baths, sanitary equipment, gas retorts and pipes, and water pipes. Glasgow's foundries at Port Dundas, Camlachie, Anderston and Maryhill met these demands in competition with ironworks at Carron and increasingly, after 1825, in Lanarkshire.[30]

Specialist products — machinery for sugar mills and rum distilleries, steam engines (which most engineering firms by 1850 made to order), cables, anchors and marine engines for the developing Clyde shipbuilding industry, locomotives and railway metal — presented few problems by the 1830s to the forges and foundries of Glasgow. Indeed, skilled labour and access to cheap iron and coal were the city's main advantages.

Urban growth also stimulated the food and drink industries. Grain milling was long established on the Kelvin at Partick, but two developments at different periods effected changes. The Forth and Clyde Canal encouraged milling, malting, brewing, and distilling to concentrate at Port Dundas — and also sugar refining — after 1800, although at Anderston and Wellpark large urban breweries maintained an impetus which was aided by the improvements in Glasgow's docks. This second development, most apparent from the 1830s, encouraged the growth of additional steam-powered flour mills at Cranstonhill and Anderston.[31]

Consumer-oriented industries increased their general significance by 1850. Glasgow by 1825 had 41 corn merchants and 2 maltsters, and by 1851 1,569 bakers, 839 butchers, 1,178 grocers, 920 drapers and 951 wine and spirit merchants.[32] The manufacture of shoes and clothing, especially hats and shirts, the expanding production of glass and pottery, the increase in the number of carpenters and cabinet makers, manifest in the *Directories*, all confirm the impression that the city had a diversified economic structure.

In analysing the employment effects of Glasgow's economic growth, the impression that textiles were still dominant in 1851 remains. The number of handloom weavers dropped sharply in the 1840s, but by then Glasgow firms were exporting fancy work to the Belfast area, and the application of the power loom undoubtedly had taken its toll of plain weaving. Among male workers in 1851, about 15,000 were engaged in the 'cotton manufacture', and there were over 22,000 females so employed. Three groups of male workers fell between 4,000 and 5,000 — labourers, shoemakers and iron workers. Falling between 3,000 and 4,000 were the masons, carpenters and porters, and groups over 2,000 included, in addition, tailors, car men, commercial clerks, engine and machine makers, and blacksmiths. For women the main occupation after 'the cotton manufacture' was domestic service, with 11,600. Clearly, the skilled metal trades and engineering were growing in significance as employers, but spinning and weaving and unskilled and semi-skilled work were more representative.[33]

Visitors to Belfast in the late eighteenth century, such as Arthur Young, were undoubtedly impressed by the fact that the town was the principal regional market for linen. Its linen drapers formed an extremely important cohort within the mercantile élite to add to the shipowners and foreign traders whose wealth was clearly obvious. Connections with the West Indies had led to the establishment of three sugar refineries; as a port Belfast had its ropeworks, canvas-making, ship-fitting and provisioning; its commitment to linen and its finishing supported the production of bleaching agents, notably sulphuric acid.[34] Indeed, in many respects it mirrored in 1790, within a smaller image, the earlier experience of Glasgow.

To supply the needs of an affluent élite, wine, tobacco and books were among its imports; its consumer industries included pottery and glass. Growing affluence was marked by improved domestic architecture and increased numbers of public buildings — churches, schools, the Poorhouse, the Academy and the Linen Hall. Transport improvement more generally in Ulster had served to increase competition from Dublin's merchant class, but slowly and surely Belfast exerted its economic power and advantages. Its hinterland regularly produced a surplus of food, part of which was processed in the town. This clearly had long-term implications for the cost of living, employment and labour costs. With more land available to maintain farmer-weavers in its vicinity and more scope for leasing land at lower rents than in Dublin, Belfast attracted men of enterprise, keen to extend the putting out system. They had long been backed by most landowners who saw the linen industry as a means of increasing their rentrolls and the town of Belfast as a growing market for food and a source of goods and services.[35]

Thus, Belfast established itself as a market for fine linen, and its businessmen set the price levels for a wider range of commodities and factors of production, including labour, in an autonomous but growing region. Whereas Glasgow's fine linen production declined as her cotton trade grew, this was not the case in Belfast. In 1820 Belfast exported to Britain 12.8 million yards of linen cloth or 34 per cent of total Irish exports, compared with 8.6 million yards in 1790 or 23 per cent. The advent of cotton served simply to supplement the fine linen trade. Dublin also took up the new industry and indeed outstripped Belfast in terms of cotton wool and yarn imports until the middle of the first decade of the nineteenth century. Thereafter Belfast gradually left the capital behind, and by 1835 accounted for 73 per cent of Irish imports of cotton wool and yarn.[36]

Robert Joy, merchant, Thomas McCabe, watchmaker, and Joy's brother-in-law John McCracken, a retired sea-captain with about twenty years' experience in rope and canvas making, employed Nicholas Grimshaw, a Lancastrian, as their technical expert and in 1778 began cotton production in premises rented from the Belfast Charitable Society's Poorhouse, using the pauper children as piecers. Grimshaw, in association with Nathaniel Wilson, a Belfast linen manufacturer, established the Whitehouse spinning mill in 1784, but this was on a rather larger scale than most of the early mills. After 1800 larger firms such as John McCracken's Francis Street mill (*c.*1803), John Milford and Company (1805) and McCrum, Lepper and Company (1811) were established. Cotton handloom weaving tended to replace linen weaving because the weavers found that by producing muslins they could earn greater incomes. Probably, Glasgow merchants began to seek agencies in Belfast in the 1790s and introduced muslin weaving from Scotland. The diffusion of mule spinning to Ulster after 1800 was probably a consequence of the wartime demand for fine muslins in the British market, and in the neighbourhood of Belfast steam-powered mills became relatively common in the first decade of the nineteenth century.[38]

Glasgow after 1800 gradually began to dominate the Belfast cotton trade, finding Ulster weavers a cheaper substitute at a time when Scottish weavers' combinations were forcing up piece-rates and challenging their employers in the Courts. The celebrated Scottish weavers' strike of 1812 further accelerated this process.[39]

In the vicinity of Belfast there were 33 cotton mills *c.*1811; by 1824 there were 22, and in 1840 only 10. Lancashire and the West of Scotland dominated the cotton industry, as Belfast reverted to an increasing specialisation in linen, only this time under factory conditions. The removal of protection from the Irish industry began the movement away from cotton which, in any case, after 1810 was increasingly threatened by British dumping when foreign markets collapsed. Wet spinning was developed as a technique in 1825 and placed the traditional Irish linen industry in danger. Significantly, the leading firm in flax spinning were Thomas Mulholland and Sons, originally muslin manufacturers, who lost a mill by fire in 1828. They decided because of English and Scottish competition to turn to spinning flax in their new mill, and in the 1830s their example was rapidly followed. By 1840 there were 18 flax-spinning firms in Belfast and its environs, and by 1852 there were another 6. The change to power weaving of linen was much slower, and by 1850 there were only 100 power looms in Belfast.[40]

Belfast's base in the metal trades in 1790 was much more fragile than that of Glasgow. Nail-making was a specialisation at Newtownbreda, not far away; the clock and watchmakers were used to precision work, and a number of them were to contribute to the development of mechanical engineering in the town; iron founding was represented by two firms: one founded by Stewart Hadskis in 1760, and the other in 1783 by Benjamin Edwards near his Ballymacarret glassworks. Although the number of foundries increased significantly by 1840, Dublin was a more important centre of iron founding in the first half of the nineteenth century. However, the range of products widened considerably from pots and pans to machinery for paper mills and bleachfields. Steam engines and textile machinery gradually became significant items in output, particularly in the 1830s and 1840s, but there was extensive competition from Scotland and England for the market in light castings. Most steam engines were made for local customers, and in 1838 Belfast had 50, about a third of the total number in Ireland, working in linen and cotton factories, foundries, grainmills and in a miscellany of other industrial establishments. At that date the nine foundries probably employed about 500 men.[41]

A foretaste of a brilliant future in shipbuilding might have been noticed by an exceptional observer. Belfast Lough had been a small-scale shipbuilding centre ever since the seventeenth century, but the only shipbuilder of note was William Ritchie, who came from Saltcoats, Ayrshire in 1791. The Clyde was the pioneer in the production of iron steamboats, but in 1820 Ritchie and his Dumbarton partner, MacLaine, built a steamboat, a wooden vessel with an engine made at Coates and Young's Lagan Foundry (established *c.*1799). Before 1850 only three firms built wooden sailing vessels in Belfast: Ritchie and MacLaine, Thompson and Kirwan, and Charles Connell and Sons. Between them they produced only about 50 ships in the period from 1820 to 1850. Iron shipbuilding was carried on in the 1840s, but only on a small scale. However, by 1850 Belfast had acquired some experience of marine engine design, and its shipyards had begun to exploit the structural material of the future.[42]

Like Glasgow's merchants who were heavily involved in railway finance, Belfast's merchants were not simply content to improve local roads and the Lagan Canal. They were also the main suppliers of capital for the Ulster Railway, completed in 1842, and continued to support transport improvements throughout the 1840s.[43]

An indication of Belfast's abundant local food supply was the development of an export trade in corn, potatoes, cattle and general provisions, particularly hams, bacon and butter. This occurred at the same time as a substantial growth in the town's population and the expansion of the local distilling and brewing industry.[44]

Both Glasgow and Belfast by 1850 controlled their regional capital markets, and their business community, especially the bankers, was calling on capital and supplying credit over a wide area. Banking facilities emerged much more rapidly in Glasgow than in Belfast. Despite the fact that Belfast bankers claimed to operate on Scottish principles, they appear to have been much more independent of Dublin than could be fairly claimed about Glasgow's relationship with Edinburgh. Maybe the chaos of the 1790s in the south of Ireland and the close adherence to strict credit controls in the north which led to differential rates of exchange with London provide the explanation for this financial autonomy. Certainly, Belfast and Glasgow seem to have participated equally in the growth of joint-stock banking in the 1830s.[45]

Both Glasgow and Belfast demonstrated the pressures which urbanisation produced for the social fabric. There was great social progress in both places by 1850: better control of street cleansing and sanitation, increasingly effective factory inspection, improved educational facilities and greater public philanthropy. Yet the problems in both cities were very grave. Population growth was accompanied by slum dwelling on a greater scale. In this respect, Glasgow had a worse problem than Belfast, with generally poorer housing conditions for its working people. Cholera exposed the inadequacies of sanitary provision in both places, but was most severe in Glasgow.[46] After *Rob Roy* made its first journey from Glasgow to Belfast on 13 June 1818, the transport connection between the two cities became swift, regular and cheap, for competition between rival steamer companies became intense. Harvest men and paupers in 1825 could travel for 10p., and by 1833 a steerage passenger could cross for 2½p. Belfast became the main port of embarkation for many Irishmen and women making for Glasgow.[47]

REFERENCES

1. Cf. R. Forsyth, *The Beauties of Scotland* (Edinburgh, 1806), III, pp. 185ff.; C. E. B. Brett, 'The Georgian Town: Belfast about 1800', in J.C. Beckett and R.E. Glasscock, eds., *Belfast: The Origin and Growth of an Industrial City* (Belfast, 1967), pp. 67ff.

2. *Census* 1851.

3. H. Hamilton, *An Economic History of Scotland in the Eighteenth Century* (Oxford, 1963), pp. 19–21; J. E. Handley, *The Irish in Scotland 1798-1845* (Cork, 1945), pp. 64ff.

4. J. R. Kellett, 'Property Speculators and the Building of Glasgow, 1783–1830', *Scottish Journal of Political Economy*, VIII, 3 (1961), pp. 211–232; J. Galloway, *William Harley: A Citizen of Glasgow* (Glasgow, 1901), pp. 21–60.

5. J. Cleland, *The Rise and Progress of the City of Glasgow* (Glasgow, 1820), p. 108.

6. Brett, 'Georgian Town', pp. 69–73.

7. T. M. Devine, *The Tobacco Lords* (Edinburgh, 1975), *passim*; *idem*, 'Glasgow Merchants and the collapse of the tobacco trade', *Scottish Historical Review*, LII, (1973), pp. 50–74; H. Hamilton, 'The Founding of the Glasgow Chamber of Commerce in 1783', *Scottish Journal of Political Economy* (1954), pp. 33–48; W. H. Crawford, 'The Evolution of Ulster Towns, 1750-1850', in *Plantation to Partition: Essays in Ulster History in Honour of J. L. McCracken*, edited by P. Roebuck (Belfast, 1981), p. 149.

8. Hamilton, *Eighteenth Century*, p. 282; Mitchell Library, Chamber of Commerce Statistics, Jan–Feb 1840, Exports of Cotton Yarn from Scotland 1835–9.

9. R. H. Campbell, *Scotland since 1707: The Rise of an Industrial Society* (Oxford, 1965), pp. 126–7.

10. E. R. R. Green, 'Early Industrial Belfast', in Beckett and Glasscock, *Belfast*, pp. 78–87 and his 'Belfast Entrepreneurship in the Nineteenth Century', in L. M. Cullen and P. Butel, eds., *Négoce et Industrie en France et en Irlande aux XVIIIe et XIXe Siècles* (Paris,1980), pp. 137–142.

11. *P.P.*, 1837–8 (145) XXXV, Second Report of the Commissioners on a General System of Railways for Ireland, *passim*.

12. *Pamphlets relating to the City of Glasgow and the River Clyde* (Glasgow, 1858), *passim*.

13. R. E. Glasscock, 'The Growth of the Port', in Beckett and Glasscock, *Belfast*, pp. 98ff.

14. Cleland, *Rise and Progress of Glasgow*, p. 91.

15. J. Butt, 'The Scottish Cotton Industry during the Industrial Revolution', in L. M. Cullen and T. C. Smout, eds., *Comparative Aspects of Scottish and Irish Economic and Social History 1600-1900* (Edinburgh, 1976), pp. 116–124.

16. T. M. Devine, 'The Colonial Trades and Industrial Investment in Scotland, *c.*1700–1815', *Econ. Hist. Rev.*, second series, XXIX (1976), pp. 9–11.

17. *Old Statistical Account*, edited by Sir John Sinclair (Edinburgh, 1791) xii, p. 116; G. Stewart, *Curiosities of Glasgow Citizenship* (Glasgow, 1881), pp. 214–15.

18. Cleland, *Rise and Progress of Glasgow*, p. 96.

19. Birmingham Reference Library, Boulton and Watt MSS, Box 19, Boulton and Watt to Pattison, 10 May, 1799; Pattison to Boulton and Watt, 24 April and 14 May 1799.

20. Ibid., Box 3M, McTaggart's Note of Engines and Horse Gins now erected at Glasgow, August 1798; London Guildhall Library GH11937/12/21 Jan. 1796, Thomas Moffat of Anderston, cotton spinner and grocer insures stock and household goods for £100; GH11937/9/23 July 1795, Peter Buchanan of Glasgow, cotton spinner insures machinery, utensils and stock, clothes and household goods for £1,200; GH11937/16/17 April 1797, Alexander Borvie insures machinery, stock and household goods for £1,000.

21. Cleland, *Rise and Progress of Glasgow*, p. 95.

22. *Census* 1831.

23. Cleland, *Rise and Progress of Glasgow*, pp. 95–6.

24. H. Hamilton, *The Industrial Revolution in Scotland* (Oxford, 1932), pp. 139ff.

25. A. and N. Clow, *The Chemical Revolution* (Edinburgh, 1952), pp. 130–150, and pp. 165–255.

26. G. MacIntosh, *A Memoir of Charles MacIntosh F.R.S. of Campsie and Dunchattan* (Glasgow, 1847); G. Stewart, *Curiosities*, pp. 37–43, 65–92.

27. Hamilton, *Eighteenth Century*, p. 172; Stewart, *Curiosities*, pp. 181–3.

28. Hamilton, *Industrial Revolution*, p. 184.

29. A. Brown, *History of Glasgow* (Glasgow, 1795), p. 262.

30. J. Butt, 'The Scottish Iron Industry before the Hot-Blast', *Journal of the West of Scotland Iron and Steel Institute* (1965-6), pp. 193-206; J. Butt, *The Industrial Archaeology of Scotland* (Newton Abbot, 1967), pp. 115ff.

31. Butt, *Industrial Archaeology of Scotland*, p. 50; J. R. Hume, *The Industrial Archaeology of Scotland* (London, 1976), I, pp. 162ff.

32. I. Donnachie, *A History of the Brewing Industry in Scotland* (Edinburgh, 1979), p. 50; S. G. E. Lythe and J. Butt, *An Economic History of Scotland* (Glasgow, 1975), p. 247.

33. L. J. Saunders, *Scottish Democracy 1815-1840* (Edinburgh, 1950), pp. 396-7.

34. R. B. McDowell, 'The late Eighteenth Century', in Beckett and Glasscock, *Belfast*, pp. 55-7; E. R. R. Green, *The Lagan Valley* (London, 1949), *passim*; *idem*, 'Business Organisation and the Business Class', in T. W. Moody and J. C. Beckett, eds., *Ulster since 1800* (1957), pp. 110-118.

35. C. E. B. Brett, 'Georgian Town', pp. 70ff; Crawford, 'Evolution of Ulster Towns', pp. 145ff; *idem*, 'Ulster Landowners and the Linen Industry', in J. T. Ward and R. G. Wilson, eds., *Land and Industry* (Newton Abbot, 1971), pp. 117-144.

36. Crawford, 'Evolution of Ulster Towns', p. 148; D. Dickson, 'Aspects of the rise and decline of the Irish Cotton Industry', in Cullen and Smout, *Comparative Aspects*, pp. 105, 108.

37. Green, 'Belfast Entrepreneurship', p. 138 and 'Early Industrial Belfast', pp. 79-83.

38. D. Dickson, 'Irish Cotton Industry', pp. 106, 109.

39. N. Murray, *The Scottish Handloom Weavers 1790-1850* (Edinburgh, 1978), pp. 182ff; Dickson, 'Irish Cotton Industry', p. 110.

40. Green, 'Early Industrial Belfast', pp. 84-86; J. L. McCracken, 'Early Victorian Belfast', in Beckett and Glasscock, *Belfast*, pp. 88-9.

41. W. E. Coe, *The Engineering Industry of the North of Ireland* (Newton Abbot, 1969), pp. 15, 20-1, 22-5, 39-41.

42. Beckett and Glasscock, *Belfast*, pp. 99-103; Coe, *Engineering Industry*, pp. 77ff.

43. Lythe and Butt, *Economic History*, p. 197; J. Butt and J. T. Ward, 'The Promotion of the Caledonian Railway Company', *Transport History*, III (1970), pp. 164-192 and 225-257; Crawford, 'Evolution of Ulster Towns', pp. 149-150; W. A. McCutcheon, *The Canals of the North of Ireland* (Newton Abbot, 1965), pp. 45-6.

44. Crawford, 'Evolution of Ulster Towns', pp. 153-4.

45. S. G. Checkland, *Scottish Banking* (Glasgow, 1975), pp. 95ff., 323-374; Green, 'Belfast Entrepreneurship', p. 138, F. W. Fetter ed., *The Irish Pound* (London, 1955), pp. 12, 16; E. D. Harley, *The Northern Banking Company Limited, Belfast* (Belfast, 1925), pp. 1-88; W. J. Knox, *Decades of the Ulster Bank* (Belfast, 1965).

46. McCracken, 'Early Victorian Belfast', pp. 91-97; M. W. Flinn, ed., *Edwin Chadwick's Report on the Sanitary Conditions of the Labouring Population of Great Britain* (Edinburgh, 1965), pp. 9-10 and 97-9; Robert Cowan, *The Vital Statistics of Glasgow* (Glasgow, 1838); *Vital Statistics of Glasgow, Illustrating the Sanitary Condition of the Population* (Glasgow, 1840); J. D. Marwick, *Glasgow — The Water Supply and Various Developments of the City Till the Close of 1900* (Glasgow, 1901).

47. Handley, *Irish in Scotland*, pp. 24ff.

16

The Coming of Joint-Stock Banking in Scotland and Ireland, c. 1820-1845

Charles W. Munn

IN the years between 1820 and the passing of the Bank Acts in 1845 the banking systems of Scotland and Ireland experienced extensive change.[1] Beginning from substantially different structures, the two systems altered and developed into remarkably similar entities. The fact that the Irish adopted many Scottish practices and organisational forms is easily demonstrable, but the Scottish system too underwent a metamorphosis of structure and, to some extent, of function which was almost as dramatic.[2]

In 1820 the Scottish banking system, based on the free issue of notes, branch banks and unrestricted association of members, was a mixture of four elements. The system was dominated and policed by the three Edinburgh-based public banks — Bank of Scotland, Royal Bank of Scotland and the British Linen Company, all of whom were founded either by Act of Parliament or Royal Charter and all of whom operated branches in the provinces, although the Royal had only one — at Glasgow. None of these concerns had any monopoly power. Secondly, several small private bankers in Edinburgh acted as retailers of credit from the public banks but also accepted and lent deposits on their own account. Thirdly, there were the provincial banking companies.[3] These were roughly analogous to the English country banks but differed from them in that they were not bounded by the law which restricted English banks to a maximum of six partners. As a result of this freedom the provincial banking companies developed in two ways — some were simple, small partnerships like the English country banks, while others were much larger, often with as many as 50 or 60 partners. Some of the provincial banks had a few branches. In many ways these concerns were like joint-stock banks but in point of fact they differed from them in several details and so, for the purpose of analysis, it is necessary to maintain a distinction between them. Sir John Clapham claimed that the banks which were founded in the Scottish provinces were 'joint-stock companies, co-partneries of many partners with unlimited liability'.[4] These banks certainly had no limited liability, but to describe them all as 'joint-stock' is misleading, as the shares in these concerns were seldom freely transferable. The problems of definition are acute but they are very important, for the fourth element in the Scottish banking system, the joint-stock banks, with which this essay is concerned, represented a clear break with past experience. The major distinguishing feature of the joint-stock banks compared with the provincial banking companies was that they were very much bigger in terms of capital, deposits, numbers of shareholders and numbers of branches. By 1820 only one joint-stock bank, the Commercial, was in business. Table 1 sets out the numbers of banks in each group in 1820.

TABLE 1. *The Scottish Banking System, 1820*[5]

1. Public Banks	3
2. Private Banks	7
3. Provincial Banks	25
4. Joint-stock Banks	1
	36

By 1845 this situation had changed dramatically.

Table 2 sets out the number of banks in each group:

TABLE 2. *The Scottish Banking System, 1845*

1. Public Banks	3
2. Private Banks	1
3. Provincial Banks	3
4. Joint-stock Banks	13
	20

All except the private banks had note issues and branch networks. Most of the provincial and private banks had been taken over by the public and joint-stock banks during the period, although a few had failed. In addition several joint-stock banks had flourished for a time and then merged their interests in the business of a larger bank. The provincial banks which had survived were the larger concerns which approached the joint-stock banks in size, and some of the joint-stock banks over the period achieved a size which was as great as the public banks. The result of this was a substantial homogeneity of structure and function within the system.

In Ireland the changes which occurred were even more strking. By 1820 the system of banking which had evolved was broadly similar to that which had emerged in England. At the apex, in Dublin, was the Bank of Ireland whose monopoly powers were comparable to those of the Bank of England. At the time the Bank was granted its Charter in 1783, it was also enacted that 'no other corporation or partnership, exceeding six in number could issue notes payable on demand or for any period less than six months'.[6] The effect of this legislation was to 'confine all other note-issuing banks to a maximum of six partners'.[7] Of the six private banks in Dublin, some were note issuers and some not but, like Edinburgh equivalents, all were fairly small-scale affairs when compared to the public bank. The third element in Ireland was the country banks. These were generally note-issuing concerns with six or fewer partners and no branches. Table 3 sets out the situation in 1820:

TABLE 3. *The Irish Banking System, 1820*[8]

1. Public Banks	1
2. Private Banks	6
3. Country Banks	18
	25

By 1845 there had been substantial change in the system. Table 4 sets out the number of banks in each group:

TABLE 4. *The Irish Banking System, 1845*

1. Public Banks	1
2. Private Banks	6
3. Country Banks	0
4. Joint-Stock Banks	9
	16

The figures for the numbers of private banks conceal the fact that there had been considerable change in the composition of this group. The most notable feature in the comparison between Tables 3 and 4 is the complete disappearance of the small country banks and their replacement by large-scale, multi-ownership banks, most of which were note issuers and had branches.[9]

In comparing Scotland and Ireland it is clear that the two started from very different bases in 1820 and that by 1845 they had been transformed but had moved much closer in structure and, as we shall see, in function. The purpose of this essay is to explain the nature of that change.

I

When Thomas Joplin, polemicist and company promoter, began his campaign in favour of freer banking with the publication of his pamphlet *An Essay on Banking in England and Scotland* in 1822, he was already very conscious of the success achieved by the Scottish banking system. He claimed that

> the Scotch banks never fail, nor is any danger ever apprehended from them; and . . . in consequence Banking is carried on in that kingdom to an extent unknown, and of course, with advantages totally unfelt in our own (England).[10]

This view of Scottish banking, although not entirely accurate — for there had been some failures — was reinforced several years later when, after the crisis of 1825–6, a Parliamentary enquiry into the issuing of bank notes in Scotland and Ireland found that Scottish banking was a system admirably calculated . . . to economise the use of Capital, to excite and cherish a spirit of useful Enterprise, and even to promote the moral habits of the people, by the direct inducements which it holds out to the maintenance of a character for industry, integrity and prudence.[11]

Joplin was not unaware of the Irish situation but confined his polemic to Scotland and England. Nevertheless he was to play a substantial role in the early development of joint-stock banking as first secretary to the Provincial Bank of Ireland. The 1826 report was much more equivocal about Irish banking than it had been about Scottish. Much was made of the failures of private and country banks in the resumption crisis of 1820, but the enquiry was not so much about the structure of banking as about the issue of small notes. Irish bankers were able to convince the commissioners that for the time being, like the Scots, they should retain their £1 note issues, and from thenceforward the Scots and Irish were able to issue notes from £1 upwards while the English had to make do with £5 and larger notes. The existence of a small note issue in Scotland and Ireland helped greatly in the popularising of the banking habit.

Despite the success of the Scottish banking system and because of the relative failure of the Irish system, pressure for change was building up in both countries. Change in Scotland was first made manifest as early as 1810 with the formation of the Commercial Bank of Scotland. This was an Edinburgh-based, large-scale, joint-stock bank with note issue and, soon, with branches. As such it was a halfway house between the provincial banking companies and the public banks. It differed from the former in that it was Edinburgh-based and much larger, and from the latter in that it had not been founded by public authority, although it was clear from the outset that it aspired to a Royal Charter. One of its founders, Henry Cockburn, argued in his memoirs that its foundation had been necessitated by the illiberal lending policies of the Public Banks, especially the Bank of Scotland and the Royal Bank. 'No men,' he wrote, 'were more devoid of public spirit, and even the proper spirit of their trade, than our old Edinburgh bankers.' Clearly political rivalry also entered into the equation, for he described the old bankers as 'the conspicuous sycophants of existing power'.[12] Although the example of the Commercal Bank, which was soon successfully established,[13] was not followed by other banks for a number of years, the importance of this concern cannot be exaggerated, for it became the model for other joint-stock banks, not just in Scotland but throughout the British Isles.

The list of total joint-stock bank formations between 1810 and 1845 is contained in Appendix A, and those still in existence in 1845 are listed in Appendix B.

One major difference between the Scottish and Irish banking systems as they had evolved over the years lay in a contrasting degree of legislative interference in each. In Scotland the system had developed almost completely free of controlling and limiting legislation. An Act of 1765 had been regulatory but had not limited the banks' abilities to lend money, accept deposits, issue notes or to have more than six partners. Nor was there any geographial limitation or public bank monopoly. The result was the system of banking outlined in Table 1. Yet when the pressures developed in the 1820s and 1830s to have bigger banks offering larger advances, there were no legislative barriers to be overcome and the change was accomplished fairly smoothly.[14]

In Ireland, as in England, however, matters were not nearly so simple. Before the country could be provided with a set of joint-stock banks similar to those which were developing in Scotland, several obstacles had to be overcome. A major obstacle was the monopoly power, or special privileges, of the Bank of Ireland. So great was this special position of the Bank that its privileges could not be removed easily or quickly without causing severe dislocation, not just to the bank but also to the Government's financial machinery and, indeed, to the whole Irish economy. In the event the monopoly powers of the Bank were gradually whittled away over the years covered by this essay. The first breach arose out of the crisis of 1820, when several of the Dublin and country banks had failed and it became evident that Ireland was in need of stronger banks.

Negotiations with Government went on for some months, and when an Act was finally passed in July 1821, the Bank lent a further £500,000 to the Government and increased its capital by the same amount, but its special position was reduced to the extent that banks with any number of partners were henceforward free to establish themselves in any part of Ireland outwith a radius of fifty Irish miles of Dublin. It seems clear that there were different levels of expectation regarding this legislation. Vansittart (Chancellor of the Exchequer), in a letter to the Bank, wrote:

> It is understood that the permission to establish Banking Companies exceeding six partners at the distance of not less than fifty miles from Dublin shall . . . not be construed to extend to such companies any privileges and immunities beyond those to which common partnerships are by law entitled excepting that of suing and being sued in the name of the Treasurer or Secretary if they should be sufficiently numerous to require such a Privilege.[15]

The expectation of the Chancellor, and indeed of the Bank, was that what would develop would be a series of strong country banks perhaps on the model of the Scottish provincial banking companies.

The advocates of joint-stock banking, however, were dissatisfied with the 1821 Act, and so when the economy began to pick up in the mid-1820s their advocacy of change in the banking system became stronger and, ultimately, more successful. Before they achieved success, however, they had to overcome several other legislative problems, most of which were the residue of older Acts. The first proposal for a joint-stock bank in Ireland came from the Northern Banking Company of Belfast in 1824, but their petitioner in the House of Commons, Sir Henry Parnell, was aware that, before the bank could be established successfully, further amending legislation was required. Specifically, two clauses of an Act of 1756[16] had to be repealed. These required the names of all partners in a bank to be on its notes and prohibited merchants engaging in foreign trade from being bankers. The second of these was likely to close membership of a bank to many leading businessmen. In Scotland and England, where no such legislation had been imposed, foreign merchants comprised an important part of the banking fraternity.[17] The removal of this restriction was therefore of great importance to Irish banking. The requirement that the names of all partners be inscribed on all notes and documents issued by a bank was clearly vexatious in a country bank, but it would render the operations of a large-scale joint-stock bank quite impossible, as the names of partners changed every few days. It was therefore not just the powers of the Bank of Ireland which inhibited the growth of joint-stock banking in Ireland. The power of the Bank of Ireland was doubly vulnerable at this time because it was a natural target for those advocating Catholic emancipation.

The solution was to repeal both sections of the offending legislation, and this was accomplished in June 1824 despite the opposition of the Bank of Ireland, which viewed the new arrival with deep suspicion and heartfelt misgivings. The hostile reaction of the Bank is entirely in keeping with the experience of leading banks in other systems when confronted with arrivistes. In Scotland the Public Banks reacted hostilely to the arrival of the provincial banking companies in the 1750s and with only slightly less energy to the arrival of the Commercial Bank of Scotland in 1810.[18] What is evidenced here is the exercise of a territorial imperative where established banks are genuinely concerned that the stability of their system will be undermined by the new arrivals. In all of these cases, however, the established banks, usually having failed to forestall the arrival, meet the competitive challenge in a direct way and settle down to a relatively peaceful co-existence. This is certainly what happened in Scotland and Ireland. Over the 1820s and 1830s the Bank of Ireland developed central banking functions, especially as a lender of last resort, which enabled it to establish a moderating influence over the rest of the banking system.[19]

When the arrival of the Northern Banking Company was closely followed by that of the Provincial Bank of Ireland, the Bank of Ireland responded quickly to the competitive challenge by moving outwards from its Dublin base and setting up branches in several towns throughout the country, notably those in which the Provinical had announced its intention of establishing branches. The result of these moves was to introduce into Ireland the elements of competition for business on a national scope which had been such a notable feature of the Scottish banking system for many years, competition which was to be further intensified with the growth of joint-stock banking.

The Provincial Bank of Ireland was also important for two other reasons. Firstly it was London-based. Although no banking was done in London, that was where its administrative centre was located. This was due to the remaining exclusive privilege of the Bank of Ireland which kept joint-stock, note-issuing banks out of Dublin and is indicative of the distortions which that privilege introduced into the development of the Irish system.[20] Secondly, the Act which accompanied the formation of the Provincial repealed another piece of antique legislation which had prevented non-residents in Ireland from becoming partners in Irish banks. These two features of the Bank's formation were closely linked, as a quotation from the Bank's minutes reveals:

> As the capital of the Society was chiefly to be raised in Britain, and indeed as the Society itself was called into existence by the very circumstances that capital adequate to such an undertaking could not be found in Ireland, there was an obvious expediency in making London the principal seat for directing the operations of the Bank, had there even existed no legal impediment to the principal Board being established in Dublin.[21]

The removal of the restraint on British capital in Irish banking was important for the formation of the Provincial, yet the claim that the capital required 'could not be found in Ireland' should not be interpreted to mean a shortage of money in Ireland but perhaps a degree of unwillingness to invest in joint-stock companies until there was evidence of the ability to pay good dividends.[22] This unwillingness was not evident in Ulster, where all three northern banks were founded, almost entirely, on local capital, as in Scotland, where the vast bulk of banking capital in both old and new banks was locally owned. In fact the market was not tested in Dublin, and it may be that if it had been, then the Provincial could have been launched with predominantly Irish capital.

The passing of the Act of 1825 for Ireland cleared the legislative way for the formation of joint-stock banks whose only limitation was that they could not open an office within a fifty (Irish) mile radius of Dublin. Their Scottish counterparts were not similarly encumbered, but in both countries multi-partnered, note-issuing branch banks could now be formed with almost equal facility (see appendices for lists). The facility to open joint-stock banks was, with the exceptions already noted, received in a rather half-hearted way, for the crisis of 1825–6 had broken and a damper was placed on all company promotions until the economy began to revive.

II

The opening of the first joint-stock banks raises the questions of what form they took, what was their model and how they conducted their business.

In Scotland these were not questions which were consciously asked or answered. The Scottish joint-stock banks were simply large-scale provincial banking companies — larger in the senses that their capital was bigger and they had many more partners. Also there were great similarities between the joint-stock banks and the public banks. Although the former were smaller than the latter at first, several soon came to rival them in size. The only important difference between them was that the public banks were formed by Act of Parliament or Royal Charters which were assumed to confer limited liability on them, while the joint-stock banks were simply large unincorporated partnerships in which the liability of members was unlimited.

In their internal organisation too there was broad similarity between the new joint-stock banks on the one hand and the public and provincial banks on the other. Deposits were taken at interest; lending was carried on by discount and cash account; notes from £1 upwards were issued; cash remittances were undertaken for customers; and branches were opened. Several of the provincial banking companies had no branches, and those which opened them had only a few, mostly in satellite towns giving them a purely local character. The Bank of Scotland and the British Linen Co., however, had extensive branch networks throughout Scotland.[23] By 1833 the Bank of Scotland had 18 branches and the British Linen Co. had 33, but two of the early joint-stock banks had moved very rapidly to establish branch networks. By that time the Commercial had 36 branches while the National had 27.[24] Most of the joint-stock banks which established branches set up networks which, if they were not national in scope, were at least supra-regional, and this distinguished them very markedly from the essentially local provincial banking companies.

In short, the Scottish joint-stock banks did not have to look very far for the model on which to build their enterprises. By contrast the Irish seem to have made an almost complete break with their past and looked furth of Ireland for a model for their new joint-stock banks. As in Scotland, some of the joint-stock banks were formed to take over the businesses of private or country banks.

The model which the Irish chose for their banking system was the Scottish example. The directors of the Northern Banking Company of Belfast described their enterprise as having been established 'on principles which have proved so eminently successful in Scotland'.[25] Similarly the Provincial Bank of Ireland thought that

> the Scotch system of Banking being that upon which this Company intends to proceed it would be desirable to obtain persons of ability and experience from the Scotch Banks to fill the situations of Managers and Accountants.[26]

Thus began the great exodus of Scottish bankers from Scotland to Ireland and England. But it was not just the experience of the Scots which was required in Ireland. The Provincial Bank directors thought that

> from the small salaries which the Scotch Banks are in the habit of giving their officers, a higher degree of talent and experience can be purchased upon more moderate terms than elsewhere.[27]

Clearly economy was just as much a feature of Irish banking as of Scottish. Junior officers, however, were recruited locally.

The remaining privileges of the Bank of Ireland prevented the two Dublin-based joint-stock banks from issuing notes, and as they were important to the total operation of banking, this prevented the complete adoption of the Scottish model by the Dublin-based Hibernian and Royal Banks. When the Royal was established in 1836, its prospectus contained many references to the banks of Scotland but it was conscious that it could not fully adopt the Scottish system and instead it was decided to 'form a Joint Stock Bank on an extensive scale, similar in its constitution to the London and Westminster Bank'.[28] The London and Westminster, however, had been founded by a Scot on the Scottish model adopted to the peculiar situation of London[29] which, because of the special position of the Bank of England, was not unlike the situation prevailing in Dublin. The major problem within the London and Dublin areas was that joint-stock banks were not permitted to issue notes and so had to find alternative sources of profit. In general terms, however, the Scottish model was uppermost in the minds of the Irish joint-stock banks.

It should not, however, be imagined that what was attempted was a slavish copying of the Scottish banking system. Indeed where Irish bankers felt that the model could be improved or that some variant of it was more appropriate to the Irish situation, then the model was amended accordingly. It is not, however, without significance that the most spectacular failure in Ireland, the Agricultural and Commercial Bank, almost completely ignored the Scottish example and chose instead to follow the structure of the equally ill-starred Northern and Central Bank of England.[30]

Some other attempts to deviate, although in a minor way, from the Scottish system were similarly unsuccessful. One of Joplin's favourite ideas, which he included in the original plan for the Provinical Bank, was to have each branch constituted as a separate bank with the head office holding half the shares. This plan, however, which had never been tried in a Scottish bank, was dropped in favour of a local board of directors at each branch but with very limited powers. The scheme as originally conceived was likely to cause considerable friction between local board and head office, as O'Connell's National Bank found to their cost when they attempted to form these semi-independent banks. The National soon abandoned the attempt.[31]

Elsewhere variants on the Scottish model met with more success. In Ulster all three banks were constituted with boards of supervision who oversaw the intromissions of a board of permanent directors who were not permitted any other business interest. The government of the Ulster Bank was vested in two directors and two assistant directors 'aided by the services of a manager and the control of a committee'.[32] Similarly the management of the business of the Northern Bank was entrusted to three partners, who were appointed directors for life, and a committee comprising a chairman, appointed for life, and six others.[33] This appears to have been an expensive system to operate: it cost the Belfast Banking Co. £4157 in 1828,[34] when compared with the Scottish system of having a part-time board of directors who oversaw the activities of the full-time manager (cashier) and secretary. In the North of Scotland Bank (Aberdeen) total salaries for top officials plus attendance allowances for directors probably did not exceed £2000 per annum.[35] Nevertheless the system worked well in Ulster, as is attested by the success of the three banks. In evidence to the 1858 Parliamentary enquiry James Bristow, director of the Northern Bank, argued that the Ulster system of management was necessitated by the public's dislike of dealing with a bank under fluctuating management.[36] This dislike, however, was not manifest elsewhere, so the real reason for having permanent directors may have been an attempt to retain control of the bank in the hands of those who had operated the private banks which had preceded the joint-stock concerns.

In nearly every other respect the Scottish system was adopted in an unadulterated way by the Irish banks. Although local variations may be found, most Irish joint-stock banks became note-issuing, branch-operating, deposit-taking and interest-allowing companies at some stage in the 1820s and 1830s. The Bank of Ireland, too, although often looking to the Bank of England as its model, met the challenge of competitive banking by opening branches throughout the country. In this case the model roles were reversed, for in 1826 the Bank of England asked the Bank of Ireland for advice on how to operate branches.[37] The Bank of Ireland, however, was slow to offer interest on deposits and did not do so until 1864.[38] In many respects it saw its role as being guardian of the system, and this is reflected in its many efforts as lender of last resort from the 1820s to the 1840s.[39] A similar role was played by the Bank of England in London and by the Public Banks in Edinburgh.

One of the most striking features of Scottish banking as it had evolved was the cash credit form of lending. This precursor of the modern overdraft was very popular in Scotland, although it was not the major form of lending, as has sometimes been alleged. The applicant for credit was required to sign a bond and to have two or more cautioners (guarantors) sign with him. No security other than this purely personal obligation was required. Borrowers could draw or repay the balance, or any part thereof, at will and interest was charged only on the daily balance outstanding. If the account passed into credit at any time, then interest was allowed at the current rate for deposits. The cash account was intended to be a revolving credit which would be drawn and repaid and drawn again quickly and so keep the banks' notes in circulation. It was, however, open to abuse, being a form of accommodation credit, as customers could draw the amount of credit and neglect to turn over the balance at the speed required by the bank. Such customers sometimes had their credits withdrawn.

The Provincial claims to have been the first bank to introduce the cash credit into Ireland, but it did so with 'great caution'[40] because of the potential abuse of the system. The claim in 1841 by an official of the Provincial that cash credits were not popular because, unlike Scotland, the bond had to be registered and became an encumbrance on the estate of all parties,[41] should not be interpreted to mean that this *type* of lending was not popular, for in the 1830s and 1840s joint-stock banks in Scotland and Ireland developed variants on the theme either by awarding simple overdrafts or by taking heritable or moveable property as security in lieu of, or in addition to, the personal bond.[42] Nevertheless it cannot be ignored that the cash credit was not ideally suited to agricultural finance which, because of its longer-term nature, was unable to meet the banks' requirements of rapid turnover. It was, however, admirably suited to industry and trade.[43] Banks certainly preferred awarding cash accounts to discounting accommodation bills.[44]

The Scottish model of banking was therefore adopted and adapted by the Irish joint-stock banks and, to a lesser extent, by the Bank of Ireland. But it is slightly misleading to think of a model in anything other than a simple sense, for the Irish were acutely aware of their own particular circumstances and adjusted the system to suit their own requirements. Furthermore the model was itself changing. Not only was the average size of Scottish bank growing, but the model was altering particularly with respect to lending (see above). Substantial growth in the size of advance and change in the nature of security was evident in this period, and many modern techniques of lending were developed at this time. There is no evidence to suggest that the Irish copied anyone in this regard, but rather it seems that, like the Scots, they made their own way in evolving these new techniques.

III

The Scots developed a system of joint-stock banking between 1810 and 1845 because there was a growing feeling that the existing banking system, for all its success, was increasingly inadequate to finance the developing trade and industry of the country. This was especially so in the 1830s and 1840s with the substantial growth of the iron and textile industries and the very considerable urban development which was then taking place. It does, however, seem that there were times when the supply of banking services outran the demand for them, but generally the Scottish banking system achieved its metamorphosis with relative tranquillity and almost no failures. That this was achieved with such ease was due in large measure to the long experience of banking enjoyed and practised by the Scottish people.

The Irish, however, had a more difficult job to do. In England the monopoly of joint-stock banking granted to the Bank of England in 1708 had 'done much harm by depriving the country of a banking system commensurate with a period of rapid economic growth'.[45] In Ireland the problem was not so much the special privileges granted to the Bank of Ireland in 1782 but the legislation of 1756 which prevented foreign merchants from becoming bankers and insisted on the names of all partners being on bank notes. If that particular piece of legislation had not been passed, then, given the broad similarity of Scotland and Ireland in the mid-eighteenth century, it does seem that Ireland might have developed a range of provincial banking companies similar to those which developed in Scotland and which quickly grew to have an important role in the country's growth. Such banks might have been able to forestall or, at least, minimise the special privileges granted to the Bank of Ireland, thus giving to the country a much more broadly based banking system.[46]

Nevertheless when pressure came, as it did in the 1820s, for the repeal of the offending Acts, the day was relatively easily carried by the proponents of joint-stock banking. An historian of the period indicated that the legislation of 1821, 1824 and 1825 'made the growth of joint-stock banking possible, but even had legal facilities existed before 1824 they would not have been used'.[47] It remains possible, if not probable, that banks of the Scottish provincial type would have emerged. Whatever the speculations of historians, however, many Irishmen of the times were in no doubt that there was a need for change in the banking system. In 1824 the House of Commons was told by George Robert Dawson that:

> All parties, Protestant and Catholic, are only of one opinion; and that opinion is founded not alone on the advantages expected from an improved system, but in dire experience of the great mischiefs occasioned by the failure of the banks in the south-west of Ireland some few years back.[48]

Dawson may have overstated his case, but he was right to stress the dual nature of the demand for joint-stock banks. Not only was there a revulsion against the experience of 1820, but there was also a hope that the new system of banking might repeat the successes achieved in Scotland.

Although there was economic expansion in Ireland in the 1820s and 1830s,[49] it was neither so extensive nor so well sustained as it was in Scotland. Nevertheless it was a period of growth which required a larger and more liberal banking system, and although the emergence of joint-stock banking in Ireland was not without its traumas,[50] Ireland was provided with a system of banking commensurate with a developing economy.

By 1845 both Scotland and Ireland were equipped with joint-stock banking systems which were similar in many ways and which, in their scale of operation and manner of doing business, were appropriate to a maturing industrial economy. The failure of the Irish economy to mature in that way was due to factors other than its banking system.

Appendix A

Scottish Joint-Stock Banks Created, 1810-1845

Name of Bank	Date of Formation	Remarks
1. Commercial	1810	
2. National	1825	
3. Aberdeen Town & County	1825	
4. Glasgow Union	1830	became Union Bank of Scotland, 1843
5. Ayrshire Banking Company	1830	
6. Western	1832	
7. Central (Perth)	1834	
8. North (Aberdeen)	1836	
9. Eastern (Dundee)	1838	
10. Southern (Dumfries)	1838	to Edinburgh and Leith, 1841
11. Clydesdale	1838	
12. Caledonian (Inverness)	1838	
13. Edinburgh and Leith	1838	became Edinburgh and Glasgow, 1844
14. Paisley Commercial	1838	to Western, 1844
15. City of Glasgow	1839	
16. Greenock Union	1840	to Clydesdale, 1844
17. Glasgow JSB	1843	became Edinburgh and Glasgow, 1844 — with 13
18. Bank of Glasgow	1843	to National, 1844
19. Glasgow Banking Company	1843	to Western, 1844
20. Glasgow Bank (2)	1844	to Clydesdale, 1944
21. Edinburgh and Glasgow	1844	13 and 17

Scottish Joint-Stock Banks in Operation, 1845

1. Commercial	8. North
2. National	9. Eastern
3. Aberdeen Town and County	10. Clydesdale
4. Union	11. Caledonian
5. Ayrshire	12. City of Glasgow
6. Western	13. Edinburgh and Glasgow
7. Central	

Appendix B

Irish Joint-Stock Banks Created, 1824-1845

Name of Bank	Date of Formation	Remarks
1. Northern	1824	
2. Hibernian	1824	no note issue
3. Provincial	1825	
4. Belfast	1827	
5. Agricultural and Commercial	1834	failed 1840
6. National	1834	
7. Ulster	1836	
8. Royal	1836	no note issue
9. Southern	1837	closed 1837
10. Tipperary	1838	issued Bank of Ireland notes
11. London and Dublin	1842	to National, 1848; no note issue

Irish Joint-Stock Banks in Operation, 1845

1. Northern
2. Hibernian
3. Provincial
4. Belfast
5. National

6. Ulster
7. Royal
8. Tipperary
9. London and Dublin

REFERENCES

1. I am grateful to the Irish Bankers' Federation and the Carnegie Trust for the Universities of Scotland whose financial assistance supported the research for this paper. Philip Ollerenshaw, Ulster Polytechnic, kindly directed my attention to several references on the Ulster banks. I am happy to record my thanks to those banks which permitted me to have access to their archives.

2. S. G. Checkland, *Scottish Banking: A History 1695-1973* (Glasgow, 1975) and G. L. Barrow, *The Emergence of the Irish Banking System 1820-1845* (Dublin, 1975).

3. C. W. Munn, *The Scottish Provincial Banking Companies 1747-1864* (Edinburgh, 1981).

4. Sir J. H. Clapham, *The Bank of England* (London, 1944), Vol 2, p. 91.

5. Checkland, *Scottish Banking*, Table 9, pp. 320-1.

6. F. G. Hall, *The Bank of Ireland 1783-1946* (Dublin, 1949), p. 37.

7. Barrow, *Emegence of the Irish Banking System*, p. 2.

8. *Ibid.*, p. 14, and Appendix 2.

9. Only the Dublin-based Hibernian and Royal banks had no branches. The monopoly of the Bank of Ireland prevented these concerns from having note issues, and it may be speculated that, as most banks regarded branches as useful outlets for their notes then, the Hibernian and Royal felt branches to be unnecessary.

10. T. Joplin, *An Essay on Banking in England and Scotland* (London, 1822).

11. *P.P.*, Report from the Commons Select Committee on Promissory Notes, 1826, p. 12.

12. H. Cockburn, *Memorials of His Time* (Edinburgh, 1856), pp. 252-3.

13. See Commercial Bank of Scotland, Directors' Minutes, Royal Bank of Scotland, Edinburgh.

14. Munn, *Provincial Banking Companies*, Ch. 5.

15. Bank of Ireland Minutes, 19/4/1821, Bank of Ireland, Dublin.

16. 29 Geo II, c 16.

17. Munn, *Provincial Banking Companies*, Ch. 7 and L. S. Pressnell, *Country Banking in the Industrial Revolution* (Oxford, 1956), Ch. 3.

18. Checkland, *Scottish Banking*, Chs. 5 and 10, and Munn, *Provincial Banking Companies*, Ch. 1.

19. Hall, *Bank of Ireland*, and C. W. Munn, 'The Bank of Ireland as a Central Bank 1820–1945', unpublished article.

20. The same consideration applies to the National Bank of Ireland founded in 1835.

21. Provincial Bank of Ireland Minutes, 18/5/1826, Allied Irish Banks, Dublin. I am indebted to Miss V. Stapleton of the Research Department, Allied Irish Banks, Dublin, for drawing my attention to this and other references from Provincial and Royal Bank of Ireland archives.

22. J. Lee, 'Capital in the Irish Economy', in L. M. Cullen, ed., *The Formation of the Irish Economy* (Cork, 1969), pp. 53–4.

23. Checkland, *Scottish Banking*. The Royal Bank of Scotland had only one branch at Glasgow.

24. *Ibid.*, p. 357.

25. Northern Banking Company Minutes 19/9/1824, Public Record Office of Northern Ireland (P.R.O.N.I.), D3145.

26. Provincial Bank of Ireland Minutes, 4/2/1825.

27. Ibid.

28. Royal Bank of Ireland Prospectus, 1836, Allied Irish Banks, Dublin.

29. T. E. Gregory, *The Westminster Bank Through a Century* (London, 1936), p. 26.

30. *The Origins and Principles of the Agricultural and Commercial Bank of Ireland*, Dublin, 1835, National Library of Ireland, p. 641 (1) and S. E. Thomas, *The Rise and Growth of Joint Stock Banking* (London, 1934), Ch. 7.

31. Barrow, *Irish Banking System*, pp. 78–9 and 126. The system of having local, but heavily circumscribed, boards of directors was one which was operated to good effect by many insurance companies.

32. Ulster Bank, Minutes of directors committee, 5/9/1842, Ulster Bank, Belfast, now in P.R.O.N.I. Appointments for life were gradually phased out in the Ulster banks, and in practice assistant directors were often permitted to have other business interests.

33. Northern Banking Co., Deed of Co-partnery, P.R.O.N.I., T1503/2.

34. Belfast Banking Co., Private Ledger, P.R.O.N.I., D3145.

35. A. Keith, *The North of Scotland Bank Ltd 1836–1936* (Aberdeen, 1936), p. 26.

36. Parliamentary Committee on Bank Acts, 1858, QQ 5214–5, evidence of James Bristow, quoted in Barrow, *Irish Banking System*, p. 67.

37. Bank of Ireland Minutes, 28/3/1826, Bank of Ireland, Dublin.

38. Hall, *Bank of Ireland*, pp. 241–3.

39. See note 19.

40. Provincial Bank of Ireland Minutes, 26/8/1825.

41. *P.P.*, 1841, Committee on Note Issuing Banks, Q 3054, evidence of Robert Murray, Inspector, Provincial Bank of Ireland.

42. C. W. Munn, 'Bank Finance for Industry: Scotland and Ireland 1820–1845', Précis in *Business History* 1982.

43. Munn, *Provincial Banking Companies*, Part 3.

44. Provinical Bank of Ireland Minutes, 15/12/1826.

45. L. S. Pressnell, *Country Banking in the Industrial Revolution* (Oxford, 1956), pp. 5–6.

46. L. M. Cullen, 'Merchant Communities Overseas, the Navigation Acts and Irish and Scottish Responses', in L. M. Cullen and T. C. Smout, eds., *Comparative Aspects of Scottish and Irish Economic and Social History 1600–1900* (Edinburgh, 1977), p. 173, for a discussion of why this did not happen.

47. L. M. Cullen, 'Germination and Growth', in B. Share, ed., *Root and Branch: Allied Irish Banks — Yesterday, Today and Tomorrow* (Dublin, 1979), p.29.

48. B. Share, *Root and Branch*, p.17.

49. L. M. Cullen, *An Economic History of Ireland since 1660* (London, 1972), Ch. 5.

50. Barrow, *Irish Banking System, passim.*

Part VI

The Question of Religion

17

The Influence of Religion on Economic Growth in Scotland in the Eighteenth Century

R. H. Campbell

THE emphasis on disputes on church order in the voluminous writings of ecclesiastical historians of Scotland limits their potential usefulness to economic historians. It leads to a narrow conception of differences in church order, which fails to stress how the differences may have reflected, or been reflected into, wider differences in society. It also leads to a relative neglect of theological attitudes, even of those which lay behind some of the passionate defences of differences in church order. Since how an individual thinks theologically is more likely to affect behaviour than how he is organised ecclesiastically, ecclesiastical historians have not, then, illuminated those intellectual attitudes which can affect human behaviour in all fields, including the economic.

A plea that ecclesiastical history should turn to intellectual history is merely a way of suggesting an approach long associated with the work of Weber. Attempts to set his theory in a Scottish context were of minor importance until Dr Marshall's recent study.[1] Unlike many who have worked in the field, Dr Marshall distinguishes the nature of the ethos or the spirit of capitalism, which Weber and others sought to explain or refute, from its relative contribution to economic growth. He recognises that the religious factor was not a sufficient cause of economic growth, perhaps not even a necessary one. Consequently he does not adopt the facile argument that, since Scotland did not experience its most striking economic growth when religious fervour, protestantism, or Calvinism were at their most potent, then they were not influential factors. On the other hand, the detailed textual study of writings on pastoral theology and of business records, in which Dr Marshall tried to determine religious influences on economic attitudes, courts the danger, inherent in any retrospective analysis, that it may lead to attitudes being read into the past when they never existed.

Overestimating religious influences in personal or social life may be understood but is dangerous. Not even detractors or misinterpreters of Weber offer a crude causal link, but a study such as the present has the inherent tendency to assume too readily that the single cause is the influence of religion. Entertaining any such monocausal explanations is particularly dangerous in relation to Scotland in the eighteenth century because of the existence of stimuli similar to those which might be derived from religious influences. They came from secular forces which can be attributed in large measure to the parliamentary union with England. The Union encouraged a growing belief in influential circles that economic development was necessary to sustain the expansion of a more refined form of human life and achievement, which could itself be expressed in economic improvement; more simply, the Union removed political opportunities within Scotland, which left those who were unable to move to the wider, but more expensive, political scene of London with no alternative but to engage in economic enterprise; more simply still, the strengthening links with England boosted a practical desire to emulate the richer, and in many ways the economically more advanced neighbour. Such influences could provide an intellectual, almost a spiritual, influence very similar to that of religious ideas.[2]

The contribution of religious influences by the stimulus given to the growth of a new spirit of enterprise or to the evolution of new social institutions has then to be set against other factors to judge — and preferably that means in modern scholarship to measure — its relative effectiveness. Measurement of such an imponderable is impossible; even less precise attempts to judge its effectiveness are no more likely to be successful. Emphasis must then be placed on how religious factors may influence economic growth. If religious influences cannot be shown to be of any significance — favourable or otherwise — in economic growth, then there is no need to try to judge their relative effectiveness. If they are significant, though to an uncertain extent, it is still possible to consider that the existence or not of similar forces in another society — Ireland compared with Scotland — may be one factor explaining differences in their economic experiences.

A clue to how to incorporate religious influences into explanations of economic growth may be found in some Scottish economic writers of the late eighteenth and early nineteenth centuries. It is in Lauderdale's criticism that Smith failed to allow for the effect of different levels of knowledge and ability, especially in different countries, on the productivity of capital.[3] In 1834 John Rae made the point even more clearly: 'the increase of general wealth is connected with the general spread of invention'.[4] Schumpeter developed the idea further in his additional stress on the need for a theory of innovation. A warning which must be heeded in developing such a theory lies in Smith's attitude to projectors, who approximate most closely to Schumpeter's innovators, but whom Smith grouped with 'prodigals' and set in opposition to 'sober people'.[5] He feared they dissipated the capital he regarded as essential to economic growth. Consequently he sought to impede rather than encourage their activities through fixing a high legal rate of interest, a proposal which Bentham criticised because, among other grounds, he believed, in almost diametrical opposition to Smith, that it would impede the enterprise so necessary for economic growth.[6] The confusion arose because most economic writers before John Stuart Mill, even Lauderdale, did not distinguish in economic growth between the contribution of capital and the more personal contribution of the entrepreneur, who might apply the capital well or badly. It is, however, through the entrepreneur that the influence of religious forces on economic growth operates, and the historian must evaluate how theological attitudes may have encouraged the development of appropriate entrepreneurial qualities in the individual and how theological attitudes and religious organisation may have affected the social environment in ways which allowed these entrepreneurial qualities to operate freely, fully and effectively.

II

It is possible to accept that religious influences were strong and important and yet to conclude that they had detrimental effects on both the entrepreneur and the environment in which he worked. At the simplest level it can be maintained that Scots were so obsessed with religious issues that they had little time for any other activities and, more seriously and more tendentiously, that their obsession led to an argumentative and disruptive society, which did not provide the social stability on which economic growth could be based.[7]

The seventeenth century, especially the later part, provides the foundations for this socially disruptive interpretation of Scottish theological thought. The key lay in the basic protestant claim of the right, or more accurately of the duty, of the individual to judge social and political institutions by the light of his conscience. The power of civil government was always recognised. It could not be other, given the scriptural authority[8] that '. . . the powers that be are ordained of God. Whosoever . . . resisteth the power, resisteth the ordinance of God.' The ruler is 'the minister of God'. Or, to quote Calvin, 'it is perfect barbarism to think of exterminating [civil government], its use among men being not less than that of bread and water, light and air, while its dignity is much more excellent'.[9] But conscience implied at least the possibility of moral and political challenge in an attempt to determine the source and objectivity of the authority being claimed. Calvin counselled to 'distinguish with sufficient accuracy between what is called the external *forum* and the *forum* of conscience . . .; this sense which sists [man] before the bar of God, is set over him as a kind of sentinel to observe and try out all his secrets, that nothing may remain buried in darkness. Hence the ancient proverb, Conscience is a thousand witnesses.'[10] The Westminster Confession was equally strong: 'God alone is Lord of the conscience, and hath left it free from the doctrines and commandments of men which are in any thing contrary to his word.'[11] The challenge which followed was at its most evident in the doctrine of the two kingdoms and in the political writings of the Scottish divines of the later seventeenth century and was perpetuated in the series of secessions, generally over the authority of the state, particularly in determining the method of appointing parish ministers in the eighteenth and nineteenth centuries. In the years from the restoration of patronage in 1712 to its final abolition in 1874, the issue was a perpetual source of challenge to the authority of the state, even by those who supported the principle of an established church. The paradox in such a situation is that demands for individual judgement can lead to such social ferment that no economic growth is possible, and that is the strong basis to the case which stresses only the disruptive influence of theology, and which proceeds to suggest that the necessary social stability did not apply in Scotland until such disruptive influences had been removed. It was not merely that the Scots were obsessed with religious affairs; their argumentative, metaphysical nature meant that their effort was directed into refined religious disputation.

The disputatious attitude of individuals was heightened by the social position and influence of the Church. It would be difficult to find a group who between them wrote more vitriolic political science, challenging established political systems, than the eleven names to whom H. T. Buckle in his study of the 'Scotch Intellect' applied his famous description of a 'monkish rabble'.[12] The presbyterian hierarchy, if such a phrase is permissible, had an authoritarian view of its position in society, but it was one which was then challenging existing social and political power, and doing so in the name of God. The institutionalising of the individual's right, even duty, to protest increased the disruptive elements in society. That was the legacy on which the eighteenth century was to build, and it is easy to see how in such conditions a case may be advanced that religious disputes prevented the social stability necessary for economic growth.

The case can then be developed further into the eighteenth century, holding basically that it was the diminution of the religious influence in Scottish life which provided the stability on which the economic growth of the later eighteenth century was built. Yet the case for a decline in religious fervour has to be made carefully, for two reasons. First, the most obvious change was in how the religious enthusiasm of the earlier centuries gave way in the more settled ecclesiastical conditions of the eighteenth century to scholastic Calvinism, to a dead orthodoxy, to the dry legalism, which so annoyed and depressed John Wesley on his visits to the General Assembly.[13] The characteristic can be seen even among the seceders who were most aware of its existence in the establishment. Two examples come from the early 1740s. The Associate Presbytery so disapproved of revivalism that it called for a public fast because of the 'awful work upon the bodies and spirits of men going on at Cambuslang',[14] and they disowned George Whitefield because of his refusal to be bound to confine his ministry in Scotland to them alone.[15] Suspicion of evangelical revivalism has long characterised those in Scotland who have been most careful to try to protect the purity of their evangelical doctrine. But as the contrast between Whitefield and Ralph Erskine, who invited Whitefield to Scotland, shows, much more so the contrast between Whitefield and some more vitriolic seceders, legalism was liable to engender most rancorous disputes. John Wesley saw so at the General Assembly in 1764, when he commented on a discussion on whether Mr Lindsay should be removed to Kilmarnock parish or not: 'If then the real point in view had been, as their law directs, *'Majus bonum Ecclesiae'*, instead of taking up five hours, the debate might have been determined in five minutes.'[16]

The second way in which the consequences of the rise of moderate influence has to be qualified is through the possibility that historians have overestimated the influence of the rise of the Moderates because it was confined to a narrow group and was very often limited to the highest levels of ecclesiastical politics. Partly because it is very difficult to determine, historians have given inadequate attention to finding out how deeply the influence of the Moderates affected Scottish ecclesiastical life and even more so Scottish society in general.[17] The few investigations which have been made of more local ecclesiastical politics show a lack of penetration. In addition Moderate ministers were often little different from others in the discharge of their routine parochial duties. If the differences between the ecclesiastical parties at national level did not penetrate to local level, then too much can be made of their influence. Even at the level of national politics the strength with which they maintained their position, and the increasing effectiveness with which they organised it, especially under William Robertson, was as responsible as the activities of their opponents for ensuring that the contentious issues of the relationship of church and state, especially on patronage, continued to dominate Scottish ecclesiastical life throughout the eighteenth century.

III

Though Schumpeter's innovator had to possess a combination of personal qualities, which enabled him to accept risk and uncertainty willingly, Schumpeter did not explain why these qualities appear in some individuals but not in others, and — the really critical issue — why some societies are more adequately endowed with entrepreneurial ability than others. The psychologist's answer is that the qualities are more likely to be acquired in a society which inculcates a strong motivation towards high achievement in economic ends.[18] How such qualities can be inculcated by religious influences can be explained only by some form of historical psycho-analysis. It is then possible to suggest that some characteristics of their theological interest gave the Scots a high motivation to achieve in economic activities.

Given the reformed tradition of which the Scots were part, they followed Calvin into social action rather than Luther into private spiritual communion. Calvinist conscience — in his own words 'a sincere desire to live piously and holily' — and Calvinist calling — again in his own words, 'the commencement of good is only with God, and . . . none but the elect have a will inclined to good'[19] — gave national politics a sense of purpose, while at a local level his acceptance of a denunciatory role for the prophetic office strengthened the activities and authority of many parish ministers.[20] The social action and denunciation which followed was often revolting or unattractive, as in trials for witchcraft, the execution of Thomas Aitkenhead, and the disciplinary activities of many kirk sessions, but even the petty tyranny into which the activities of a session frequently degenerated was aimed at encouraging the Christian living which was the fruit of the Christian faith.

A more direct contribution can be suggested from the psychological effects of two doctrines which, though they have been used to show the inhibiting effects of religious factors on economic action, can be interpreted to show how they encouraged entrepreneurial initiative instead. The first is the influence of conscience, which is central to any contention that the strength of religious sentiment in Scotland was disruptive. The second is predestination.

The role of conscience cannot easily be illustrated in ways which satisfy the historian. The individual is alone able to expose and expound the workings of his conscience, and his interpretation is so subjective that it is highly prejudiced. Only a genius with the literary ability of Boswell can demonstrate the fearsome psychological pressures which a bad conscience can exert. Boswell is the exception. For other illustrations it is better to use a source of which historians have often been wary, but which in the hands of perceptive writers can be illuminating, and that is historical fiction. The Scottish novel reaches its greatest achievement in an examination of the problem of the Scot and his conscience, nowhere more effectively than in *The Heart of Midlothian*.[21] Jeanie Deans and her father both have their individual crises of conscience — she of whether to tell a falsehood to save her sister, he whether to recognise the Courts of an uncovenanted government. So Jeanie held, 'we are cruelly sted between God's laws and man's. What shall we do?' And, after a conversation at cross-purposes, comes David Deans' reply, 'if ye are na free in conscience to speak for her in the court of judicature, follow your conscience Jeanie, and let God's will be done'. It is even more interesting to see how neither Scott nor Galt could avoid accepting the role of conscience in their contrasting novels of *Old Mortality* and *Ringan Gilhaize*.[22] Galt published the latter to correct Scott's unsympathetic interpretation of the covenanters, but both express the same views on the dominating influence of conscience; the difference lies in the characters they use to express the sentiments. In Scott it is the near-comic figure of Mause Headrigg, who explains her refusal to allow Cuddy to attend the wappenschaw quite simply, but finally, because 'I can find nae warrant for them whatsoever'. In Galt, the sentiment is the same, but is expressed more fully and nobly, as befits his sympathetic interpretation of religious enthusiasm. The patriarchial figure of Ebenezer Muir expresses the issues almost as a benediction: 'Neither king, nor priest, nor any human authority, has the right to interfere between you and your God; and allegiance ends where persecution begins . . . the right to resist in matters of conscience is the foundation-stone of religious liberty.' Gilhaize himself holds, when on trial: '. . . if I, knowing both the laws of God and the laws of the land, find the one contrary to the other, undoubtedly God's laws ought to have the preference in my obedience'. In each case the doctrine of the two kingdoms is clear.

In these examples the drama of the individual's conscience is enacted in a religious context, the tussle between God's laws and man's laws, and that was how most Scots saw it, but, as far as everyday living was concerned the problem was virtually identical for the individual in later generations for whom the context became secular and not religious. An example may be culled from Smith's moral theory. Smith held that conduct was controlled by the 'man within', the desire for approbation, which forced man to act in ways of which the 'man without', the Impartial Spectator, would approve. To equate the 'man within' with the older theologically determined definition of conscience is not possible, because Smith's morals were not normative but scientific, and the rules of morality, adherence to which alone gave rise to positive virtue, were socially determined.[23] But the practical everyday effects on the individual were similar in the pressure for conformity. It was Smith, not Burns, who first held that 'if we saw ourselves in the light in which others see us . . . a reformation would generally be unavoidable'.[24] Smith's stress on the 'demi-god within the breast' leads in terms of practical everyday living to views remarkably similar to those of Calvin. Hence theological and secular thought led to a constant self-criticism, perhaps — as shown so clearly in the case of Boswell — with attendant psychological dangers, but requiring an unending, serious-minded analysis of accountability in all aspects of life. The Scot could never escape from a constant series of awful judgements on how others saw him, and for most in pre-industrial Scotland that meant how One Other saw him.

Similarly, the doctrine of predestination, which so absorbed Scottish interests, has provided interpretations which are psychologically destructive of character. At the lowest level a thoroughly passive form of fatalism may result, always attractive in a near-subsistence economy, but discouraging entrepreneurial action or risk-taking of any kind. At the other extreme it can lead those who are effectually called to emphasise the several benefits which accompany or flow from justification, adoption and sanctification in this life[25] that they are led to some of the more bizarre heresies of sinlessness, which seem to have been much more common in the south of England than in Scotland, perhaps because they usually require a certain measure of affluence in which to flourish. Though few in Scotland followed extreme heresy, their assurance led to action. Scottish literature again provides an illustration of the active side of pre-destination, often in a macabre form, and never more so than in Hogg's *Confessions of a Justified Sinner:*

> I conceived decreed, not that I should be a minister of the Gospel, but a champion of it, to cut off the enemies of the Lord from the face of the earth; and I rejoiced in the commission, finding it more congenial to my nature to be cutting sinners off with a sword, than to be haranguing them from the pulpit, striving to produce an effect, which God, by his act of absolute pre-destination, had for ever rendered impracticable.

The assurance and stimulus cannot be denied, even when Holy Willie reflected on how he was:

> . . . a pillar 'o thy temple,
> Strong as a rock,
> A guide, a ruler and example
> To a' thy flock.

The 'unco guid' may be unattractive in many ways, but they have the assurance needed to be successful entrepreneurs.

Whatever their unattractive aspects, conscience and predestination implanted in the individual a high motivation towards achievement. The reformation had opened the way for achievement to lie in economic affairs by its rejection of any sacerdotal tradition which demeaned economic enterprise or some aspect of it. The refusal to draw a distinction between the religious and the secular is fundamental to much reformation theology. The test was not the occupation or the activity but the way it was done. The Pauline injunction to the Colossians had been 'whatsoever ye do, do it heartily, as to the Lord',[26] so that, as Calvin put the matter clearly, 'in following your proper calling, no work will be so mean and sordid not to have a splendour and value in the eye of God'.[27] Or, to cite from one of many sermons on the theme by an eighteenth-century parish minister, 'if, by your abilities, you have gained wealth, and raised yourself to an honourable station among your brethren, so far you have done well . . . It was heaven bestowed the talents, the industry, the abilities, by which you rose.'[28]

If the negative contribution of the withdrawal of any imputations of moral inferiority to economic affairs was the central contribution of reformed theology to the economic environment, it is possible to ignore two evident sources of confusion. First, even when accepting the legitimacy of the pursuit of material gain, many reformed theologians equivocated when they viewed its possible consequences for the individual. Economic enterprise could so easily lead to the accumulation of wealth, and theologians were only too well aware of the camel's difficulty in going through the eye of the needle. Ralph Erskine warned:[29]

> If a man desires to be religious, God must have his whole heart; and he through grace must give it, and make a continual trade of religion; if a man desire to be rich, the world will oblige him to rise early and sit up late and eat the bread of carefulness; yea, and employ his head and his heart, and all about the world. And therefore God and the world cannot be served by one and the same man.

But the spiritual danger lay not in money but in the love of it. One minister warned in a sermon entitled, significantly, 'On the Deceitfulness of the Heart, in the Abuse of Prosperity': '. . . ye *who are at ease in Zion,* consider that you do not, you cannot receive God's mercies in vain. To you they must either prove a real blessing or a dreadful curse.'[30] Better then to follow Calvin and regard riches as of the same moral worth as poverty, for to do other would be 'to murmur against God, at whose pleasure riches and poverty, contempt and honours, are dispensed'.[31] Though man's chief end was 'to glorify God and enjoy him for ever',[32] economic action was a completely legitimate activity and even one through which man's chief end might be realised.

The other possible source of confusion lies in the difficulty of knowing the extent to which the flock followed the alleged shepherd and pastor. In Scotland there is a vast difference between the Calvin of the *Institutes,* which identifies the majesty and glory of God at the heart of society, and the arid theology of Calvin's sons, whose spiritual guns were more frequently deployed on the logical exposition of a particular point of view than on any conclusion relevant to life and thought. To judge from the possibly unreliable evidence of published sermons, even deliberate applications remained abstract and general. But all were at one in accepting the removal of the distinction between the religious and the secular.

The removal of the distinction is only a negative factor. A more positive inducement to express high motivation in economic terms is also necessary. A comparison with English experience provides a possible pointer. Explanations of the Quaker domination of many early industrial ventures suggest that one reason behind their success, and one only indirectly linked to their religious faith, lies in the way in which they were excluded from many walks of life, especially from certain political, professional and civil activities. Hence their energies and effort had to be directed into economic action, almost because they had no other choice open to them. The analogy with the position in Scotland is not on the same level, for occupations were not similarly closed, but it is possible that one field of creative activity was restricted through public, and especially ecclesiastical, disapproval, that of the creative arts and so — again to some extent because there was nothing left for them to do — Scottish enterprise flowed into economic channels. The extent of the disapproval was noted in the eighteenth century as a characteristic trait of Scottish reformed theology, notably by Hume,[33] and tangentially by Smith, when he suggested 'public diversions', 'painting, poetry, music, dancing . . . all sorts of dramatic representations and exhibitions' as one way of countering the 'dangerously rigorous and unsocial' morals of narrow sects.[34] The criticism has been sustained by modern commentators, but disapproval of the imaginative arts may have encouraged Scots to realise their motivation to achievement in activities of obvious economic importance.

IV

In the eighteenth century a positive encouragement was given to the entrepreneur, as the old religious interests and the new secular thought accommodated each other in ways which enabled the beneficial effects of the theological motivation outlined to be applied in a stable environment. Much Scottish historical writing has concentrated on the antagonism rather than on the accommodation, but an examination of four diverse challenges to ecclesiastical stability, both direct and indirect, shows their confined nature.

The most direct challenge to the generally secure nature of the religious settlement after 1690 came from several bodies whose rejection of the ecclesiastical settlement usually implied a political rejection. They influenced much Scottish life but did not affect the growing cohesion of society. The Cameronians, most uncompromising of all in their opposition to an uncovenanted state, struggled to survive after 1690, without even an ordained minister in their ranks for some time, and, forming a presbytery only in 1743, existed only in small pockets in their traditional strongholds. At the end of the century they held they had 'nothing to boast, with respect to the numbers of either their ministers or people', with only sixteen congregations, including five vacant pastorates in Scotland, twelve in Ireland with two vacant, and nine or ten in America with four or five vacant.[35] The vitriolic literature of the Cameronians has given them a reputation for awkwardness, which they probably did not deserve in their private lives, but, however they may be viewed, they were of no importance nationally after 1690. Equally small groups of Roman Catholics were similarly isolated geographically, in the Highlands and Islands. Their potential challenge to the cohesion of the establishment was regarded with greater concern, leading to special efforts by the General Assembly to provide in these neglected areas pastoral care which regarded the inculcation of presbyterian truth as a way to temporal as well as eternal salvation.[36] The last of the minority groups in outright opposition were the episcopalians, split in the early eighteenth century, partly because of dissension in their own ranks, especially among clergy who were increasingly non-juring and liturgical in ways not in keeping with native traditions. Consequently the episcopalians were already declining into a remnant, not significantly removed in influence from the Cameronians and the Roman Catholics even before an act of 1746 required an oath of loyalty from their clergy and before the declaration that all orders conferred by Scottish bishops after 29 September 1748 were invalid.

The political challenge of the minority groups of Roman Catholics and non-juring episcopalians came to a head in the Jacobite rebellions, especially in 1745. The tragedy of the rebellions for the economic development of Scotland was not that they ended in defeat, but that they ever happened. They were deplored and opposed by most Scots, especially by those in the economically progressive lowlands. The bias of Scottish historiography, though less so among professional historians, to concentrate on the world that was being lost in which they were encouraged notably by Scott, as in *Waverley,* though not in the character of Bailie Nicol Jarvie in *Rob Roy,* underestimates the growing strength of the new forces. More symptomatic of the changing nature of Scottish society at the time is the rising influence of the opponents of the old order, of such a family as the Dalrymples of Stair among the new arrivals and the dominance of the House of Argyll among the greatest. Unpopular they may have been for a number of reasons (jealousy being a major one), which their own self-seeking ruthlessness did not discourage, but they were indicative of the possibility of social and economic advance in Scotland by a new breed, especially by those who accepted the presbyterian settlement, whether through theological conviction or political expediency.

Another direct challenge to the establishment, narrowly based on church order but penetrating Scottish society more deeply, came with the secessions, though their challenge was slight and was blunted by their tendency to engage in disputes and further secessions among themselves. The secessions reflected the growing influence of the moderate party in the established church. Openly they demanded conformity: 'there can be no society where there is no subordination . . . no church or ecclesiastical society can exist, without obedience required from its members, and informed by proper sanctions'.[37] More subtly it is possible to suggest that their rise meant a greater insistence on subordination from the traditionally orthodox than from enlightened liberals. A contrast was frequently drawn between the different treatment meted out to John Simson, the allegedly heretical professor of divinity at Glasgow, and to those who upheld the English puritan work of *The Marrow of Modern Divinity,* condemned by the General Assembly in 1720. It is then not surprising that attitudes to secession should harden, between the more generous treatment of Ebenezer Erskine when he left the establishment to form the Associate Presbytery in 1733 and that meted out in the deposition of Thomas Gillespie in 1752, which led to the formation of the Relief Presbytery in 1761. Gillespie was personally attractive, but early training at Doddridge's Academy and initial ordination by English Independents (which left him, and the Relief Presbytery in due course, with a lasting suspicion of the connection between the church and state) marked him out as someone to whom many in the General Assembly, though of different standpoints, were antagonistic. But unlike Cameronians, Roman Catholics and non-juring episcopalians, the dissenters were not suspect politically. On the political settlement after 1688, the parliamentary union of 1707, and even on many matters of church and state there was a fundamental measure of agreement between the dissenters and the national church. Seceders, of many hues, long upheld the view of one of their distinguished ministers that they seceded 'not from the constitution of the church of Scotland, but from the *prevailing party in her judicatures*'.[38] Unlike their English equivalents, the Scottish dissenters did not suffer from significant disabilities. They were not, for example, excluded from the universities, and there was often co-operation at local level.[39] The underlying unity was because the disputes, however strong they may have been, were narrowly theological.

Neither of these two groups of what were theological challenges in origin had the social or political power to dislodge the established church from its supremacy. The landed proprietors had such power, especially because of their responsibilities as heritors and their rights as patrons after its restoration. Their relationship with the established church was, however, critically different from that in Ireland. Their insistence on their rights as patrons was to be a festering issue in the church throughout the eighteenth century and beyond, and not surprisingly, practically no landowner supported dissenting bodies. When the Scottish landed proprietors moved from supporting the established church, as they did increasingly in the eighteenth century, they moved to episcopalianism, but, since much indigenous episcopalianism in Scotland was politically suspect, they regarded themselves as members of the Church of England in Scotland and did not project their personal ecclesiastical affiliation into attempts to alter the nature of the establishment. Those who remained personally loyal to the Presbyterian establishment did not regard it, however, as offering the political, economic or social opportunities which the established churches offered in the other parts of the British Isles. The parochial emoluments in Scotland, while passing rich by comparable Scottish equivalents, such as the lowly paid parochial schoolmasters, were paltry compared with the plum parishes in England, or the possibilities of preferment in Ireland. And the ministry of the Church of Scotland did not offer a path to political power. The landed proprietors, therefore, did not seek to dominate the Church; they accepted it, and within broad limits, especially regarding patronage, left it in peace. The Church may be accused of servility to the landowners but it could not be regarded as their agent. In a way quite different from elsewhere in the British Isles, the established church was a church of the people. It was a truly national church as it had never been in the seventeenth century, when the nature of the settlement was in bitter dispute, or subsequently in the nineteenth century, when it was seriously, though temporarily, ruptured by dissent in 1843 and when its position as a national institution was more permanently challenged by Irish Roman Catholic immigration.

Retrospectively, a church in such a dominating position socially might seem a major target for the increasingly secular thought of the eighteenth century, but its challenge, while directed to the theological tenets of the church, was muted as far as its institutional power and influence was concerned. It is possible that historians have underestimated the common ground between the believers and those who queried, or even denied, the faith. The common ground lay in the acceptance of much of what the church stood for in practice. The common ground is evident in the work of Smith. His sources and authorities show the drastic intellectual change from the previous century. His library had all the classical authors and a wide range of the most obscure travellers' tales, but practically nothing on Christian theology. It seems to provide an excellent example of the substitution of the authority of the classical tradition for that of Judaic/Christian thought. Even more significant still is the way he deleted in a later edition of the *Theory of Moral Sentiments* a passage which commended the doctrine of the Atonement, though only because of the psychological benefits offered by some form of substitutionary sacrifice to a repentant sinner troubled by feelings of guilt.[40] The change of authority and emphasis may seem to lead to the elimination of religious influences entirely, but, before coming to that conclusion, another interpretation is possible.

It is too easy to assume that the secular thinkers of the eighteenth century encouraged the introduction of a more stable social order because they divested themselves and those they influenced of religious prejudices. Care must be assumed not to attribute all the credit for social stability in that way, as though it came only when secular thought took over from religious prejudice. To begin with, the intellectual luminaries of the eighteenth century were unrepresentative. Intellectually and geographically the influence of the Enlightenment was narrow, yet its influence may well have been as significant for what it did not do as for what it did. The secular writers may have had a greater influence if their social thought had been thrown on the side of destruction and revolution. That it was not. For all their close links with French and other continental thinkers, and for all the intellectual revolution of scepticism which they produced, the revolutionary change was confined to an intellectual position and did not transform itself into a major attack on property rights or into an attack on many aspects of social life.

Secular and theological thought may have avoided collision because of some aspects of the Scottish theological background. First, because — in following Calvin — the Scots, even of an earlier generation, had supported a social system in which the individual passed moral and political judgments, and so they left less room, or desire, for criticism in the field of political order and property rights by the secular thinkers of the eighteenth century. Second, because church order and clerical behaviour in Scotland could not easily engender any shrill form of anti-clericalism. Smith believed that 'there is scarce to be found anywhere in Europe a more learned, decent, independent, and respectable set of men than the greater part of the Presbyterian clergy of . . . Scotland'. 'It is accordingly in Presbyterian countries only that we ever find the common people converted without persecution, completely, and almost to a man to the established Church.'[41] Though Smith always tried to avoid giving offence, his views were not unique, and stood out in sharp contrast with the views of some of his friends on the Continent. The new secular thought was not spoiling for a fight with the theologians over social order.

Some hold that the ecclesiastical authorities were less tolerant, that, having achieved a position of influence, they were unwilling to allow social deviance to others. It must always be remembered that some of the most critical commentators on ecclesiastical practice in the eighteenth century, and those whose accounts are most commonly used as sources — Burns and Hume are the classic examples — were thoroughly prejudiced witnesses. In spite of the opposition to Hume, he was able to live and work happily in Edinburgh and be honoured there. The failure of Hume's candidature for a chair at Edinburgh in 1745 and his unacceptability at Glasgow in 1752 were more than the outcome of clerical opposition.[42] Quite simply David Hume was not a suitable person to be responsible for the education of the young in a society in which most, irrespective of their religious opinion, sought social stability. In short, the nature of the Church's enthusiasm for a heresy-hunt was changing if not declining. Even the orthodox who remained in the establishment were criticised by the seceders for their *'moderation and tameness'*, 'a subject of convivial merriment among the genteel and fashionable circles of those who have not the shadow of religion' and a 'matter of regret, and of lamentation, to serious Christians of all denominations'.[43] But even the heretic blasts, which so alarmed the consciences of the orthodox, especially in the west, were narrowly confined to theological issues. They were not related to any form of economic action, except at trivial levels, nor did they significantly inhibit the development of any qualities of individual motivation in economic affairs which may have been necessary for economic progress. Even those aspects of the Church most criticised in the eighteenth century — the apparently petty victimisation of the discipline of the Kirk Session, and the Session's failure to put down the mighty from their seats — whatever other defects those aspects may have had — produced a Church which, irrespective of the theology of its different parties, had no longer any desire to destroy, or even to challenge, the existing social and political order. It was socially conservative; it made no disrupting contribution to Scottish society.

To many historians and theologians that is no commendation of the influence of religion in society, but that is another matter. It is enough to conclude that while personal religion of a characteristic Scottish form was still strong, a variety of factors ensured that religious issues did not disrupt the general fabric of society in the eighteenth century. It was then possible to apply the motivation derived from a strong personal faith and apply it in a socially stable environment. That was one, but only one, ingredient in Scotland's economic prosperity.

REFERENCES

1. Gordon Marshall, *Presbyteries and Profits: Calvinism and the development of capitalism in Scotland, 1560·1707* (Oxford, 1980). For different responses to Dr Marshall's work see reviews in *Economic History Review*, xxxiv (May 1981) by S. G. E. Lythe; *Scottish Journal of Sociology*, 5 (1981) by R. H. Campbell; *Scottish Historical Review*, lx (October 1981) by David Stevenson.

2. A considerable literature has gathered around these topics. An interesting interpretation, though not necessarily one which would command general acceptance, is in G. E. Davie's Historical Association pamphlet, No. 99 (General), *The Scottish*

Enlightenment. Two new studies which deal with similar topics are I. Hont and M. Ignatieff, eds., *Wealth and Virtue: The Shaping of Political Economy in the Scottish Enlightenment* (Cambridge, 1982) and R. H. Campbell and A. S. Skinner, eds., *The Origins and Nature of the Scottish Enlightenment* (Edinburgh, 1982).

3. James Maitland, 8th Earl of Lauderdale, *An Inquiry into the Nature and Origin of Public Wealth* (1804), pp. 162f.

4. John Rae, *New Principles of Political Economy* (London, 1834), reprinted as *The Sociological Theory of Capital* (ed. C. W. Mixter, 1905).

5. Adam Smith, *An Inquiry into the Nature and Causes of the Wealth of Nations* (1776), eds. R. H. Campbell, A. S. Skinner, W. Todd (Oxford, 1976), I.x.b.43; II.iii.26.27; II.iv.15.

6. *Jeremy Bentham's Economic Writings* (ed. W. Stark, London, 1952), vol. i, pp. 167–87.

7. For an interesting example among many which follows this interpretation, see David Daiches, *The Paradox of Scottish Culture* (Oxford, 1964) especially pp. 40f.

8. Rom. 13.1, 2, 4.

9. John Calvin, *Institutes of the Christian Religion* (1536), translated by H. Y. Beveridge (London, 1953), IV.xx.3.

10. *Ibid.*, III.xix.15.

11. *Westminster Confession,* XX.II.

12. H. T. Buckle, *The History of Civilization in England* (London, 1857–1861). Later editions usually divided the work into three volumes, with the Scottish material in the third. Most of the relevant Scottish material was reprinted in H. T. Buckle, *On Scotland and the Scotch Intellect* (ed. H. J. Hanham, Chicago, 1970), p. 385.

13. John Wesley, *Journal* (Everyman edn.), vol. iii, p. 180.

14. Arthur Fawcett, *The Cambuslang Revival* (London, 1971), p. 189.

15. Even a sympathetic account cannot absolve the seceders on this issue: Donald Fraser, *The Life and Diary of the Reverend Ralph Erskine* (Edinburgh, 1834), especially pp. 330–1.

16. Wesley, *Journal* (Everyman edn.), vol. iii, p. 180.

17. Valuable work in this field has been done by Ian D. L. Clarke in his unpublished Cambridge University Ph.D. thesis (1964), 'Moderatism and the moderate party in the Church of Scotland, 1752–1805' and in his essay, 'The Moderate Regime in the Church of Scotland, 1752–1805', in N. T. Phillipson and R. Mitchison, eds., *Scotland in the Age of Improvement* (Edinburgh, 1970), pp. 200f. I am also indebted to work undertaken in this field by Mr J. McIntosh for his M.Litt. degree of the University of Stirling.

18. D. C. McLelland, *The Achieving Society* (Princeton, 1961); E. E. Hagen, *On the Theory of Social Change* (Homewood, 1964).

19. Calvin, *Institutes,* IV.x.4 and II.iii.8.

20. Michael Walzer, *The Revolution of the Saints: a study in the origins of radical politics* (London, 1966), 2; Richard L. Greaves, *Theology and Revolution in the Scottish Reformation* (Grand Rapids, 1980), esp. Ch. 7.

21. For a full discussion, see David Craig, *Scottish Literature and the Scottish People 1680–1830* (London, 1961), Ch. VI. For an examination of the use of literature and history, see James Anderson, *Sir Walter Scott and History* (Edinburgh, 1981).

22. I am indebted to work by Mrs J. Milligan on this contrast when studying for her M.Litt. in the University of Stirling.

23. T. D. Campbell, *Adam Smith's Science of Morals* (London, 1971), pp. 157 and 175f.

24. Adam Smith, *The Theory of Moral Sentiments* (1759), eds. D. D. Raphael and A. L. Macfie (Oxford, 1976), II.4.6.

25. As stated in the answer to the thirty-second question on effectual calling in *The Shorter Catechism* (1648).

26. Col. 3.23.

27. Calvin, *Institutes,* III.x.6.

28. George Goldie, *Sermons* (Edinburgh, 1805), p. 189.

29. Ralph Erskine, *Works* (Glasgow, 1764), vol. ii, pp. 541–2.

30. John Jamieson, *Sermons on the Heart* (Edinburgh, 1789), vol. i, p. 407.

31. Calvin, *Institutes,* III.vii.9.

32. *The Shorter Catechism,* answer 1.

33. David Hume, *The History of Great Britain* (1754), ed. Duncan Forbes, Pelican edn. (London, 1970), pp. 146–7.

34. Smith, *Wealth of Nations,* V.i.g.15.

35. *A Short Account of the Old Presbyterian Dissenters,* published by the authority of the Reformed Presbytery of Scotland (Edinburgh, 1806), p. 44. An interesting example of their local importance is in John Leopold, 'The Levellers Revolt in Galloway in 1724', *Journal of the Scottish Labour History Society,* No. 14 (May 1980), pp. 4f.

36. General Assembly Papers of 1777 explain the reason for government support of itinerant preachers and catechists: 'Popery and Ignorance do increase and prevail in the Highlands and Islands . . . Now as the Evil thereof may be of dangerous Consequence to our Government . . .'. Scottish Record Office [SRO] CH 1/2/119.

37. Reasons of dissent from the judgment and resolution of the commission of assembly, 11 March 1752. Reprinted in *Scots Magazine,* vol. xiv (1752), p. 192.

38. *An Historical Account of the Seceders,* from a real Friend of the Church of Scotland (Edinburgh, 1766), p. 25.

39. See, for example, John Mitchell, *Memories of Ayrshire about 1780,* in *Miscellany VI* (Scottish History Society, 1939), pp. 298–9.

40. See Appendix II of Raphael and Macfie edn. of *Theory of Moral Sentiments.*

41. Smith, *Wealth of Nations,* V.i.g.37 and 38.

42. For Hume's own comments on the relevance of a man's 'philosophical Speculations' when 'concern'd in the Instruction of Youth', see *The Letters of David Hume,* ed., J. Y. T. Greig (Oxford, 1932), vol. 1, p. 34; and for Smith's concern with public opinion, see *The Correspondence of Adam Smith,* eds. E. C. Mossner and I. S. Ross (Oxford, 1977), p. 5.

43. James Robertson, *Overture concerning Dr McGill's errors . . . to the Associate Presbytery of Glasgow* (Paisley, 1792), p. 90.

18

Religion, Work-Discipline and Economic Attitudes: The Case of Ireland

S. J. Connolly

'THE earliest improvement and step towards civilization which is known to have taken place in the manners, morals and customs of the people in this as well as in all the neighbouring parishes was the settlement of the Scots and English in it in the reign of James I, and the consequent establishment of the Protestant religion.'[1] In the century and a half since this confident sentence was written, the notion of a link between religious affiliation and the habits and attitudes most conducive to economic growth has risen to the status of a major controversy and then, to a certain degree, receded. In part this decline may reflect a sense among economic historians that their discipline has achieved self-sufficiency, resulting in a reduced regard for imports from other subject areas. But the main reason clearly lies in the methodological problems which have plagued all discussion of the topic: the difficulty of isolating, among a welter of other factors — many of them themselves the subject of debate — a relationship between religion and economic behaviour; and the near impossibility, even where this can be done, of determining which of the two is influencing the other.

These difficulties are formidable. Nevertheless, when one turns to the case of Ireland in the eighteenth and early nineteenth centuries, the question of the link between religion and economic performance continues to demand attention. For whatever refinements are added to our picture of regional variations in economic and social development, the basic distinction remains that between eastern Ulster, with its Protestant majority and its nineteenth-century industrial revolution, and the remainder of the country. Of the many possible lines of thought to which this might give rise, the present essay will concentrate on two. First, it will discuss the attitudes and teachings of the Catholic clergy of this period, and the extent to which these might have been an obstacle to economic progress. Second, it will examine certain contrasts, principally in the area of work-discipline, which contemporaries claimed to discover in the attitudes and behaviour of Catholic and Protestant laymen.

I

Contrary to what has been suggested for other denominations, Catholic religious doctrine — at least as understood by its Irish representatives — prescribed no one distinctive attitude to worldly success and failure. The man who regulates himself according to the law of God, the future Archbishop Cullen wrote to his father in 1822, 'will be ever enjoying a prosperous tenor of fortune'; if he should meet with calamities, however, 'he will bow down his head, submissive to the Lord, and will suffer every affliction with the greatest patience and resignation'. By the end of the nineteenth century, Irish Catholic churchmen were to show signs of inclining in the latter direction, idealising the simple virtues of a society of small agricultural occupiers and expressing uneasiness about the moral degeneration which might accompany any increase in its prosperity.[2] But this was clearly a response to prolonged economic stagnation. The outlook of churchmen in earlier periods, before the economic fortunes of the greater part of Ireland had diverged so unmistakably from those of Great Britain, was very different.

Catholic churchmen of the late eighteenth and early nineteenth centuries were not given to extended analysis of social theory. When called upon to condemn popular disturbances, for example, they preferred to rely on purely religious arguments concerning the sinfulness of resistance to established authority, and on the pragmatic consideration that such resistance was always futile, rather than on any discussion of general political principles. On the rare occasions when they did go further than this, however, they emerge as a body of men who accepted, without much thought, the conventional social and political ideas of their day. Thus Catholic churchmen generally subscribed to the view that a hierarchical organisation of society was essential to its proper workings. 'Society,' Archbishop Troy of Dublin proclaimed in 1793, 'implies different classes and orders of men, necessarily subordinate and dependant.' Bishop Doyle of Kildare and Leighlin, writing in 1822, compared society to the human body: 'The different ranks and orders which compose it are ordained of God, that the whole may be preserved entire. If any of them should seek to usurp the place of the other, discord would ensue.' At the same time this acceptance of social inequality as God-given and inevitable was not a licence for fatalism. Instead there was a clear link between virtue and worldly success. Archbishop Carpenter of Dublin responded to the distress of 1771 by calling for alms for the poor, but also by exhorting all those who worked for a daily wage to be industrious and avoid drink, 'it being justly apprehended that the distresses of the poor arise in a great measure from idleness and drunkenness'. Bishop Coppinger of Cloyne and Ross reproved the United Irishmen in 1798 with the argument that, even if every individual in the country were to be given an equal share of property, a lapse of twelve months would see the restoration of social gradations. 'The industrious, the thrifty, the honest, the temperate would soon surpass the idle, the profligate, the squanderers and the licentious.'[3]

A similar acceptance of conventional moral and economic attitudes may be seen in the association of Catholic churchmen with attempts to devise measures of poor relief which would not prove prejudicial to the maintenance of labour discipline. When the Association for the Suppression of Mendicity in Dublin was set up in 1818, defining its main object as being 'to prevent the necessitous poor, capable of labour, from procuring subsistence without useful industry', it included among its vice-presidents Archbishop Troy and his coadjutor, Daniel Murray. In 1821 Troy was one of the two signatories to an address to the inhabitants of Dublin circulated by the Association, lamenting 'the too-prevalent practice of public alms-giving', and warning that the 'mistaken benevolence' which led to money being given in this way 'only encourages idleness and vice'. In the same year the annual report of the Association paid tribute to 'the zeal and intelligence of the Roman Catholic clergy of this metropolis', which had been shown both in collecting funds for the organisation and in 'repeated exhortations to their flock on the true nature of charity'. In the same way Bishop Blake of Dromore, writing in 1833, argued in favour of a scheme to suppress street-begging in Newry and relieve strolling beggars 'in the manner best adapted to reconcile them to a life of labour and to virtuous habits'.[4]

This is not to suggest that the doctrines taught by the Catholic clergy never imposed restrictions on the economic activities of their flocks. The most obvious example is the prohibition of usury, which continued to be enforced on some occasions, at least in the province of Munster. The practice of leasing milch cows to tenants along with land, and the charging of higher prices for goods bought on credit, were condemned on these grounds in the diocese of Cloyne and Ross in 1755, and the former prohibition was also noted in the diocese of Kerry about three years later. In 1824 Bishop Coppinger of Cloyne and Ross announced his intention of forbidding as usury certain practices connected with the sale of flax seed. Edward Wakefield, visiting Co. Cork in 1808, was told that guineas were hoarded, 'especially as some of the Catholics are scrupulous in receiving interest'.[5] Yet even here one should not exaggerate the potential or actual damage done to trade. If some clergymen interpreted church law literally, others were anxious to take as flexible a view as possible. This was made clear in 1784, when Archbishop Butler of Cashel suggested to the speaker of the Irish Commons an act which would help to undo the damage caused to trade by 'the sentiments of several of the R[oman Catholic] clergy', who 'deter numbers from placing their money at interest'.[6] Bishop Coppinger's proposed condemnation of usury, equally, came only after Rome had refused to accept the reasons he had proposed for regarding the practice concerned as legitimate. Outside Munster the question of interest appears to have attracted less attention. However, one suggestive glimpse of the attitudes of both clergy and laity is provided by a document drawn up in 1761 by the Dominican community in Galway city, in which they acknowledged the receipt of £50 from Martin Blake and undertook 'to discharge as many masses as the lawful interest from thence arising will at any time bear at the rate of one shilling Irish each mass'.[7]

Whatever their later attitudes, then, it is unlikely that the influence of the Catholic clergy in eighteenth and early nineteenth-century Ireland would have been a serious obstacle to economic progress. The majority of Catholic churchmen appear to have fully absorbed the conventional economic and social doctrines of their day, and there is little to indicate that their outlook on most issues would have been sigificantly different to that of their Protestant counterparts. Continued scruples over the question of interest may have caused some inconvenience, but against this must be set the obvious concern of Archbishop Butler and others for the welfare of Irish commerce. Nor is there much to suggest that Catholic teaching encouraged either a negative attitude to work or an excessive concern with the next world at the expense of the present. When Bishop Blake of Dromore was approached in 1833 by a correspondent anxious lest a new job might interfere with certain non-obligatory religious duties, his reply was unequivocal: 'You can sanctify yourself by other means which are easily practicable, and your conscience should not reproach you when it is not your own fault. Remain therefore in [the situation] and make your example as edifying as possible by your exactness, punctuality and assiduity, and by showing always a well governed and charitable temper.'[8]

II

An examination of the direct teachings of Catholic priests and bishops, however, cannot tell the whole story. It is also necessary to ask whether, despite the best efforts of these churchmen, there might not have been significant differences in the economic attitudes and behaviour of Catholic and of Protestant laymen. This question can be approached in two ways. Historical writing on the role of religion in economic development has been concerned mainly with the middle classes, the potential or actual entrepreneurs. Contemporary comment, on the other hand, concentrated more on the qualities, or lack of qualities, seen among the lower classes, the potential or actual labour force.

Where the first of these approaches is concerned, the material does not as yet exist for a detailed discussion. However, it is possible to distinguish two separate lines of argument. The first of these is the view that Irish Catholicism somehow emasculated its adherents as economic agents. Thus Sir Horace Plunkett, writing in 1904, maintained that Irish Catholics were characterised by a lack of self-reliance, and 'a listlessness and apathy in regard to economic improvement which amount to a form of fatalism'.[9] Such suggestions can be relatively easily disposed of. Professor Cullen's account of the activities of Irish Catholic merchants overseas, and his analysis of attitudes to trade among different sections of the Irish landed class; Professor Lee's pen-picture of the character of commercial life in nineteenth-century Dublin; Professor Connell's vivid portrayal of the mercenary character of marriage in late nineteenth-century rural Ireland: all these make it impossible to believe that Irish Catholicism can have had any such general effect.[10] But this still leaves the more subtle, and more plausible, of the two possible lines of argument, developed elsewhere in this volume by Professor Campbell. This is the view that certain types of Protestantism may have helped to create in their adherents habits and inner drives particularly conducive to economic success. Here the debate is a complex one, turning on issues of psychological analysis which are unlikely to be resolved, one way or another, from the Irish evidence.

Contemporary views on the link between religion and economic behaviour were concerned less with the middle than with the lower classes. Here many claimed to find a close association. A Co. Armagh rector, writing in 1816, commented on 'the superior industry and orderly conduct of the Protestant settlers of all denominations' in his parish. Ulster Catholics, Rev. Henry Cooke agreed in 1825, were 'not generally so industrious as the Protestants', and 'less inclined to adopt improvement'. Others expanded the comparison to a contrast between eastern Ulster and the remainder of the country. The rector of Ahoghill, Co. Antrim, writing in 1799, attributed the prosperous state of his county to the fact that 'our northerns are not like Dublin tradesmen, who, when trade is good, work one day and drink two'. An agent for the Marquis of Downshire, writing in 1824, contrasted the tenants in Co. Wicklow with those in Co. Down: 'The people are of another nature and habits, what is wanted here is industry, which is chiefly the cause of the poverty among the working people.'[11]

How are these claims to be assessed? Serious problems of labour-discipline did exist in eighteenth and early nineteenth-century Ireland. However, these must be seen in perspective. Recent studies, in Great Britain and elsewhere, have done much to reveal the distinctive characteristics of work in societies which have not yet been affected by the transition to large-scale, factory-based industry: the emphasis on tasks to be completed rather than on time to be spent working; the regulation of both wages and pace of work by customary standards rather than by calculations of what the market will bear; the irregular rhythm of labour, in which the long hours are relieved by frequent breaks and holidays, and in which those not subjected to a strict time-discipline alternate between bouts of intense work and periods of idleness.[12] The problems of labour-discipline complained of by Irish observers are recognisably part of this general pattern. Thus it has been pointed out that Irish workers in Great Britain in the early nineteenth century did not manifest any innate aversion to hard work. On the contrary they proved to be particularly suited to precisely those types of heavy physical work, demanding violent but irregular effort, for which the native labour force, conditioned by a different work-discipline, was no longer so well adapted.[13]

This is not to suggest that the problems of labour-discipline encountered in Ireland were not particularly serious ones. However, there were reasons for this. The great majority of the population, in the first place, was employed in agriculture, and thus in work which by its very nature could not be subordinated to a routine of fixed and regular hours, but had to be performed as the seasons and the weather dictated. 'Under strong exciting circumstances,' it was observed in 1840, 'the Irish peasant will work harder than the labourer of any other country, but his toil is neither steady nor continuous. The season of total inactivity comes as regularly as the season of violent exertion; and the character of the peasant is rendered all the worse by the striking magnitude of the vicissitude.' Added to this was the problem of chronic underemployment. The Irish Poor Enquiry calculated in 1836 that agricultural labourers had on average only 135 days of paid employment each year. Even so stern a commentator as George Nicholls, the designer of the Irish poor law, recognised in these circumstances the main cause of the 'desultory and idle habits' of the rural lower classes: 'The work required upon their small holdings is easily performed, and may, as they say, 'be done any day'. Their work for wages is uncertain; hence arises a total disregard of the value of time, a desultory and sauntering habit, without industry or steadiness of purpose.'[14]

Problems of labour discipline, however, were not confined to agriculture. The working conditions of most urban dwellers permitted a much lesser degree of flexibility than was the case with cottiers or smallholders. Some trades, it is true, retained traces of the task-oriented pattern of work which continued to dominate rural labour. A Newry newspaper proprietor testified in 1838 that up to two years before his employees had not worked for clearly defined hours: 'I was indulgent with them when they wished indulgence; and when the hurry was great and business pressing they were not particular with me; we went on amicably together.' Even after 1836, when the men demanded extra payment for time worked in excess of ten hours a day, 'they added, upon my remonstrance, that on post-nights, the night before publication [i.e. three nights a week] . . . they would not mind stopping until the work went to press'. The great majority of artisans, however, were subjected by this time to strictly defined hours of work. The secretary of the Dublin Plasterers' Society recalled in 1838 that one of his employers

> had a clerk that used to mind the men's time in going in and out, and I considered it a very harsh thing that a man would be returned back and lose a quarter of a day for being merely four or five minutes beyond his three-quarters of an hour at breakfast, and the man proposed that he would work during his dinner hour, he would give that time if he might be allowed, and he was not allowed to work his dinner hour for that five minutes.

Yet if employers were able to impose a strict working day, they experienced greater difficulties in imposing on their workers a regular working week. According to Joseph Archer, writing in 1801, 'the working manufacturers [of Dublin], even when work is in abundance, mostly idle on Mondays, though they will be often obliged to pinch themselves the remainder of the week, or run in debt'. 'There are few instances,' a Dublin timber merchant complained in 1838, 'in which you do not find a sawyer take the first day of the week to himself and part of the second.' Even in 1868, it was claimed, 'Monday is a very idle day for many of the artisans in Dublin', although a former magistrate maintained that those for whom this was true were 'not one-fourth of the number that it was in my boyhood'. This Monday absenteeism, he added, was not simply a matter of recovering from the heavy drinking of the day before: 'I think that the Monday amongst those people is a continuation of the idleness of the Sunday.'[15]

Two points are involved here, both of them characteristic of a society which has not yet been affected by the large-scale development of factory industry. From the employers' point of view absenteeism of this kind may on occasion have been inconvenient. But as long as it was not necessary to co-ordinate the movements of workers with the operation of expensive machinery, it could be tolerated and allowed for. Where the worker was concerned, the question was one of responsiveness to financial incentives. When men chose to work less than a full six-day week, whether through observing 'Saint Monday' or by some other means, they were opting for increased leisure rather than maximum cash earnings. The same attitude was encountered as late as the 1880s by the management of a jute spinning company set up to provide employment in Co. Galway. The employees, the chairman complained, were perfectly satisfactory when at work, but the company was 'dreadfully bothered' by absenteeism. A girl who could earn 18s in a full week's work preferred to settle for 5s and a greater degree of freedom, 'leaving my loom idle, robbing me and herself too'. When wages were reduced by 10 per cent, however, productivity actually improved: 'I suppose they found it was necessary to work harder to make sufficient wages.'[16]

The idea of a simple causal link between religion and the presence or absence of habits of industry, then, does not stand up to examination. The problems of labour discipline experienced in eighteenth and early nineteenth-century Ireland were the result, not of any innate aversion to hard work associated with the dominance of Catholicism, but of attitudes and patterns of behaviour characteristic of a society at this level of development. However, this still leaves the question of whether these attitudes and patterns of behaviour might have been more influential, or might have persisted longer, among some groups than among others. In particular, Ulster Protestants differed from Catholics in Ulster and elsewhere both in their economic circumstances and in the cultural influences to which they were exposed. Did they also differ in their work psychology? The rector of Dungiven, Co. Londonderry, writing in 1814, contrasted the working habits of his 'Scotch' and 'Irish' parishioners in terms which in many ways anticipate modern discussions of the problem. Both groups, he found, were industrious, 'but the industry of the Scotch is steady, patient and directed with great foresight; while that of the Irish is rash, adventurous and variable'. While the Scotch engaged in linen weaving, the Irish showed an 'indisposition to the slow but regular profits of manufacture', preferring 'the less regular and certain, but to them more interesting gain, which arises from the quick transition of property, and the frequent fluctuations in the cattle trade'.[17]

The rector's comment is an interesting one, particularly since it presents the issue, not in terms of vice and virtue, but of contrasting ways of life. And it may well be that some distinction of the type he outlined did exist. At the same time there are grounds for suggesting that any differences in working habits between Ulster Protestants and their Catholic neighbours were by no means as clear-cut as he believed. The custom of Saint Monday was well known in Ulster as well as in Dublin. In Belfast, the Rev John Edgar reported in 1834, 'it is . . . a very general complaint, in reference to whole classes of tradesmen, that they spend in idleness and dissipation the Monday, and very frequently the Tuesday'. Among coachmakers in the city of Derry one firm had succeeded by 1836 in eliminating Monday absenteeism, but in another the journeymen 'sometimes . . . only work half a day of a Monday, and sometimes not at all'. Linen weaving, despite the rector's reference to 'slow but regular profits', was a typical pre-industrial occupation, in which the worker chose both the amount of work he did and the time at which he did it, and Ulster weavers availed themselves of this flexibility as freely as workers elsewhere. When food was cheap, Arthur Young noted in a well-known passage, the weavers of Co. Down produced less cloth than when food was expensive: like the jute spinners of Co. Galway a century later, their preference was for increased leisure rather than higher real wages. Both Young and other observers noted the willingness with which weavers abandoned their looms for hunting and other pastimes, making up for time lost by extra work later in the week. Yet all these groups of workers — skilled tradesmen in Belfast and Derry, linen weavers in Co. Down and elsewhere — would have been predominantly Protestant. Edward Wakefield, writing in 1812, made the comparison explicit. The northern Presbyterian, he maintained, spent as much time on horse-races, gambling, cockfighting and other amusements as the Catholic did on saints' days and visits to holy wells, and the superior prosperity of the weaver was the result, not of any particular industry on his part, but of the fact that his whole family were employed and contributed to the general support. By 1840 concern over the irregular working habits of weavers had led to the establishment, in Belfast and elsewhere, of weaving factories, in which weavers, while still operating hand looms, could be brought under the discipline of fixed hours and constant supervision.[18]

III

This essay cannot claim to have examined all the possible links between religion and economic action in eighteenth and early nineteenth-century Ireland. To present a complete analysis, for example, it would be necessary to compare, not just the outlook of Catholics and of Protestants, but also that of Protestants of different denominations. It would also be necessary to look at the ways in which religion might have had an indirect influence on economic life: for example, through the educational activities of different churches, or by acting as a cultural barrier, impeding the adopting of new skills or forms of employment.[19] In the areas which have been examined, however, the evidence collected here suggests that the influence of religion on economic performance was at best a limited one. Catholic and Protestant churchmen subscribed to and sought to propagate the same attitudes to economic life and to society generally. Among the laity, equally, any variations in attitudes and behaviour appear to have been relatively minor — too much so, certainly, to be seen as evidence of radically different work psychologies. At the same time it would be wrong to present too static a picture. This last section will look briefly at certain developments which were beginning only towards the end of the period considered here.

The willingness of Ulster weavers to give up their independence and submit to the uncongenial discipline of a 'lock-up' was only one symptom of a wider change in the tone of popular social life. The reports on parishes in Antrim and Londonderry collected during the 1830s by investigators for the Ordnance Survey confirm earlier accounts of the wide variety of traditional amusements kept up by the Protestant population of these counties. At the same time these reports also comment frequently on the sharp decline seen in recent years in enthusiasm for such amusements. The main reason suggested for this decline is economic: falling real incomes meant both that there was less money available to spend on amusements and that people had to work longer hours to maintain an acceptable standard of living. However, there are also suggestions of a change in outlook and habits. In Camlin, Co. Antrim, for example, amusements had declined, partly because there was less money in circulation, 'and partly from their habits having become more settled and steady'. Elsewhere too there are accounts of traditional amusements being replaced by quieter and more respectable forms of recreation, such as book clubs and singing schools devoted to sacred music. This was also a period which saw the growing strength of evangelicalism within the different Protestant denominations, and some reports explicitly link the change in habits to religious influences. In various parishes, for example, it is the clergy who are credited with having brought about the abandonment of card-playing, cock-fighting and other recreations, while in Lisburn handball and similar sports had been given up within the previous forty years 'and religious practices instituted in their stead'.[20]

So there was after all one way in which religion may have had a part in the economic development of nineteenth-century Ireland, even if not the one assigned to it by most contemporaries. In England, it has been argued, evangelical religion, and in particular Methodism, played a major role in the process by which men and women adapted themselves to the new work-discipline required by industrialisation, partly by providing an outlet for suppressed or diverted energies, and partly by its emphasis on a strict and constant self-control.[21] Evangelicalism in Ulster, these reports suggest, may have done something similar. If so, however, the emergence of a distinctively Protestant work-ethic is something which came about only after the economic development of the north-east had already diverged unmistakably from that of other parts of Ireland. And it follows that any such ethic must be seen as the by-product of successful industrialisation rather than as its cause.

The other main point which can be made about this development takes us back to the earlier discussion of the role of the Catholic clergy. By the 1830s, it appears, Presbyterian and other Protestant churchmen in parts of Ulster had succeeded in suppressing or modifying the traditional amusements of their congregations, and thus in clearing the way for a new and more rigorous labour discipline. But if so, they had merely succeeded (in more favourable circumstances) in achieving something which their Catholic counterparts, both in Ulster and elsewhere, had also been attempting. Already by the late eighteenth century there had been signs that Catholic churchmen were becoming critical of many traditional forms of recreation. Around 1780, for example, a new priest appointed to the parish of Carlow 'set about reforming every abuse that came within his reach . . . such as bull-beating [*sic*], cockfighting, manfighting, gambling and everything of that description'.[22] Such efforts intensified in the years after 1800, as priests and bishops increasingly threw their weight against a wide range of popular amusements, from traditional festivals such as St John's Eve or the pattern days at holy wells to roadside dancing and casual assemblies for amusement on Sunday afternoons. Most striking of all, the holy days of the Catholic church itself came in for strong criticism, their number being reduced in 1778 and again between 1829 and 1831, each time in response to petitions from the Irish hierarchy to Rome.[23] In all this, of course, Catholic churchmen were motivated by concern for the moral welfare of their flocks, rather than by economic considerations. And it is also true that their efforts to bring about a restructuring of popular attitudes and behaviour never achieved more than limited results. But this should not obscure the fact that they had shown themselves to be more than ready to make the attempt. If things had been otherwise — if their efforts had been reinforced by the sort of social change which was taking place in contemporary England — then the Catholic church and its clergy might today be seen as having had a role in Ireland similar to that which historians of British development have assigned to Methodism or to the Association for the Suppression of Vice. It was not their fault that other actors were not so ready to play their parts, and that the whole project never got beyond the early stages of rehearsal.

REFERENCES

1. Royal Irish Academy, Ordnance Survey Memoirs, 10/V/5, sect. 3, James Boyle's memoir of Dunluce, Co. Antrim, 1835.

2. Peadar MacSuibhne, ed., *Paul Cullen and his Contemporaries* (Naas, 1961–77), I, 106. For attitudes in the later nineteenth century and after see D. W. Miller, *Church, State and Nation in Ireland 1898–1921* (Dublin, 1973), pp. 70–6.

3. J. T. Troy, *A Pastoral Instruction on the Duties of Christian Citizens* (Dublin, 1793), p. 5; J. W. Doyle, *Pastoral Address against the Illegal Associations of Ribbonmen* (Dublin, 1822), pp. 22–3; M. J. Curran, ed., 'Instructions, Admonitions etc of Archbishop Carpenter 1770–86', *Reportorium Novum*, II, 1 (1958), pp. 153–4; P. F. Moran, ed., *Spicilegium Ossoriense* (Dublin, 1874–84), III, pp. 591–2. For a more detailed discussion of these points, see S. J. Connolly, *Priests and People in Pre-Famine Ireland 1780–1845* (Dublin, 1982), pp. 220–9.

4. *Association for the Suppression of Mendicity in Dublin, First Report* (Dublin, 1819), p. 23; *Third Report* (Dublin, 1821), p. 27; *Dublin Evening Post*, 19 July 1821; Public Record Ofice of Northern Ireland, Dio(RC)3/1 (formerly T.3371), pp. 30–31, draft letter to *Newry Commercial Telegraph* [November 1833]. The generosity shown to beggars and vagrants by the Irish poor, frequently commented on by contemporary observers, has led one recent writer to distinguish between 'Catholic' and 'Protestant' attitudes to charity in early nineteenth-century Ireland (Timothy P. O'Neill, 'The Catholic Church and Relief of the Poor 1815-45', *Archivium Hibernicum*, XXXI (1973), p. 134). However, the habits of indiscriminate alms-giving so disapproved of by Catholic churchmen like Troy were as common among the predominantly Presbyterian farmers, smallholders and weavers of Co. Antrim as they were among poorer Catholics elsewhere in Ireland (see *Commissioners for Enquiring into the Condition of the Poorer Classes in Ireland* [hereafter *Poor Enquiry, Ireland*], Appendix A (Parl. Papers, 1835, XXXII, Part 1, pp. 702–30). In this, as in other matters, the real line of division was social class rather than religion.

5. Michael Manning, 'Dr Nicholas Madgett's *Constitutio Ecclesiastica*', *Kerry Archaeological & Historical Society Journal*, 9 (1976), pp. 72–3; Cashel Diocesan Records, Archbishop's House, Thurles [National Library of Ireland, MIC P5998–6013], Everard and Laffan Papers, 1824/10, Coppinger to Robert Laffan, 11 Oct. 1824; Edward Wakefield, *An Account of Ireland, Statistical and Political* (London, 1812), II, p. 603.

6. Cashel Diocesan Records, James Butler II Papers, 1784/2, Butler to Edmund Pery, 17 April 1784 (copy). Butler's argument was that these clergymen had been trained in continental countries, where the rate of interest was fixed by law in order to prevent usury, and so did not appreciate that in Ireland, a more commercial society, the rate was fixed as a premium to encourage investment. The act he suggested received the royal assent on 14 May 1784 (*H. of C. Journals (Ireland)*, XXI, p. 597).

7. Public Record Office of Ireland, Ballyglunin Papers, M6935/73(3).

8. P.R.O.N.I. Dio(RC) 3/1, p. 9, Blake to ——— Vernon, 27 June 1833.

9. Horace Plunkett, *Ireland in the New Century* (London, 1904), p. 110.

10. L. M. Cullen, *The Emergence of Modern Ireland 1600-1900* (London, 1981), pp. 115-20, 124-8; Joseph Lee, *The Modernization of Irish Society 1848-1918* (Dublin, 1973), pp. 16-17; K. H. Connell, *Irish Peasant Society: Four Historical Essays* (Oxford, 1968), pp. 113-61.

11. W. S. Mason, ed., *Statistical Account or Parochial Survey of Ireland* (Dublin, 1814-19), II, p. 82; *Select Committee on the State of Ireland* (Parl. Papers, 1825, VIII), p. 373; *H.M.C. Report 13, Appendix 8* (Charlemont Mss), p. 354, Edward Hudson to Charlemont, 5 July 1799; W. A. Maguire, *The Downshire Estates in Ireland 1801-45* (Oxford, 1972), pp. 229-31.

12. See for example Keith Thomas, 'Work and Leisure in Pre-Industrial Society', *Past & Present*, 29 (1964); E. P. Thompson, 'Time, Work-Discipline and Industrial Capitalism', *Past & Present*, 38 (1967); E. J. Hobsbawm, 'Custom, Wages and Work-Load in Nineteenth-Century Industry' in *Labouring Men* (London, 1968); Sidney Pollard, 'Factory Discipline in the Industrial Revolution', *Economic History Review*, XVI, 2 (1963); D. A. Reid, 'The Decline of Saint Monday 1766-1876', *Past & Present*, 71 (1976); Ian Blanchard, 'Labour Productivity and Work Psychology in the English Mining Industry', *Econ. Hist. Rev.* XXXI, 1 (1978).

13. E. P. Thompson, *The Making of the English Working Class* (Harmondsworth, 1968), pp. 473-8.

14. *Assistant Hand-Loom Weavers Commissioners*, Part III (Parl. Papers, 1840, XXIII), pp. 594-5; *Poor Enquiry, Ireland*, Appendix H (Parl. Papers, 1836, XXXIV), p. 12; George Nicholls, *Poor Laws — Ireland: Three Reports* (1838), pp. 10-11.

15. *Select Committee on Combinations of Workmen, Second Report* (Parl. Papers, 1837-8, VIII), pp. 71-2; *ibid.*, p. 137; Joseph Archer, *Statistical Survey of the County Dublin* (Dublin, 1801), p. 221; *S.C. Combinations, Second Report*, p. 13; *Select Committee on the Sale of Liquors on Sunday (Ireland) Bill* (Parl. Papers, 1867-8, XIV), p. 69. As late as 1872 Cardinal Cullen complained that 'the bad part of the people', under the guidance of trade unions, now refused to work on Saturday afternoons, while 'they devote Monday as usual to dissipation' (P. J. Corish, ed., 'Irish College, Rome: Kirby Papers', *Arch. Hib.* XXXII (1974), p. 56).

16. *Select Committee on Industries (Ireland)* (Parl. Papers, 1884-5, IX), pp. 302-3, 308.

17. Mason, ed., *Statistical Account of Ireland*, I, pp. 307-8, 340.

18. *Select Committee on Enquiry into Drunkenness* (Parl. Papers, 1834, VIII), p. 71; *Poor Enquiry, Ireland*, Appendix C (Parl. Papers, 1836, XXX), pp. 62-3; Arthur Young, *A Tour in Ireland* (1892 ed.), I, pp. 132, 127; Mason, ed., *Statistical Account of Ireland*, II, p. 528; Wakefield, *Account of Ireland*, II, p. 740; *Hand Loom Weavers' Commissioners*, Part III (P.P. 1840, XXXIII), pp. 633-5, 641, 666, 717-18.

19. See for example the comments of Robert Stevenson on the reluctance of Ulster Catholics prior to 1740 to become involved in linen weaving: 'They considered it as a manufacture introduced by the Protestants or Huguenots tending to change their religion and they preferred for many years being labourers to that of being weavers' (P.R.O.N.I. D562/1270, View of Co. Armagh, 1795).

20. Ordnance Survey Memoirs, 6/I/2, pp. 26-7 (Camlin); 12/I/5, p. 31 (Kilbride, Co. Antrim); 9/III/3, pp. 54-5 (Doagh, Co. Antrim); 12/V/4 (Kilraughts, Co. Antrim); 16/IV/2, p. 62 (Templecorran, Co. Antrim); 29/V/2, p. 49 (Artrea, Co. Londonderry); 37/I/3, pp. 6a, 11 (Desertlyn, Co. Londonderry); 1/II/2, p. 64 (Aghagallon, Co. Antrim); 5/II/5, p. 178 (Blaris, Co. Antrim).

21. Thompson, *Making of the English Working Class*, Ch. 11. See also R. W. Malcomson, *Popular Recreations in English Society 1700-1850* (Cambridge, 1973), pp. 100-7.

22. Roger McHugh, ed., *Carlow in '98: The Autobiography of William Farrell of Carlow* (Dublin, 1949), p. 39.

23. For a fuller discussion of these points see Connolly, *Priests and People*, Ch. 4.

Part VII

The Long View

19

Incomes, Social Classes and Economic Growth in Ireland and Scotland, 1600–1900

L. M. Cullen

COMPARATIVE exercises in history can be presumptuous because they lead an historian to make reflections on the history of a country about which he knows a good deal less than his own. Indeed, even for his own country, such comparisons lead him onto the ground where the scholarly foundations are most shaky — social structure, incomes, and the reasons which account for growth or stagnation. However, the attempt can be justified because it involves emphasis on an analytical rather than descriptive approach, and because some features which domestic historians take for granted can seem immediately striking to an outsider.

Irish and Scottish history alike have been obscured in whiskey, mist and misery. The mists and the whiskey may be regarded without controversy as part of the common history of both countries. But it is surprising that misery looms larger in the telling of at least some periods in the history of Scotland than of Ireland, and that Ireland is frequently, for the seventeenth century in particular, represented in an unexpectedly positive light. However, to the outsider the emphasis by the Scots on the social problems of their seventeenth century seems excessive. Scottish difficulties in the 1690s were not unique: in that decade famine was general in many parts of Europe, and Ireland was in a relatively happy position in escaping demographic disaster. Likewise, Scotland's problems in foreign trade were not novel in the closing decades of the century, and some of the staple exports of both countries were in difficulties. Scottish consignments of cattle to England may already have peaked in 1682–3;[1] in Ireland, whose foreign trade in this period is generally regarded as expanding, the last good year was 1684 and though the volume of exports may not have peaked until 1687, prices were by that time disastrously low.[2] The Irish downturn was a consequence of abundance in the French market, which led French policy towards pastoral products to become protective in 1685 and 1688. Thereafter, war from 1689 to 1697, the most prolonged hostilities experienced for half a century and the first sustained war at sea, disastrously affected the foreign trade of both countries. If the price effects of war on Irish agriculture were mitigated, it was only because livestock numbers had been decimated in the military campaigns of 1689–91; the prices of livestock products did not slump until the outset of the new century (except for the vital commodity butter, whose prices plummeted in 1699). Even in the advance of sheep farming, reflected in turn in the abrupt rise in exports of wool and woollens in the second half of the 1690s, a pessimistic appraisal by the larger landholders of alternative uses of land can be detected. In fact, if exports in 1698 are netted of the additional exports of wool and woollens and windfall profits in butter, the long-term evolution of Irish foreign trade since the 1680s was less rosy than a crude comparison of gross export figures suggests. Paradoxically, in Ireland's case, the difficulties of the livestock industry helped to account for the growth in cereal cultivation in the 1690s and may explain both the country's freedom from famine and a grain surplus for export, both to France, despite the war, and, more substantially to Scotland in 1696 and again in 1699.

If the conditions in the 1680s and 1690s in the two countries are compared, it is difficult to see Scotland's position as being exceptional. Indeed, it seems to have been ahead of Ireland. The scale of Scottish immigration indicates underdevelopment in Ireland, just as the character of this movement suggests that the migrants were leaving a richer or better developed economy. Scottish settlers were able to finance their own passage and installation, they were largely pastoral — which implies that they possessed some assets — and cattle ownership was general among them, whereas in Ireland many indigenous rural dwellers did not own cattle. It was this latter rural category who, profiting from the inability of livestock farmers to stock lands in the 1690s, expanded tillage strikingly. Economic recovery in the north-east was helped by the fact that the military campaigns ceased there a year earlier than in the rest of the country: however, the resources of existing Scottish settlers and new investment by a further influx in the 1690s were also vital to Ulster's comparative success. Its position in dairying had been improving since the 1660s, and its relative importance in the economy was noticeably greater in the post-1660 decades than in the first half of the century, when a self-sufficient classic cider-and-grain economy had been established in parts of the region by settlers from south-west England. The emerging 'Scottish' economy of north-east Ireland first experienced crisis in the opening two decades of the next century, and the abrupt ending of Scottish immigration after 1700 was a response to the change which took place as soon as war in 1702 again plunged the Irish livestock economy into depression.

Some attention to the 1690s is warranted by the need to emphasise that Scotland's problems at that time do not seem to constitute grounds for a pessimistic appraisal of Scotland's development. Foreign trade in particular is a dangerous basis for assumptions about comparative development. Higher per capita levels of foreign trade in Ireland at the end of the seventeenth century[3] reflect, as will be argued later, a higher level of commercialisation rather than greater wealth. Scottish incomes throughout the period were consistently higher than Irish; and Scotland's social structure was already more *developed* than the Irish which was *primitive*, and more *rigid* than the Irish which was *fluid*. Indeed, it is likely that relative incomes changed little over the period from 1600 to 1900. Kuznets observed many years ago that the growth rate of per capita incomes in America and European countries since 1844 did not vary greatly,[4] suggesting that the disparity in absolute levels was there at the outset. It is hard to push comparisons back beyond 1844, but both practical evidence and theoretical considerations support the idea that relativities in income or its distribution tend to be persistent over very long intervals, and especially if short-term fluctuations are discounted. Hence disparities existing in the eighteenth and nineteenth centuries should have been there even at an earlier date. England's lead over other countries at the time was exaggerated by contemporaries and by later writers, partly indeed because of the weight attached to its more commercialised character and the novelty of some of its production methods. O'Brien and Keyder's recent study of England and France is an interesting corrective to the widely held view that the gap in living standards between the countries was large.[5] Moreover, even in their case, the difference is overstated in the case of production in current prices, because France as a cereal producer suffered disproportionately in its agricultural terms of trade in the nineteenth century.

Parallel to the difference in income levels between both Scotland and Ireland is the existence of wider disparities within incomes in the poorer country. The reason for this is obvious: skills are scarcer, hence the more skilled occupations command higher rates of remuneration, whereas low productivity ensures much lower returns for unskilled work. In Ireland agricultural incomes compared unfavourably both with the corresponding incomes in Scotland, and with non-agricultural incomes at home. On the basis of the 1908 agricultural census, the wide gulf between Scotland and Ireland in gross output per gainfully occupied worker in agriculture is evident: £109 in Scotland, £46 in Ireland. On the other hand, the disparity in both countries was slight in the case of non-agricultural incomes. The English corn merchant Cropper commented in 1825 on the wide gap between wages of skilled and unskilled in Ireland.[6] While agricultural incomes in Scotland were more than twice the level of those in Ireland, Scottish per capita national income was only a half higher in 1911, despite a greater dependency rate in Ireland.[7] Even without aggregate income data, similar disparities can be traced in the late eighteenth century. The disparity can be gauged in Arthur Young's data in 1776: masons typically earned two shillings *per diem (p.d.)* in Ireland, whereas labourers' wages averaged 6½d., i.e. a ratio of almost 4:1. In the Statistical Account, Scottish masons' wages in the 1790s were typically two shillings *p.d.* and labourers' wages one shilling: a much closer ratio of 2:1.

If labourers' wages are taken crudely as some indication of earnings in the agricultural sector, agricultural earnings in Scotland were twice the level of Irish on the basis of comparison of rates in the 1790s. This relationship was not greatly different on the basis of Bowley's data in the early 1830s,[8] the levels in the 1790s and 1830s thus broadly matching the disparity in agricultural incomes in 1908. The gap was wider in the interval — in the 1850s and subsequent decades. But the sharp rise in Scottish wages at that time can not be construed as a rise from Irish-type levels previously; the level was already higher and, over the period from the 1770s to 1908 as a whole, the long-term disparity remained surprisingly rigid. In other words, the gap in relative agricultural incomes preceded the economic changes in nineteenth-century Scotland.

Other evidence supports the contention that the disparity between Scottish and

Irish living standards already existed well before the agricultural changes of the early nineteenth century. De la Tocnaye's accounts of his sojourn in Scotland in the mid-1790s and in Ireland in 1796–7, if we accept a French arbiter, give a clear impression that Scotland was the richer country.[9] If Scottish wages were higher, we would expect better techniques and more labour-saving investment. This seems to have been the case, and in Ireland even in the rich farming areas a surprisingly high degree of cultivation was by spade. Again, the image of Scotland's agriculture has suffered because its methods were traditional. But to De la Tocnaye, coming from a country with a rich traditional agriculture, they were not a source of comment. On the other hand, seventy years earlier, Defoe, though he described parts of lowland Scotland as fertile, and even allowed the region between Dunbar and Edinburgh to be as rich 'as most in England', was patronising about Scottish agriculture because of 'setting their corn up in great numbers of small stacks without doors, not making use of any barns'.[10] De la Tocnaye, though aware of very different methods in France, was not in the least surprised at this practice which was still general in Scotland, thinking it quite effective.[11] Scotland already had better ability to survive bad years than Ireland. The Scottish experience in 1782–3 was perhaps similar to Ireland's, but what is striking in the Irish context is the degree to which supplies were transferred out of Ireland in the autumn of 1782 when prices were everywhere high, whereas in Scotland surpluses were retained at home. The painful memory of the 1782 season was present to compilers of the Scottish Statistical Account in the 1790s, but the terms in which the evidence is presented suggest that there was less pressure to put supplies on the market and a consequent ability to retain supplies at local level. Indeed, in the parish of Lethnot in Forfar, survival was said to have been assured by the surplus in the previous year's harvest.[12]

Too much emphasis can be put on nineteenth-century changes in Scottish agriculture. Contemporaries who exalted advances deprecated the old as barbarous and inefficient. This view of the past was much more general in Scotland than in Ireland, where the Enlightenment was not comparable, and where the rejection of the old was articulated less. In Scotland, rejection of the past led to an exaggerated adverse picture of earlier Scottish agriculture as, for instance, in the misrepresentation of the pre-Union cattle trade. In Greenlaw in Berwick, the memoir in the Statistical Account went as far as claiming that 'before the union, Scotland had no foreign market for her sheep and black cattle'.[13] The fact is that by comparison with Ireland changes in Scottish agriculture came very late, and the changes in the early nineteenth century are so striking because more compressed. Indeed, accounts of Scottish improvement seem to lump together both changes in land arrangement and labour-saving and cropping techniques, which are not necessarily at all closely related. Ian Whyte's arguments on agriculture and society in seventeenth-century Scotland are an invaluable support to the argument of this essay, but are most relevant if we see Scottish agriculture as relatively developed to start with rather than as advancing progressively on a broad front.

Whether one takes 1760 or 1790, enclosure was far less complete in Scotland than in Ireland, and the survival of rundale villages far more common. In fact, Ireland bore far more evidence of innovation between 1600 and 1800, and on that account appeared to passing contemporary visitors at least in the seventeenth century the more modern country. The Lancashire visitor Brereton who travelled in both countries in 1635 is in the present context the most appropriate example of this. He was clearly impressed by much of what he saw in Ireland, finding the district from Belfast to Lisburn 'a paradise in comparison of any part of Scotland'.[14] But the Lagan corridor along with north Armagh was the centre of the most intense settlement by English colonists in Ireland. Indeed, comparing Edinburgh and Dublin, he found the latter 'far beyond Edinborough'.[15] From the little we know of the two cities, it is doubtful whether Dublin at this date was larger than Edinburgh, and Brereton made a point of noting that Dublin had no street comparable with Edinburgh's High Street, but unquestionably Dublin was growing very rapidly. From the pictorial map of 1647, Edinburgh was still a city of wynds reaching off the High Street and of tall tenement houses,[16] whereas Dublin was already building in brick as well as expanding. Both the newness of the city and the modernity of its buildings must have been very striking to a visitor freshly arrived from Scotland and intent on comparing Dublin with an Edinburgh at once more static and conservative.

A second contrast between the two countries is that there was a much more sustained creation of fairs, markets and villages in Ireland. While there are some arresting similarities between village creation in eighteenth-century Scotland and Ireland, there is no Scottish parallel for the sustained growth of villages in Ireland in the seventeenth century. Moreover, the fairs and markets created at that stage in Scotland, as Whyte has shown, were intended to service existing *local* markets, as for instance in the case of the market at Painstown (East Lothian), established to cater for 80 colliers and their families.[17] Ireland's market structure was more closely geared to trade, and especially to the livestock trade. Irish exports of cattle and beef in the 1660s were the equivalent of 72,000 head of cattle; Scotland's exports at their seventeenth-century peak were only 20–30,000. Moreover, Scottish livestock trade was concentrated on the south-west of the country; Ireland's, despite being geographically more dispersed, integrated rearing and fattening regions across the island. Indeed, the more intense creation of markets in the remoter areas was precisely for this reason.[18]

The third contrast, closely related to the two preceding ones, was the much greater force of commercialisation in Ireland. The end-product of this force was immediately evident to the French consul in Dublin in 1834: the contrast between abundance at local level in France, and in Ireland the export of virtually all the food.[19] Commercialisation began very early, and was reflected in the change in Irish diet between the seventeenth and eighteenth centuries: consumption of butter and grain declined, giving way to the potato. There was no comparable change in Scotland: the potato was well-established in Ireland in 1740 (even if some of the claims for it at that date have been fanciful); in Scotland it appeared only after 1750. A position was emerging in Ireland where much of the food supply was marketed. A high level of consumption would have held back trade and development, the point hinted at on the Scottish side in the comment on owner-occupiers at Slamannan in Stirling who, 'though they and their families live very comfortably upon the produce, yet they cannot spare any money to lay out in improvements'.[20] Grain-growing districts everywhere were more self-sufficient than pastoral ones: a much higher proportion of the output was consumed locally and markets were frequently close at hand. A memoir on a cattle-raising parish, Rerrick in Galloway, drew the contrast with tillage regions, noting that the farmers 'often led out in the world [had] an illumination to their minds, and a polish to their manners, which those, in a mere grain country, are absolute strangers to'.[21] In fact, the significance of the crisis in Scotland's foreign trade in the late seventeenth century is all the more likely to have been exaggerated if the importance of 'autoconsumption' and local markets is not taken into account. To some extent, the crisis may have been overstated by those involved in foreign trade who were anxious to identify their own interests with Scotland's at large and to press home as strongly as possible the case for union which would promote or protect Scotland's nascent colonial interests. Overall, Ireland, relative to income much more dependent on foreign trade, was a greater sufferer from the trade crisis in the 1680s and 1690s; it also experienced a marked stagnation in trade in the early decades of the new century and showed signs of greater social vulnerability at that stage: Ireland, not Scotland, experienced famines in the 1720s and 1740s. It can even be argued that it was the depth of the crisis which made Irish society ready consciously to espouse further change and innovation.

Commercialisation can be measured in terms of: (i) the degree of self-sufficiency on holdings; (ii) the proportion of sales outside the region; (iii) the proportion of production marketed outside the economy altogether. These aspects are closely interrelated, although each can be distinguished in its own right. In all three respects Ireland was the more commercialised country. In the first case, subsistence was less evident in Ireland in the sense that per capita food sales were very large. A corollary of this was that payments in produce for land or services ceased at an early date. Nor was food consumed profusely by the families who produced it: diet became progressively sparser. Superficially, 'autoconsumption' seems fairly large in the estimate of Irish agricultural output in 1908, because farms were smaller and incomes much lower than in Scotland. But in relation to the low absolute levels of income, the proportions of 'autoconsumption' were modest. Consumption of what Irish farmers produced was sparing and purchases were indispensable. The importance of imported maize especially in the poorer regions and the substitution of cheap imported American bacon for farm-produced bacon in the comfortable regions is a striking measure of the progressive penetration of commercialisation to the very core of Irish diet in the nineteenth century. In fact, in the eighteenth century, food purchases by the poor were relatively more significant than those by the better-off. Indeed, even cloth was purchased by poor and well-off alike in rural Ireland: the bad clothing of the Irish was a comment on the lack of textile makers in rural Ireland before the eighteenth century; and the success, though not perhaps all the origins, of the linen industry, lies in the fact that the Scots who came to Ulster were adaptable and able to switch to textiles. The market for imported second-hand clothes which emerged in the eighteenth century is an indication of reliance on purchases by those too poor to buy new Irish-manufactured cloth. In his visit to

Ireland, Sir Walter Scott in 1825 noted how badly clothed the Irish were, though as he also noticed a generation gap between the badly dressed old people and the young, one can detect a change.[22] Ironically, this may be related to the changing fortunes of the textile industry in which goods produced within Ireland were beginning to be replaced with massive imports of cheap cloth from Britain.

On the second point, sales outside regions, there is little doubt that these were more marked in Ireland. While local circuits of exchange existed in Ireland, they were weaker than in Scotland, both because sales to distant markets were relatively more important than in Scotland, and because the low incomes of rural inhabitants ensured that their purchase of consumer goods was very sparing. The marked orientation in Ireland towards sales outside the region was thus a parallel to the high degree of dependence by the individual producer on sales. In Scotland, much grain which paid rent was re-purchased by farmers, and the proportion even increased in times of crisis. This is a striking contrast with Ireland, where high prices usually served to draw grain out of a region or even out of the country. Whyte illustrates the rise in local consumption in the 1690s,[23] and indeed high prices both in 1696 and 1699 led to a massive upsurge in exports from Ireland. In the Scottish livestock trade, highland sales to the lowlands were comparatively slow to develop, and much of the livestock trade was contained within the south-west.[24] The Irish livestock trade from an early stage consisted of an intricate structure which created the means whereby several farmers or smallholders successively made a profit on the same beast. There was no comparable market structure in Scotland linking together the interests of smallholders in remote areas and graziers in rich areas. There was considerable fattening of locally reared cattle not only in the rich Lothians but even in the poorer south-west. Landowners played a large role in the trade in Scotland: they not only marketed cattle, but sometimes even purchased them at Falkirk expressly for droving to England.[25] Indeed, the very existence of drove roads in a less pastoral economy than the Irish is a testimony to a concentrated trade more geared to final markets. In Ireland, by contrast, drove roads were not evident, but the intricate network of fairs multiplying intermediate transfers of livestock is a dominant characteristic of much of the economy. Moreover, if the rise of specialist dairying regions is allowed for — an activity which re-directed the use of land from local food supply towards production for export — almost the entire pastoral economy of the island was interlocked in the mutual dependence of regions in the matter of the disposal of surplus male calves.

Scotland had thus a more self-sufficient agriculture, and a less specialised or more mixed one, than Ireland: much grain was retained regionally for human or animal use, markets were usually closer to hand, and the buying in of livestock was far less general or intricate than in Ireland. The relative absence of a strong internal livestock trade in Scotland is reflected in the progressive dependence in the nineteenth century of Scottish farmers on Irish stores.[26] In 1908 the gross output of British agriculture should be netted of some £7 million on this score: in other words Scotland's gross agricultural output of £23 million should be reduced by almost £3 million. It is indeed on this basis that Scottish agriculture created its classic pattern in the eighteenth and nineteenth centuries. The mixed pattern of Scottish agriculture rather than its innovativeness seems to have been its source of strength. But precisely because so much of the production was retained locally, sales outside the region were less important than in Ireland, where the effort to take advantage of changes in prices had seen some striking shifts over time between products, dictated more by relative prices on distant markets than by the conditions of the soil or by local demand.

The pattern of a dominant market structure is evident in linen also: both yarn markets and cloth markets played a major role in the early Irish linen trade. In Scotland, by contrast, the fact that much yarn was imported created a more centralised control of yarn supplied to spinners, and hence ultimately of cloth sales as well. Even whiskey was more commercialised in Ireland than in Scotland. In both countries, there was a process of substitution of whiskey for ale, and the change was slowest in the richest regions: in Ayr, whisky was said not to be a genteel drink, and the better sort of person preferred ale.[27] But though Scots drank more whisky per head, it was more market-oriented in Ireland, and especially in the southern half of the country, where whiskey drinking spread late, the large distilleries popularised the product.

Overall, Irish agriculture was much more export-oriented than Scottish. Quite apart from the ecological limits on mixed agriculture in Ireland, the country lacked consumer markets either within rural areas or the towns on the same scale as in Scotland. By 1900 one half of output was exported, and the process of commercialisation had been carried to the extreme limits experienced in European agriculture: imported maize widespread both as an animal and human food, as much bacon imported as was exported. This extreme commercialisation in Ireland and the comparative success of Scottish lowland farmers at the same period in maintaining a pattern of mixed farming drew on long-standing forces, and both features were in harmony with long-standing patterns in the character of agriculture in each country.

Because Ireland had the more commercialised economy, rents were paid in cash to a greater extent and from an earlier date than in Scotland. Rents had been paid in kind in Ireland in many instances as late as the 1620s,[28] but from the 1650s cash payments were increasingly general. Dairying was the one sector where payment in cash lagged, even in the case of seventeenth-century dairying in the hands of English immigrants who organised their production on patterns familiar to those in south-west England and whose English dairyman-tenants in the early stages paid their rents in produce.[29] But the diffusion of dairying in the eighteenth century geographically into new regions and socially from immigrant to native dairymen was accompanied by a rapid commercialisation of payments. Dairying itself, however, was a complex activity in which tenants, often even small ones, rented cows to one or more dairymen: the payment in kind from the dairyman presupposed a marketing role on the part of the tenant who received butter and whose own rent was a cash one. In Scotland by comparison, rents in kind were still widespread in the 1690s,[30] and in the Statistical Account in the 1790s the emphasis on payments in kind seems very striking to an Irish reader: he is at a loss to find parallels as extensive or as numerous in contemporary Irish conditions. The greater importance of arable in Scotland is one factor accounting for this, but one can find these conditions not only in the arable Lothians (where despite the proximity of markets payment in kind was common) but in the pastoral south-west. The only payment in kind in Ireland which remained common was the exchange of labour for land, a payment which put the recipient of the land at an acute disadvantage, as will be argued presently, and which both reflected and reinforced the pattern of low incomes among agricultural labourers.

Though Ireland was more commercialised, in the sense that relatively more output was placed on national or external markets, cash other than for rent and farm purchases must have been acutely scarce, as payments in kind did not supplement incomes as in Scotland. Consequently it is reasonable to infer a very limited use of cash for purposes of purely local and retail exchange. If the volume of trade was large (and though per capita total exports fell below Scottish, per capita *agricultural* exports were larger) and money was scarce, sufficient currency was available for wholesale trade only because consumer purchases were limited, and indeed a pronounced trend towards greater food purchases in rural areas in the second half of the nineteenth century must have handicapped the growth of other consumer outlays. The recurrent comment on the general possession of a watch in rural Scotland in the 1790s is a significant indication as to how conditions in the less commercialised but richer society left some surplus for consumer goods. Clothing is a yet more striking instance. Per capita bank deposits and note circulation, a proxy measure over time of comparative living standards, support inferences about the low level of Irish incomes. Not only was banknote circulation lower than in Scotland in 1851, but the upward trend subsequently in per capita banknote circulation — in contrast to stagnation in Scotland and England — is itself a commentary on the low levels of cash before the 1850s. The conduct of a very high level of per capita wholesale trade on the basis of extremely low levels of both note circulation and bank deposits is consistent only with very modest retail purchases, and suggests that local exchanges in Ireland had been dominated by wholesale transactions for distant markets. The fact that the rise in note circulation after 1851 is combined with an upturn in bank deposits illustrates both how low the level of Irish incomes was in the middle of the nineteenth century and how the disposal of consumer income on retail purchases was still at a formative stage.

	Per Capita Banknote Circulation		Per capita Bank Deposits	
	Ireland £	Scotland £	Ireland £	Scotland £
1851	0.7	1.2	1.3	n.a.
1861	1.1	1.4	1.6	n.a.
1871	1.4	1.8	4.8	20
1881	1.3	1.5	5.5	21
1891	1.4	1.4	7.2	23
1901	1.5	1.8	9.3	24
1911	1.7	1.5	12.8	24

All this is not an argument that Ireland was a non-monetised society before 1851. Quite the reverse. Cash purchases loomed large in the outlays of eighteenth-century Irishmen, because their incomes were low while cash purchases grew modestly but inexorably from the middle decades onwards. In Scotland, purchases were made out of a cash income which significantly under-represented total income because, if rent was paid in kind, there were no overriding demands on it, or because there were significant supplements in kind, appreciating in their cash value, to basic wages. In particular, given the importance of rent payments in kind and of income in kind, the Scottish pattern of income was more likely to leave a surplus for expenditure on non-food items. It is significant too that payments in kind in Scotland were frequently expressed in commodity terms, not in cash terms, whereas in Ireland the universal expression in the eighteenth century of payments in kind in terms of cash (with lingering exceptions among dairymen) underlines the progressive erosion by commercialisation of the foundations of older relationships.

The relative position of Scottish households was enhanced if anything by the fact that wages were often paid in kind. Not only were living-in servants a much more important feature of the Scottish rural economy (they were boarded even by rich farmers, whereas in Ireland they were common only among the small farmers, were young, and had to exist on a diet even more meagre than the poor one of their employer), but many Scottish farm workers living out received a stipulated amount of food in addition to their other remuneration.[31] In Ireland cottagers were much more important than in Scotland, in many instances paying by their labour for the land which they occupied. In a period of rising prices, the value of payments in kind such as Scottish labourers received tended to rise, whereas the Irish labourer was caught in the scissors-like effect of nominal money wages which were depressed by competition for employment and rising rents for land as inflated produce prices pushed upwards farmers' valuations of the land let to labourers.

Rural Scotland in 1800 seems in several respects much more archaic than Ireland: enclosure was belated, multure to mill-owners was much more common, duty labour was more general in leases. Indeed, precisely because its social structure was well-defined and organic in its development, its rigidity helped to preserve many of the past characteristics of Scottish society. In Ireland, on the other hand, social organisation was open to change and also failed to shelter archaic features in existing society. In Scotland, small heritors were, by Irish standards, common, and in some regions, especially in the south-west, surprisingly numerous. In Ireland, the survival of archaic patterns was less in evidence, and their absence provided an autonomous social factor which compounded the purely economic ones making for commercialisation. Rural Scotland's social structure was the more rigid of the two, in that in lowland farming the categories of landowner, farmer and landholding cottager were well-defined, and access to all three categories was becoming more difficult: small landowners and farmers tended to disappear, while farmers were more and more able to replace cottagers with unmarried living-in servants. Many of the writers in the Statistical Account commented on the adverse effect that the change had on population growth, and certainly the evidence of stagnant or falling

population in many lowland parishes is impressive. The Irish land system, by
contrast, was far more fluid, and its social categories, which are much more difficult
to systematise, have been a fruitful source of confusion for historians. Indeed, the
number of distinct social categories, and the number of individuals within them,
increased. Cottagers became more numerous while their numbers fell in Scotland.
Landed estates were on average larger than in Scotland, but the creation of large
holdings below owners in fee meant that the gentry class if anything increased,
middle tenures drawing both younger sons of Protestant gentry and Catholics who
had lost land in the upheavals of the seventeenth century. These tendencies from
both below and above militated against a widespread emergence of large farmers
comparable with those of lowland Scotland. The diffusion of gentry-type classes or
gentry-influenced social values in Ireland was unparalleled in Scotland, where on
the evidence of the Statistical Account the minor gentry had disappeared in many
parishes, sometimes even to a dramatic degree. In fact so fluid was Irish rural
society that the number of substantial farmers increased significantly in the
eighteenth century. But the very fact that such farmers were increasing in number
in Ireland, while they were decreasing in number in Scotland but holding large
acreages, is a reminder of how late was Ireland's start in developing a rigid or stable
social structure.

    A rigid rural structure like Scotland's provided scope for mobility because it
squeezed out many, and also because those who left, if their incomes were higher, as
is argued in this essay, departed with some resources to aid their advancement
elsewhere. Evidence for mobility abounds at all social levels in Scotland. Many
gentry and farmers moved out of agriculture, and employment beyond their home
region, careers abroad and education were all responses to the pressures which
compelled Scots to be increasingly mobile.[32] In Ireland, on the other hand, access to
large intermediate tenures offered an avenue to gentry status, limiting the pressure
to move away. The success of upper-class Irish emigrants before 1800, while
impressive, was very much the work of a limited, relatively unchanging social
group, and on balance it was more a case of Catholic gentry mobility in the age of
the Penal Laws than of a wider trend among the landed classes. However, the
post-1800 decline of middlemen was accompanied by an accelerated migration of
Protestants. By contrast, mobility and its effects reached deep into Scottish society,
and the higher economic returns could even attract individuals into farming
whereas in Ireland the social structures ensured that before 1800 the highest
rewards were either in middle tenures, or outside farming altogether, and
individuals made the right decision in leaving it. In Scotland farming was profitable
enough, as in Creich in Fife, for rich farmers to become owners in fee,[33] and at a
more modest level in Strachan in Kincardine, where farmers were said to consist of
people who made money in service.[34] The point of illustrations such as these is that
they show that returns on capital in farming were high enough to attract people
with a knowledge of farming conditions more deeply into farming, whereas in
Ireland returns in farming (quite apart altogether from its low social esteem)
compared unfavourably with those elsewhere in rural society or outside it
altogether. In the last analysis, it can be said that Scotland entered its agricultural

revolution with an already highly developed social structure. In Ireland, by contrast, not only had shortage of sunshine and a wetter climate made the country more pastoral, but its social structure was also less conducive to economic progress. In Scotland a more advanced social structure made it much easier to respond positively to the opportunities created by the Industrial Revolution.

REFERENCES

1. I. Whyte, *Agriculture and Society in Seventeenth-century Scotland* (Edinburgh, 1979), p. 239.

2. L. M. Cullen, 'Economic trends, 1660–91', in T. W. Moody, F. X. Martin and F. J. Byrne, eds., *A New History of Ireland* (Oxford, 1976), iii, pp. 403, 405.

3. L. M. Cullen and T. C. Smout, 'Economic growth in Scotland and Ireland', in Cullen and Smout, eds., *Comparative aspects of Scottish and Irish economic and social history, 1600–1900* (Edinburgh, 1977), p. 5.

4. S. Kuznets, 'Notes on the pattern of U.S. economic growth', *Modern Economic Growth and Structure* (London, 1965), p. 311.

5. P. K. O'Brien and C. Keyder, *Economic Growth in Britain and France 1780–1914* (London, 1978); 'Voie brittanique et voie française vers la société industrielle (1780–1914)', *Annales*, XXXIV (1979).

6. J. Cropper, *The present state of Ireland* (Liverpool, 1825), quoted in G. O'Brien, *The economic history of Ireland from the Union to the Famine* (Dublin, 1921), p. 395.

7. Cullen and Smout, 'Economic growth in Scotland and Ireland,' in Cullen and Smout, *Comparative Aspects*, p. 13.

8. A. L. Bowley, 'The Statistics of Wages in the United Kingdom during the last hundred years. Part IV. Agricultural Wages — earning and general averages', *Journal of Royal Statistical Society* (September, 1899).

9. De la Tocnaye, *Rambles through Ireland* (Cork, 1798), 2 vols; *Promenade d'un Français dans la Grande Bretagne* (Dublin, 1797).

10. D. Defoe, *A Tour thro' the Whole Island of Great Britain in 1727*, ed. G. D. H. Cole (London, 1928), i, pp. 693, 699.

11. De la Tocnaye, *Promenade . . . ,*p. 206.

12. *Statistical Account of Scotland*, iv, p. 12.

13. *Statistical Account of Scotland*, xiv, p. 505.

14. Sir William Brereton's *Travels in Ireland, 1635*, in C. L. Falkiner, *Illustrations of Irish History and Topography* (London, 1904), p. 370.

15. *Ibid.*, p. 377.

16. Huntly House, Edinburgh, 'Bird's eye view of Edinburgh, 1647'.

17. Whyte, *Agriculture and Society*, p. 187.

18. See Patrick O'Flanagan's essay earlier in this volume.

19. Archives nationales, Paris, AE 13^{III} 436, Quelques notes sur l'Irlande, Dublin, 29 June 1834.

20. *Statistical Account*, xiv, p. 84.

21. *Statistical Account*, xi, p. 58.

22. *The Letters of Sir Walter Scott, 1825–1826*, ed. H. J. C. Grierson (London, 1935), IX, pp. 196, 201.

23. Whyte, *Agriculture and Society*, pp. 179, 248.

24. *Ibid.*, pp. 239, 240, 242.

25. *Ibid.*, pp. 241, 161, 179; and Defoe, *Tour*, ii, pp. 137–8.

26. L. M. Cullen, 'The Regions and Their Issues: Ireland', in G. Mingay, ed., *The Victorian countryside* (London, 1981) i, pp. 94–102.

27. *Statistical Account,* vi, p. 111.

28. *Calendar of State papers, Ireland, 1625–1632,* p. 148.

29. For an interesting early example, see Brereton, *Travels in Ireland,* p. 403.

30. Whyte, *Agriculture and Society,* pp. 179, 194, 248, 252; H.M.C., *Laing MSS.,* ii, p. 137.

31. T. M. Devine, 'Social Stability and Agrarian Change in the Eastern Lowlands of Scotland 1810–1840', *Social History,* iii, no. 3, pp. 331–346.

32. See T. M. Devine's essay 'The Social Composition of the Business Class in the larger Scottish towns, 1680–1740', earlier in this volume.

33. *Statistical Account,* iv, p. 228.

34. *Statistical Account,* v, p. 377.

20

In Pursuit of Comparative Aspects of Irish and Scottish Development: A Review of the Symposium

T. M. Devine and David Dickson

THE numberless seventeenth- and eighteenth-century merchants and migrants, sailors and students who got to know both Scotland and Ireland have apparently left no record of their impressions of the differences between the two societies. Occasionally general and rather ambiguous comparisons were made by travellers such as Brereton, Varley and De la Tocnaye,[1] and also by political writers, notably during the great debate in Ireland in 1798–9 on the proposed union between Britain and Ireland, when some of those opposing the measure contrasted Ireland's rapid eighteenth-century development, particularly since parliamentary independence, with the supposedly less vigorous performance of the Scottish economy since 1707.[2] That particular assessment became much harder to sustain in the early ninteenth century as statistical evidence and parliamentary inquiries revealed the more advanced character of the Scottish economy, and the growing contrast between an industrialising society and one where the agricultural sector not only remained dominant but was probably increasing in relative importance.

One of the tasks for the three dozen historians who assembled at Strathclyde University in September 1981 to discuss the papers that now appear in this volume was to investigate how deep were the roots of the visibly different nineteenth-century economies and social structures of the two countries: did Scotland's economy pull ahead decisively at the close of the eighteenth century, or had Scottish society developed the potential for growth during a long apprenticeship?

Scotland and Ireland by the 1780s had both enjoyed some three generations of peace, economic expansion and demographic growth, albeit punctuated during the first half of the eighteenth century by Jacobite diversions in Scotland and mortality crises in Ireland. The land area under cultivation had never been greater and the leading cities were reaching a new order of magnitude: both societies were on the move. Economic expansion over the century had rested in both countries on massive growth in the volume of exports of linen, livestock and livestock products. Scotland in addition had the re-export trade in colonial goods, an option denied to

T

the Irish traders before 1780, but this was not an advantage of strategic proportions. Overall, the two economies had up to then a similar basket of products with which to compete in English and Atlantic markets.

Participants at the symposium tended to look beyond this common experience, to search for structural differences which might explain the subsequent divergence. Contrasts in the ownership and management of landed property and in tenurial structure became one of the favoured areas for comparative analysis.

It has often been assumed that the social consequences of the seventeenth-century revolution in Irish land ownership were traumatic and long lasting, although the degree to which management practices and tenancy arrangements actually changed has hardly been investigated. *Rosalind Mitchison*, in the paper printed earlier in this volume, has suggested that with the new proprietorial élite came a total revision in attitudes to land ownership, the old social and political functions of landed wealth being superseded as the new owners sought to maximise commercial returns. New landlords with new attitudes created a new economy. In Scotland, according to *Ian Whyte*, new attitudes to estate management on the part of Lowland landowners were also the catalyst of seventeenth-century agrarian innovation, but significantly this shift in *mentalité* came without a change in the personnel of the landlord class, and occurred gradually and with less social disruption.

Yet, the close causal link in the Irish case between proprietorial change and economic transformation was not accepted without reservation at the symposium. *Aidan Clarke* pointed to the shadowy evidence indicating that the Irish economy in the sixteenth century had had some dynamic qualities, and that 'the gradual loosening up process' visible in early modern Scotland was not entirely absent even in Gaelicised Ireland. In *Clarke's* view the pattern of evolutionary development was weakened in the early seventeenth century by the growing ascendancy of new English interests across Ireland, and destroyed in the wake of the 1641 rising; he suggested that the distinctiveness of the new English lay more in their approach to the use of cattle than in their concept of the functions of land ownership; cattle in the old Gaelic system had been

> regarded as capital goods rather than as a consumer product . . . the basis of social relationships and the life style of the Gaelic community . . . the resource which was made available to tenants and clients.[3]

The extensive production and sale of store cattle and, later, butter were to become the hall-marks of a new pastoral order. The role of cattle underwent the same transformation in the Scottish Highlands, if rather more imperceptibly, as the old military structure began to decay and the region became increasingly responsive to the demand of the Lowland towns and English markets.

There was a further qualification of the thesis that the commercialisation of Irish land-use came as a result of changes in landlord attitudes. *Peter Roebuck*, commenting on the ability of Irish landlords in the seventeenth and eighteenth centuries to direct change, argued that prevalence of tenancy by leasehold — with long lease terms by Scottish standards — substantially reduced the discretionary powers of landowners, and that the arbiters of agricultural change were generally the lease-holding tenants:

> The Irish landlords' bad press has become almost indelibly printed on the national consciousness. However, though the record needs to be set straight, current work will not produce a story replete with Ernle-like heroics. Rather the Irish landlord will emerge as tangential, if not irrelevant, to the main flow of agricultural change.[4]

Might not the Scottish improvers, so long the object of hagiographical treatment, also have been credited with more economic significance than their contribution merits?[5] It would seem that research on eighteenth-century Scotland is rediscovering the crucial innovative role of the Lowland tenantry, although it is probable that with the later development of the agricultural lease in Scotland, landowners there had a stronger financial base and a greater interest in agricultural intervention.

The social distance between landowner and tenant in seventeenth-century Scotland, according to *Whyte,* had been 'such a yawning gulf . . . that there were very limited opportunities for social mobility'. In Ireland there seems to have been no such clear distinction between property owners and chief tenants — who as time passed were increasingly lessors themselves, tenurial middlemen who sublet parts or even all their tenancies to smallholders. Middlemen of sorts had existed in sixteenth-century Gaelic Ireland, and of course tacksmen were pivotal in eighteenth-century Highland society. But examination of the ubiquitous middlemen of eighteenth-century Ireland reveals much of the peculiarities of the land system before 1780: the predominance of 'planter' chief tenants of English or Scottish extraction in many parts of the country and under them the evolution of a rural social order where undifferentiated cottier tenancy (involving family farming and intermittent labour services) was giving way to a more stratified arrangement of 'snug' farmers and near-landless smallholders, labourers and artisans. *L. M. Cullen's* paper stresses an essential dichotomy between this fluidity of Irish rural society, and a more rigid, less volatile social structure in Scotland. But even if Scottish society was more tightly stratified, it appears that before the end of the seventeenth century there was a sufficiently large number of affluent tenants across the Lowlands to sustain an embryonic rural money market where farmers' surpluses were lent out to tradesmen or even to proprietors. In Ireland the level of rural saving and its destination is less clear: many landowning families had merchant connections, many chief tenants had siblings in urban occupations, yet the eighteenth-century market in rural property and unexpired lease interests seems to have been sufficiently accessible and inviting to draw much of the mobile savings of larger Irish tenants.

Whatever the debate on tenurial structures, there was little dispute at the symposium that mean farm size in eighteenth-century Lowland Scotland was larger than in Ireland and that the contrast was becoming more pronounced, although within each country variations in farm size — between regions and across farming systems — may have been even greater; for example, Irish farms on prime soils and in advantageous locations, especially where stock-farming remained the norm during the era of high cereal prices, do not appear to have shrunk much, whereas holding size fell rapidly in the regions of rural domestic industry. In general, however, the opposition of Scottish and Irish trends in farm size is striking:

> Irish society for a variety of reasons was willing to accommodate more people on the land in the eighteenth century, while Scottish Lowland society . . . believed that improved farming meant facing the social cost of excluding small tenants from the land.[6]

Why should this have been so? The issue surfaced at a number of points during the symposium, and three types of explanation were advanced: tenurial, ecological and demographic.

The first explanation was that Scottish landlords for historical and economic reasons were able to keep tighter control over their tenants and over land-use practices than could their Irish counterparts, once the custom of preferential dealing with large tenants had been established in the socially precarious environment of seventeenth-century Ireland. Where head tenants on long leases were tempted to sublet or to facilitate subdivision by under-tenants, there was little landlords could do in the short term, however much they might regard farm fragmentation as the antithesis of 'improvement'. The tenurial system may thus have 'lubricated' the supply of small farms, but the question remains, why were large farms apparently less profitable in eighteenth-century Ireland than in Scotland? The Smithian answer would have been that this was a function of the relative scarcity of capital in Ireland, or at least of under-investment, but did Irish agriculture suffer from being undercapitalised?

The ecological explanations for the growing contrast in farm size focused on the opportunities for flax and potato cultivation in the two societies. *T. C. Smout* sensed a basic difference in the ease with which flax could be cultivated:

> In Scotland the linen trade . . . was advantageously pursued in towns and villages where the weavers (or spinners) had little or no access to the land, and this was because flax grew badly in the country and was best imported and distributed to urban and semi-urban nodes. Excluded tenants therefore had something to do outside the agrarian sector. In Ireland the linen trade was most advantageously followed in the countryside where the flax grew so well, so there was an incentive to subdivide the farms to accommodate the spinning and weaving cottiers, especially in Ulster . . .[7]

The precocious adoption of the potato as a major subsistence crop in the south, midlands and west of Ireland has also been explained in ecological terms: most of the nutritious varieties of the plant available in the early eighteenth century seem to have thrived best in damp and relatively frost-free habitats which had a long growing season — more common in Ireland than virtually anywhere else in Europe.[8] The potato's introduction by definition reduced the acreage (but probably not the labour) required for family subsistence, and *ceteris paribus* removed an obstacle to the creation of smaller farm units.

The demographic explanation for the downward drift in Irish farm size rests on the assumption that the rates of natural increase in the two countries were quite unlike. Statistical data on eighteenth-century Scottish population are by Irish standards excellent, but estimates of total population for Scotland before the 1750s, as for Ireland over most of the century, are very tentative. But however the figures are computed, there can be no doubt that population growth in eighteenth-century Ireland was decidedly faster. At the end of the century, Irish population at five millions was roughly three times that of Scotland, whereas around 1700 it is most unlikely to have been even double Scotland's total of about one million.[9] As *Michael Anderson* pointed out, it is Scottish population growth at this stage that is out of line, growing slowly by English as well as Irish standards.[10] It is inherently improbable that Scottish mortality levels were higher than Irish ones, and as emigration levels were modest in both countries, presumably Irish marital fertility, female age of marriage or nuptiality rates differed markedly from Scottish ones. The only observed economic factor which might explain the fertility difference is the contrasting organisation of the rural labour market: the Scottish unmarried living-in servant — already a feature in many parts of the country in the late seventeenth century as the *Whytes'* paper shows — had no real parallel in Ireland, where the great majority of rural labourers in the eighteenth and early nineteenth centuries were married and maintained a separate household, potato ground etc., even those who were regular 'bound' labourers working for larger farmers or the gentry.

Whatever the mechanisms underlying Irish population growth, the multiplication of households in the countryside after 1750 affected both the intensification of subsistence production (enlarged potato cultivation) and the character of the labour market. But the key problem remains the direction of the causal link between farm fragmentation and population growth. Opinions at the symposium remained divided on this issue.

A lively debate on the character of pre-industrial commercialisation was initiated by *Cullen's* paper: did the rapidity of socio-political change in seventeenth-century Ireland lead to a precocious and traumatic penetration of market forces into agriculture, to such an extent that, at the beginning of the eighteenth century, Ireland was actually more commercialised than Scotland, despite the fact that the latter was probably the more affluent country? *Smout* was sceptical: if Irish rural society was more commercialised, why did the gains from trade not lead to higher incomes?

> Is it because in some sense the Irish economy was very seriously distorted by English imperialism, that Irish trade was disadvantageously monopolised in the hands of English merchants, that the structure of the Irish economy was in some Wallersteinian sense being distorted and exploited by the pressure of the core on the periphery to its long-term cost?[11]

There was no one willing to take up the challenge to apply a 'world-economy' model to Anglo-Irish relations, but *Clarke* suggested that the profits of economic development in post-Cromwellian Ireland had only increased income inequalities; the spread effects of growth failed to reach the great 'inert sector', the majority who had no control over resources.

Visible symptoms of rapid Irish commercialisation were the many new fairs, market places and landlord-sponsored villages, examined here by *Patrick*

O'Flanagan and *D. G. Lockhart*. *Cullen* suggested that the number of Irish estate-village foundations was in fact considerably greater than *Lockhart's* estimate, and while new market and estate villages were being established in parts of Scotland during the period, it was on a smaller scale and more regionally defined than in Ireland. *Raymond Gillespie* queried, however, whether the legal process of fair and market creation was not more a measure of landowners' aspirations than a sign of commercial development on the ground, or — as with some 'new' Connaught markets in the early seventeenth century — the legal recognition of traditional points of exchange in the old Gaelic economy.

Doubts about the quality of Irish commercialisation in the pre-1780 era were expressed by *Joel Mokyr*, drawing on later evidence from the pre-Famine period: commercialisation may have extended across the country but it was superficial, and he speculated that perhaps five-eighths of the country's population in the 1840s performed no more than five cash transactions per annum, the sale of the staple crop or animal, and the payment of rent obviously being the principle ones. This picture of surface commercialisation did not go unchallenged, and discussion of *Robert Dodgshon*'s paper revealed that commercialisation could be a reversible process: the decline of wool production in the Southern Uplands from its late fifteenth- and early sixteenth-century peak and the growth in rural population were probably associated with a greater subsistence orientation on the part of tenants.

The greater survival of non-cash arrangements in Scotland — payments in kind by tenants and by employers of labour — well into the eighteenth century was taken as one of the pointers to the relatively less monetised character of rural Scotland. But a lower level of monetisation, if true, is not necessarily a sign of weaker commercialisation. *Smout* argued that

> the case for the under-commercialisation of Scotland is partly illusory: Skye, after all, was sending animals to London in the first half of the seventeenth century, and receiving in turn the visits of Lowland chapmen selling petty consumer goods at Portree fair. And the impression of lower per capita exports from Scotland than from Ireland in the eighteenth century is partly a function of Anglo-Scottish trade not going into the statistics of the customs service while Anglo-Irish trade did.[12]

The debate over relative commercialisation remained inconclusive. There was, however, consensus on a related topic, the differing patterns of urban development. *Leslie Clarkson* highlighted the contrast between the two urban systems in the eighteenth century, Ireland's dominated by Dublin and the three Munster ports, with few local and regional urban centres, Scotland's with nothing to rival Dublin but relatively rich in middle-rank towns. *Clarkson* estimated that at the end of the eighteenth century one-fifth of Scotland's population lived in the thirteen towns of 7,000 or more, whereas less than one-tenth of Irishmen lived in the eleven or twelve such towns, with half of these urban dwellers residing in Dublin. The leading cities in both countries were major ports, but physical topography as much as economic organisation determined this. Scotland's greater urbanisation by the end of the eighteenth century was not because of the expansion of these port cities so much as the rise of new centres of workshop industry such as Paisley, mushrooming at a time when Ireland's proto-industrialisation remained pre-eminently rural. Furthermore Scotland's somewhat larger rural middle-income groups created a strong local demand for urban goods and services; in Ireland the rentier classes' spending power was directed towards Dublin, and provincial social centres were slow to emerge. Was Dublin's fourfold growth over the eighteenth century really such 'a spectacular achievement in a pre-industrial society'[13] and Edinburgh's far more sedate growth a sign of relative retardation? It was pointed out that in late medieval Scotland, Edinburgh had dominated Scottish towns as eighteenth-century Dublin did within Ireland, and that a primate city of Dublin's gargantuan proportions could be taken as a sign of relative Irish backwardness.

The port towns in both societies were dominated by their general merchant élites. Even Dublin, though possibly not Edinburgh, was governed by men of trade. The response to *Tom Devine's* paper on Scottish merchant communities in the eighteenth century revealed less points of difference than might have been expected between the economic behaviour of Scottish merchants and that of Irish merchants. The real contrast was one of scale: the level of capital accumulation among Irish merchants was generally less impressive, multiple partnerships fewer and family survival in trade possibly shorter. Underlying this was the independent character of Scottish international commerce and the commission character of Irish Atlantic trade — which at least in part was a consequence of the limited access Irish merchants had to American and Caribbean markets under the Navigation Acts. *Gordon Jackson* doubted whether even without the Acts the Irish economy could have maintained its own long-distance trades 'for the same reason that . . . the Humber ports could not or the ports of Tyne and Wear . . .',[14] a rather pessimistic assessment of Irish resources in the eighteenth century. *Cullen* pointed out that whereas British shipping dominated Anglo-Irish trade and Irish transatlantic commerce, Irish ships and principals controlled the country's trade with France and southern Europe. Nevertheless were Irish merchants and, by extension, entrepreneurs more risk averse, less 'enterprising' than their Scottish counterparts? It is perhaps significant that sizeable colonies of Scottish merchants became established in Irish ports, notably in Dublin and Cork, in the later eighteenth century, and these were more than just groups of factors for Glasgow tobacco houses. There was no comparable Irish presence in Scotland, although considerable numbers of merchants of Irish origin were based by mid-century in London and of course in the main French and Iberian ports.

The possibility that the ethos of Calvinism assisted the development of Scottish commercial capitalism was introduced into the discussion by *Roy Campbell's* paper. When pressed by a sceptical *Bruce Lenman* who refused to accept the validity of any Weberian hypothesis, *Campbell* spelt out why the dominant theology of eighteenth-century Scotland may have been conducive to development:

> Where I think there *may* have been a difference between Scotland and Ireland . . . is in the environmental effects of religion within which the entrepreneur had to operate; . . . in Scotland in the eighteenth century, almost uniquely, there were few theological disputes that spread into political or social disputes . . . religious and theological factors produced unique social stability.[15]

Irish merchants of course operated in an urban society where denominational divisions were explicit, if less acutely sensed in the second half of the eighteenth century. And while particular denominations dominated the trade of individual ports, the overall Anglican commercial pre-eminence (outside Ulster) reflected the distribution of rural wealth. Within the northern province the rural gentry were mainly Anglican, but in the towns the merchant communities were dominated by those with a dissenting background; *W. H. Crawford* indicated that even in the countryside there was a relative decline in the number of Anglicans and Quakers involved as bleachers and drapers in the linen industry after its initial development; dissenters were foremost as there was almost no Catholic involvement in linen entrepreneurship. Had Ulster Presbyterianism — with its largely Glasgow-trained clergy — a social philosophy that positively affected group economic behaviour?

Throughout the discussion on the two societies prior to Scottish industrialisation the contrast between the gradual character of social, demographic and agrarian change in Lowland Scotland and the rapidity of Irish movement was generally accepted. Most participants at the symposium agreed that an explanation of the differential rates of change must proceed beyond the economic sphere. The major area of disagreement lay in interpreting the consequences of this differential. Was the apparent economic failure of early nineteenth-century Ireland determined by the manner of its earlier growth? Was the unprecedented economic growth of Scotland after the 1780s directly related to the smoothness of earlier social and cultural adaptation?

Geological determinism certainly found little favour at the symposium: before the cost of coal became a pressing factor in industrial location, underemployment was proving a heavy drain on the Irish economy. The absence of strategic industrial raw materials in Ireland and their presence in Lowland Scotland certainly guaranteed different development paths for the two countries after 1800, but why was Ireland apparently excluded from exploiting the new organisational and technological opportunities of the nineteenth century?

One inherited difference between the two economies was in the nature of their labour markets. In the eighteenth and early nineteenth centuries internal migration of a permanent kind seems to have been much more strongly developed in Lowland Scotland than in Ireland: about 5 per cent of those enumerated in Ireland in 1841 were living in counties other than their native one, whereas in Scotland in 1851 the figure was over 30 per cent. *Malcolm Gray's* judgement that 'the readiness of the rural population to move into industrial work and towns must surely have been a prime factor in industrialisation',[16] with small towns acting as collecting points for rural migrants, implies that immobility was a major impediment to Irish development. But, despite low levels of internal migration, the volume of Irish emigration to Britain and to North America by the 1840s had reached massive proportions: was this an indication of the failure of the Irish economy, or at least of 'some sort of surplus getting out?'[17] *Cormac Ó Gráda's* paper suggests that many emigrants were coming from declining industries, but as *Mokyr* observed, it was the better-off counties with less population pressure that were the main contributors to pre-Famine emigration; elsewhere exodus was constrained by the costs of the move.

Why, then, was short-distance movement not more resorted to? *Anderson* wondered whether the lack of smaller market centres almost forced Irish migration either towards large cities — as in the eighteenth century — or overseas:

> in Scotland the more diverse response [was] . . . made possible by the availability of lots of little . . . local sinks into which migrants [could] . . . fall.

In seeking to explain the contrasting levels of local migration he asked whether

> the tenancy arrangements are significant, or have we got a very different life cycle pattern with children in Ireland tending to stay at home and work on the local plot . . . while the Scots go into farm service and are thus less inhibited about their subsequent migration? If this was so . . . might it be something to do with . . . inheritance practices, might it be something to do with growth of the poor laws?[18]

But some questioned whether willingness to migrate was the heart of the matter. Irish towns and urban industry do not seem to have encountered labour scarcities, and seasonal harvest migration from many western and upland parts of Ireland had a long history. Low internal migration in Ireland in fact reflected the reluctance of the poorer elements in Irish rural society to break their links with cultivation and to become a true rural proletariat, a reluctance, *Peter Solar* suggested, that may have been reinforced by the absence of a comprehensive poor law before 1838. There were of course additional factors strengthening the urban or quasi-urban location of industrial employment in Scotland and its rural character over much of Ireland; and it was this abortive rural expansion of industrial employment which had profound demographic and agricultural consequences.

But the assumption that rural Ireland 'failed' in the early nineteenth century is challenged in *Solar's* paper. His provocative thesis that Irish agriculture, measured in terms of its total productivity, was as efficient as that of Scotland, forced some re-evaluation of received wisdoms. If Ireland had become a strategic bread basket for industrial Britain (accounting in the case of Scotland for about 17 per cent of domestic grain requirements in the 1830s in *Solar's* estimate), if yields were relatively high, and if selective agricultural improvement had been incorporated without major organisational changes on the land, why was Ireland poor? The skewed distribution of farm size over much of the south of Ireland, with well over half of the profitable land area in farms of over thirty statute acres in the 1850s, meant that the numerical dominance of minuscule farms was less economically damaging than socially problematic. Congestion and efficient farming co-existed. Critics of *Solar's* approach were sceptical about the value of divorcing the social crisis in rural Ireland from agricultural performance; *Mokyr*, for instance, while conceding that 'in a certain way . . . the Irish economy was well organised and [the Irish] . . . were not throwing away resources', added that 'that is not quite the same as saying they were not poor . . .'[19]. Capital remained the problem for Irish agriculture; with greater investment much uncolonised land could, in *Mokyr's* view, have successfully been reclaimed. By the 1840s, when no Lowland county in Scotland had a majority of its householders in farming, Irish agriculture was supporting a train of petty producers and underemployed labourers, a problem exacerbated by the shrinking earnings in rural domestic industry. The contrast therefore appears between Scottish society's ability to soften income inequalities through the expansion of industrial employment and the maintenance (over the long run) of wage levels, and the polarisation in Ireland between landowners and farmers on the one hand and those without access to adequate land who had neither the means to migrate to employment nor the fall-back until 1838 of a local public relief system.

The discussion on nineteenth-century agriculture highlighted the problems of glossing over regional variation. *Gray's* and *Dodgshon's* papers serve as warnings to the generaliser, but overall it would seem that variations in farming systems and agrarian structures were wider in Scotland than in Ireland, even leaving out of consideration the central and west Highlands. *Gray* and *Campbell* picked out the south-west of Scotland, the dairy zone, as having particularly distinctive if elusive qualities — were its Irish associations partly responsible? And parts of the wealthy mixed farm districts of Leinster, as profoundly influenced by Dublin as the Lothians were by Edinburgh, were unusual in preserving a considerable element of social continuity (by Irish standards) while incorporating some technical innovations.

Rural disorder in each country had pronounced regional patterns, parts of the Highlands having the most notorious record in Scotland, a westward shifting belt of counties in the case of Ireland. *Eric Richards'* claim that 'for a peasant society in terms of pre-industrial violence . . . Ireland was right at the top of the league . . .'[20] was countered by *Joseph Lee*, who remarked that social stability in Ireland was entirely the norm between 1750 and 1900 over four-fifths of the country at any one period. Nevertheless rural Scotland was decidedly more tranquil than Ireland (or England); no lingering 'sub-cultures of violence' seem to have existed in the Lowlands and there was nothing in modern Scottish history to compare with the peasant fury that swept Leinster in May 1798, nor with the more politically radical, Presbyterian-dominated rebellion that agitated east Ulster in the next month. If the reasonable assumption is made that social dislocation within rural communities usually generates collective expressions of grievance, Scottish social stability was remarkable; as *Devine* noted:

> before 1815 . . . eviction, radical surgery on an estate, was much more widespread in Scotland . . . than it was in Ireland, so in a sense one particular variable, the force making for violence, was actually greater [in Scotland].[21]

Lee suggested that the regional pattern of Irish agrarian disorder indicated a critical tension between commercialisation and a certain stage of social development, and districts at that stage were particularly prone to disturbance; no similar geographical shift appears to have occurred in Scotland. One explanation put forward for the different histories of social disorder was related to internal migration:

> If there are opportunities to retain your place at the same social level . . . through migration internally, then that removes a great incentive to taking extreme measures on the spot.[22]

But even if Scotland had more efficient social safety-valves, the capacity of society south of the Highlands to adjust to profound social change without visible internal conflict was also a measure of the tightness of social control within the affected communities.

Religion may have helped, at least up to the early nineteenth century; denominational controversies thereafter once again became socially divisive. The more acutely sectarian character of Irish rural disorder after 1800 has been somewhat misinterpreted; certainly neither religious teaching nor religious teachers encouraged social confrontation. As *Sean Connolly's* paper shows, Catholic social teaching in the early nineteenth century was highly conventional and conservative. Indeed the causal link at that stage between religion and economic behaviour appears to have been very weak, despite the contemporary belief that the reverse was true. It was religious prejudice, so prevalent then in both societies, that heightened social grievances and social inequality:

> If enough people believe that Catholics are bad workers, then they will end up being hired for on the whole lower quality jobs; Protestants will be preserved . . . capital will end up flowing to non-Catholic regions . . . [23]

By the 1840s, when it was coming to be recognised that the 'factory system' was taking root in east Ulster, the region's success seemed to some to demonstrate the superiority of Protestant culture. Certainly the financial resources of the Belfast region were in Protestant hands despite the growing relative importance of the town's Catholic population; a contemporary estimate *c.*1820 computed that Protestant capital employed in Belfast trade and industry exceeded Catholic capital nearly forty-fold.[24] *Lenman,* however, argued that Belfast's industrial transition was largely unconnected with the Protestant character of its entrepreneurs; location vis-a-vis Ayrshire, the Clyde and north-west England was a more powerful determinant. But was the social structure of Belfast's hinterland distinctive? This possibility was considered in discussion of *Crawford's* paper. It remains unclear whether the rate of capital formation in the region was much greater than elsewhere in Ireland. *Charles Munn* noted that interest rates on bank deposits in Ulster did indeed differ from the rest of the country in the 1830s and 1840s, but they were higher, not lower, reflecting presumably the greater credit needs of an industrialising region. This feature was paralleled in Scotland at the time; deposit rates in the Glasgow region were generally higher than in other areas.

Only one dimension of our symposium has been surveyed here. Much of the concrete discussion concerned local or methodological issues, but those occasions when 'internal' controversies were stirred up by provocative contributions were always entertaining and usually educational for the non-combatants. The pursuit of a comparative perspective inevitably made some discussions rather speculative because of imbalances in the current state of research, or in the evidence available. But consciousness of such imbalance assists the planning of future research — one of the dividends of the comparative method according to Marc Bloch. Hopefully the papers in this volume have helped fulfil Bloch's other expectations of the comparative approach:

> [international comparisons] provide a means of confirming or rejecting explanations which might seem irrefutable if viewed in a single historical or geographical setting . . . [and] underline singularity by revealing the inadequacy of general explanations of local phenomena.[25]

REFERENCES

1. See above pp. 251-2, and (Charles Varley), *The Unfortunate Husbandman,* Desmond Clark, ed. (London, 1964).

2. See, for example, *An Address to the People of Ireland against an Union* (Dublin, 1799), pp. 28-30; Charles Bell, *An Union neither Necessary nor Expedient for Ireland,* 3rd ed. (Dublin, 1799), pp. 37-8. For a contrary judgement on Scotland's relative progress, see *Reasons against a Union . . .,* 2nd ed. (Dublin, 1798), pp. 19-20.

3. Aidan Clarke on Rosalind Mitchison's paper. Verbal (and sometimes unscripted) comments made by participants at the symposium and cited here are reproduced from tapes made of the proceedings. These are temporarily deposited in the Library of Trinity College, Dublin.

4. Peter Roebuck on Joel Mokyr's paper.

5. See T. M. Devine, 'The English Connection and Irish and Scottish Development', above, pp. 23-4.

6. T. C. Smout on L. M. Cullen's paper.

7. Ibid.

8. P. M. A. Bourke, 'The Potato, Blight, Weather and the Irish Famine' (unpublished Ph.D. dissertation, National University of Ireland, 1965), pp. 19-24.

9. Scottish population estimates are taken from L. M. Cullen and T. C. Smout, eds., *Comparative Aspects of Scottish and Irish Economic and Social History 1600-1900* (Edinburgh, 1977), pp. 4-5; for Irish estimates, see Stuart Daultrey, David Dickson and Cormac Ó Gráda, 'Eighteenth-Century Irish Population: New Perspectives from Old Sources', *Journal of Economic History,* XLI, 3 (Sept. 1981), pp. 624-5.

10. In discussion of Tom Devine's paper on 'The English Connection'.

11. T. C. Smout on L. M. Cullen's paper.

12. Ibid.

13. L. A. Clarkson on David Dickson's paper.

14. Gordon Jackson on Laura Cochran's paper.

15. Roy Campbell in discussion of his own paper.

16. Malcolm Gray in discussion of his own paper.

17. Michael Anderson on Cormac Ó Gráda's paper.

18. Michael Anderson on Malcolm Gray's paper.

19. Joel Mokyr on Peter Solar's paper.

20. Eric Richards on Joseph Lee's presentation.

21. Tom Devine on Joseph Lee's presentation.

22. Joseph Lee in discussion with Michael Anderson on Malcolm Gray's paper.

23. Joel Mokyr on Sean Connolly's paper.

24. British Library, Liverpool papers, Add. MS 38368, pp. 159-68. We are grateful to Peter Solar for bringing this document to our attention.

25. A. G. Hopkins' summary of Marc Bloch's argument appears in Clive Dewey and A. G. Hopkins, eds., *The Imperial Impact: Studies in the Economic History of Africa and India* (London, 1978), pp. 5-6.

Index ⋆

⋆(Ir.) denotes a reference specifically to Ireland, (Sc.) a reference specifically to Scotland, and (cf.) where a comparison or association between the two countries is made.